Anne-Christin Mittwoch | Anne-Marie Weber [eds.]

The Interest of the Company – A Driving Concept for Sustainable Business?

A European Inquiry Inspired by a Polish-German Comparison

Nomos

Gefördert aus Mitteln der Deutsch-Polnischen Wissenschaftsstiftung
Projekt wspierany przez Polsko-Niemiecką Fundację na rzecz Nauki

DEUTSCH | POLSKO
POLNISCHE | NIEMIECKA
WISSENSCHAFTS | FUNDACJA
STIFTUNG | NA RZECZ NAUKI

The Deutsche Nationalbibliothek lists this publication in the Deutsche Nationalbibliografie; detailed bib http://dnb.d-nb.de
1st Edition 2026

Published by
Nomos Verlagsgesellschaft mbH & Co. KG
Waldseestraße 3–5 | 76530 Baden-Baden
www.nomos.de

Production of the printed version:
Nomos Verlagsgesellschaft mbH & Co. KG
Waldseestraße 3–5 | 76530 Baden-Baden

ISBN 978-3-7560-3103-0 (Print)
ISBN 978-3-7489-5444-6 (ePDF)
DOI https://doi.org/10.5771/9783748954446

Onlineversion
Inlibra

Preface

This volume, *The Interest of the Company – A Driving Concept for Sustainable Business? A European Inquiry Inspired by a Polish-German Comparison*, brings together a unique set of scholarly perspectives on one of the most pressing questions for corporate governance in the twenty-first century: can the interest of the company serve as a meaningful legal and conceptual anchor for sustainable business conduct? The contributions in this book reflect a collective European effort to explore this question through the lens of national company laws and their evolving role in the context of sustainability-related reforms.

The book is the outcome of the research project *The Company Interest in Germany and Poland – A Comparative Legal Analysis in the Context of the European Sustainable Corporate Governance Initiative*, generously funded by the Polish-German Science Foundation (Polsko-Niemiecka Fundacja na Rzecz Nauki / Deutsch-Polnische Wissenschaftsstiftung). The project was conceived as a bilateral scholarly collaboration, and it flourished as such – building intellectual bridges between legal systems, academic cultures, and individuals.

The volume is structured in two parts. The first part, *Sustainable Business and the Interest of the Company: Legal Perspectives from Poland and Germany*, offers a detailed bilateral analysis that reflects the project's comparative origins. The second part, *Sustainability and the Interest of the Company in Europe*, expands the discussion to include legal perspectives from across the European Union, encompassing eight jurisdictions and offering broader insights into the potential for convergence or divergence in the interpretation and function of the company's interest in a sustainability context.

We are deeply grateful for the support of the Polish-German Science Foundation, whose funding made this research possible. We also wish to express our sincere thanks to the University of Warsaw and the Martin Luther University Halle-Wittenberg, which served as institutional homes for the project and offered generous academic and logistical support throughout its duration. We would also like to thank the Publication Fund of Martin Luther University Halle-Wittenberg for supporting the open access publication of this book. Finally, we would like to express our sincere thanks to Cristina Lloyd, who has optimised the linguistic quality of the contributions in this volume through her careful and dedicated English proofreading and editing.

The project team consisted of the two lead investigators and editors of this book, Anne-Christin Mittwoch and Anne-Marie Weber, doctoral researchers Tonio Friedmann and Aleksandra Szczęsna, and student assistant Helena Kordasiewicz. Together, we worked in close cooperation with seven associated researchers who contributed jurisdictional reports from across Europe and whose expertise and dedication substantially enriched the entire project.

A highlight of the project was the international conference held on 2 October 2024, at the University of Warsaw, which provided an invaluable forum for exchange between the project team, the associated researchers, other scholars, and practitioners. The conference not only informed the final shape of this book but also underscored the enduring importance of transnational dialogue in the development of company law at the national and EU level.

Beyond its academic achievements, the project yielded something equally valuable: it deepened a sense of mutual trust, intellectual kinship, and personal friendship between the Polish and German members of the research team. The cooperation was marked not only by professionalism and scholarly commitment but also by warmth, generosity, and a shared spirit of curiosity. This seamless and enriching collaboration across borders became one of the most gratifying outcomes of our work. We look forward, with hope and enthusiasm, to continuing this path together.

Anne-Christin Mittwoch and Anne-Marie Weber
Editors

Table of Contents

1. The Interest of the Company and the Legal Fabric of Polish-German Business Relations

Anne-Marie Weber and Anne-Christin Mittwoch

A. Introduction

In most jurisdictions of the EU, the concept of "the interest of the company" lies at the heart of company law. As a doctrinal construct, the interest of the company features prominently across legal systems – in statutes, case law, and corporate governance codes – typically serving as the benchmark against which the actions of board members are evaluated.[1] Despite its widespread use, the concept of the interest of the company often lacks precise definition. Does it simply equate to shareholder interests? Does it serve as shorthand for long-term value creation? Or does it invoke a broader commitment to stakeholders or the public good? These ambiguities have become increasingly salient in light of recent crises affecting both people and planet, prompting renewed scrutiny of how sustainability objectives intersect with the legal and normative understanding of the company's interest.

While these conceptual challenges are important in themselves, they become even more intricate when examined through a transnational lens. When locally-embedded understandings of the company's interest encounter one another across borders, tensions may arise, especially where business relations are deeply integrated. A particularly instructive case emerges from the economic entanglement between Poland and Germany.

Although the two countries share close economic ties and a degree of legal proximity, their company law traditions, corporate governance cultures, and institutional trajectories diverge substantially. Germany exemplifies a mature legal system with a well-developed doctrinal framework, established jurisprudence, and a vibrant academic discourse on the board's role and the balancing of competing interests within the company.[2] Poland, by contrast, is a post-socialist legal system in which company law has evolved

1 Weber/Mittwoch RECoL 2023, 143 (152–157).
2 See chapter 3 of this volume.

swiftly over the past three decades, shaped by German, Anglo-American, and supranational (EU) influences. Yet this hybrid development has often occurred without the same level of doctrinal coherence or institutional consolidation.[3]

These divergences become particularly visible when foreign investors (shareholders) interact with Polish subsidiaries, their boards, and the legal professionals who advise them. Conflicting interpretations of the company's interest also surface in joint ventures, where board appointees representing different legal and governance backgrounds must collaborate. In such transnational settings, the company is not merely a legal entity or an economic unit: it also becomes a place where norms are contested. What is in the best interest of the company when strategic decisions must be taken by a Polish board under the influence of a German shareholder? How is the company's interest interpreted when local employment needs conflict with group-level financial optimisation? Who decides – and under what standard – whether a company should bear the costs of environmental or social compliance in a complex cross-border supply chain? Irrespective of private international law, which determines the applicable legal framework in cross-border situations, these issues bring to light differing conceptions of good corporate governance that must be harmonised in practical application.

This chapter does not attempt to answer these questions from a doctrinal point of view; that task will be taken up in the following chapters, which explore the interpretation of the company's interest in Polish and German company law, as well as other European jurisdictions. Instead, the present chapter offers the contextual groundwork for such analysis. It maps the economic interdependence between Poland and Germany and illustrates how the concept of the company's interest emerges as a potential point of friction in these cross-border dynamics. In doing so, it sets the stage for the legal inquiry that follows.

B. Poland and Germany as Interdependent Economic Actors

The origins of the economic interdependence between Poland and Germany can be traced back to Poland's dual transformation in the early 1990s: the shift from a centrally-planned economy to a market economy, and

3 See chapter 2 of this volume.

from an authoritarian regime to a democratic polity that is integrated into Western institutions. However, it took an entire generation to arrive at the level of cooperation and mutual reliance that characterises Polish-German economic relations today.

The stereotype of "Polish economy" (*polnische Wirtschaft*) dates back at least to the writings of Georg Forster in the eighteenth century.[4] In the 1990s, Forster's perception was far from extinguished: Poland was still widely associated with hyperinflation, institutional fragility, and economic disorder.[5] Popular German discourse alternated between derision, latent guilt over wartime atrocities, and sporadic admiration for the *Solidarność*-movement.[6] Rarely was Poland viewed as a stable or trustworthy economic partner.

Conversely, from the Polish perspective, the Federal Republic of Germany stood as a model of economic discipline, institutional order, and material affluence.[7] This contrast was particularly stark in the late 1980s, when the German economy experienced a "mini economic miracle," underpinned by a generous welfare state and a strong Deutsche Mark.[8] The iconic Mercedes-Benz W123, discount shopping temples like Aldi, and opportunities for seasonal work, often informal, were the object of admiration in Poland. Envisioning Poland as a credible future partner to such an advanced and competitive economy required considerable strategic foresight and political resolve.

Among the figures who demonstrated such vision was Tadeusz Mazowiecki, Poland's first democratically-elected Prime Minister.[9] In seeking a "Polish Ludwig Erhard," Mazowiecki entrusted Leszek Balcerowicz with implementing radical market-oriented reforms. The so-called "shock therapy" was accompanied by immense social costs, including the collapse of many state-owned enterprises and a dramatic surge in unemployment. Yet the market began to function – first and foremost in trade. Nevertheless, the foundations of a functioning market economy were laid, particularly in the domain of trade. With the opening of borders, informal Polish markets proliferated across Germany, while German consumer goods, es-

4 Kordel Przegląd Historyczny 202, 879 (879–902).
5 Kaluza/Traupe/Płóciennik, p. 9 (10).
6 Kaluza/Traupe/Płóciennik, p. 9 (10).
7 Kaluza/Traupe/Płóciennik, p. 9 (10).
8 D'Elia JEEH 1993, 381 (381–402).
9 Kaluza/Traupe/Płóciennik, p. 9 (10).

pecially from Aldi, inundated street stalls in Poland.[10] Germany, with its geographic proximity, economic scale, and early trade linkages, emerged as Poland's most promising trade partner. Yet the German market also posed formidable challenges, requiring adaptation to exacting quality standards and unfamiliar capitalist principles.

Initially, German investment gravitated more readily toward the Czech Republic and Hungary. In the early 1990s, Poland's political volatility and underdeveloped legal-institutional frameworks fostered a degree of scepticism among German business actors.[11] This was compounded by the burden of the foreign debt Poland had accumulated.[12] Only after the 1994 agreement on partial debt relief[13] did confidence in Poland begin to grow. Western financial institutions and multinational corporations turned their gaze east of the Oder, discovering, just an hour's drive from Berlin, a rapidly-expanding market with competitive labour costs and a well-educated workforce.

The deepening of trade and investment ties was greatly accelerated by the process of European integration. Poland's association agreement of 1991,[14] followed by EU membership in 2004,[15] provided a stable regulatory framework and substantial structural funds, stimulating domestic demand for investment goods. German firms were ideally positioned to benefit.

10 Kaluza/Traupe/Płóciennik, p. 9 (10).
11 Deszczyński RPEiS 2004, 79 (79–91).
12 Piech/Bodo, p. 183 (183–194).
13 Tiongson East European Quarterly 1997, 55 (55).
14 Europe Agreement establishing an association between the European Communities and their Member States, of the one part, and the Republic of Poland, of the other (OJ L 348, 31.12.1993, p. 2–180).
15 Treaty between the Kingdom of Belgium, the Kingdom of Denmark, the Federal Republic of Germany, the Hellenic Republic, the Kingdom of Spain, the French Republic, Ireland, the Italian Republic, the Grand Duchy of Luxembourg, the Kingdom of the Netherlands, the Republic of Austria, the Portuguese Republic, the Republic of Finland, the Kingdom of Sweden, the United Kingdom of Great Britain and Northern Ireland (Member States of the European Union) and the Czech Republic, the Republic of Estonia, the Republic of Cyprus, the Republic of Latvia, the Republic of Lithuania, the Republic of Hungary, the Republic of Malta, the Republic of Poland, the Republic of Slovenia, the Slovak Republic, concerning the accession of the Czech Republic, the Republic of Estonia, the Republic of Cyprus, the Republic of Latvia, the Republic of Lithuania, the Republic of Hungary, the Republic of Malta, the Republic of Poland, the Republic of Slovenia and the Slovak Republic to the European Union (OJ L 236, 23.9.2003, p. 17–930).

Bilateral trade rose from nearly €35 billion in 2004 to over €66.5 billion by 2008, with Germany maintaining a consistent trade surplus.[16]

Paradoxically, the global financial and economic crisis that erupted in 2008 further strengthened Polish-German economic ties. In response to collapsing demand, German firms rationalised their supply chains, increasingly replacing higher-cost suppliers in Southern Europe with cost-efficient, capable partners in Central and Eastern Europe. This reconfiguration of intra-European trade disproportionately benefitted Poland. Indeed, economists from Southern Europe have argued that one of the crisis's more enduring consequences was the diversion of German trade and investment flows from the South to Eastern Europe. Data supports this claim: by 2016, bilateral trade between Germany and Poland exceeded €100 billion. At the same time, Poland distinguished itself within the EU through sustained GDP growth, prudent fiscal management, and declining unemployment. The outdated stereotype of the "Polish economy" began to fade, especially among younger German business leaders.

Since the early 1990s, Polish-German economic relations have evolved into one of the densest and most strategically consequential bilateral partnerships within the EU. Germany gained access to an increasingly-skilled labour force and a nearby production base, enhancing its global competitiveness. Poland, for its part, benefited from access to German capital, technology, and logistics infrastructure, while Polish firms acquired crucial experience through integration into German-led corporate structures.

Today, Germany remains Poland's largest trading partner in goods, both in terms of exports and imports.[17] Conversely, Poland has emerged as Germany's fourth-largest trading partner.[18] Bilateral trade is dominated by medium- and high-technology products embedded in global value chains. In 2021, such goods accounted for 46 percent of Polish exports to Germany and 53 percent of Polish imports from Germany.[19] Key sectors include electrical equipment (such as automotive batteries and household appliances), vehicles and automotive components, and consumer electronics. Germany is the primary indirect exporter of Polish value-added goods: more than

16 Kaluza/Traupe/Płóciennik, p. 9 (12).

17 Central Statistical Office, Foreign Trade Statistical Yearbook 2024, p. 18–19; see also Ebenroth/Boujong/Joost/Strohn/Poelzig/Sander/Grundmann/Denga, Vor. § 343 HGB, mn. 75.

18 Statistisches Bundesamt, Außenhandel. Rangfolge der Handelspartner im Außenhandel der Bundesrepublik Deutschland 2024, p. 2.

19 Ambroziak/Gniadek/Kopiński/Sierocińska/Wąsiński, p. 5.

22 percent of Polish value-added goods that are ultimately exported to other countries is channelled through German firms. As a result, Polish components and services reach markets worldwide, including the United States, through Germany-based production and distribution systems.

Germany is also Poland's largest investor when measured by location of the ultimate controlling entity, and the second-largest when measured by ultimate beneficial ownership, and second only to the Netherlands when measured by formal legal registration. According to data from the National Bank of Poland, German direct investment in Poland totalled around €60 billion by the end of 2023.[20]

Flagship German investments in Poland include the Volkswagen factory near Września, completed in 2016 at a cost of nearly €1 billion, still the largest foreign investment in Poland to date. Beyond the automotive sector, German firms are active in virtually all areas of the Polish economy: grocery retail, banking, insurance, home appliances, construction materials, food production, telecommunications, and transport.[21] Germany's presence in Poland is not limited to large corporations such as Volkswagen, Mercedes-Benz, Siemens, or Bosch. Thousands of small- and medium-sized German enterprises operate in Poland, often as subsidiaries embedded within larger corporate groups or as partners in production networks.

In recent years, Polish firms have also begun to engage in cross-border investment and strategic partnerships, albeit on a smaller scale. Some have entered the German market through acquisitions or joint ventures, while others have integrated into German-led European networks of production, logistics, and innovation.

Today, the economic interdependence between Poland and Germany is no longer defined solely by trade volumes or capital flows. Rather, it reflects a high degree of structural integration. The two economies are intricately connected through cross-border supply chains and transnational corporate networks that operate within and across distinct legal and institutional frameworks. The density of bilateral economic activity has been accompanied by the emergence of a professional infrastructure that facilitates translation and coordination between legal systems. Transnational law firms, notarial chambers, chambers of commerce, and bilateral legal associations all contribute to the governance of this complex interface. More

20 National Bank of Poland, Foreign direct investment in Poland and Polish direct investment abroad in 2023, Warsaw 2024, p. 17.

21 Ambroziak/Gniadek/Kopiński/Sierocińska/Wąsiński, p. 26.

recently, the intensifying regulatory focus on sustainability, human rights, and corporate due diligence has added new layers of legal and institutional complexity. In this evolving landscape, mutual legal understanding and alignment are becoming indispensable foundations of the Polish-German economic partnership.

C. The Company's Interest in Polish-German Business Relations

Understanding Polish-German business relations entails more than tracking trade flows or foreign direct investment. It requires close attention to the legal and normative infrastructures companies operate in, especially when corporate responsibilities are shared or contested across borders. Applying a transnational lens reveals that the modalities of cooperation are not static or self-contained, but are shaped by mutual observation, legal transplantation, and the selective adaptation of practices within processes of decision-making. In this context, the concept of the interest of the company assumes particular importance. Although both Polish and German corporate law formally ground directors' duties in reference to the company's interest, doctrinal interpretations and practical applications often diverge, particularly in transnational constellations.

Polish-German business interdependence typically manifests in three principal forms: (1) cross-border contractual relationships, (2) joint ventures, and (3) vertically integrated group structures involving subsidiaries. Across all of these, the company's interest functions as both a legal standard and a practical heuristic. It guides board-level decisions, frames strategic considerations, and provides the vocabulary through which competing financial, regulatory, or sustainability-related priorities are articulated and negotiated.

I. Contractual Cooperation: autonomous yet interdependent entities

The most foundational form of Polish-German economic engagement is constituted by cross-border contractual relationships. These are usually structured through long-term agreements between legally-independent companies. In such settings, each party retains formal autonomy, and the concept of the company's interest remains internal to each legal entity.

Nevertheless, legal and reputational interdependencies often mean that one company's operational decisions materially affect the other's risk exposure.

Sustainability-related obligations illustrate this dynamic clearly. For example, a German manufacturer subject to the German Lieferkettensorgfaltspflichtengesetz (Act on Corporate Due Diligence Obligations in Supply Chains) may require its Polish supplier to adopt stringent environmental and labour standards, even where such standards exceed those mandated by Polish law. The Polish company may view such requirements as burdensome and cost intensive. However, a broader, pluralistic conception of the company's interest could more easily justify compliance beyond mere value-enhancement arguments.

Frictions nonetheless emerge. When cost pressures incentivise Polish suppliers to compromise on compliance, and German clients insist on strict adherence to mitigate their own regulatory and ESG-related obligations and aspirations, tensions may escalate. Legal advisors play a critical role in these situations, translating expectations into locally-actionable terms. In this setting, the company's interest functions not merely as a doctrinal standard, but as a lens through which sustainability becomes aligned, or fails to align, with commercial viability.

II. Co-governance in joint ventures

Joint ventures between Polish and German partners represent a more integrated and complex form of cross-border cooperation. These entities are typically characterised by shared equity participation and co-determined governance structures. Board composition is often reflective of national origin, with members appointed by both sides, thus institutionalising cross-jurisdictional negotiation within the company's decision-making framework.

Divergences may surface in board discussions over long-term strategy, capital allocation, or responses to regulatory pressures. For instance, a dispute might arise over whether to allocate resources to a decarbonisation initiative in response to EU sustainability regulations. The German partner may regard this as essential for aligning the joint venture with evolving ESG benchmarks and safeguarding future financing opportunities. The Polish partner, by contrast, may question the economic feasibility or the urgency of such measures, especially in light of domestic regulatory laxity or political opposition to rapid green transitions.

Such disagreements highlight the ambiguity inherent in the notion of the company's interest. Is it best understood as a compromise between shareholder positions? Or does it instead require an autonomous articulation grounded in the long-term sustainability and profitability of the joint venture itself? When sustainability measures are supported by clear commercial rationales, such as securing access to green financing or safeguarding export eligibility, then their incorporation into the company's strategic agenda can be framed as fully aligned with financial interests. But where these benefits are more diffuse or speculative, internal contention becomes more likely. In this setting, the interest of the company serves not only as a normative guidepost but also as a platform for articulating divergent visions of the joint venture's role for and within society.

III. Subsidiaries in Corporate Groups: legal Autonomy under strategic command

In vertically-integrated corporate groups, the interpretive tensions surrounding the interest of the company reach their most acute form. For instance, if a Polish company functions as a wholly-owned subsidiary of a German parent, it is subject to both national legal constraints and transnational strategic imperatives. Under Polish law, the management board of the subsidiary has a duty to act in the interest of the company it serves – not of its shareholder *per se*. However, doctrinal interpretations in Polish company law and group governance practices often blur this distinction.[22]

Conflicts commonly arise in areas such as profit distribution, investment strategy, and restructuring. Consider a German parent company demanding high-dividend payouts to support group-level financial consolidation, while Polish managers argue for reinvestment in local operations to maintain competitiveness or comply with emerging regulatory standards. In such cases, the company's interest becomes contested terrain and could become both a legal shield and a strategic lever: the company's interest may be invoked either to resist shareholder demands or to justify compliance with them.

Sustainability pressures add further layers of complexity. German parent companies, particularly those listed or otherwise exposed to global ESG reporting obligations, may impose uniform environmental or social standards

22 See chapter 2 of this volume.

across their group operations. A Polish subsidiary may be asked to phase out fossil-fuel-based production methods or implement costly labour protections. These measures may well serve the long-term interest of the group and even align with emerging EU legislation. Yet, for the local entity, they may generate immediate financial strain or conflict with the expectations of domestic stakeholders.

Illustratively, consider the planned closure of a Polish manufacturing site as part of a German-led, group-wide consolidation aiming to reduce the carbon footprint. While this may serve the group's sustainability goals and improve its ESG ratings, the Polish management board faces a legal and ethical dilemma: does acting in the interest of the company require resisting closure to preserve local employment and maintain operational solvency? Or does loyalty to the group take precedence?

IV. The Company's Interest as a Normative Compass

Across all three constellations of Polish-German business cooperation – contractual relationships, joint ventures, and corporate group structure – the concept of the interest of the company emerges as a central but contested standard. It provides a normative anchor for board members' duties and a vocabulary for resolving cross-border tensions. Yet its meaning is neither fixed nor self-evident. Especially in light of the growing regulatory emphasis on sustainability, human rights, and due diligence, the interpretation of the company's interest requires constant renegotiation between legal regimes, commercial priorities, and stakeholder expectations.

What unites these different scenarios is the recognition that sustainable corporate behaviour, though increasingly necessary, is not automatic. It often requires justification, contention, and translation, particularly when transnational governance structures are involved. In this regard, the company's interest remains a vital legal and practical construct, one that enables corporate actors to navigate the complex interplay between profit, purpose, and responsibility in Polish-German economic relations.

D. Outlook

The analysis undertaken in this chapter reveals that the concept of the company's interest, far from being a static or self-evident legal principle, plays a central role within the broader legal fabric of Polish-German business relations. As economic integration deepens, transnational business constellations become increasingly complex, and challenges around sustainability objectives intensify, the need for mutual legal understanding becomes more urgent.

Against this backdrop, divergences in how Polish and German actors interpret and apply the company's interest are not merely technical differences: they are symptomatic of deeper tensions within the normative architectures of the two legal systems. These tensions surface most acutely in cross-border contractual relationships (including supply chains), joint venture companies, and vertically-integrated group structures, where board members and advisors must navigate plural legal expectations and reconcile them with strategic and operational imperatives. The company's interest functions in such cases not as a universally accepted north star, but as a site of translation – where doctrinal abstractions are rendered into actionable standards.

Yet it is precisely this interpretive friction that renders the concept of the company's interest so vital. In an era marked by rising regulatory complexity, shifting geopolitical alignments, and intensifying demands for corporate accountability, the company's interest acts as a crucial mediating device. It compels boards, shareholders, and regulators to confront fundamental questions of purpose, responsibility, and legitimacy. Within the Polish-German context, it becomes a normative interface, a zone where legal traditions, economic pragmatism, and sustainability aspirations converge and sometimes collide.

Thus, the "legal fabric" that binds Polish and German corporate actors is not a seamless weave, but rather a dense and evolving tapestry of mutual influence, adaptive learning, and normative contestation. While the following chapters will explore in greater doctrinal detail how the interest of the company is understood in Poland, Germany, and other European jurisdictions, this chapter underscores a critical point: as an open-ended legal concept, the company's interest acquires concrete meaning only through the practices of those who invoke, interpret, and operationalise it – often across borders.

Therefore, to see the interest of the company through a transnational lens is to recognize that economic actors do not simply apply a fixed rule: they engage in a process of framing, translating, and adapting the concept to concrete situations, often drawing on legal ideas, institutional templates, and discursive practices from beyond their national borders. In doing so, they contribute to the ongoing redefinition of what the company is for, and whom it is meant to serve. Ultimately, to examine the interest of the company from a transnational perspective is to acknowledge that company law is not simply a system of neutral rules, but a site of normative struggle over the meaning of the legitimate role of private power in society.

References

Ambroziak, Łukasz/Gniadek, Joanna/Kopiński, Dominik/Sierocińska, Katarzyna/Marek Wąsiński, Współpraca handlowo-inwestycyjna Polski z Niemcami, Warsaw 2022, p. 5

Bodo, Monika, The International Debt of Poland, in Piech (ed.) Economic Policy and Growth of Central and East European Countries, London 2003, p. 183

D'Elia, Costanza, Miracles and Mirages in the West German Economy: A Survey of the Literature of the 1980s, JEEH 1993, 381

Deszczyński, Przemysław, Inwestycje bezpośrednie RFN w Polsce w okresie transformacji, Ruch Prawniczy, Ekonomiczny i Socjologiczny 2004, 79

Ebenroth, Carsten T./Boujong, Karlheinz/Joost, Detlev/Strohn, Lutz/Poelzig, Dörte/Sander, Volker (eds.), Handelsgesetzbuch, Band 2: §§ 343-475h, München 5th Edition 2024

Kordel, Jacek, Zur Entstehung des Begriffs 'polnische Wirtschaft', Przegląd Historyczny 2020, 879.

Płóciennik, Sebastian, Besser geht's nicht? Die deutsch-polnischen Wirtschaftsbeziehungen, in Kaluza/Traupe (eds.), Jahrbuch Polen 2020 – Polnische Wirtschaft, Wiesbaden 2020, p. 9

Tiongson, Erwin, Poland and IMF conditionality programs: 1990–1995, East European Quarterly 1997, 55

Weber, Anne-Marie/Mittwoch, Anne-Christin, Harmonizing duties of board members in the Anthropocene: When expectations meet reality, RECoL 2023, 143

2. The Interest of the Company in Poland: Dismantling the Narratives for Sustainability

Anne-Marie Weber and Aleksandra Szczęsna

A. Introduction

The concept of "the interest of the company" plays a central role in company law, shaping decision-making frameworks and governance structures. In Poland, like in many other European countries, the interest of the company is firmly and explicitly embedded in the legal framework, yet it remains undefined in statutory provisions. As a result, the application of the concept requires interpretative effort, posing challenges for decision-makers within the company, their legal advisors, and, ultimately, the adjudicating courts. The outcome of this interpretation process is crucial, as it determines the substance of board members' duty of care.

The debate in Polish scholarship and jurisprudence concerning the company's interest has thus far primarily centred on issues related to conflicts between minority and majority shareholders, as well as related issues within corporate groups. This focus is understandable, given that companies in Poland typically have majority shareholders, resulting in a heightened risk of horizontal conflicts between shareholders.[1] From this discourse a prevailing narrative has emerged, framing the company's interest as "a resultant of the shareholders' interests" (see Sec. 4 below), which situates the understanding of the company's interest in Poland squarely within the framework of the shareholder value model.[2]

The recent removal of a provision on board members' duties from the European Commission's initial CSDDD proposal has hindered a *quasi*-definition of the company's interest at the European level;[3] accordingly, renewed attention has been directed toward the extent to which national company law can accommodate sustainability objectives. Unlike developments in other EU Member States, the sustainability challenges of our time

1 Opalski, Przegląd Prawa Handlowego 2008/11, 16 (19).
2 Mazur, Państwo i Prawo 2022/7, 114 (120).
3 Weber/Mittwoch, RECoL 2023/1, 143 (161–162).

have yet to generate significant interest in Polish company law, let alone inspire legislative initiatives. The potential of the company's interest as a gateway for integrating sustainability objectives into corporate governance remains underexamined in legal scholarship.[4] This chapter seeks to address this gap in the literature.

Our aim is to critically examine and dismantle the narratives that have surrounded the company's interest in Polish legal discourse to assess whether they facilitate or impede the pursuit of corporate sustainability. Corporate sustainability envisions corporate conduct as: (1) *environmentally sustainable*, ensuring long-term stability and resilience of ecosystems; (2) *socially sustainable*, upholding human rights and promoting good governance; and (3) *economically sustainable*, meeting the economic needs essential for stable and resilient societies.[5]

To this end, we examine how the narratives on the company's interest intersect with sustainability challenges to determine whether a sustainability-oriented reconceptualization of the company's interest requires legislative intervention. Our inquiry focuses on the Polish joint-stock company (*spółka akcyjna*, S.A.), including public and private joint-stock companies whose shares are not traded on an organised market.

The chapter is arranged in six sections. Following this introduction, Section 2 provides context on the historical detachment of the narratives on the company's interest. Section 3 explores the normative function of the company's interest within Polish company law, while Section 4 reconstructs the prevailing contemporary interpretations of the concept. Section 5 investigates the extent to which these narratives are receptive to sustainability objectives. Finally, Section 6 evaluates whether legislative intervention is necessary to redefine the company's interest in alignment with the sustainability paradigm.

---

4 Preliminary threads of an emerging discussion related explicitly to Polish company law can be found in: Opalski, Przegląd Prawa Handlowego 2025/4, 4; Olszak/Stokłosa, Prawo i Więź (Law & Social Bonds) 2025/1, 346; Weber/Mazur/Szczęsna, Przegląd Prawa Handlowego 2022/6, 20; Chałaczkiewicz-Ładna/Sójka/Jerzmanowski, European Business Law Review 2023/4, 665; Dumkiewicz/Szczotka/Kopaczyńska-Pieczniak/Weber-Elżanowska, p. 218 (226); Weber/Mittwoch, Review of European and Comparative Law 2023/1, 143; Radwan/Regucki, International and Comparative Corporate Law Journal 2012/32, 1 – 48.

5 Liao/Sjåfjell/Argyou/Liao/Sjåfjell/Argyou, p. 1 (2).

B. *Disconnected origins of the company's interest*

The evolution of company law in Poland is intricate, shaped by the nation's turbulent history.[6] A nuanced understanding of how the company's interest is interpreted today requires analysis that goes beyond contemporary legal frameworks and doctrinal views. This section examines whether historical interpretations of the company's interest can offer insights into contemporary analysis and to what extent historical developments may, in fact, constrain the applicability of the historical method.

I. *Early developments.*

The growing presence of trade companies (*kompanie handlowe*), the immediate precursors to joint-stock companies,[7] on Polish territory can be traced back to the second half of the 18th century.[8] A defining characteristic of these entities was their strong connection with the state – or more specifically, with the royal court. The privilege of establishing a trade company was reserved for the monarch. In practice, it was common for founding acts to be approved by parliamentary statutes (*konstytucje sejmowe*), which granted these companies public-law concessions, land endowments, and other privileges.[9] The prevailing doctrinal view is that the founding acts of joint-stock companies – referred to at the time as "laws" (*ustawy*) – functioned as *lex specialis* to the general substantive and procedural private law.[10] Simultaneously, all companies were subject to state oversight, initially by the Treasury Commissions (*Komisje Skarbowe*) and later by the Treasury Department of the Permanent Council (*Departament Skarbowy Rady Nieustającej*). In the absence of specific regulations, these bodies were also responsible for resolving company-related disputes.

6 Frąckowiak, Acta Universitatis Wratislaviensis 2015/101, 45 (45).

7 Dąbrowska, Zeszyty Prawnicze 2019/4, 7.

8 Michalski, Monitor Prawa Handlowego 2017/2, 6 (8). Some authors refer to these entities as joint stock companies (*spółki akcyjne*), see Kula, p. 56; Mądzik, Rocznik Lubelski, 1979, 77 (84).

9 Bałtruszajtys, Czasopismo Prawno-Historyczne 1959/2, 85–110.

10 Bałtruszajtys, Czasopismo Prawno-Historyczne 1959/2, 85–110; Michalski MPH 2017/2, 6 (10).

II. *Partitions and legal fragmentation.*

The end of the 18th century marked the beginning of the partitions of Poland by the neighbouring empires, resulting in an increasingly fragmented legal landscape that persisted for over a century.[11] Following the restoration of independence in 1918, five distinct legal regimes governed commercial matters in different parts of Polish territory:[12] (1) Napoleon's Commercial Code of 1807 (with its respective amendments),[13] (2) the Digest of Laws of the Russian Empire of 1835,[14] (3) the German *Handelsgesetzbuch* of 1897, (4) the Austrian *Allgemeines Handelsgesetzbuch* of 1863, and (5) Hungarian commercial law, which applied in the regions of Spiš and Orava.

As a result of the profoundly fragmented legal landscape, doctrinal discourse on commercial law and theories of the legal person were influenced by multiple legal systems. The fragmentation of the legal landscape had a lasting impact on the development of legal thought, making it difficult to identify a singular, coherent tradition regarding the company's interest. While key writings from that era offer insights, they remain isolated contributions rather than a unified doctrinal foundation. For example, writing in Polish and engaging with German scholarship, *Longchamps de Bérier* developed his own theory of the legal person, explicitly distinguishing the interest of a joint-stock company from the individual interests of its shareholders.[15] However, such context-specific and fragmented scholarly contributions do not constitute a cohesive intellectual heritage that could serve as a meaningful historical foundation for later interpretations of the

11 Following the first partition in 1772, Russia, Austria, and Prussia annexed large parts of Poland. The second partition in 1793 further reduced Poland's territory, with Prussia and Russia taking more land. In 1795, the third partition led to the total erasure of Poland from the map of Europe, as the remaining Polish lands were divided among the three powers, and Poland ceased to exist as an independent state.

12 See: Górnicki, Prawo i Więź 2022/4, 618 (618–619); Janczewski, p. 15; Michalski, Monitor Prawa Handlowego, 2017/2, 6 (14).

13 See in detail: Michalski/Michalski, pp. 65–81. After the first partition, the Duchy of Warsaw (*Księstwo Warszawskie*), a French client state, was created in 1807 under the influence of Napoleon Bonaparte. It was a semi-independent entity with its own constitution and legal system but still heavily influenced by France. The Duchy served as a significant symbol of Polish sovereignty. However, it lasted only until 1815, when the Congress of Vienna redrew Europe's borders, and most of the Duchy's territory was incorporated into the Russian Empire as the Congress Kingdom of Poland (*Królestwo Kongresowe*).

14 See in detail: Michalski/Tarkowski, pp. 105–125.

15 Longchamps de Bérier, pp. 165–199.

company's interest. Thus, it was the absence of a shared doctrinal tradition, rather than its presence, that characterized the legal landscape prior to the unification of modern Polish company law.

III. *Independence and unification.*

The Act on Joint-Stock Companies (*Prawo o spółkach akcyjnych* – AJSC), enacted in 1928, was the first modern Polish company law to regulate joint-stock companies uniformly across the entire Polish territory.[16] It introduced a registration-based system (*system meldunkowy*) under which a joint-stock company was formed and acquired legal personality upon its entry into the register, without requiring an administrative concession or prior approval.[17] However, the AJSC made an exception for companies deemed to be of national importance or public utility, requiring their formation and charter to be approved by the Minister of Industry and Trade.[18] This provision made clear that public utility considerations did not apply universally to all joint-stock companies: rather, they only applied to a select category of joint-stock companies. By incorporating elements of the concessionary system, these regulations sparked criticism from both the business community and legal scholars, who viewed them as a constraint on entrepreneurial freedom and legal certainty.[19]

Parallel to the adoption of the AJSC, the Polish Codification Commission (*Komisja Kodyfikacyjna*) was actively working on unifying the commercial law, a process that culminated in the enactment of the Commercial Code (*Kodeks handlowy*, "CC").[20] Like the AJSC, the CC did not generally condition the establishment of a joint-stock company on public utility requirements.

16 Regulation of the President of the Republic of Poland of 22 March 1928 – Law on Joint Stock Companies (Journal of Laws No. 39, item 383). Dz. U. Nr 39, poz. 383. The text of the regulation with the justification of the Codification Commission of the Republic of Poland appeared in the study by Namitkiewicz: Polish Stock Law, Warsaw 1928.

17 Michalski, Monitor Prawa Handlowego 2017/3, 6 (9).

18 This exception also applied to companies engaged in banking and insurance activities, requiring their statutes to be approved by the Minister of the Treasury in consultation with the Minister of Industry and Trade.

19 Bloch, Przegląd Prawa Handlowego 1928/3, 116; Benis, p. 13.

20 Regulation of the President of the Republic of Poland of 27 June 1934 – Commercial Code (Journal of Laws No. 57, item 502).

The concept of the company's interest was embedded in specific provisions of the CC. It appeared as a prerequisite for depriving shareholders of their pre-emptive rights (Article 435 § 2 CC), in the plural form (*interesy spółki*, "company's interests") when addressing conflicts of interest between the company and a management board member (Article 373 CC), and as a criterion for the annulment (*uchylenie*) of a resolution of the general meeting (Article 414 CC).[21] Despite these explicit references, the CC did not provide a legal definition of the company's interest, nor did the legislative materials elaborate on its meaning.

Given the abrupt cessation of the CC's applicability in 1939 due to the outbreak of the Second World War, its brief period of enforcement did not permit the development of a substantial body of doctrinal analysis or jurisprudence interpreting the concept of the company's interest. Consequently, only a few scattered references to the concept exist in the legal literature of that period.

Allerhand, one of the drafters of the CC, explained that a company's interests are harmed when "its revenues are diminished, or the company's survival is at risk".[22] Referring to Article 435 § 2 CC, which stipulated that shareholders could be deprived of their pre-emptive rights only in the company's interest, *Allerhand* emphasized that such deprivation could occur solely "for the benefit of the company, not merely for a specific group of shareholders".[23] Consequently, *Allerhand* attributed a notion of separation and autonomy to the company's interest, explicitly distinguishing it from the interests of shareholders. However, aside from referencing economic indicators (such as revenues), *Allerhand* did not elaborate further on the substance of the company's interest.

Similarly, in discussing the annulment of general meeting resolutions that violate the company's interest, *Dziurzyński* asserted that a resolution could be contested if it infringed upon "the interest of the company as such" (*interes spółki jako takiej*).[24] As an example of such conduct infringing the interest of the company, *Dziurzyński* cited a situation in which shareholders act to benefit a competing company in which they also hold

21 Current literature distinguishes the singular form "company's interest" (*interes spółki*) from the plural form "company's interests" (*interesy spółki*), arguing that the latter describes the areas of the company's business activities, relationships with contractors, financial institutions, and other partners, see: Opalski/Pabis Art. 422 CCC mn. 83.

22 Allerhand, pp. 380, 642.

23 Allerhand, pp. 380, 664.

24 Dziurzyński/Fenichel/Honzatko/Dziurzyński, Art. 240 CCC note 6.

shares, prioritizing their personal gain over the well-being of the company. This interpretation clearly indicates that *Dziurzyński* viewed the company's interest as conceptually distinct from the interests of its shareholders.

Although *Namitkiewicz*, another prominent legal scholar of the time, did not explicitly address the concept of the company's interest, his work provides an important interpretative backdrop. *Namitkiewicz* defined commercial law as "a set of normative provisions that lead to a balancing of economic interests, resulting from activities aimed at generating profit through the exchange of goods, thereby guiding the moral and economic conduct of the individuals involved in such activities, in line with a sense of appropriate social ends".[25] In this view, commercial law functions as a system of rules that shape the behaviour of economic actors in accordance with broader societal objectives. *Namitkiewicz* further argued that ensuring morally sound conduct through commercial law is essential for both the safety and efficiency of commerce.[26] He emphasized that commercial law should incorporate "social-service norms" (*normy społeczno-służbowe*) that seek to advance broader social objectives, particularly by protecting weaker parties in legal relationships whose interests might otherwise be insufficiently safeguarded.[27]

A similar broad contextual perspective emerges in the writings of *Dniestrzansky*, who stressed that "the focus of economic law is not the individual with their needs and aspirations, but society itself, which seeks ways to realise its interests, even if this contradicts the selfishness of individuals or the abuse of state power".[28] This perspective underscores the idea that economic regulation must balance private interests with broader public objectives, reflecting a fundamental tension between individual economic freedoms and societal welfare in shaping legal norms.

Taken together, these context-specific perspectives offer valuable insights but fall short of forming a cohesive doctrinal foundation for interpreting the company's interest through the historical method. While scholars such as *Dziurzyński, Namitkiewicz,* and *Dniestrzansky* addressed issues related

25 Namitkiewicz, Przegląd Prawa Handlowego 1992/1, 24 (26) – reprint of article from Przegląd Prawa Handlowego 1925/2; translation by the authors.

26 Namitkiewicz, Przegląd Prawa Handlowego 1992/1, 24 (27).

27 This may be the reason why Namitkiewicz critiqued the CC for minimising the provisions of public policy – Namitkiewicz Przegląd Prawa Handlowego 1992/1, 24 (28); Górnicki, Acta Universitatis Wratislaviensis 2015/101, 63 (89–90).

28 Dniestrzański, Czasopismo Prawnicze i Ekonomiczne 1932/1, 340 (361); translation by the authors.

to corporate governance, economic regulation, and the balance between private and public interests, their analyses remained limited in scope and often indirect in relation to the company's interest as a distinct legal concept. As a result, while these writings can be cited to support specific arguments, any attempt to construct a coherent historical doctrine of the company's interest from them would be misplaced, underscoring the limitations of relying on historical interpretations as an authoritative basis for defining the company's interest in Polish company law today.

IV. *Dormancy in a planned economy.*

Although the CC formally remained in effect after 1945, its practical application was systematically curtailed in response to the political and economic transformations that occurred as Poland fell within the Soviet sphere of influence. The new political and economic system, built on the principles of special protection of state property, nationalization of private ownership, and a centrally planned economy, left little room for the traditional commercial law framework. As a result, commercial law as outlined by the CC was effectively replaced by economic law (*prawo gospodarcze*),[29] or more accurately "socialised trade law" (*prawo obrotu uspołecznionego*), which was founded on the differentiation of the category of social property.

The marginalization of commercial law reached its peak with the introduction of the Civil Code,[30] the enactment of which also revoked the bulk of the CC.[31] Although certain provisions from the CC remained in force, including those regulating joint-stock companies, the dominant political and economic system rendered commercial law largely obsolete. As a result, commercial law entered a prolonged period of dormancy, with its function markedly diminished. During this time, neither meaningful academic discourse nor jurisprudence on the concept of the company's interest emerged, further reinforcing the absence of a coherent doctrinal foundation for its historical interpretation.

29 Kułak, Studia nad Autorytaryzmem i Totalitaryzmem 2021/3, 73 (81).

30 Act of 23 April 1964 – Civil Code (Journal of Laws No. 16, item 93).

31 See: Article VI of the Act of 23 April 1964 Introductory provisions of the Civil Code (Journal of Laws No. 16, item 94, as amended).

V. *Transition to a market economy.*

The transition to a market economy in Poland, initiated in 1989, served as a catalyst for the revival of commercial law. This transformation was set in motion by the efforts of the Independent Self-Governing Trade Union "Solidarność" (*Niezależny Samorządny Związek Zawodowy "Solidarność"*),[32] whose negotiations with the government led to significant legal and economic reforms.[33] However, this momentum was temporarily disrupted by the imposition of martial law in December 1981, which delayed the restructuring process. The process of transformation resumed with negotiations between the resurgent *Solidarność* and state authorities, culminating in the Round Table Talks of April 1989. Legislative reforms, including the Act of 23 December 1988 on Economic Activity,[34] laid the foundation for Poland's transition to a market economy and the re-emergence of commercial law as a vital framework for regulating economic relations in Poland.

As Poland transitioned to a market economy, the dormant provisions of the CC that had remained in effect, including the provisions regulating joint-stock companies, gradually regained relevance through practical application. However, during this period of rapid economic transformation, scholarly attention was directed less toward doctrinal issues like the company's interest and more toward the broader question of whether a new codification of commercial law was necessary and if so, what form it should take. This debate gained prominence following the establishment of the Codification Commission (*Komisja Kodyfikacyjna*) in 1997.[35]

---

32 In 1980, on August 30 in Szczecin, August 31 in Gdańsk, September 3 in Jastrzębie, and September 10 at the Katowice Steelworks, representatives of the strike committees and the ruling party signed the August Agreements (*Porozumienia Sierpniowe*). As a result, on September 17, 1980, in Gdańsk, workers' representatives from across Poland established the nationwide Independent Self-Governing Trade Union "Solidarność".

33 A gradual transition began, moving away from a management system for state-owned enterprises dominated by administrative directives, toward a more market-oriented approach. A significant influence on the functioning of economic entities was gained by employee self-management, which ceased to be dependent on party-controlled and union-controlled bodies closely linked to state power, instead becoming a true representation of workers.

34 Act of 23 December 1988 on economic activity (Journal of Laws No. 41, item 324).

35 The members included Professor Stanisław Sołtysiński, Professor Andrzej Szajkowski and Professor Janusz Szwaja. Later Professor Janusz Szwaja was replaced by Professor Andrzej Szumański.

Legal commentary on the CC during its revival in the 1990s reinforced the general understanding of the distinction between the company's interest and the interests of its shareholders but remained limited to specific contexts. *Sołtysiński,* analysing the annulment of shareholder resolutions, underscored that the company's interest is compromised when shareholders – particularly those with significant influence over management – diminish the company's assets through improper or fictitious transactions.[36] He further emphasized that the misuse of corporate resources to benefit only a select group of shareholders violates both the company's interest and the rights of other shareholders. *Sołtysiński* observed that "the capital invested by all shareholders and the results of the company's activities are exploited in the interest of only some shareholders, thereby violating both the company's interest and the interests of the remaining shareholders".[37] This reasoning affirmed the company's interest as an independent legal concept, separate from the aggregate interests of individual shareholders.

Similarly, *Frąckowiak* argued that a resolution of the general meeting contravenes the company's interest when it prioritizes the interests of shareholders or third parties at the expense of the company itself. This perspective further reinforces the idea that the company's interest is a distinct legal concept, separate from both shareholder interests and external considerations.[38] However, like *Sołtysiński*'s analysis, *Frąckowiak*'s interpretation remained confined to specific contexts, without advancing a broader doctrinal framework for defining the company's interest within Polish company law.

In jurisprudence, the consideration of non-shareholder interests in defining the company's interest was embodied in the Łódź Court of Appeal's judgment of 7 March 1994.[39] The case concerned a capital increase for a bank, and the court was tasked with assessing whether the safeguarding of the company's interest was a crucial prerequisite for depriving shareholders of their pre-emption rights under Article 435 § 2 CC. The court ultimately ruled that the exclusion of existing shareholders' pre-emption rights was justified if the exclusion facilitated the efficient supply of capital and strengthened the bank's financial condition. Notably, the judgment emphasized that strong supply of capital would also benefit the bank's account

36 Sołtysiński/Szajkowski/Szwaja/Sołtysiński, p. 77.
37 Sołtysiński/Szajkowski/Szwaja/Sołtysiński, p. 108.
38 Frąckowiak/Kidyba/Kruczalak/Pyzioł/Weiss/Frąckowiak, p. 594.
39 Appeal Court 7.03.1994 – ACr 21/94 published in Wokanda 1994/11, p. 54.

holders (depositors), suggesting that stakeholders, not just shareholders, could be considered in the interpretation of the company's interest.[40] While this ruling indicated that the company's long-term stability and financial health might, in certain contexts, require taking non-shareholder interests into account when interpreting the company's interest, it did not establish a systematic framework for integrating non-shareholder considerations into the general understanding of the company's interest.

VI. *The new Commercial Companies Code.*

The Commercial Companies Code ("CCC"), developed by the Codification Commission (*Komisja Kodyfikacyjna*), was adopted in 2000 and remains in force today, albeit with numerous amendments.[41] The Codification Commission adhered to the "continuation directive", which sought to maintain the core concepts, terminology, and structure of the earlier CC wherever possible.[42] However, in the case of joint-stock companies, several fundamental aspects were revised. Notably, the partial concession system was entirely abandoned, allowing for joint-stock companies to be established for any economic or non-economic purpose without the need for prior administrative approval.

The primary objective of the CCC was to swiftly revive company law and establish a legal framework that would facilitate economic activity while ensuring alignment with the standards required for Poland's anticipated accession to the European Union.[43] As a result, legislative discussions prioritised practical considerations over abstract or theoretical debates.[44] Consequently, it is unsurprising that the legislative materials contain no substantive discussion on the concept of the company's interest. Instead, the focus remained on creating a functional and investor-friendly regulatory environment, leaving the interpretation and development of the company's interest largely to judicial decisions and scholarly discourse.

---

40 Okolski/Modrzejewski/Gasiński, Przegląd Prawa Handlowego 2000/8, p. 11; Okolski/Modrzejewski/Gasiński PPH 2002/10, p. 24; Radwan, p. 275.

41 Act of 15 September 2000. Commercial Companies Code (i.e. Journal of Laws of 2024, item 18, as amended).

42 Justification of the CCC, p. 2; Sołtysiński, Państwo i Prawo, 2000/11, pp. 4–6.

43 Justification of the CCC, p. 9.

44 For a description of the main features of the CCC, as well as of the sources of foreign inspiration in its drafting, see: Baums/Hopt/Horn/Sołtysiński, p. 533; Drobnig/Hopt/Kötz/Mestmäcker/Sołtysiński, pp. 70–72.

Although the CCC is clearly influenced by the German legal tradition that carried over from the CC, and German experts were consulted by the Codification Commission,[45] there is no indication of an intent to fully transplant German legal principles into the CCC. The drafting process also drew inspiration from various other legal systems, including French, Italian, Austrian, Dutch, Swiss, and American company law.[46] Given this diverse set of influences, it is not feasible to argue that German, or any other foreign academic discussions, can be directly applied to interpretation of the company's interest within contemporary Polish company law. Instead, the company's interest must be understood within the specific historical, economic, and legal context that has shaped Poland's company law.

VII. *Interim conclusion.*

The evolution of Polish company law has been shaped by shifting legal regimes, economic transformations, and legislative pragmatism rather than by stable doctrinal tradition. The historical trajectory of the concept of the company's interest in Polish law is marked by fragmentation and discontinuity. The practical priorities that influenced both legislation and legal scholarship – particularly during the drafting of the currently-applicable CCC – led to the concept of the company's interest being introduced in an undefined and "naked" form, without a cohesive theoretical foundation. As a result, attempts to reconstruct the meaning of the company's interest by drawing on historical sources are inherently flawed. On the one hand, claims that the concept of shareholder primacy is "strongly rooted" in the Polish corporate governance tradition[47] are not supported by historical analysis. On the other hand, the explicit rejection of shareholder primacy or the adoption of an alternative theoretical model are not supported either. The absence of a clear and traceable doctrinal lineage means that any contemporary interpretation of the company's interest must be developed independently, rather than derived from an inconsistent and often disjointed historical record.

45 Prof. Marcus Lutter led the team of German experts that participated in the work.

46 Justification of the CCC, p. 22; Oplustil/Radwan, pp. 466–69.

47 As supported by Opalski, Przegląd Prawa Handlowego 2022/4, p. 9.

C. The normative function of the company's interest

I. *Terminological Foundations*

To begin with, it is essential to note that under the contractual basis of the joint-stock company, shareholders commit to pursuing a common objective (*wspólny cel*) through the contribution of assets and, if stipulated by the company's charter, through cooperation in other specified forms (Article 3 CCC). The legislature does not specify any ramifications as to the common objective. The prevailing view is that in a joint-stock company, the common objective may encompass any legally-permissible aim – whether economic, such as profit generation, or non-economic, including scientific, cultural, or social (including charitable) goals.[48]

The idea of the shareholders' common objective, as mentioned in Article 3 CCC, should be distinguished from the objective of the contractual obligation (*cel umowy*), which corresponds to what can be called the company's objective (*cel spółki*).[49] However, while these concepts are distinct, the common objective of the shareholders is inherently reflected in, and informs, the company's objective.[50]

The company's objective is further solidified through the determination of the object of the company's activity (*przedmiot działalności spółki*), which must be outlined in a joint-stock company's charter (Article 304 § 1 sec. 2 CCC).[51] The object of the company's activity can be formulated in a descriptive manner in the charter.[52] Designation of the object of the com-

48 Opalski/Wiśniewski, Art. 3 CCC mn. 16; Sołtysiński/Szajkowski/Szumański/Szwaja/Szajkowski Art. 3 CCC mn. 28; Szumański/Włodyka, p. 4; Michalski, p. 19; an opposing view was presented by Romanowski, who argues that a joint stock company may only be founded to conduct economic activity, see: Szajkowski/Romanowski, pp. 170–173.

49 Opalski//Wiśniewski, Art. 3 CCC mn. 20. Certain authors also equate the common objective with the company's objective, see: Kidyba/Skubisz/Okolski/Wajda, p. 257; Szumański, Przegląd Prawa Handlowego 2010/5, 9 (12).

50 Romanowski, SPP 2015/3, 63 (63).

51 Sołtysiński/Szajkowski/Tarska, p. 144; Michalski, p. 26.

52 The prevailing interpretation that a joint-stock company's charter must strictly use PKD (*Polska Klasyfikacja Działalności* – Polish Classification of Activities) terminology is based on a fundamental misunderstanding of the PKD's function, which is meant for statistical analysis. Nevertheless, this rigid approach, imposed by most registration courts, has influenced business practice, leading to the widespread use of PKD terminology in describing the object of a company's activities in charters – see Opalski/Wiśniewski, Art. 304 CCC mn. 13.

pany's activity also plays an auxiliary role in interpreting the company's interest.[53]

II. *Diverse Normative Applications*

The concept of the company's interest (*interes spółki*) is explicitly referenced in several provisions of the CCC. However, neither the CCC itself, the legislative materials related to its adoption, nor any other legal act provides a formal legal definition or explicit guidance on the interpretation of the company's interest. Similarly, the corporate governance code issued by the Warsaw Stock Exchange (*Dobre Praktyki Spółek Notowanych na GPW 2021* („DPSN2021")[54] mentions the company's interest without offering a definition. Consequently, under the current legal framework, the concept remains open to interpretation, giving rise to challenges stemming from competing narratives and the uncertainties surrounding their coexistence.[55]

Additional complexity arises from the conceptual and linguistic distinctions between the common objective (*wspólny cel*), the company's objective (*cel spółki*), and the object of the company's activities (*przedmiot działalności spółki*) on one hand, and the company's interest (*interes spółki*) on the other. While the former offer valuable insights into how the company's interest might be understood, drawing clear distinctions between them is often challenging. Notably, the company's interest is frequently described as functionally linked to the company's objective – meaning that any actions taken to achieve the company's objective must align with the company's interest.[56] Conversely, some have argued that the company's interest plays a defining role in shaping the company's objective.[57]

The concept of the company's interest serves as a fundamental criterion in several key areas of Polish company law. The company's interest determines the duty of joint-stock company management board members to abstain from decision-making in cases where a conflict of interest arises between the member and the company (Article 377 CCC). Additionally,

53 Opalski/Wiśniewski, Art. 304 CCC mn. 11.

54 Warsaw Stock Exchange, Dobre Praktyki Spółek Notowanych na GPW 2021, 2021, https://www.gpw.pl/pub/GPW/pdf/DPSN_2021.pdf. The code applies to issuers of shares listed on the WSE's main market.

55 Szajkowski/Romanowski, p. 141; Opalski/Pabis, Art. 422 CCC, mn. 56.

56 Kidyba/Skubisz/Okolski/Wajda, p. 264.

57 Szajkowski/Romanowski, p. 131.

the company's interest functions as a standard for judicial review of shareholder resolutions, guiding the proper exercise of voting rights at the general meeting (Article 422 § 1 CCC). Furthermore, pursuant to Article 433 § 2 CCC, the general meeting may only partially or entirely deprive shareholders of their pre-emptive rights to subscribe for shares if it is in the company's interest. Finally, in the context of cross-border mergers, divisions, and conversions under the provisions of from the Company Law Directive, the company's interest also provides a basis for courts to proceed with a cross-border reorganization despite a pending claim for annulment of the underlying resolution (for mergers, see Article 516^{18} § 2 CCC).[58]

III. *Normative Implications for Board Members' Duties*

The company's interest serves as a normative principle that shapes the responsibilities of a joint-stock company's governing bodies and their members.[59] Although neither the CCC nor the DPSN2021 explicitly mandate decision-making in accordance with the company's interest, it is widely accepted that all corporate decisions must be guided by this principle.[60] The interpretation of the company's interest, therefore, determines the fundamental standard for assessing the propriety of board members' actions.[61]

The appointment of a member of the management or supervisory board establishes an organizational relationship (*stosunek organizacyjny*) between the individual and the company.[62] This relationship forms the basis of the duties vested in a board member in their capacity as a board member: the obligation to diligently (i.e. with due care)[63] and loyally[64] perform one's

58 Motives 10 and 12 of the Directive (EU) 2019/2121 of the European Parliament and of the Council of 27 November 2019 amending Directive (EU) 2017/1132 as regards cross-border conversions, mergers and divisions (OJ L 321, 12.12.2019, p. 1–44).

59 Opalski Przegląd Prawa Handlowego 2008/11, 16 (17); Opalski/Opalski, Comments before Art. 368 CCC mn. 59.

60 Davies/Hopt/Nowak/Van Solinge/Sołtysiński, p. 538; Opalski Przegląd Prawa Handlowego 2008/11, 16 (17).
Opalski/Opalski, Art. 368 CCC mn. 14; Kappes, p. 3; Chałaczkiewicz-Ładna/Sójka/Jerzmanowski, European Business Law Review 2023/4, 665 (674).

61 Opalski/Opalski, Comments before Art. 368 CCC mn. 59.

62 Opalski/Opalski, Art. 368 CCC mn. 16.

63 In other legal systems: *duty of care, Sorgfaltspflicht, devoir de diligence.*

64 In other legal systems: *duty of loyalty, Treuepflicht, devoir de loyauté.*

duties in the interest of the company.[65] Importantly, Polish company law does not treat management or supervisory board members as direct or indirect representatives of their appointing parties or as representatives of the majority shareholders.[66] Board members are granted independent and sovereign authority to make decisions in the interest of the company on matters within the competencies of their respective boards.[67] While shareholders may utilise legal instruments to limit the discretion of board members – especially through the right of dismissal – they cannot undermine the decision-making autonomy of the board members.[68] Individuals appointed by minority shareholders, specific shareholders, or employees are equally obliged to fulfil their duties in the company's interest.

In the two-tier board structure of the joint-stock company,[69] the company's interest informs both the duties of the management board members, which include administering the company's affairs and representing it vis-à-vis third parties, and the oversight and control responsibilities of the supervisory board members. Therefore, understanding the company's interest helps clarify the duty of care (*wzorzec należytej staranności* – Article 483 CCC) and the content of the duty of loyalty required of board members, which provides guidelines for the decision-making processes.[70] Thus, the interpretation of the company's interests is decisive for shaping board members' conduct and, as a result, the conduct of the company itself.

The decision-making processes of board members that contravene the interest of the company may constitute grounds for their dismissal. Responsibility for dismissal of a management board member lies with the supervisory board unless stipulated otherwise by the statute (Article 368 § 4 CCC). However, the general meeting can always conduct a dismissal (Article 368 § 4 CCC). A specific "important cause" (*ważny powód*) for dismissal must only be provided if the company's charter contains such a requirement (Article 370 § 2 CCC). In such cases, depending on the severity of the violation, misalignment of the decision-making process with the company's interests may meet the criteria for an important cause.[71]

---

65 Opalski/Opalski, Comments before Art. 368 CCC mn. 42, 44–47.

66 Opalski, Przegląd Prawa Handlowego 2008/11, 16 (22).

67 Opalski/Opalski, Comments before Art. 368 CCC mn. 57.

68 Opalski, Przegląd Prawa Handlowego 2008/11, 16 (22).

69 Davis/Hopt/Nowak/Van Solinge/Sołtysiński, pp. 524–531; Vicari/Schall/Oplustil, pp. 706–738; Fleckner/Hopt/Sołtysiński, pp. 764–776.

70 See Stefanicki, pp. 172–230.

71 Szumański, Przegląd Prawa Handlowego 2006/5, 4 (5).

Similarly, supervisory board members may be dismissed by the general meeting at any time (Article 370 § 1 CCC and Article 386 § 2 CCC). If the company's charter stipulates that dismissal requires an important cause, violating the company's interest may be adequate grounds for such action. In 2007, the Supreme Court issued a contentious resolution, holding that a dismissed board member lacks standing to challenge the resolution of the general meeting regarding their dismissal, even when the board member claims that the resolution was adopted in violation of the law – for example, without the necessary quorum or majority of votes.[72]

Article 483 § 1 CCC stipulates that a board member is accountable to the company for damages caused by actions or omissions that violate legal requirements or the company's charter unless the board member can prove that they were not at fault. This provision governs civil liability arising from the failure to fulfil, or the improper fulfilment of, duties stemming from the organisational relationship between the company and the board member. To hold a board member liable, a claimant must establish: (i) the unlawfulness of the board member's actions or omissions, demonstrated by a breach of duties arising from their organisational relationship with the company; (ii) the existence and extent of the damage suffered by the company; and (iii) a causal link between the board member's actions or omissions and the damage incurred by the company. Notably, Article 483 § 1 CCC provides for a presumption of fault, requiring the board member to prove that the harm faced by the company resulted from factors outside their control.

Under Article 483 § 1 CCC, unlawfulness includes violations of any generally applicable legal provisions that govern the operations of the company, as well as breaches of the company's charter or the board's internal regulations.[73] Crucially, unlawful conduct that triggers liability under Article 483 § 1 CCC includes a board member's negligent performance of their duties.[74] The nature of a board members' duties vis-à-vis the company is addressed by Article 377[1] § 1 CCC (management board) and Article 387[1] § 1 CCC (supervisory board). According to these provisions, board members, in fulfilling their responsibilities, must exercise the diligence that corresponds to the professional nature of their activities and uphold loyalty to the company. This broadly-defined standard must be specified

72 Supreme Court 1.03.2007 – III CZP 94/06, OSNC 2007, No. 7–8, item 95.
73 Opalski/Opalski, Art. 483 CCC mn. 15.
74 Opalski/Opalski Art. 483 CCC mn. 17.

and "filled with substance" in each specific case. The boundaries of "loyalty" are determined by the company's interest.[75] In other words, when assessing the duties of board members in the context of their relationship with the company, a key factor is determining the company's interest as "a creditor".[76] Therefore, interpreting the notion of the company's interest is of paramount significance in evaluating board members' performance of duties and potential civil liability for actions infringing upon the company's interest.[77]

As detailed above, a board member's failure to act in accordance with the company's interest may serve as the basis for civil liability under Article 483 CCC.[78] If the company fails to file a lawsuit for damages within one year of when the board member's violation of the company's interest was disclosed, Article 486 § 1 CCC provides that any shareholder may file such a lawsuit (the so-called *actio pro socio*). Standing to sue is granted to shareholders regardless of the size of their shareholding.

It must be noted that, as in many other jurisdictions, the actual enforceability of a specific understanding of the board members' duty of care through civil liability is significantly limited by the protective function of the business judgment rule. In Poland, the business judgment rule was introduced as an explicit statutory provision in 2019.[79] According to Art. 483 § 2 CCC, a board member does not breach the duty of care if, in acting loyally towards the company, they operate within the bounds of justified business risk. Actions that are within the bounds of justified business risk include those that are based on information, analyses, and opinions that should be taken into account when making a diligent assessment.

---

75 Opalski, p. 145; Opalski, Przegląd Prawa Handlowego 2008/11, 16 (22); Supreme Court 24.7.2014. – II CSK 627/13, Lex/el, in which the Supreme Court stated that when making decisions concerning the management of the company's affairs, a member of the management board should be guided exclusively by the company's interest, and culpable actions carried out in excess of the limits of economic risk are contrary to the company's interests and constitute unlawful action.

76 Opalski/Opalski, Art. 483 CCC mn. 17.

77 Szajkowski/Romanowski, p. 142.

78 Opalski, Przegląd Prawa Handlowego 2008/11, 16 (16); Szajkowski/Romanowski, p. 142.

79 Act of 9 November 2018 amending certain acts to simplify tax and economic law for entrepreneurs (Journal of Laws of 2018, item 2244) *(Ustawa z dnia 9 listopada 2018 r. o zmianie niektórych ustaw w celu wprowadzenia uproszczeń dla przedsiębiorców w prawie podatkowym i gospodarczym (Dz.U. z 2018 r. poz. 2244)).*

This, however, should not be understood as rendering the concept of the company's interest irrelevant to board members' conduct. On the contrary, the way the company's interest is defined fundamentally shapes the content of the duty of care, irrespective of the availability or effectiveness of sanctions. Moreover, civil liability is not the sole mechanism through which compliance or breach of the duty of care may be addressed. Other relevant consequences include reputational damage and internal disciplinary measures, such as dismissal.

Finally, even if the imposition of civil liability based on a particular understanding of the company's interest remains limited, the explicit anchoring of the definition of the company's interest in law may function as an enabling mechanism: it may reduce legal uncertainty, which could facilitate the practical adoption of that interpretation by board members. For example, a definition of the company's interest that incorporates sustainability considerations may decisively affirm the legitimacy of taking environmental and social factors into account in corporate decision-making.

D. Dominant narratives on the company's interest

Given the role of the company's interest in shaping board members' duties, it is unsurprising that efforts to concretely define the company's interest have sparked controversy. In the following discussion, we categorize the emerging interpretative efforts into dominant narrative streams.

At a broad conceptual level, the company's interest can be understood as its "sphere of aspirations" (*sfera dążeń*).[80] Disagreements surrounding the definition of the company's interest arise from attempts to delimit this sphere – essentially, there are differing opinions as to what the substantive content of "the company's interest" is, though all are aimed at providing a clear guiding principle for board members in the execution of their duties.[81]

A more granular distinction can be drawn between the *abstract* company's interest and the *concrete* company's interest.[82] The latter refers to a specific company and is associated with a particular decision or course

80 Opalski, p. 145.
81 Opalski, p. 145.
82 Kappes, p. 5; Bilewska, pp. 63–65, who similarly distinguishes between a company's material and formal interest.

of action the company is about to undertake.[83] In this sense, the concrete company's interest is not a static concept; instead, it evolves throughout the course of the company's existence.[84] The concrete understanding of the company's interest naturally builds upon the foundational assumptions derived from the common objective, the company's objective, and the object of the company's activity (see Sec. 3 above).[85]

This chapter explores the emerging narratives surrounding the interpretation of the abstract company's interest, which applies universally to all joint-stock companies and reflects a shared understanding of their nature.[86] The abstract company's interest functions as an "instruction manual", providing guidelines for the companies and context for the company's decisions that clarify their concrete interest. Thus, the framework for understanding the abstract company's interest is indispensable in determining a company's concrete interest.

The debate surrounding the abstract company's interest in Polish law centres on two key questions. First, does the company, as an entity, possess an independent interest, or is its interest merely a derivative of the interests of shareholders or other stakeholders? Second, if the concept of an autonomous company interest is rejected, should determination of the abstract company's interest be confined to shareholder interests alone, or should it also account for the interests of other stakeholders[87] – more specifically, do the interests of stakeholders directly compete with those of shareholders? Or, alternatively, are governing bodies required to consider stakeholder interests only to the extent mandated by legal provisions? In such case, does this imply that stakeholder interests can only be considered if they serve to advance shareholder interests?

---

83 Opalski, Przegląd Prawa Handlowego 2008/11, 16 (17); Romanowski, Przegląd Prawa Handlowego 2015/7, 8 (14).

84 Oplustil, p. 147 et seqq.; Gębusia, pp. 38–41.

85 Kappes, p. 6; Supreme Court 5.11.2009 – I CSK 158/09, OSNC 2010, No. 4, item 63, in which the court indicated that the interest of the company is a resultant of the interests of all groups of its partners, defined in the light of the common goal, the realisation of which the partners undertook to achieve in the light of Article 3 of the CCC.

86 While several scholars in the literature have denied the existence of an abstract company's interest, they simultaneously offer abstract definitions of the company's interest that align with the understanding of the term in this chapter. See: Szajkowski/Romanowski, p. 145; Opalski, p. 151; Olszak, p. 222.

87 Weber-Elżanowska, p. 127 and the literature referenced therein.

The answers to these foundational questions, as developed in Polish legal doctrine and jurisprudence, give rise to three principal narratives regarding the interpretation of the company's interest.

I. *The autonomous company's interest*

Polish pre-war scholarship viewed the company as a genuine social phenomenon – an entity legally distinct from its shareholders and capable of possessing its own interests that may diverge from those of both shareholders.[88] Several modern scholars advocate for a similar stance. They argue that the company's legal personality, combined with the inherently normative character of the company's interest, underscores the autonomous nature of that interest.[89]

According to these perspectives, the legal personality granted to a company implies the existence of its own distinct interest, which may, in certain instances, conflict with the interests of its shareholders, particularly the specific interests of individual shareholders.[90] In line with this narrative, a proposal has been made to introduce an explicit reference to the legal person's interest in the provisions of the Polish Civil Code, emphasizing that the statutory grant of legal personality to a company establishes an interest that is legally distinct from the economic interests of its shareholders.[91] It was argued that such an amendment would strengthen the company's interest as a general standard for assessing the legality of actions undertaken by its governing bodies, even in cases where the CCC does not explicitly reference this criterion.[92]

However, the autonomy of the company's interest as a legal concept does not predetermine whether, or to what extent, the substantive content of such an autonomous interest diverges from the shareholders' interests.[93] An autonomous company's interest still requires substantive definition, which must be drawn from an external source. Guidance certainly flows from

88 Longshamps de Bérier, pp. 161–165; for contemporary approval of this view – Safjan/Frąckowiak, pp. 1012–1013.
89 Szumański, Przegląd Prawa Handlowego 2010/5, 9 (12); Gronau, Kancelaria 2011, 34 (34); Modrzejewska/Olechowski, p. 673; Okolski/Wajda, p. 755; Bryłowski/Kidyba, Przegląd Prawa Handlowego 2005/10, 4 (10); Dąbrowska, p. 68.
90 Szumański, Przegląd Prawa Handlowego 2010/5, 9 (12).
91 Domański/Pietrusińska, p. 506.
92 Domański/Pietrusińska, p. 506.
93 Domański/Pietrusińska, p. 506.

the company's overall objective and the object of a company's any given activity, which indirectly connects to the shareholders' interests that consequently "transpire" into the autonomous company's interest. Typically, an autonomous view of the company's interest tends to simplify the focus on the "economic survival" of the company and the protection of its assets.

II. *As a resultant of shareholders' interests*

An opposing narrative, which is currently the prevailing narrative in Polish company law, was introduced by *Opalski* in his seminal 2008 article, which conceptualises the company's interest as a resultant (*wypadkowa*) of the interests of the persons involved in the functioning of the company, specifically rejecting the notion of an autonomous company's interest.[94] *Opalski*'s perspective rests on the premise that a legal person is an artificial construct of the legal system[95] that lacks its own internal will[96] and that the mere attribution of legal personality does not establish its autonomous interest.[97] From this standpoint, the company is considered to have an interest only in relation to external parties, rather than an internally distinct interest of its own.[98]

A key argument advanced by proponents of this view is that recognizing an autonomous company interest in absolute terms would lead to problematic conclusions. For instance, resolutions concerning dividend payouts, company dissolution, or reductions in share capital could consistently be deemed detrimental to the company's interest, potentially rendering them subject to annulment under Article 422 § 1 CCC.[99] Similarly, it is argued

94 Opalski, Przegląd Prawa Handlowego 2008/11, 16 (16); later expanded in: Opalski, p. 145; Romanowski, Przegląd Prawa Handlowego 2015/7, 8 (14); Radwan/Regucki, International and Comparative Corporate Law Journal 2012/32, 15.

95 Romanowski, Przegląd Prawa Handlowego 2009/3, 10 (13); Szajkowski/Romanowski, p. 134.

96 Opalski, Przegląd Prawa Handlowego 2008/11, 16 (17).

97 Romanowski, Przegląd Prawa Handlowego 2015/7, 8 (14).

98 Opalski, Przegląd Prawa Handlowego 2008/11, 16 (17).

99 Opalski/Pabis, Art. 422 CCC mn. 83.

that the company's very existence is contingent on its shareholders, as demonstrated by their ability to pass a resolution dissolving the company.[100]

Further, this narrative maintains that the company's interest cannot be understood as an objective or abstract concept independent of its shareholders, who seek to advance their own subjective interests.[101] Some contend that in reality, "the determinant of the company's interest is essentially the interest of its shareholders".[102] This perspective underscores the contention that those who wield decision-making and appointment powers within the company effectively define the company's interest by determining which interests it will pursue.[103]

Moreover, the CCC does not include any provisions supporting the recognition of the interests of groups other than shareholders as an independent component in defining the company's interest.[104] Excluding stakeholders from shaping the company's objectives is justified by concerns that including them in a CCC provision would afford governing bodies excessive discretion in evaluating the interests of the company, which could lead to negative consequences.[105] If governing bodies were granted unrestricted authority to consider stakeholder interests, virtually any action could be justified as serving the company's interest – except in cases of clear mismanagement.[106]

As a result, within the examined narrative, it is argued that the company must consider stakeholders' interests only when (1) legally required to do so, or (2) when consideration of stakeholder interests is necessary to further shareholders' interests.[107] Stakeholder interests should thus be accounted for solely incidentally – that is, to the extent that they align with, and further, the interests of shareholders. At the same time, it is argued that defining the company's interest requires acknowledging the interests

100 Oplustil, p. 171 et seqq.

101 Szajkowski/Romanowski, pp. 139–140.

102 Opalski, Przegląd Prawa Handlowego 2008, 16 (22); Romanowski, Przegląd Prawa Handlowego 2009/3, 10 (13); translation by the authors.

103 Chałaczkiewicz-Ładna/Sójka/Jerzmanowski, European Business Law Review 2023/4, 665 (676); Opalski, PPH 2008, 16 (18).

104 Opalski, Przegląd Prawa Handlowego 2025/4, pp. 10, 14, 16; Opalski, Przegląd Prawa Handlowego 2008/11, 16 (18); Wajda, p. 39; Opalski, p. 167; Radwan/Regucki, International and Comparative Corporate Law Journal 2012/32, 18.

105 Opalski, Przegląd Prawa Handlowego 2008/11, 16 (18); Cejmer/Napierała/Sójka/Stroiński, p. 363.

106 Opalski, Przegląd Prawa Handlowego 2008/11, 16 (18).

107 Opalski, Przegląd Prawa Handlowego 2008/11, 16 (18).

of shareholders alongside those of other groups, such as creditors, employees, and local communities. However, these non-shareholder interests are "non-autonomous" and may only be considered insofar as they serve shareholders' interests.[108]

This approach to the company's interest, as a resultant of shareholder interests, was partially reaffirmed in the Supreme Court's resolution of 22 October 2009. Echoing *Opalski*'s reasoning, and using his explicit wording, the Court stated that the company's interest constitutes "a compromise, a resultant between the often-conflicting interests of minority and majority shareholders".[109] Similarly, in its judgment of 5 November 2009, the Supreme Court stated that the company's interest is "resultant of the interests of all the groups of shareholders",[110] further asserting that these shareholders should be regarded as the economic owners of the company.[111] This interpretation was upheld in subsequent jurisprudence.[112] However, neither of these judgments offers a specific account of how shareholder interests should be balanced against other stakeholder interests. Their focus lies primarily in establishing a functional connection between shareholder interests and the company's interest, leaving broader conceptual questions unresolved.[113]

If the company's interest is viewed as a resultant of the interests of all shareholder groups' interests, the principle of majority rule suggests that, in practice, the interests of the majority shareholder (or shareholder group) will typically prevail.[114] This raises a critical question: what guidelines should members of the company's governing bodies follow when weighing the interests of minority shareholders in shaping this resultant? This issue remains unresolved in legal scholarship. As the Constitutional Tribunal

108 Jara/Bilewska, Art. 422 CCC.

109 Supreme Court 22.10.2009 – III CZP 63/09, OSNC 2010, No. 4, item 55; translation by the authors.

110 Supreme Court 5.11.2009 – I CSK 158/09, OSNC 2010, No. 4, item 63; translation by the authors.

111 See a broader discussion in Stefanicki, pp. 31–35.

112 Supreme Court 3.6.2015 – V CSK 592/14, OSNC 2016, no. 5, item 65; Supreme Court of 22.10.2015 – IV CSK 738/14, OSNC 2016, no. 10, item 120; Appeal Court in Poznań 2.10.2019 – I AGa 364/18, Legalis no 2285532; Appeal Court in Białystok 20.09.2019 – I AGa 5/19, Legalis no 2264366; Appeal Court in Warsaw 4.12.2013 – VI ACa 290/13, Legalis no 776042.

113 Weber, Przegląd Prawa Handlowego 2025/7, p. 41–42.

114 Chałaczkiewicz-Ładna/Sójka/Jerzmanowski, European Business Law Review 2023/4, 665 (676); Olszak, p. 237.

stated in its judgment of 21 June 2005, the company's interest should not be equated solely with the majority shareholder's interest.[115] The Tribunal also stressed that the principle of majority rule must be balanced with the principles of equal treatment of shareholders and the protection of the legitimate interests of minority shareholders. Similarly, in its judgment of 5 November 2009, the Supreme Court stated that the principle of majority rule does not imply that the company's interest is identical to that of the majority shareholder.[116]

III. *The resultant of shareholders' and stakeholders' interests*

Another narrative, primarily attributed to *Sołtysiński*, builds upon the concept of the company's interest as a resultant of various interests, broadening the scope of the company's interest to include not only shareholders but also stakeholders. According to this perspective, the company's interest should be understood as the outcome of both shareholder and stakeholder interests.[117] In this view, the primary duty of board members is to act in alignment with the company's interest rather than exclusively in the interests of the shareholders.[118]

While acknowledging that shareholders' interests remain predominant, *Sołtysiński* argues that board members must consider stakeholder interests as required "in light of the concept of the company's interest".[119] He contends that board members "may not avoid their social responsibilities"[120] and rejects the notion that stakeholder interests exist merely as a subset of shareholder interests, to be considered only when they align with shareholders' objectives. In his view, such an interpretation effectively nullifies any meaningful obligation to respect stakeholder interests.[121]

This notion of the company's interest was reflected in a previous version of the corporate governance code of the Warsaw Stock Exchange, which came into force in 2005 (*Dobre praktyki w spółkach publicznych 2005 –*

115 Constitutional Tribunal 21.06.2005 – P 25/02, OTK-A 2005, No. 6, item 65.
116 Supreme Court 5.11.2009 – I CSK 158/09, OSNC 2010, Nr 4 poz. 63.
117 Sołtysiński/Sołtysiński/Moskwa, p. 41; Szmid, p. 19.
118 Sołtysiński/Sołtysiński/Moskwa, p. 38.
119 Davies/Hopt/Nowak/Van Solinge/Sołtysiński, p. 538.
120 Davies/Hopt/Nowak/Van Solinge/Sołtysiński, p. 538.
121 Sołtysińki/Sołtysińki/Moskwa, p. 38–39.

"DPSP2005")[122] but was repealed in 2007.[123] The first general principle of DPSP2005 stated that the primary objective of a company's governing bodies is to pursue the company's interest. It defined the company's interest as increasing the value of the assets entrusted to it by shareholders, while also taking into account the rights and interests of other stakeholders involved in the company's operations, particularly its creditors and employees. In addition, rule no. 33, which addressed the duties of management board members, specified that in determining the company's interest and making corporate decisions, due consideration should be given to the legitimate long-term interests of shareholders, creditors, employees, and other entities engaged in the company's business activities, as well as the interests of local communities.

E. *Sustainability objectives and the dominant narratives*

In Polish company law, sustainability objectives have thus far played a marginal role at best in shaping the understanding of the company's interest.[124] This limited attention highlights the need for a thorough analysis of the three dominant narratives on the company's interest, examining their implications through the lens of sustainability.

I. *Sparse prospects*

Under the prevailing view, which defines the company's interest as a resultant of shareholders' interests (see Sec. 4.2. above), the integration of sustainability objectives is significantly constrained. From this perspective, sustainability considerations can only be integrated into the company's

122 Warsaw Stock Exchange, Dobre Praktyki Spółek Notowanych na GPW 2005, 2005, https://www.gpw.pl/pub/GPW/files/PDF/dobre_praktyki/dp2005.pdf.

123 Warsaw Stock Exchange, Dobre Praktyki Spółek Notowanych na GPW 2007, 2007, https://www.gpw.pl/pub/GPW/files/PDF/dobre_praktyki/dobrepraktyki2007.pdf.

124 Weber/Mazur/Szczęsna, PPH 2022/6, 20 (22); Dumkiewicz/Szczotka/Kopaczyńska-Pieczniak/Weber-Elżanowska, p. 226; Weber/Mittwoch, RECoL 2023/1, 143 (156–157); Radwan/Regucki, International and Comparative Corporate Law Journal 2012/32, 1 – 48.

interests if they align with shareholders' interests.[125] While such alignment may occur in cases where unsustainable practices pose financial risks that directly impact shareholder value, these "win-win" scenarios do not capture all instances where sustainability should be prioritized. Indeed, there are many situations in which sustainability goals might conflict with shareholder interests, raising critical questions about how such competing considerations should be balanced within the framework of board members' duties.

Even within the prevailing narrative that equates the company's interest with that of its shareholders, it is widely acknowledged that the freedom to define this interest is subject to certain limitations. Beyond explicit legal constraints – such as the principle of equal treatment of shareholders – a key restriction arises from the obligation to adhere to the principle of fairness (*dobre obyczaje*).[126] Accordingly, when aligning the company's interest with shareholders' interests, the resulting decisions must not violate the moral norms contained in the principle of fairness. This perspective suggests that any company action affecting stakeholders must consider their interests to the extent necessary to uphold the principle of fairness.[127] However, while this reasoning may restrict decisions that clearly and egregiously breach the moral norms that constitute the principle of fairness, it clearly does not provide a reliable framework for guiding board members toward sustainability-oriented practices. The principle of fairness remains underdeveloped in the context of sustainability, leaving decision-makers without a clear interpretative foundation. From a judicial standpoint, it is unlikely that a sustainability-inclusive interpretation of the principle of fairness will be applied in a meaningful or consistent manner.

Moreover, given the dominant understanding of the company's interest, there is significant legal uncertainty regarding the permissibility of voluntary commitments to integrate sustainability goals into corporate governance.[128]

Based on the foregoing, attempts to incorporate sustainability considerations into the company's interest – when that interest is viewed solely as a derivative of shareholders' interests – are unlikely to result in a meaningful

125 Opalski, Przegląd Prawa Handlowego 2025/4, p. 10, 14, 16; Olszak/Stokłosa Prawo i Więź (Law & Social Bonds) 2025/1, 346.

126 Opalski, Przegląd Prawa Handlowego 2008/11, 16 (21); Weber-Elżanowska, p. 137; Weber/Mazur/Szczęsna, PPH 2022/6, 20 (24); Dumkiewicz/Szczotka/Kopaczyńska-Pieczniak/Weber-Elżanowska, p. 227; Kappes, p. 6.

127 Weber-Elżanowska, pp. 137–138.

128 See Weber, Przegląd Prawa Handlowego 2025/7, pp. 43–45.

shift capable of genuinely advancing the objective of corporate sustainability.

II. *Glimmers of potential and their challenges*

The remaining two narratives, the autonomous company's interest (see Sec. 4.1 above) and the company's interest as a resultant of both shareholders' and stakeholders' interests (see Sec. 4.3 above) provide more potential for integrating sustainability considerations. In theory, the narrative that describes the company's interest as autonomous could serve as a potential gateway for corporate sustainability. Since an autonomous company's interest asserts that the company's interest is not merely derived from shareholders or any other external interests, the question arises as to whether the substance of this autonomous interest could encompass sustainability objectives. This opens the door for broader interpretations of the company's interest, where sustainability considerations could be integrated as a core component.

Similarly, the view of the company's interest as a resultant of both shareholders' and stakeholders' interests could, in theory, accommodate sustainability objectives. In this framework, stakeholder interests, which could include environmental concerns alongside traditional interests such as those of employees and the local community, may provide a basis for integrating sustainability into the company's decision-making. However, it is important to note that this perspective, which is grounded in the dichotomous debate between shareholders and stakeholders, may face criticism.[129] Specifically, the challenge lies in balancing often competing or divergent interests, which could limit the extent to which sustainability objectives are pursued. The company's interest as a resultant of both shareholders' and stakeholders' interests may not offer sufficient guidance on prioritising or weighing these interests, particularly when conflicts arise between financial goals and sustainability objectives.

Both of these narratives, while they provide "hope", share a fundamental challenge: they require moving away from the dominant perspective that defines the company's interest as a mere function of shareholders' interests. To integrate sustainability into these frameworks, significant interpretative effort is required to fundamentally reimagine the company's role in soci-

129 Sjåfjell/Mähönen, Bond Law Review 2022, 69 (69–113).

ety and develop new concepts that reflect this broader role – concepts that are not yet widely accepted in legal discourse, doctrine, or judicial practice. As mentioned earlier, the often-significant aspect of the historical examination of legislative materials fails to provide substantial insight for Poland. While pre-war legal literature may offer some theoretical support for an autonomous conception of the company's interest, incorporating sustainability considerations into this model – or within a framework that balances shareholders' and stakeholders' interests – remains a difficult interpretative leap. Robust methodological justification is needed to establish a sustainability-conscious understanding of the company's interest within these theoretical models that would allow companies to meaningfully embrace sustainability objectives.

Certain valid interpretative directives can, however, be drawn from EU law. In particular, the adoption of several legal acts in the field of sustainable finance[130] helps to shape a certain vision of the desired role of a company within European society.[131] This holds true even for companies that are not directly within the scope of these regulations, since EU provisions still carry significant interpretative value.[132]

Additionally, the DPSN2021 could be consulted as an interpretative source in both the autonomous company's interest approach and the company's interest as a resultant of the shareholders' and stakeholders' interest approach. According to rule 1.3 of the DPSN2021, a company incorporates "ESG considerations" into its business strategy, focusing on environmental issues, including metrics and risks associated with climate change and sustainable development. It also addresses social and labour matters, such as ensuring gender equality, providing adequate working conditions, respecting employees' rights, maintaining dialogue with local communities, and building customer relationships. Furthermore, according to rule 6.2. of the DPSN2021, incentive programs should be designed to

130 Such as the Regulation 2019/2088 of the European Parliament and of the Council of 27 November 2019 on sustainability-related disclosures in the financial services sector ("SFDR"), the Directive 2022/2464 of the European Parliament and of the Council of 14 December 2022 amending Regulation (EU) No 537/2014, Directive 2004/109/EC, Directive 2006/43/EC and Directive 2013/34/EU, as regards corporate sustainability reporting ("CSRD"), as well as the Directive 2024/1760 of the European Parliament and of the Council of 13 June 2024 on corporate sustainability due diligence and amending Directive (EU) 2019/1937 and Regulation (EU) 2023/2859 ("CSDDD") which addresses due diligence in value chains.

131 Weber/Mazur/Szczęsna, Przegląd Prawa Handlowego 2022/6, 20 (24–30).

132 Weber/Mazur/Szczęsna, Przegląd Prawa Handlowego 2022/6, 20 (25).

link the remuneration levels of the company's management board members and key managers to the company's actual long-term performance, both financial and non-financial. These programs should also reflect long-term value creation for the company's shareholders, sustainable development, and operational stability.

Despite these important interpretative guidelines, any progress ultimately depends on key actors' willingness to pursue these avenues of reasoning and undertake the necessary shifts in thinking – most notably, decision-makers at the company level. However, because the company's interest plays a crucial normative role in determining board members' responsibilities and potential liability, adopting a progressive reinterpretation within corporate decision-making presents significant risks. If shareholders do not recognize or support the necessity for such a reinterpretation, board members could face consequences ranging from civil liability to dismissal. This creates a substantial barrier to integrating sustainability into corporate governance, as board members must navigate both legal risks and shareholder expectations, which may not align with sustainability-oriented approaches.

Furthermore, a revision of the understanding of the company's interest would also need to be embraced by other actors involved in a company's decision-making processes in a broad sense. This includes lawyers, other advisers, and judges adjudicating disputes involving the application of the concept of the company's interest. For this transformation to take place, awareness and openness to integrating sustainability considerations must become an integral part of legal education and professional training.[133] Incorporating sustainability concepts into academic curriculum and ongoing professional development would help establish a foundation for rethinking corporate governance and the responsibilities of those shaping it.

Consequently, achieving a meaningful shift in the interpretation of the company's interest in Poland would require a long and demanding process involving multiple actors, including academia, the judiciary, and – most importantly – board members and shareholders. Frankly, at this point, such an interpretative shift is unlikely to materialize in a timeframe that aligns with the urgency of the matter at hand.

133 See more on the role of education in relation to corporate sustainability Melon/Weber, pp. 239, 243.

F. Reframing the company's interest for sustainability – the way forward

As demonstrated in this chapter, black-letter Polish company law does not provide a clear definition or explicit guidance on the concept of the company's interest. Instead, its meaning is shaped through interpretation, influenced by competing narratives within legal doctrine and jurisprudence.

The prevailing view equates the company's interest with that of its shareholders, effectively restricting the integration of sustainability considerations to "win-win" scenarios where sustainability aligns with shareholder interests. This narrow interpretation limits the broader potential for embedding sustainability into corporate governance as it confines sustainability initiatives to those that provide direct financial benefits to shareholders, reducing sustainability goals to economic calculations rather than recognizing their wider social and environmental significance. Consequently, this view offers little room for meaningful integration of sustainability goals in cases where they conflict with shareholder interests.

While the other two alternative narratives on the company's interest hold theoretical potential for integrating sustainability, the practical, interpretative shift they necessitate would represent a paradigmatic transformation. Achieving this shift would require corporate decision-makers and the broader legal community – including scholars, advisors, and judges – adopting an entirely new framework of understanding akin to a Kuhnian scientific revolution[134]. Given the pressing nature of the sustainability challenge, waiting for such a shift to unfold naturally is neither realistic nor sufficient.

Therefore, we conclude that in the context of the joint-stock company, legislative intervention is necessary to explicitly align the concept of the company's interest with corporate sustainability. Such an intervention would provide clearer guidance and a stronger legal foundation for integrating sustainability objectives into corporate governance, effectively addressing the gaps and legal uncertainties that currently hinder meaningful progress in this area.

References

Allerhand, Maurycy, Kodeks handlowy: komentarz, Lviv 1935

134 Kuhn.

Bardach, Juliusz, Historia państwa i prawa Polski do roku 1795, Warsaw 1957

Benis, Artur, Studia Akcyjne, Warsaw 1933

Bilewska, Katarzyna, Dochodzenie roszczeń spółki kapitałowej przez jej wspólników, Warsaw 2008

Bloch, Józef, Na marginesie projektu ustawy o spółkach akcyjnych, PPH 1928/3, 116

Bryłowski, Paweł/Kidyba, Andrzej, Kategoria interesu w kodeksie spółek handlowych, PPH 2005/10, 4

Chałaczkiewicz-Ładna, Katarzyna/Sójka, Tomasz/Jerzmanowski, Jędrzej, To Whom Polish directors Owe their duties – Between Shareholder Primacy and Political Agenda, European Business Law Review 2023/4, 665

Dąbrowska, Justyna, O początkach spółki akcyjnej, Zeszyty Prawnicze 2019/4, 7

Dąbrowska, Justyna, Zaskarżanie uchwał zgromadzeń spółek kapitałowych, Warsaw 2016

Dniestrzański, Stanisław, O istocie prawa gospodarczego, Czasopismo Prawnicze i Ekonomiczne 1932/1, 340

Domański, Grzegorz/Pietrusińska, Ewa, Interes spółki jako atrybut jej osobowości prawnej, in Mróz/Stec (eds.), Instytucje prawa handlowego w przyszłym kodeksie cywilnym, Warsaw 2012, p. 506

Dziurzyński, Tadeusz/Fenichel, Zygmunt/Honzatko, Mieczysław, Kodeks handlowy. Komentarz I-II, Łódź 1992

Frąckowiak, Józef in Safjan (ed.), System prawa prywatnego. Prawo cywilne – część ogólna, Warsaw 2007

Frąckowiak, Osiemdziesiąt lat polskiego prawa handlowego – wzloty, upadki oraz mozolna reaktywacja, Acta Universitatis Wratislaviensis 2015/101, 45

Frąckowiak, Józef in Frąckowiak/Kidyba/Kruczalak/Pyziol/Weiss (eds.), Kodeks handlowy. Komentarz, Warsaw 1998, p. 594

Gębusia, Iwona, Interes spółki w prawie polskim i europejskim, Warsaw 2017

Górnicki, Leonard, Założenia i koncepcja kodyfikacji prawa w II RP, Prawo i Więź 2022/4, 618

Górnicki, Leonard, Przewodnie konstrukcje i pojęcia kodeksu handlowego z 1934 roku, Acta Universitatis Wratislaviensis 2015/101, 63

Gronau, Mateusz, Quo vadis interesie grupy spółek?, Kancelaria 2011, 34

Janczewski, Stanisław, Prawo handlowe, wekslowe i czekowe, Warsaw 1946

Jara, Zbigniew, Kodeks spółek handlowych. Komentarz, Warsaw 2022

Jastrzębski, Robert, Prawo handlowe i gospodarcze II Rzeczypospolitej, Warsaw 2019

Kappes, Aleksander, Naprawienie szkody wyrządzonej wspólnikom mniejszościowym. Majątkowa ochrona mniejszości w spółkach kapitałowych, Warsaw 2024

Kuhn, Thomas, The Structure of Scientific Revolutions, Chicago 2012

Kułak, Krzysztof, Skazane na zapomnienie – prawo handlowe w PRL, Studia nad Autorytaryzmem i Totalitaryzmem 2021/3, 73

Liao, Carol/Sjafjell, Beate/Argyrou,Aikaterini, Innovating business for a sustainable post-pandemic future, in Liao/Sjåfjell/Argyou (eds.), Innovating Business for Sustainability. Regulatory Approaches in the Anthropocene, Cheltenham 2022, p. 1

Longchamps de Bérier, Roman, Studya nad istotą osoby prawniczej, Lviv 1911

Longshamps de Berier, Roman, Wstęp do nauki prawa cywilnego, Lublin 1922

Maliszewski, Wacław/Okolski, Józef/Opalski, Wiesław, Prawo obrotu uspołecznionego: podstawowe instytucje, Warsaw 1976

Mazur, Paweł, Nowy paradygmat ładu korporacyjnego. Globalne tendencje w dyskusji o interesie spółki i ich możliwy wpływ na prawo polskie, PiP 2022/7, 114

Mądzik, Marek, Powstanie i pierwsze lata działalności Kompanii Czarnomorskiej (1782–1785), Rocznik Lubelski 1979, 84

Michalski, Marek, O wprowadzeniu Kodeksu handlowego Napoleona do systemu prawa polskiego, czyli początkach uregulowanej spółki akcyjnej w Polsce, in Michalski (ed.), Kształtowanie się spółki akcyjnej a doświadczenia polskie, Warsaw 2020

Michalski, Marek, Geneza spółki akcyjnej w obrocie prawnym w Polsce oraz w prawie polskim do 1918 r., MPH 2017/2, 6

Michalski, Marek, Spółka akcyjna w obrocie prawnym w Polsce oraz w prawie polskim od 1918 r. do 1939 r., MPH 2017/3, 6

Michalski, Marek, Spółka akcyjna, Warsaw 2014

Namitkiewicz, Jan, Próba charakterystyki i i określenie prawa handlowego, Przegląd Prawa Handlowego 1992/1, 24

Okolski, Józef/Wajda, Dominika, Cel spółki akcyjnej, in Skubisz/Kidyba (eds.), Współczesne problemy prawa handlowego. Księga jubileuszowa dedykowana Marii Poźniak-Niedzielskiej, Cracow 2007, p. 255

Okolski, Józef/Wajda, Dominika, Zasada rządów większości i ochrona akcjonariuszy mniejszościowych wobec pojęcia „interesu spółki akcyjnej" in Frąckowiak (ed.), Kodeks spółek handlowych po pięciu latach, Wrocław 2006, p. 750

Okolski, Józef/Modrzejewski, Jerzy/Gasiński, Łukasz, Zasada równego traktowania akcjonariuszy na gruncie k.s.h., Przegląd Prawa Handlowego 2002/10, 24

Olechowski, Marcin, Interes spółki kapitałowej wobec relacji kontraktowych w grupach spółek (zagadnienia wybrane) in Modrzejewska (ed.) Prawo handlowe XXI wieku. Czas stabilizacji, ewolucji czy rewolucji. Księga jubileuszowa Profesora Józefa Okolskiego, Warsaw 2010, p. 667

Olszak, Krzysztof, Interes spółki akcyjnej i spółki z ograniczoną odpowiedzialnością w prawie polskim oraz hiszpańskim, Warsaw 2022

Olszak Krzysztof, Stokłosa Angelina, Prawo i Więź (Law & Social Bonds) 2025/1, 346

Opalski, Adam (ed.), Kodeks spółek handlowych. Komentarz. Spółka akcyjna IIIA, Warsaw 2016

Opalski, Adam, Kodeks spółek handlowych. Spółka akcyjna IIIB, Warsaw 2016

Opalski, Adam (ed.), Kodeks spółek handlowych. Spółki osobowe, Komentarz. Art. 1–36 IA, Warsaw 2024

Opalski, Adam, O pojęciu interesu spółki handlowej, Przegląd Prawa Handlowego, 2008/11, 16

Opalski, Adam, For Whom Corporate Managers Are Trustees, czyli niekończący się spór o wykładnię kategorii interesu spółki handlowej, Przegląd Prawa Handlowego 2025/4, 4

Opalski, Adam, Prawo zgrupowań spółek, Warsaw 2012

Oplustil, Krzysztof, Instrumenty nadzoru korporacyjnego (corporate governance) w spółce akcyjnej, Warsaw 2010

Oplustil, Krzysztof, Stock corporations: corporate governance, in Vicari/Schall (eds.), Company Laws of the EU. A Handbook, München, Oxford, Baden-Baden 2020, p. 706

Oplustil, Krzysztof/Radwan, Arkadiusz, Company Law in Poland: Between Autonomous Development and Legal Transplants in Jessel-Holst/Kulms/Trunk (eds.), Private Law in Eastern Europe, Tubingen 2010, p. 445

Radwan, Arkadiusz, Prawo poboru w spółce akcyjnej, Warsaw 2004

Radwan, Arkadiusz/Regucki, Tomasz, The Possibilities for and Barriers to Sustainable Companies in Polish Company Law, International and Comparative Corporate Law Journal 2012/32, 1

Romanowski, Michał, W sprawie pojęcia i natury spółki publicznej, Przegląd Prawa Handlowego 2009/3, 10

Romanowski, Michał, Znaczenie sporu o metodę odczytywania pojęcia "interes spółki kapitałowej", Przegląd Prawa Handlowego 2015/7, 8

Romanowski, Michał, Cel spółki i charakter prawny umowy spółki, SPP 2015/3, 63

Sjåfjell, Beate/ Mähönen, Jukka, Corporate Purpose and the Misleading Shareholder v Stakeholder Dichotomy, Bond Law Review 2024/2, 69

Sołtysiński, Stanisław (ed.), System Prawa Prywatnego XVIIA, Warsaw 2015

Sołtysiński, Stanisław, Corporate Boards in Poland, in Davies/Hopt/Nowak/Van Solinge (eds.), Corporate Boards in Law and Practice: A Comparative Analysis in Europe, Oxford 2013, p. 511

Sołtysiński, Stanisław, Kodeks spółek handlowych. (Podstawowe założenia), PiP 2000/11, 4

Sołtysiński, Stanisław, Sources of foreign inspiration in the draft of the Polish Company Law in Baums/Hopt/Horn (eds.) Corporations, Capital Markets and Business in the Law, London, Boston 2000, p. 533

Sołtysiński, Stanisław, Transfer of Legal Systems as seen by the "Import Countries": A View from Warsaw in Drobnig/Hopt/Kötz/Mestmäcker (eds.), System Transformation in Mittel-und Osteuropa und ihre Folgen für Banken, Börsen und Kreditsicherheiten, Tübingen 1998, p. 70

Sołtysiński, Stanisław, Poland: Corporate governance of joint-stock companies, in Fleckner/Hopt (eds.), Comparative Corporate Governance: A Functional and International Analysis, Cambridge 2013, p. 753

Sołtysiński, Stanisław, Wynalazek spółki kapitałowej: o krok od wieczności, PiP 1998/11, 14

Sołtysiński, Stanisław/Szajkowski, Andrzej/Szumański, Andrzej /Szwaja, Jacek (eds.), Kodeks spółek handlowych. Komentarz I, Warsaw 2005

Sołtysiński, Stanisław/Szajkowski, Andrzej/Tarska, Monika (eds.), System Prawa Prywatnego XVIIA, Warsaw 2015

Stefanicki, Robert, Należyta staranność zawodowa członka zarządu spółki kapitałowej, Warszawa 2020

Stroiński, Rafał, Zasady dobrych praktyk w spółkach publicznych notowanych na Giełdzie Papierów Wartościowych w Warszawie S.A. – wybrane zagadnienia na tle prawno-porównawczym, in Cejmer/Napierała/Sójka (eds.), Europejskie prawo spółek. Corporate Governance III, Cracow 2006, p. 363

Symonowicz, Antoni, Śp. Jan Namitkiewicz, Palestra 1958/9, 73

Szmid, Kamil, Natura Spółki Akcyjnej jako Delimitacja Zasady Swobody Umów w Prawie Polskim i Amerykańskim, Warsaw 2015

Szumański, Andrzej (ed.), System prawa handlowego. Prawo spółek IIA, Warsaw 2019

Szajkowski, Andrzej, Prawo spółek osobowych. System Prawa Prywatnego XVI, Warsaw 2016

Szumański, Andrzej, Prawa „szczególne" wspólnika spółki kapitałowej a zasada odwołalności członka zarządu przez wspólników oraz zasada wyboru członków rady nadzorczej grupami, Przegląd Prawa Handlowego 2006/5, 4

Szumański, Andrzej, Spór wokół roli interesu grupy spółek i jego relacji w szczególności do interesu własnego spółki uczestniczącej w grupie, Przegląd Prawa Handlowego 2010/5, 9

Tarkowski, Mikołaj, Spółka akcyjna w poglądach prawniczych Gabriela Szerszeniewicza (18663–1912). Przyczynek do historii prawa handlowego w Imperium Rosyjskim, in Michalski (ed.) Kształtowanie się spółki akcyjnej a doświadczenia polskie, Warsaw 2020

Wajda, Dominika, Obowiązek lojalności w spółkach handlowych, Warsaw 2015

Wajda, Dominika, Ochrona akcjonariuszy mniejszościowych w kodeksie spółek handlowych, Warsaw 2007

Warsaw Stock Exchange, Dobre Praktyki Spółek Notowanych na GPW 2021, 2021, https://www.gpw.pl/pub/GPW/pdf/DPSN_2021.pdf (last accessed: 10 January 2025)

Warsaw Stock Exchange, Dobre Praktyki Spółek Notowanych na GPW 2005, 2005, https://www.gpw.pl/pub/GPW/files/PDF/dobre_praktyki/dp2005.pdf (last accessed: 10 January 2025)

Warsaw Stock Exchange, Dobre Praktyki Spółek Notowanych na GPW 2007, 2007, https://www.gpw.pl/pub/GPW/files/PDF/dobre_praktyki/dobrepraktyki2007.pdf (last accessed: 10 January 2025)

Weber, Anne-Marie, O interesie spółki w kontekście postulatów zrównoważonego rozwoju – polemika, Przegląd Prawa Handlowego 2025/7, 35

Weber, Anne-Marie, (In)corporate sustainability – what's the role to be played by corporate law academics?, in Melon (ed.) Sustainability in Public Procurement, Corporate Law and Higher Education, Routledge 2023

Weber, Anne-Marie/ Mazur, Zofia/Szczęsna, Aleksandra, Zrównoważony ład korporacyjny (sustainable corporate governance) -kierunek ewolucji polskiego prawa spółek?, Przegląd Prawa Handlowego 2022/6, 20

Weber, Anne-Marie/Mittwoch, Anne-Christin, Harmonizing Duties of Board Members in the Anthropocene: When Expectations Meet Reality, RECoL 2023/1, 143

Weber-Elżanowska, Anne-Marie, Postulat zrównoważonego wzrostu gospodarczego jako wyzwanie dla polskiego prawa handlowego, in Dumkiewicz/Szczotka/ Kopaczyńska-Pieczniak, Sto lat polskiego prawa handlowego. Księga jubileuszowa dedykowana Profesorowi Andrzejowi Kidybie, Warsaw 2020, p. 218

Weber-Elżanowska, Anne-Marie, Wpływ instytucji prawnych rynku kapitałowego na efektywność Spółek Skarbu Państwa, Warsaw 2017

Zoll, Fryderyk, Prawo cywilne, Poznań 1931

3. A Perfect Match? The German Concept of the Company's Interest and the EU Sustainable Corporate Governance Agenda

Anne-Christin Mittwoch and Tonio Friedmann

A. Introduction

Sustainability is the defining planetary challenge of our time. International commitments such as the Paris Agreement and the UN Agenda for Sustainable Development 2030 are shaping the global direction of sustainability policy. The ecological transformation of the economy is at the top of the European legislature's agenda, with climate change being the most urgent task in this context. According to the findings of natural and social science research, sustainability issues are not limited to climate change but rather are complemented by several other ecological concerns that form a framework of planetary boundaries[1] and are complemented by a social foundation.[2] The equality of the three dimensions of sustainability – ecological, social, and economic – is emphasised by recent declarations of the United Nations (UN),[3] which built on the Brundtland Report,[4] a foundational document in the formation of the modern sustainability concept. The intent of

1 See Rockström/Steffen et al., Ecol. Soc. 14 (2) 2009, 32; Rockström/Steffen et al., Nature (461) 2009, 472 et seqq.; Steffen/Rockström et al., Science 347 (6223) 2015, 1259855.

2 Leach/Raworth/Rockström p. 84; Raworth, Oxfam Discussion Papers, p. 9; Raworth, chapter 1 et passim.

3 United Nations, Report of the United Nations Conference on Environment and Development, Annex I., Declaration on Environment and Development, 12.8.1992, UN-Doc. A/CONF.151/26 (Vol. I); United Nations, Report of the United Nations Conference on Environment and Development, Annex II, Agenda 21, 12.8.1992, UN-Doc. / CONF.151/26 (Vol. II); United Nations, transforming our world: the 2030 Agenda for Sustainable Development, 25.12.2015, UNDoc. A/RES/70/1/L.1.

4 UN-General Assembly, Report of the World Commission on Environment and Development, 11.12.1987, UN-Doc. A/RES/42/187; WCED, our Common future, p. 43.

the European Green Deal[5] and the resulting European Climate Law[6] was to pave the way for a sustainable economy, while regulatory measures are designed to address human rights abuses in transnational company supply chains.[7]

Although public law instruments, such as direct regulatory emission controls, or market solutions, like emission fees or tradable emission rights, have a long tradition as political instruments for environmental protection, recent legislative efforts for a more comprehensive sustainability transformation emphasise the role of private law in the implementation of climate policy goals.[8] Since transformation towards incorporation of the sustainability goals requires an adaptation of prevailing economic behaviours, companies as central market actors need to be analysed.[9] Initially, financial reporting was seen as the means of choice at the union level,[10] but with the progressing legal formalisation of corporate responsibility, the Commission increasingly relies on real compliance and behavioural obligations. At the heart of these European sustainability approaches to company law is the Corporate Sustainability Due Diligence Directive (CSDDD); its adoption

5 European Commission, Communication from the Commission to the European Parliament, the European Council, the Council, the European Economic and Social Committee and the Committee of the Regions, The European Green Deal, 11.12.2019, COM(2019) 640 final.

6 Regulation (EU) 2021/1119 of the European Parliament and of the Council of 30 June 2021 establishing the framework for achieving climate neutrality and amending Regulations (EC) No 401/2009 and (EU) 2018/1999.

7 Directive (EU) 2024/1760 of the European Parliament and of the Council of 13 June 2024 on corporate sustainability due diligence and amending Directive (EU) 2019/1937 and Regulation (EU) 2023/2859, PE/9/2024/REV/1, OJ L, 2024/1760, 5.7.2024 (CSDDD) and various national initiatives, see for example French and Swiss reforms Fleischer/Danninger DB 2017, 2849.

8 In addition to the CSDDD, in particularly Directive (EU) 2024/1799 of the European Parliament and of the Council of 13 June 2024 on common rules promoting the repair of goods and amending Regulation (EU) 2017/2394 and Directives (EU) 2019/771 and (EU) 2020/1828, PE/34/2024/REV/1, OJ L, 2024/1799, 10.7.2024.

9 See also Weber/Mittwoch RECol 2023, 143.

10 Directive 2014/95/EU of the European Parliament and of the Council of 22 October 2014 amending Directive 2013/34/EU as regards disclosure of non-financial and diversity information by certain large undertakings and groups, OJ L 330, 15.11.2014, which exists already in the second generation: Directive (EU) 2022/2464 of the European Parliament and of the Council of 14 December 2022 amending Regulation (EU) No 537/2014, Directive 2004/109/EC, Directive 2006/43/EC and Directive 2013/34/EU, as regards corporate sustainability reporting, PE/35/2022/REV/1, OJ L 322, 16.12.2022.

was the result of the broader EU Commission's Sustainable Corporate Governance Initiative that was launched in 2020.[11] This initiative, as well as the CSDDD, sparked the discussion about sustainability and company law in the EU.

The CSDDD propelled one of the core concepts of company law – the interest of the company – to the centre of the corporate sustainability discussion. One of the most controversial provisions of the CSDDD was the proposed Art. 25, which stated in para. 1 that, in fulfilling their duty to act in the best interest of the company, directors take into account the consequences of their decisions for sustainability matters. Under Art. 25 para. 2 CSDDD, Member States would have been required to ensure that their rules on breaches of the duties of directors reflected Art. 25 para. 1 CSDDD. Member States would also be required to extend their sanction regimes to the duty to consider sustainability concerns. In German company law, the proposed Art. 25 CSDDD was directly connected to Section 76 para. 1 and Section 93 para. 1 and 2 of the German Stock Corporation Act (AktG),[12] which would have needed to be revised to implement the CSDDD.[13] However, Art. 25 CSDDD and the duty to act in the best interest of the company were removed from the CSDDD before adoption and are not part of its final version.[14] Adoption of the proposed Art. 25 CSDDD would undoubtedly have caused a paradigm shift in company law and been a milestone in the development of sustainable corporate governance.

Thus, irrespective of the deletion of Art. 25 CSDDD, it is worth looking at the legal concept of the company's interest as a cornerstone of the sustainability discussion in company law. The company's interest is the guiding principle for management behaviour and thus is the starting point for the discussions about the nature of the company and its relation to

11 Proposal for a Directive of the European Parliament and of the Council on Corporate Sustainability Due Diligence and amending Directive (EU) 2019/1937, 23.2.2022, COM/2022/71 final (CSDDD-draft), on the regulatory content of the CSDDD-draft and in particular on the company law provisions from a German perspective Hübner/Habrich/Weller NZG 2022, 644.

12 Stock Corporation Act of 6 September 1965 (Federal Law Gazette I, p. 1089), as last amended by Article 7 of the Act of 22 February 2023 (Federal Law Gazette 2023 I no. 51), https://tinyurl.com/m2apyrwk, herein after referred to as "AktG".

13 See Hübner/Habrich/Weller NZG 2022, 644 (650); Fest AG 2023, 713 (718 et seqq.).

14 Directive (EU) 2024/1760 of the European Parliament and of the Council of 13 June 2024 on corporate sustainability due diligence and amending Directive (EU) 2019/1937 and Regulation (EU) 2023/2859, PE/9/2024/REV/1, OJ L, 2024/1760, 5.7.2024.

society. The company's interest is also directly connected to the current dichotomy between the shareholder primacy model and the stakeholder value system in defining the company's interest – a discussion that is largely informed by the Anglo-American corporate governance debate. The debate on the company's purpose, which is also more pronounced in the Anglo-American legal discussion, is connected to the concept of the company's interest. Finally, the concept of the company's interest is based on various economic theories that may need to be re-evaluated in the light of the current sustainability transformation. This chapter examines the German perspective and attempts to answer the question of whether the concept of the company's interest from a German perspective is compatible with the current EU approaches to fostering sustainable corporate governance. The concept of the company's interest is first assessed from a historical and economic perspective (B.). Drawing on this historical background, recent developments are then reviewed to clarify the extent to which sustainability-related duties of the board could be implemented in German company law (C). Following analysis of these modern approaches, the central question as to what extent the legal concept of the company's interest can serve as a vehicle for sustainable corporate governance is then addressed (D).

In international discussions, the German corporate governance system is usually characterised as a prime example of the pluralistic interest or stakeholder value system to the company's interest, particularly regarding the right of co-determination and the legal construct of the company's interest.[15] But is the German system truly an example of the stakeholder value system? And if it is, does this mean German company law and sustainability are a perfect match?

B. The evolution of the company's interest in Germany

In German company law, the legal concept of the company's best interest has traditionally served as an unwritten guideline for the actions of a company's executive bodies: both the management and supervisory board must base their decisions on the company's best interest.[16] Making deci-

15 Keay, p. 42; Ireland MLR 1999, 32 (32); Salacuse L. & Bus. Rev. Am. 2003, 33 (47); Wen JIBLR 2011, 325 (326).

16 German company law traditionally provides for a two-tier board system.

sions in the company's best interest is primarily a behavioural maxim for management and supervisory board members that reflects the brief legal requirement in Section 76 para. 1 AktG that the management board must manage the company on its own responsibility. The formulation of the best interests of the company as an explicit requirement of the business judgment rule in Section 93 para. 1 sentence 2 AktG provides a clearer indication of the relevance of the company's interests. But how can this legal concept be given substance, and to what extent is it relevant in practice? Questions about the company's interest are usually connected to corporate governance of a stock corporation: while the managing directors of a German Limited Liability Company (GmbH) can be significantly restricted in their freedom of decision or be subject to instructions by the articles of association and shareholder resolutions, the management board of a German Stock Corporation is shielded from the shareholders in its management duties by Section 119 para. 2 AktG, which provides that the general meeting may only take a decision regarding matters of the management of the company's affairs if the management board requests it. According to Section 111 para. 4 AktG the measures to be taken by the management may not be transferred to the supervisory board. For this reason, the concept of the company's interest is of considerable importance in stock corporations in Germany. Yet, German company law traditionally has been controversial as to which interests the board must consider when managing the company. Determination of which interests to include is not simple, as it is linked to fundamental questions of company law, namely the nature and purpose of the company, its relationship to society, and ultimately, the relationship between the market and the state. In Germany, this discussion on which interests a board must consider when managing a company has a long tradition and was initially started under the broader heading of whether companies must serve the common good (I.1). Discussion about the nature of the common good laid the groundwork for debate about the concept of the company's interest (I.2). More recently, discussion about the company's interest has been economised and somewhat simplified (II.), which does not seem to fit well with the historical developments. The current sustainability transformation illustrates this dichotomy of shareholder primacy and stakeholder value approach and sheds new light on key issues of corporate governance.

I. The market and state: a historically significant relationship

1. Serving the common good

Historically, the relationship between the state and the market has been discussed mainly in the context of the obligation of companies to serve the common good, a discourse that dates to the beginnings of company law.[17] At the end of the 18th century, during the period of the octroi system, the Prussian state was somewhat suspicious of company founders, particularly due to the introduction of the principle of limited liability. Due to concerns about abuse of power, market-dominating positions, and actions at the expense of the common good, the Prussian legislature attempted to link public and private interests through regulation by establishing public benefit of a German stock corporation as a requirement for its formation.[18] Accordingly, II 6 § 25 of the General Prussian Land Law of 1794[19] stipulated that corporations required state approval and had to be incorporated for the purpose of a lasting public benefit.[20] However, what exactly constituted a public benefit was not universally clarified. The law did not provide a definition, nor did case law use the term consistently.[21] The public benefit was regularly recognised in cases where the enterprise was rooted in a general economic interest of the State.[22] The concept of public benefit at that time can certainly not be equated with the modern understanding of public benefit, especially considering the emergence of the US Benefit Corporation and other related ideas. However, the concept of public benefit historically intended to express the consideration of public interests in the broadest sense. Furthermore, the appointment of commissioners or governors entrusted with representing state interests in the late 18th century, who could oversee, and directly intervene in, the company management highlights the regulatory connection of state interests and public interests.

17 For an overview in the context of the current sustainability transformation, see also Mittwoch, p. 296 et seqq.

18 At this time, the General Prussian Land Law of 1794 already recognised the legal form of the corporation, which can be compared in its legal characteristics with today's German stock company; the invention of the German limited liability company did not follow until around 100 years later.

19 Reprinted in: Hattenhauer, p. 433.

20 Hattenhauer, p. 433.

21 Mittwoch, p. 301.

22 For example, in the motives for the regulation on joint-stock companies of 31 January 1840, printed in: Baums, p. 54 et seq.; Weber, p. 28 et seqq.

To safeguard public benefit interests, the state was also entitled to send representatives to the general meeting.[23] Such personnel instruments are indeed being discussed again today with a view to promoting corporate sustainability.[24]

As liberalisation progressed and the state's influence on the formation of companies diminished, reference to the public benefit disappeared from German company law when the General Commercial Code was amended in 1870.[25] Neither the introduction of the Commercial Code in 1897 nor the Civil Code in 1900 brought it back.

However, at the beginning of the 20th century, the debate on the "theory of the enterprise as such", initiated by *Walther Rathenau*, reintroduced the link between the company and the public interest, primarily due the high macroeconomic importance of large companies.[26] Rathenau suggested that the stock corporation should no longer be seen as a creation of private law interests only, but rather as a national economic factor which, despite its private economic characteristics as a profit-making enterprise, also served public interests.[27] The subsequent discussion of a theory of the enterprise as such did not immediately find normative expression, but it decisively shaped the recognition of the independence of the corporation and its detachment from various individual interests.[28]

Only a few years later, the National Socialist legislature introduced Section 70 para. 1 in the 1937 amendment to the German Stock Corporation

---

23 Lehmann, 1898, p. 286; Lehmann, 2018, p. 82–88; in this context, see section 46 of the Royal Prussian Railway Act of 3 November 1838.

24 European Commission, Public consultation on the Sustainable Corporate Governance Initiative between October 2020 and February 2021, https://ec.europa.eu/info/law/better-regulation/have-your-say/initiatives/12548-Sustainable-corporate-governance/public-consultation_en; in the context of Benefit Corporations and Certified B Corporations in US corporate law Möslein/Mittwoch RabelsZ 2016, 399 (417 et seqq); on the current debate in Germany see C. III (Footnote 83 et seq.).

25 The amendment of 11 June 1870 also removed the requirement for joint-stock companies to hold a concession, cf. article 208 para. 2, reprinted in: Schubert/Hommelhoff, p. 115; more about the first amendment to company law in 1870 Bayer/Habersack/Lieder, p. 318 et seqq.

26 Rathenau; Rathenau himself never advocated the doctrine of the enterprise as such (*Lehre des Unternehmens an sich*), but his writing never got rid of this misconception after Haussmann supposedly recognised the doctrine in Rathenau's writing, see Haussmann JW 1927, 2953; Laux, p. 59 et seq.

27 Rathenau, p. 38 et seq.

28 Haussmann Bank-Archiv 1930, 57 (64); Habersack AcP (220) 2020, 594 (624); Mittwoch, p. 332.

Act, which required the management board to manage the company on its own responsibility, in the way the "welfare of the company and its successors and the common good of the people and the empire require".[29] Reference to the common good meant that the common good should act as an unwritten preamble and guideline for the whole of company law.[30] Of course, the National Socialist legislature also sought to enshrine its ideology – such as the principle of "common good before individual good" – in German company law.[31] Although the clause on the common good still bears the stamp of National Socialism, its roots can be traced back even further in German history, to the Weimar Republic and the debate on the theory of the enterprise.[32]

Regardless of origin, the concept of the common good was removed again by the 1965 company law reform and has not been reintroduced since. Interestingly, removal of the common good in the 1965 reform was justified on the grounds that the orientation of the board towards the common good was self-evident – its explicit normative formulation was therefore considered dispensable.[33] The lawmakers referred to the German constitution (Grundgesetz), namely to Art. 20 para. 1 on the social obligation of property under its Art. 14 para. 2, and to the social market economy as the applicable economic policy system.[34] Sixty years later, the orientation of the stock corporation towards the common good is anything but self-evident. In fact, the unwritten commitment of company law to the common good has diminished considerably.[35] Despite the discussion about its implicit continued validity, importance of the common good has decreased due to a

29 Printed in: Schröder, p. 46.

30 Schlegelberger/Quassowski, § 70 mn. 8.

31 Official commentaries openly refer to the "Führer principle" and the National Socialist principle of "common good before individual good" ("Gemeinnutz vor Eigennutz"), see: Danielcik, § 70 mn. 6; Schlegelberger/Quassowski, § 70 mn. 1, 8.

32 The official explanatory memorandum to the standard refers to the principle of responsible economic management, see in this context Mittwoch, p. 314; Schubert, p. 26 et seq., in particular Fn. 41; Ballerstedt/Hefermehl/Schilling, p. 159 (161); Jahn/Kempf/Prittwitz/Schmitt-Leonardy/Spindler, p. 249 (263).

33 Explanation of the government's draft printed at Kropff, p. 97; to this Bayer/Wöbbeking/Poppe/Langlet/Sommerer/v. Maltitz/Mittwoch, p. 54 (71).

34 Baas, p. 79 et seqq., 164; Reuter AcP (179) 1979, 509 (552); Münchner Kommentar zum Aktiengesetz/Spindler, § 76 mn. 78; Rittner JZ 1980, 113; Rittner, p. 132; critical of this Großmann, p. 117 et seqq.; Birke, p. 172, different view especially Mülbert AG 2009, 766 (770).

35 Beck'scher Online-Großkommentar Aktiengesetz/Fleischer, § 76 mn. 23; similar Mittwoch/Klappstein/Botthof/Bühner/Figge/Schirmer/Stöhr/Wolff/Weber, p. 419

lack of significant practical impacts[36] and was absorbed into the debate on the company's interest.

The question of the company's purpose is inherently tied to the issue of whose interests the company's management must take into account. Since the 1970s, this question has been examined through the legal concept of the company's interest. As the debate on the common good of the company faded, its values were internalised in the debate on the company's interest.

2. From co-determination to legal doctrine: the shaping of the company's interest

A key moment in the development of the concept of the company's interest was the introduction of co-determination rights on supervisory boards in Germany. The Co-Determination Act of 1976 established equal employee representation for companies with more than 2,000 employees that were not part of the coal, iron, or steel industry.[37] Employee participation on supervisory boards contributed to be a growing debate about which interests management can or should account for when exercising their discretion for the company. The institutionalisation of employees' interests led legal scholars to argue that these interests must play a role in company decision-making.[38] As a result, the co-determination movement was strongly associated with the company's interest and came to be seen as a reflection

(433) stating that there is no clear result of the historical interpretation from today's perspective.

36 Koch, § 76 mn. 30; Schubert, p. 27 et seq.; Fleischer ZGR 2017, 411 (415 et seq.); Reuter AcP (179) 1979, 509 (525); Fischer/Gessler/Schilling/Serick/Ulmer/Raisch, p. 347 (352 et seqq.); Ballerstedt/Hefermehl/Schilling, p. 159 (168 et seq.); disapproving Münchner Kommentar zum Aktiengesetz/Spindler, § 76 mn. 79; Rittner JZ 1980, 113 (113) instead derives the common good obligation from Art. 14 para. 2 GG; particularly opposing Mülbert AG 2009, 766; Baas, p. 68 et seq.

37 Co-determination Act of 4 May 1976 (Federal Law Gazette I p. 1153), last amended by Article 17 of the Act of 7 August 2021 (Federal Law Gazette I p. 3311), section 1, herein after referred to "Co-determination Act"; in addition to the Co-Determination Act, two more co-determination laws are in force: the Coal, Iron, and Steel Codetermination Act and the One-Third Participation Act.

38 Reichert-Facilides/Rittner/Sasse/Raiser, p. 101 (114); Schilling, ZHR 1980, 136 (143); Ballerstedt, ZGR 1977, 133 (135 et seq.); Mertens, ZGR 1977, 270 (275 et seqq.); controversial Mülbert, ZGR 1997, 129 (151); cf. Paefgen, p. 115, 118.

of a pluralistic stakeholder value understanding of the company's interest in Germany and internationally.[39]

However, the controversy did not end with the passing of the Co-Determination Act. When opponents of the Act asked the Federal Constitutional Court (Bundesverfassungsgericht, in short BVerfG) to assess the compatibility of co-determination with the constitution, the court not only upheld the Act, but also explicitly acknowledged the pluralistic view of the company's interest in its reasoning.[40] Additionally, the German Federal Court of Justice (Bundesgerichtshof, in short BGH) also recognised the concept of the company's interest around the same time and used it as a benchmark for assessing the confidentiality obligations of supervisory board members, which sparked further debate about the company's interest.[41]

Both court decisions and the Co-Determination Act itself triggered a decade of academic debate about the meaning and the scope of the concept of the company's interest. Scholars approached the issue from different angels, ranging from interdisciplinary theories to procedural models enriched by material principles.[42] The debate was further fuelled by a broader discussion about the development of German enterprise law as a counterpart to company law, which directly linked these developments to the company's interest and resulted in enterprise-specific approaches in law to defining the company's interest.[43]

---

39 Schubert, p. 145, 147 et seq.; from an international perspective: Sjåfjell/Bruner/Rühmkorf, p. 232 (237 et seq.); Sjåfjell/Richardson/Millon, p. 35 (48 et seqq.).

40 BVerfG 01.03.1979 – 1 BvR 532, 533/77, 419/78, 1 BvL 21/78, NJW 1979, 699 (703).

41 BGH 05.06.1975 – II ZR 156/73, BGHZ 64, 325, NJW 1975, 1412 (1413).

42 Overview of the variety of approaches towards the company's interest, Jürgenmeyer, p. 88 et seqq.; Mülbert ZGR 1997, 129 (142 et seqq.).

43 The German academic debate still revolves around the notion "enterprise's interest" (*Unternehmensinteresse*) and not "company's interest". This is due to historical reasons, as the concept of the company's interest was closely linked to approaches to the development of a business law. These approaches argued for a shift in focus from the legal entity of the company to the broader construct of the enterprise, cf. Reichert-Facilides/Rittner/Sasse/Raiser, p. 101 (117); Schilling ZHR 1980, 136 (144). However, to this day, no consistent business law has been established in Germany. The reflection on the enterprise was used to justify an autonomous interest of the enterprise, recognising all potential interests of the stakeholders within the enterprise. Today, the difference between the two concepts is disappearing, as already pointed out by Flume, who considered the company's interest and the enterprise's interest to be identical Sandrock/Flume, p. 43 (63); lately also Koch, § 76 mn. 66 who states that the term is used as an acronym to define the board's guiding principle.

An interdisciplinary interpretation, influenced by social-science, views the company's interest as the autonomous interest of a social organisation – a group of people linked by a common economic purpose and by their means.[44] Here, the company's interest is understood as emerging through an integrative process in which the specific interests of each member of the social organisations equate to an autonomous interest of the company.[45] This understanding of the company's interest is a rather dynamic construct which can be compared to public law doctrine on the exercise of discretion: allowing a variety of lawful choices in the light of a specific individual situation.[46] The outcome of exercising this discretion does not necessarily have to be aligned with the individual interests of its members.

However, most legal scholars advocate for a procedural approach to determining the interest of the company.[47] They call for rules that clarify how interests can be managed, particularly conflicting interests. This is done by assessing and then harmonising the different interests of the stakeholders. While accounting for differing interests in this way is primarily procedural, scholars have enriched the concept so it can operate within a framework. According to most legal scholars, the guiding principle when assessing and harmonising the interests of different stakeholders is the profitability of the company.[48] Profitability is mainly understood in the long-term, as long-term profitability best meets the needs of shareholders and other

44 *Fechner* was the leading figure in shaping this concept of social organisation under company law, see Fechner, Die Treubindungen des Aktionärs, p. 67 et seq.; Fechner, Das wirtschaftliche Unternehmen in der Rechtswissenschaft, passim.

45 Boettcher/Hax/Kunze/v. Nell-Breuning/Ortlieb/Preller, p. 143 et seq.; Ballerstedt/Hefermehl/Kunze, p. 47 (47 et seqq.); Fischer/Hefermehl/Kunze, p. 333 (347 et seqq.); Kunze, ZHR 1980, 100 (102 et seqq.).

46 Cf. for instance Kunze, ZHR 1980, 100 (117).

47 With differences as to which individual interests should be taken into account, cf. Hanau ZGR 1979, 524 (544); cf. Westermann ZGR 1977, 219 (223), who considers a prevalence of the interests of the shareholders in conflicts to be legitimate; cf. also Kunze ZHR 1980, 100 (117); Schilling ZHR 1980, 136 (144); Fischer/Gessler/Schilling/Serick/Ulmer/Raisch, p. 347 (357); as well Semler, p. 33 et seq.

48 Jürgenmeyer, p. 99, 103; Kort AG 2012, 605 (609 et seq.); Hirte/Mülbert/Roth/Kort, § 76 mn. 53; Schubert, p. 32 et seq.; Fischer/Gessler/Schilling/Serick/Ulmer/Raisch, p. 347 (361, 363) understanding profitability as the long-term capital preservation; see further BGH 13.10.1977 – II ZR 123/76, NJW 1978, 104 (106) advocating a pluralistic understanding within the guiding principle of economic efficiency.

stakeholders.[49] Others defend a monistic view, arguing that public interests are best served when individuals focus on maximising their own interests.[50] Still, the prevailing pluralistic perception recognises the relevance of public interests in business decisions-making, reinforcing a pluralistic understanding of the company's interest. From a pluralistic perspective, the board **may** take into account the interests of shareholders and employees, as well as the public interests, as long as the long-term profitability is not compromised, but they are not **required** to do so.

Since the 1980s, the once-broad debate on the company interest has increasingly narrowed to primarily shareholder versus stakeholder interests. This dichotomy originates from the Anglo-American corporate governance discussion, which was widely embraced in Germany from the time it emerged and is still highly relevant to this day.

II. Economically-motivated dichotomy of shareholder and stakeholder

Today's discussion about the content of the company's interest, both nationally and internationally, is mostly limited to the dichotomy of the shareholder primacy model and the stakeholder value system or, in other words, the contrast between a monistic and a pluralistic conception.[51] The basis of this discussion is not in law but in economics.[52] Underlying microeconomic theories play an essential role in the US corporate governance discussion and have led to the approach that shareholder interests should be prioritised in relation to the interests of other stakeholders (shareholder primacy model), when defining the company's interest. The following section sketches out the microeconomic theories that support shareholder primacy and contrasts shareholder primacy with the stakeholder value system.

---

49 Already then, it was pointed out that profitability cannot be measured solely in economic terms but must also take account of 'societal' or 'social' factors, Martens AG 1976, 113 (118); Brinkmann, p. 101 et seqq.; Jürgenmeyer, p. 102 et seq.

50 Hölters BB 1978, 640 (642).

51 For the purpose of simplicity, only the currently dominant dichotomy between the shareholder and stakeholder approaches will be discussed here; other concepts, in particular mediating approaches such as enlightened shareholder value, will be excluded; for more details on enlightened shareholder value, see Mittwoch, p. 136 et seqq.

52 Mülbert ZGR 1997, 129 (134 et seqq.); Groh DB 2000, 2153; v. Colbe ZGR 1997, 271; fundamental from an economic perspective in particular Markowitz J. Finance (7) 1952, 77; Fama J. Finance 1970, 383; Friedman; Jensen/Meckling J. Financ. Econ. (3) 1976, 305.

The first microeconomic theory that supports a shareholder primacy model assumes a separation between shareholders, as the economic owners of the company, and managers, who exercise control over the company.[53] The separation of ownership and control, combined with the fact that company shares are increasingly dispersed in ownership, creates the risk that managers may not necessarily act in the interests of the owners, but might instead use their position as corporate trustees for their own benefit, engaging in opportunistic behaviour. This concept of ownership and control creates a principal-agent relationship between shareholders and the board, which comes with many problems.[54] The monistic approach aims to mitigate these problems by giving management a clear mandate: their guiding principle should always be maximal value creation for the shareholders. It should be noted however, that unlike in the US, the German shareholder landscape was never characterised by dispersed ownership of shares; instead, shares were, and still are, typically held in block ownership.

The capital market efficiency hypothesis also lends itself to a shareholder primacy model, as it finds that a company's share price simultaneously reflects all available information about the respective company.[55] For publicly-listed companies, this means the success or failure of the company should be reflected in the company's share price, and thus, members of the boards of public companies are often committed to the short-term financial interests of shareholders, with profit orientation in favour of shareholder being the primary or even exclusive goal of the company. This means that under the capital market efficiency hypothesis, specific interests of other stakeholders, such as employees, customers, and suppliers, receive less attention than the financial interests of shareholders.[56] The key advantage of

---

53 Fundamental Berle/Means; Jensen/Meckling J. Financ. Econ. (3) 1976, 305; more recently Armour/Gordon J. Leg. Anal. (6) 2014, 35; In Germany, the concept of economic ownership can be found in the explanatory memorandum to the 1965 Stock Corporation Act, but it does not provide any explicit differentiation for the complex nature of share ownership, see Schoppe, p. 88; Webering, p. 7.

54 This theory originally goes back to the so-called Berle-Dodd debate on the orientation of modern companies, Alchian/Demsetz Am. Econ. Rev. (62) 1972, 777; Jensen/Meckling J. Financ. Econ. (3) 1976, 305; Fama J. Political Econ. (88) 1980, 288.

55 Fundamental Fama J. Finance 1970, 383; Rappaport; from a German perspective Mülbert ZGR 1997, 129 (131 et seqq.); Crezelius/Hirte/Vieweg/Mülbert, p. 421 (424 et seqq.); Groh DB 2000, 2153.

56 Fundamental Rappaport; in detail Hommelhoff/Hopt/v. Werder/Fleischer, p. 185; Kuhner ZGR 2004, 244 (258, 273); Ulmer AcP (202) 2002, 143, (155 et seqq.); Groh DB 2000, 2153 (2158); using the example of reducing the number of jobs to increase

the capital market efficiency hypothesis is that it focuses business decisions on financial parameters that can be easily presented within the framework of disclosure and financial reporting obligations, and which can be subject to judicial scrutiny if disputes arise. Proponents of the shareholder primacy model state that the capital market efficiency hypothesis effectively minimises the risk of opportunistic management behaviour. The capital market efficiency hypothesis together with the portfolio theory form the second fundamental assumption of shareholder primacy.[57] The latter focusses on minimising risk or maximising return for shareholders in a diversified portfolio.[58]

A third microeconomic approach that supports the shareholder primacy model is the linking of microeconomic theory with corporate law theory. The combination of these two theories highlights questions about the nature of the company by characterising the company as a network for contracts.[59] In this network, shareholders are the only interest group that is not contractually bound to the company in such a way that their claims are contractually secured, which is typically the case for employees, suppliers, or customers. Rather, shareholders are regarded as profit beneficiaries and risk bearers (residual claimants) because any remaining profit in the form of dividend payments is allocated to them only after the contractual claims of other stakeholders have been satisfied. Since shareholders are thus seen as the economic owners and risk bearers of the company under this approach, their priority in management decisions is justified.[60]

---

the return on equity v. Werder ZGR 1997, 69 (75) and from a business perspective Bischoff, p. 83; the shareholder approach according to Rappaport is based on net present value, which in principle also takes into account cash flows in the distant future. If the capital market systematically misprices transactions in the distant future (i.e. if there is no capital market efficiency), this has an (indirect) impact on the duties of the board under the shareholder value approach.

57 Fundamental to the efficient market hypothesis Fama J. Finance 1970, 383.

58 Groundbreaking to the portfolio theory Markowitz J. Finance (7) 1952, 77.

59 Alchian/Demsetz Am. Econ. Rev. (62) 1972, 777; Jensen/Meckling J. Financ. Econ. (3) 1976, 305; for an overview see Easterbrook/Fischel; Hart; from the German perspective Groh DB 2000, 2153 (2158); instead of many Eisenberg J. Corp. L. 24 (1998), 819; critical also Kraakman et al., p. 5 et seqq., with a preference for the term "nexus for contracts"; on the various theories on the nature of the legal person Mittwoch, p. 362 et seqq.; Fleischer NZG 2023, 243 (245 et seqq.); Watson J. Corp. L. Stud. (19) 2019, 137; Watson ECGI Working Paper N° 701/2023.

60 Easterbrook/Fischel, p. 36 et seq.; Allen Wash. & Lee L. Rev. 1993, 1395 (1400); Hommelhoff/Hopt/v. Werder/Schmidt/Weiß, p. 161 (169).

Finally, proponents of the shareholder primacy model assume that prioritising shareholders is also efficient for the company as a whole and ultimately aligns with the interests of other stakeholders. Capital providers are more likely to make positive investment decisions in favour of the company if their interests are protected, which can especially be achieved by granting control rights.[61] Positive investment decisions are of paramount importance for the company's fate because capital is the only truly scarce resource in the entrepreneurial production process. All other resources, such as labour or necessary environmental goods, have either unlimited availability or – ideally – are substitutable without limit.[62] Based on these considerations, there are no arguments for prioritising the interests of other stakeholders over those of shareholders; the mere fact that stakeholders contribute to the creation of value in the company is not sufficient from an economic perspective to justify priority for them in decision-making.[63]

The countermodel to shareholder primacy is the stakeholder value system, which was significantly shaped by *Robert Edward Freeman* and further developed by *Margaret Blair* and *Lynn Stout* in the form of team production theory, sees things differently.[64] In contrast to the monistic paradigm of model, the stakeholder value system is based on the fundamental assumption that a company is generally managed in the interests of all stakeholders equally, without any abstract prioritisation of the shareholders or any other stakeholder group.[65] Shareholders are not in opposition to other stakeholder groups: they are one of several groups of stakeholders with a special economic relationship. The various stakeholder groups work together as a team for the collective benefit.[66] Under the stakeholder value system, managers are seen as trustees of the company's assets:

61 Hommelhoff/Hopt/v. Werder/Schmidt/Weiß, p. 161 (170).

62 Boubaker/Cumming/Nguyen/v. Werner/Stoner, p. 179 (182); on the problem of substitutability of environmental goods, see Mittwoch, p. 38 et seqq. and in-depth p. 43 et seqq.

63 Hommelhoff/Hopt/v. Werder/Schmidt/Weiß, p. 161 (170).

64 Freeman; Freeman/Reed Cal. Mgmt. Rev. 1983, 88; Freeman Bus. Ethics Q. 1994, 409; Blair; Blair/Stout Va. L. Rev. (85) 1999, 247.

65 With fundamental considerations Alchian/Demsetz Am. Econ. Rev. (62) 1972, 777, (779 et seqq.), who also already use the term team production (794); in addition Dean Co. Law. 2001, 66 (69); Preston/Sapienza J. Behavioral Economics 1990, 361.

66 Blair/Stout Va. L. Rev. (85) 1999, 247 (278).

they operate as mediating hierarchs and have the task of promoting the prosperity of the company as a whole, not just the profits of shareholders.[67]

There is no consensus in German literature as to which of the two approaches is superior, which is why the shareholder primacy model has not been adopted, neither in academia, nor in court decisions.[68] German company law does not decide the issue on the books, and it is also blind to the dichotomy of shareholders' and stakeholders' interests. This is because the purpose of the stock corporation and the understanding of its overall nature have historically been shaped less by economic theories and more by the socio-legal question of the relationship between the state and the market or public and private interests, as laid out above. While the shareholder primacy model's influence reached its peak in the German corporate governance debate in the late 1990s and early 2000s, the 2010s brought an increased awareness for sustainability issues in business that has reshaped the discussion, including the adoption of the European directive on nonfinancial reporting.[69]

C. Transformation of the company's interest through sustainability?

I. Implementation of sustainability-related management duties

The review of the historical roots of the company's interest in German company law has shown that sustainability-related duties of boards, insofar as they are relevant to the management's actions in the company's interests, can be easily implemented into German company law. Even before the publication of the directive proposal, various parties had proposed enshrining the stakeholder value system (pluralist model) of the company's interest as the guiding principle for the board of the German stock corporations in Section 76 para. 1 AktG;[70] some proposals even included substantive

67 Blair/Stout Va. L. Rev. (85) 1999, 247 (271, 281 et seq.); Stout U. Pa. L. Rev. (152) 2003, 667 (669); from a German perspective Grundmann/Kirchner/Raiser/Schwintowski/Weber/Windbichler/v. Werder, p. 285 (287 et seq.).

68 Yet this was the theory of Hansmann/Kraakman Geo. L. J. (89) 2001, 439 (441).

69 Directive 2014/95/EU of the European Parliament and of the Council of 22 October 2014 amending Directive 2013/34/EU as regards disclosure of non-financial and diversity information by certain large undertakings and groups, OJ L 330, 15.11.2014.

70 Schubert, p. 210 et seqq., 220 (thesis 24) calls for an adjustment to the current state of discussion; Mittwoch, p. 358 et seqq.; Hommelhoff ZGR 2001, 238 (250); cf. his more

concretization with reference to the company law binding to the common good.[71] Despite of the fact that key provisions of the Stock Corporation Act, like Section 76 or 93 AktG, have not been changed, recent developments demonstrate that sustainability aspects are increasingly shaping the pluralist approach to corporate governance in Germany, as illustrated by recent versions of the German Corporate Governance Code (GCGC). Furthermore, there have been prominent discussions among academics and practitioners: in 2024, the 74th German Jurists' Conference discussed the relationship between company law and climate change and a working group of experts in stock corporation law considered the role of sustainability in developing proposals for a comprehensive reform of stock corporation law.

II. Sustainability in the German Corporate Governance Code (GCGC)

The GCGC is separate from the Stock Corporation Act and is not enacted by a democratically-legitimised lawmaker but instead by a commission whose members are appointed by the German Federal Minister of Justice. This commission presents essential statutory regulations for the management and supervision of German listed companies and contains, in the form of recommendations and suggestions, nationally and internationally acknowledged standards for good and responsible corporate governance.[72]

The current version of the GCGC offers a definition of the company's interest ("the enterprise's best interest") in its foreword. The foreword explicitly states that "the Code highlights the obligation of [m]anagement [b]oards and [s]upervisory [b]oards – in line with the principles of the social market economy – to take into account the interests of the shareholders, the enterprise's workforce and the other groups related to the enterprise (stakeholders) to ensure the continued existence of the enterprise

recent position Hommelhoff NZG 2015, 1329 (1330 et seq.); Hommelhoff NZG 2017, 1361 (1362, 1366).

71 Relevant draft laws were introduced by the Bündnis 90/Die Grünen parliamentary group in 2012 (BT-Drs. 17/11686, Entwurf eines Gesetzes zur Änderung des Aktiengesetzes vom 18.11.2012) and by the SPD parliamentary group in 2017 (SPD-Fraktion, Entwurf eines Gesetzes zur Angemessenheit von Vorstandsvergütungen und zur Beschränkung der steuerlichen Absetzbarkeit vom 20.2.2017); in-depth analysis of the various proposals at Mittwoch, p. 324 et seq.

72 The GCGC is regularly updated and available online at https://www.dcgk.de./en/home.html.

and its sustainable value creation". By committing the management and supervisory boards to sustainable value creation, the Code goes much further than the European Commission's original proposal of Art. 25 CS-DDD, which only required management to consider the impact of their decisions for sustainability aspects – but not to act accordingly. If the foreword of the GCGC were binding law, Germany would already have sustainability-related duties of management in place[73]: the foreword connects these duties directly to the concept of the company's interest, which at the same time calls for sustainable value creation.[74] The GCGC also stipulates in Recommendation A.1 that the management board shall systematically identify and assess the risks and opportunities associated with social and environmental factors, as well as the ecological and social impacts of the enterprise's activities. In addition to long-term economic objectives, the corporate strategy should also give appropriate consideration to ecological and social objectives. According to Recommendation A.3, corporate planning should include corresponding financial and sustainability-related objectives. The internal control system and the risk management system shall also cover sustainability-related objectives, unless required by law anyway, which includes processes and systems for collecting and processing sustainability-related data.

The same concepts apply to the supervisory board under the GCGC: according to Principle 6 of the GCGC, supervision and advice also include sustainability issues. Recommendation C.1 GCGC suggests that the supervisory board's skills and expertise profile should include expertise regarding sustainability issues that are relevant to the enterprise. Such expertise is particularly important in the field of accounting. According to Recommendation D.3 GCGC, accounting and auditing also include sustainability reporting.

As important and interesting as the requirements of the GCGC are for the development of sustainable corporate governance in Germany, it is important to note that its scope is limited to listed companies, and the GCGC also has no binding legal status and is considered soft law. According to Section 161 para. 1 of the AktG, the executive board and supervisory board of the listed company must declare annually that the recommendations of the

---

73 On the distinction between the existing approaches to sustainability-related duties, cf. Harbarth AG 2022, 633.

74 See on the concept of sustainable value creation in the European Union Sjåfjell/Tsagas/Villiers.

GCGC are being complied with or which of the Code's recommendations are not being applied and why not.[75] Thus, the GCGC foreword's commitment to sustainable value creation has little effect: as a mere principle (and not a recommendation), it is not even part of the declaration of compliance pursuant to Section 161 AktG; thus the comply-or-explain mechanism does not apply. Nevertheless, the importance of the GCGC requirements should not be underestimated.[76] As the GCGC is a relatively flexible soft law instrument, it has repeatedly been used as a testing ground for innovative but controversial corporate law requirements. For example, the introduction of gender quotas for management and supervisory board appointments was tested in the GCGC before it was subsequently included in the Stock Corporation Act in 2015 and 2021.[77] The shaping of the company interest as a driver for sustainability in the GCGC can thus be considered as an important step to sustainable corporate governance for listed companies in Germany.

III. Current academic discussions

The current academic discussion points in a similar direction and it is picking up speed: the 74th German Jurists' Day 2024 analysed whether legislative measures in company law were recommended in the fight against climate change.[78] The Association of German Jurists, founded in 1860,

75 GCGC provisions can be categorised as principles, recommendations and suggestions. Only recommendations are covered by Section 161 AktG, see the foreword of the GCGC, see fn. 73.

76 According to their declarations of compliance, all 40 DAX companies comply with recommendations A.1 and A.3 of the GCGC, Gleiss Lutz, p. 5, 15 et seq. In general, empirical studies indicate a high level of acceptance of the Code, see Corporate Governance Reports on the 2017 and 2020 versions of the GCGC: v. Werder/Danilov/Schwarz DB 2021, 2097; Beyenbach/Rapp/Strenger;v. Werder/Danilov DB 2018, 1997.

77 Gesetz für die gleichberechtigte Teilhabe von Frauen und Männern an Führungspositionen in der Privatwirtschaft und im öffentlichen Dienst vom 24.04.2015, BGBl. I 2015, p. 642 ("FüPoG I"); Gesetz zur Ergänzung und Änderung der Regelungen für die gleichberechtigte Teilhabe von Frauen an Führungspositionen in der Privatwirtschaft und im öffentlichen Dienst vom 07.08.2021, BGBl. I 2021, Nr. 51, p. 3311 ("FüPoG II").

78 See the resolutions of the Business Law Division of the 74th German Jurists Association: https://djt.de/wp-content/uploads/2024/09/djt_74_Beschluesse_Wirtschaftsrecht.pdf and for more details on the Business Law Division: https://djt.de/74-djt/fachprogramm/wirtschaftsrecht/.

examines the necessity of amendments to the German and European legal system on an academic basis, presenting proposals for the further development of the law to the public, pointing out legal abuses, and encouraging lawyers from all professional groups and fields to exchange views.[79] Since the association does not represent the interests of specific professional or social groups, its word carries weight in the legal community and with the legislature.[80]

Heidelberg-based legal scholar *Marc-Philippe Weller*'s legal opinion served as a basis for the 2024 discussion. Although his legal opinion did not explicitly recommend the integration of sustainability-related duties of the board into the concept of the company's interest,[81] it presented three concrete proposals in the form of a "climate triad" for company law: first, the introduction of climate quotas for large companies as provided for in Art. 22 CSDDD; second, the introduction of the legal form "climate-neutral" that could be added to any legal form in German company law for the purpose of signalling; and third, with regard to "climate governance" there are different recommendations for the management board, the supervisory board, and the general meeting of a stock corporation.[82] Although, or perhaps because, some of the proposals were quite progressive, most of them did not meet the approval of the German Jurists' Conference. Nevertheless, *Marc-Philippe Weller*'s developments demonstrate that the sustainability discussion has arrived at the centre of company law.

In this vein, a proposal by a group of 26 prominent academics called for a major reform of German Stock Corporation Act in 2024,[83] in an effort to bring the Act up to date with the modern reality of stock corporations in honour of its 60th birthday in 2025. The cornerstones of the academics' proposal were digitalisation, artificial intelligence, and the shift towards sustainability.[84] While this working group explicitly rejected the idea of requiring management boards commit to sustainability or public interest aspects when managing the company on the basis of Sections 76, 93 AktG,

79 Section 2 para. 1 of the articles of association of the German Jurists' Day, available at https://djt.de/djt-e-v/der-verein/ueber-uns/.

80 See also the Association's website, https://djt.de/djt-e-v/der-verein/ueber-uns/.

81 74. djt I/Weller, p. F92 et seq.; see explanatory summary Weller NJW Beilage 2/2024, 58.

82 Weller/Hößl/Seemann ZGR 2024, 180.

83 Gesellschaftsrechtliche Vereinigung; see also the explanatory summary Habersack/Vetter AG 2024, 377 (379 et seq.).

84 Habersack/Vetter AG 2024, 377.

they did consider introducing an obligation for management boards to take sustainability and public interest into account. The working group rejected a change in the composition of the management and supervisory boards, to the effect that these bodies would each be supplemented by a person with sustainability expertise. However, the working group did introduce the concept of a "Say on Climate", which ultimately produces a mixed picture and results in no clear decision.

The current academic discussion on sustainability in company law has not yet led to the German legislature taking any concrete measures. Whether the German Stock Corporation Act itself will be reformed in the near future and to what extent sustainability aspects would be part of such a reform is thus questionable. However, considering the rapidly developing academic and political discussion, driven by international and European developments in the area of corporate sustainability, it is almost certain that the legal infrastructure will be changed to some extent; it just remains to be seen whether the company's interest will play a major role in this respect.

D. Conclusion: A Perfect Match?

In international discussions, the German corporate governance system is characterised as a prime example of a pluralistic interest or stakeholder value system, particularly regarding the right of co-determination and the legal construct of the company's interest.[85] From a comparative perspective, this is certainly true. Considering its historical development, the German pluralistic concept of the company's interest seems predestined to implement the European Sustainable Corporate Governance Agenda, placing sustainability at the heart of corporate law. There are two reasons for this. First, the pluralistic approach already allows for the consideration of sustainability issues, despite there generally being no requirement to do so. Second, the concept of the company's interest is linked to the debate on the commitment of stock corporations to serve the common good and thus accounts for the significant relationship between market and state. In this respect, the consideration of sustainability aspects by corporate boards is the modern successor of the traditional debate on serving the common good. Since German company law is historically aware of the integration of private and public interests into the corporate purpose and company's

85 Refer to footnote 15.

interest, it is not surprising that the academic debate on sustainability transformation has been groundbreaking for German company law.

The question of how sustainability could be more effectively implemented in German company law is already being addressed by the GCGC with regard to publicly-listed stock corporations. The concept of the company's interest plays a central role in these developments. If the GCGC were binding law, Germany would exceed the proposed requirements of the European Sustainable Corporate Governance Agenda, specifically of the (deleted) Art. 25 CSDDD. Such a development does not appear to be out of the question, as the GCGC has historically been used as an innovation hub for best practices in company law, which have led to corresponding changes in the German Stock Corporation Act.

In terms of legal policy, however, the direction in which German company law will develop is questionable; the prospects for greater integration of sustainability into the concept of the company's interest do not appear to be very promising. At the 74th German Jurists' Day in 2024, the concept of the company's interests was not addressed; instead, the focus was on "softer" measures such as a "Say on Climate" and climate-neutral labelling.[86] Similarly, the 2024 academic proposal rejected the idea of obligating management to pursue environmental or public interest under Sections 76 and 93 AktG, but did consider introducing an obligation to take environmental and public interests into account. These developments illustrate that a rapid update of these provisions in the light of the debate of corporate sustainability is possible but unlikely.

Therefore, the German concept of the company's interest and the EU Sustainable Corporate Governance Agenda are indeed a great match – this is evidenced by historical development and academic interpretation of the concept. However, there is a strong political reluctance to reshape the concept in terms of promoting sustainability. Instead, it is often suggested that the sustainability transformation should be achieved through special legal acts that do not affect company law, or at least do not affect core concepts of company law. The current omnibus initiative of the EU Commission could be a game-changer in this respect: the call for fewer regulatory and bureaucratic burdens on companies and their boards in favour of leaner solutions could push German company law to zoom out from its current focus on imposing specific legal obligations and instead

86 74. djt I/Weller, p. F76 et seqq., F101 et seqq.; see also the resolutions of the 74th German Jurists Day (fn. 79).

emphasise more general legal concepts. The concept of the company's interest could be the general principle that guides businesses on the way toward economic activity without compromising planetary boundaries and social foundations, while allowing for the reduction of bureaucracy. In this way, the concept of the company's interest could enable strategic planning and lead to corporate sustainability.

References

Alchian, Armen/Demsetz, Harold, Production, Information Costs and Economic Organization, AER 1972, p. 777

Allen, William T., Contracts and Communities in Corporation Law, WLULR 1993, p. 1395

Armour, John/Gordon, Jeffrey N., Systemic Harms and Shareholder Value, JLA 2014, p. 35

Baas, Dieter, Leitungsmacht und Gemeinwohlbindung der Aktiengesellschaft, Bern 1976

Ballerstedt, Kurt, Das Mitbestimmungsgesetz zwischen Gesellschafts-, Arbeits- und Unternehmensrecht, ZGR 1977, p. 133

Baums, Theodor, Gesetz über die Aktiengesellschaften für die Königlich Preußischen Staaten 1843, Aalen 1981

Berle, Adolf/Means, Gardiner, The Modern Corporation and Private Property, New York 1932

Beyenbach, Johannes/ Rapp, Marc Steffen/ Strenger, Christian/ Wolff, Michael, Kodexakzeptanz 2019: Analyse der Entsprechenserklärungen von DAX- und MDAX-Gesellschaften zum Deutschen Corporate Governance Kodex (Code Compliance 2019: Analysis of the Declarations of Conformity with the German Corporate Governance Code), 2019, https://ssrn.com/abstract=3391284 (last accessed: 4 April 2025)

Birke, Max, Das Formalziel der Aktiengesellschaft. Eine juristische und ökonomische Analyse der Pflicht der Organe der Aktiengesellschaft zur Berücksichtigung der Interessen von Nichtaktionären, Baden-Baden 2005

Bischoff, Jörg, Das Shareholder Value-Konzept, Wiesbaden 1994

Blair, Margarete M., Ownership and Control: Rethinking Corporate Governance for the Twenty First Century. Who's at Stake in the Governance Debate, Washington DC 1995

Blair, Margaret M./Stout, Lynn A., A Team Production Theory of Corporate Law, VLR 1999, p. 247

Boettcher, Erik/Hax, Karl/Kunze, Otto/von Nell-Breuning, Oswald/Ortlieb, Heinz-Dietrich/Preller, Ludwig (eds.), Unternehmensverfassung als gesellschaftspolitische Forderung – ein Bericht, Berlin 1968

Brinkmann, Thomas, Unternehmensinteresse und Unternehmensrechtsstruktur: Aufgaben und Grenzen eines normativen Regulativs unternehmenspolitischer Prozesse, Berlin 1982

V. Colbe, Walther B., Was ist und was bedeutet Shareholder Value aus betriebswirtschaftlicher Sicht? ZGR 1997, p. 271

Danielcik, Hans P., Aktiengesetz. Gesetz über die Aktiengesellschaften und Kommanditgesellschaften auf Aktien nebst Einführungsgesetz und Nebengesetzen, Berlin 1937

Dean, Janice, Directing public companies: Company Law and the Stakeholder society, London 2001

Easterbrook, Frank/ Fischel, Daniel, The Economic Structure of Corporate Law, Cambridge 1996

Eisenberg, Melvin A., The Conception that the Corporation is a Nexus of Contracts, and the Dual Nature of the Firm, JCL 1998, p. 819

European Commission: Directorate-General for Justice and Consumers and EY, Study on Directors` Duties and Sustainable Corporate Governance, 2020, https://op.europa.eu/de/publication-detail/-/publication/e47928a2-d20b-11ea-adf7-01aa75ed71a1/language-en (last accessed: 4 April 2025)

Fama, Eugene F., Agency Problems and the Theory of the Firm, JPE 1980, p. 288

Fama, Eugene F., Efficient Capital Markets. A Review of Theory and Empirical Work, The Journal of Finance 1970, p. 383

Fechner, Erich, Die Treubindungen des Aktionärs, Weimar 1942

Fechner, Erich, Das wirtschaftliche Unternehmen in der Rechtswissenschaft. Antrittsvorlesung der Universität Bonn Heft 7, Bonn 1942

Fleischer, Holger, Shareholders vs. Stakeholders: Aktienrechtliche Fragen, in: Hommelhoff/Hopt/v. Werder (eds.), Handbuch Corporate Governance, 2nd ed., Stuttgart 2009

Fleischer, Holger, Gesetzliche Unternehmenszielbestimmung im Aktienrecht – Eine vergleichende Bestandsaufnahme -, ZGR 2017, p. 411

Fleischer, Holger/Danninger, Nadja, Konzernhaftung für Menschenrechtsverletzungen. Französische und schweizerische Reformen als Regelungsvorbilder für Deutschland?, DB 2017, p. 2849

Fleischer, Holger, Ein Rundgang durch die Landschaft gesellschaftsrechtlicher Theorien, NZG 2023, p. 243

Flume, Werner, Unternehmen und juristische Personen, in: Sandrock (ed.), Festschrift für Günther Beitzke zum 70. Geburtstag, Berlin 1979, p. 43

Freeman, Edward, Strategic Management: A Stakeholder Approach, Cambridge 1984

Freeman, Edward, The Politics of Stakeholder Theory: Some Future Directions, BEQ 1994, p. 409

Freeman, Edward/Reed, David L., Stockholders and Shareholders: A New Perspective on Corporate Governance, CMR 1983, p. 88

Friedman, Milton, The social responsibility of business is to increase its profits, New York Times Magazine 1970

Gesellschaftsrechtliche Vereinigung, Reformbedarf im Aktienrecht. Vorschläge für eine große Aktienrechtsreform Bd. 30, Köln 2024

Groh, Manfred, Shareholder Value und Aktienrecht, DB 2000, p. 2153

Großmann, Adolf, Unternehmensziele im Aktienrecht, Köln 1980

Habersack, Mathias, Gemeinwohlbindung und Unternehmensrecht, AcP 2020, p. 594

Habersack, Mathias/Vetter, Jochen, Vorschläge für eine große Aktienrechtsreform, AG 2024, p. 377

Hanau, Peter, Die arbeitsrechtliche Bedeutung des Mitbestimmungsurteils des Bundesverfassungsgerichts, ZGR 1979, p. 524

Hansmann, Henry/Kraakman, Reinier, The End of History for Corporate Law, GLJ 2001, p. 439

Harbarth, Stephan, Corporate Sustainability Due Diligence- Richtlinie (Kein) Systemumbruch im deutschen Aktienrecht?, AG 2022, p. 633

Hart, Oliver, Firms, Contracts and Financial Structure, Oxford 1995

Hattenhauer, Hans, Allgemeines Landrecht für die preußischen Staaten, 2nd ed., Berlin 1994, p. 433

Haussmann, Fritz, Die Aktiengesellschaft als „Unternehmen an sich", JW 1927, p. 2953

Haussmann, Fritz, Der allgemeine Anfechtungstatbestand („Generalklausel") im Aktienrecht und im Recht der Berggewerkschaft. Zugleich eine Erörterung der Begriffe „Konzernzugehörigkeit" und „Unternehmen an sich", Bankarchiv XXXI (1931/31), p. 467

Hirte, Heribert/Mülbert, Peter O./Roth, Markus, Aktiengesetz: Grosskommentar Bd. 4/1, 5th ed., Berlin 2014

Hölters, Wolfgang, Der Beirat der GmbH und GmbH & Co.KG, BB 1978, p. 640

Hübner, Leonhard/Habrich, Victor/Weller, Marc-Phillipe, Corporate Sustainability Due Diligence, NZG 2022, p. 644

Ireland, Paddy W., Company Law and the Myth of Shareholder Ownership, MLR 1999, S. 32

Jensen, Michael J./Meckling, William H., Theory of the Firm: Managerial Behavior, Agency Costs and Ownership Structure, JFE 1976, p. 305

Jürgenmeyer, Michael, Das Unternehmensinteresse, Frankfurt a. M. 1984

Keay, Andrew R., The Enlightened Shareholder Value Principle and Corporate Governance, London 2013, p. 42

Koch, Jens, Aktiengesetz, 19th ed., München 2025

Kraakman, Reinier/Armour, John/Davies Paul, The Anatomy of Corporate Law, 3rd ed., Oxford 2017

Kropff, Bruno, Aktiengesetz: Textausgabe des Aktiengesetzes und des Einführungstextes zum Aktiengesetz, Düsseldorf 1965, p. 97

Kuhner, Christoph, Unternehmensinteresse vs. Shareholder Value als Leitmaxime kapitalmarktorientierter Aktiengesellschaften, ZGR 2004, p. 244

Kunze, Otto, Bemerkungen zu Inhalt und Methode einer Unternehmensrechtsreform, in: Ballerstedt/Hefermehl (eds.), Festschrift für Ernst Geßler zum 65. Geburtstag, München 1970, p. 47

Kunze, Otto, Bemerkungen zum Verhältnis von Arbeits- und Unternehmensrecht, in: Fischer/Hefermehl (eds.), Gesellschaftsrecht und Unternehmensrecht: Festschrift für Wolfgang Schilling zum 65. Geburtstag, Berlin 1973, p. 333

Kunze, Otto, Zum Stand der Entwicklung des Unternehmensrechts, ZHR 1980, p. 100

Laux, Frank, Die Lehre vom Unternehmen an sich, Schriften zur Rechtsgeschichte, Berlin 1998

Leach, Melissa/Raworth, Kate/Rockström, Johan, Between social and planetary boundaries: navigating pathways in the safe and just space for humanity, in: UNESCO ISSC (ed.), World Social Science Report. Changing Global Environments, 2013, p. 84

Lehmann, Karl, Das Recht der Aktiengesellschaften I, Berlin 1898, p. 286

Lehmann, Karl, Die geschichtliche Entwicklung des Aktienrechts bis zum Code de Commerce 1895, 2nd ed., Köln 2018

Lieder, Jan, Die 1. Aktienrechtsnovelle vom 11. Juni 1870, in: Habersack/Bayer (eds.), Aktienrecht im Wandel I, Tübingen 2007, p. 318

Markowitz, Harry, The rand Corporation, JLFIAN 1952, p. 77

Martens, Klaus-Peter, Allgemeine Grundsätze zur Anwendbarkeit des Mitbestimmungsgesetzes, AG 1976, p. 113

Mertens, Hans-Joachim, Die inneren Organe des Aufsichtsrates Zuständigkeit des mitbestimmten Aufsichtsrats, ZGR 1977, p. 270

Millon, David, Corporate social responsibility and environmental sustainability, in: Sjåfjell/Richardson (eds.), Company Law and Sustainability: Legal Barriers and Opportunities, Cambridge 2015, p. 35

Mittwoch, Anne-Christin, Nachhaltigkeit und Unternehmensrecht, Tübingen 2022

Mittwoch, Anne-Christin, Nachhaltige Unternehmen durch Recht, Herausforderungen der Nachhaltigkeitstransformation für die Rechtswissenschaft aus Sicht des Wirtschaftsrechts, in: Bayer/Butz/Langlet/Poppe/Sommerer/Maltitz/Wöbbeking (eds.), Junges Nachhaltigkeitsrecht: Selbstverständnis, Status Quo und Perspektiven, München 2022, p. 57

Möslein, Florian/Mittwoch, Anne-Christin, Soziales Unternehmertum im US-amerikanischen Gesellschaftsrecht: "Benefit Corporations" und "Certified B Corporations", RabelsZ 2016, p. 399

Mülbert, Peter O., Shareholder Value aus rechtlicher Sicht, ZGR 1997, p. 129

Mülbert, Peter O., Marktwertmaximierung als Unternehmerziel der Aktiengesellschaft in: Crezelius/Hirte/Vieweg (eds.), Festschrift für Volker Röhricht: Zum 65. Geburtstag. Gesellschaftsrecht – Rechnungslegung – Sportrecht, Köln 2005

Mülbert, Peter O., Corporate Governance of Banks, EBOR 2009, p. 411

Mülbert, Peter O., Soziale Verantwortung von Unternehmen im Gesellschaftsrecht, AG 2009, p. 766

Paefgen, Walter, Struktur und Aufsichtsratsverfassung der mitbestimmten AG, Köln 1982

Raisch, Peter, Zum Begriff und zur Bedeutung des Unternehmensinteresses als Verhaltensmaxime von Vorstands- und Aufsichtsratsmitgliedern, in: Fischer/Gessler/Schilling/Serick/Ulmer (eds.), Strukturen und Entwicklungen im Handels-, Gesellschafts- und Wirtschaftsrecht: Festschrift für Wolfgang Hefermehl zum 70. Geburtstag am 18. September 1976, München 1976, p. 347

Raiser, Thomas, Das Unternehmerinteresse, in: Schmidt/Reichert-Facilides/Rittner/Sasse (eds.), Festschrift für Reimer Schmidt, 1976, p. 101

Rappaport, Alfred, Creating Shareholder Value: The New Standard for Business Performance New York, 12th ed., New York 1986

Rathenau, Walter, Vom Aktienwesen – Eine geschäftliche Betrachtung, Berlin 1917

Raworth, Kate, A Safe and Just Space for Humanity: Can We Live within the Doughnut?, Oxfam Discussion Papers 2012

Reuter, Dieter, Die Bestandssicherung von Unternehmen – ein Schlüssel zur Zukunft des Handelsgesellschaftsrechts, AcP 1979, p. 509

Rittner, Fritz, Zur Verantwortung der Unternehmensleitung, JZ 1980, p. 113

Rockström, Johan/Steffen, Will/Noone, Kevin/Persson, Asa/Chapin, Staurt F./Lambin, Eric F./Lenton, Timothy M./Scheffer, Marten/Folke, Carl/Schellnhuber, Hans Joachim/Nykvist, Björn/de Wit, Cythia/Hughes, Terry/van der Leeuw, Sander/Rodhe, Henning/Sörlin, Sverker/Snyder, Peter K./Costanza, Robert/Svedin, Uno/Falkenmark, Malin/Karlberg, Louise/Corell, Robert W., A safe operating space for humanity, Nature 2009, p. 472

Rockström, Johan/Steffen, Will/Nonne, Kevin/Persson, Asa/Chapin, Stuart F./ Lambin, Eric F./Lenton, Timothy M./Scheffer, Marten/Folke, Carl/Schellnhuber, Hans Joachim/ Nykvist, Björn/de Wit, Cythia/Hughes, Terry/van der Leeuw, Sander/Rodhe, Henning/Sörlin, Sverker/Snyder, Peter K./Costanza, Robert/Svedin, Uno/Falkenmark, Malin/Karlberg, Louise/Corell, Robert W Planetary Boundaries: Exploring the Safe Operating Space for humanity, Ecology and Society (2009), p. 474

Rühmkorf, Andreas, Stakeholder Value versus Corporate Sustainability, in: Sjåfjell/ Bruner(eds.), The Cambridge Handbook of Corporate Law, Corporate Governance and Sustainability, Cambridge 2019, p. 232

Salacuse, Jeswald W, Corporate Governance, Culture and Convergence: Corporations American Style or with a European Touch, LBRA 2003, p. 33

Schilling, Wolfgang, Macht und Verantwortung in der Aktiengesellschaft (oder das Prinzip der Interesseneinheit), in: Ballerstedt/Hefermehl (eds.), Festschrift für Ernst Geßler zum 65. Geburtstag, München 1971, p. 159

Schilling, Wolfgang, Das Aktienunternehmen, ZHR 1980, p. 136

Schlegelberger, Franz/Quassowski, Leo, Aktiengesetz, Gesetz über Aktiengesellschaften und Kommanditgesellschaften auf Aktien, 3rd ed., Berlin 1939

Schmidt, Reinhard H./Weiß, Marco, Shareholder vs. Stakeholder: Ökonomische Fragen, in: Hommelhoff/Hopt/v. Werder (eds.), Handbuch Corporate Governance, 2nd ed., Frankfurt a. M. 2009, p. 161

Schoppe, Bastian, Aktieneigentum, Nürnberg 2011, p. 88

Schubert, Claudia, Das Unternehmensinteresse – Maßstab für die Organwalter der Aktiengesellschaft, Baden-Baden 2020

Schubert, Werner/Hommelhoff, Peter, Hundert Jahre modernes Aktienrecht, ZGR, Sonderheft 1985, p. 115

Semler, Johannes, Leitung und Überwachung der Aktiengesellschaft: Die Leitungsaufgaben des Vorstands und die Überwachungsaufgaben des Aufsichtsrates, 2nd ed., Köln 1996

Sjåfjell Beate/Mähönen, Jukka, Upgrading the Nordic Corporate Governance Model for Sustainable Companies, ECL 2014, p. 58

Sjåfjell Beate/Mähönen, Jukka, Corporate Purpose and the Misleading Shareholder vs Stakeholder Dichotomy, 2022, University of Oslo Faculty of Law Research Paper No. 2022–43, http://dx.doi.org/10.2139/ssrn.4039565 (last accessed: 4 April 2025)

Sjåfjell Beate/Tsagas Georgina/Villiers Charlotta, Sustainable Value Creation in the European Union: Towards Pathways to a Sustainable Future through Crises. Cambridge University Press, Cambridge 2022

Spindler, Gerald, Gemeinwohlorientierte Unternehmensinteressen und Kapitalgesellschaften, in: Jahn/Kempf/Prittwitz/Schmitt-Leonardy (eds.), Wirtschaft – Moral-Strafrecht, Gedächtnisschrift Lüderssen, Berlin 2023, p. 249

Spindler, Gerald, Leitung der Aktiengesellschaft, in: Goette/Habersack/Kalss (eds.), Münchner Kommentar zum Aktiengesetz, 6th ed., München 2023

Ständige Deputation des Deutschen Juristentages, Verhandlungen des 74. Deutschen Juristentages Stuttgart 2024, Band 1: Gutachten / Teile A – G: Gesamtband, München, 2024

Steffen, Will/Rockström, Johan et. al., Planetary boundaries: Guiding human development on a changing planet, Science (2015), p. 347

Stout, Lynn A., Corporate Control Transactions, UPaLRev 2003, p. 667

Ulmer, Peter, Aktienrecht im Wandel – Entwicklungslinien und Diskussionsschwerpunkte, AcP 2002, p. 143

V. Werder, Axel, Soziales Unternehmertum im US-amerikanischen Gesellschaftsrecht: "Benefit Corporations" und "Certified B Corporations, ZGR 1997, p. 69

V. Werder, Axel, Zur Stakeholderbalance des Rechts der Corporate Governance, in: Grundmann/Kirchner/Raiser/Schwintowski/Weber/Windblicher (eds.), Festschrift Schwark zum 70. Geburtstag, Heidelberg 2009, p. 285

Watson, Susan M., The Corporate Legal Person, JCL Studies 2019, p. 137

Weber, Anne-Marie/Mittwoch, Anne-Christin, Harmonizing Duties of Board Members in the Anthropocene: When Expectations Meet Reality, Review of European and Comparative Law, 2023, 52 (1), p. 143

Weber, Iris J., Die gemeinnützige Aktiengesellschaft, Nürnberg 2014

Webering, Anabel, Der verfassungsrechtliche Schutz der aktienrechtlichen Mitgliedschaft: unter besonderer Berücksichtigung der Vorgaben an den Gesetzgeber, Frankfurt a. M. 2002,

Weller, Marc-Phillipe, Empfehlen sich im Kampf gegen den Klimawandel gesetzgeberische Maßnahmen auf dem Gebiet des Gesellschaftsrechts?, in: Ständige Deputation des Deutschen Juristentages (ed.), Verhandlungen des 74. Deutschen Juristentages Stuttgart 2024, Band 1, München 2024, p. F.1

Weller, Marc-Phillipe, Klimatransformation des Gesellschaftsrechts, NJW-Beilage (2/2024), p. 58

Weller, Marc-Phillipe/Hößl, Theresa/Seemann, Camilla, Greening Corporate Law, ZGR 2024, p. 180

Wen, Shuangge, The magnitude of shareholder value as the overriding objective in the UK: the post-crisis perspective, JIBLR 2011, p. 325

Werner, Frank M./Stoner, James A. F, Sustainability and the evolution of the shareholder wealth maximization paradigm, in: Boubaker/Cumming/Nguyen (eds.), Research Handbook of Finance and Sustainability, Cheltenham 2018, p. 179

Westermann, Harm P., Rechte und Pflichten des mitbestimmten Aufsichtsrates und seiner Mitglieder, ZGR 1977, p. 219

4. Embedding Sustainability in the Interest of the Company: Unpacking the EU Sustainable Corporate Governance Initiative

Anne-Christin Mittwoch and Anne-Marie Weber

A. A European Initiative for a Sustainable Corporate Governance

In 2020, the European Commission launched the Sustainable Corporate Governance Initiative. Its aim was to improve the European regulatory framework, using company law and corporate governance as a vehicle to foster sustainable behaviour in business and finance.[1] The Commission explicitly stated that the initiative was intended to enable companies to focus on long-term sustainable value creation rather than short-term benefits and to better align the interests of companies, their shareholders, managers, stakeholders, and society.[2] In this vein, the initiative's purpose is to help companies better manage sustainability-related matters in terms of social and human rights, climate change, and the environment. The Commission launched an open public consultation which ran from 26 October 2020 until 8 February 2021 and intended to publish a proposal for a directive in the summer of 2021. However, it was not until 23 February 2022 that the proposal for a directive on Corporate Sustainability Due Diligence (CSDDD) was finally published, marking a turning point in the debate on sustainability and company law.[3] The final version of the directive was adopted in June 2024.[4]

This chapter explores the ideas and regulatory developments of sustainable corporate governance at the EU level. It sketches out the Commission's

1 Https://ec.europa.eu/info/law/better-regulation/have-your-say/initiatives/12548-Sustainable-corporate-governance_en.

2 See "About this initiative. Summary," European Commission, Https://ec.europa.eu/info/law/better-regulation/have-your-say/initiatives/12548-Sustainable-corporate-governance_en.

3 European Commission, Proposal for a Directive of the European Parliament and of the Council on Corporate Sustainability Due Diligence and amending Directive (EU) 2019/1937, COM(2022) 71 final, 2022/0051(COD) of 23.2.2022.

4 Directive (EU) 2024/1760 of the European Parliament and of the Council of 13 June 2024 on corporate sustainability due diligence and amending Directive (EU) 2019/1937 and Regulation (EU) 2023/2859, OJ L of 5.7.2024.

Sustainable Corporate Governance Initiative of 2020 and the proposal and fate of the subsequent CSDDD – particularly regarding the concept of the company's interest. The future development of sustainable corporate governance in the EU will be significantly influenced by the implementation of the European legislation by the Member States. This national implementation will in turn influence further European developments. The status quo of national implementation and sustainable corporate governance in general will be examined in detail for numerous Member States in the following chapters. However, the European perspective provides the foundation and framework for this process. The EU legislature has recently – without success – attempted to explicitly integrate sustainability into the concept of the interest of the company and is now in the process of implicitly developing this core concept of company law further towards sustainable corporate governance.

B. Contextualization: The Commission's long way to sustainability in company law

It is important to emphasize that the European debate on corporate sustainability has only been conducted within the framework of company law relatively recently. This focus is welcomed, as the transformation to a sustainable economy and thus to sustainable business law is inherently also a company law matter and should have been treated as such much earlier. In earlier years, however, the Commission strongly focused on Corporate Social Responsibility (CSR), a movement that was closely linked to information duties. For many years, CSR was also closely linked to the "business case" for corporate sustainability – it was perceived as a mere voluntary instrument by the Commission and officially defined as such in 2001.[5] Only after that was CSR gradually changed into a binding legal concept, defined as "the responsibility of enterprises for their impacts on society" in 2011.[6]

5 European Commission, Greenpaper Promoting a European Framework for Corporate Social Responsibility, COM(2001) 2001, 366 final of 18.7.2001, p. 6; on the concept of the business case for CSR S. MacLeod, European Public Law 2007, 671 (680 et seq.); Rühmkorf, p. 20.

6 Communication from the Commission, A renewed EU strategy 2011–14 for Corporate Social Responsibility, COM(2011) 681 final of 25.10.2011, p. 6.

This shift in meaning, and the fact that the Commission explicitly abandoned voluntariness as the defining characteristic of CSR, paved the way for the adoption of the Non-Financial Reporting Directive (NFRD),[7] which amended the Accounting Directive[8] in 2014. The NFRD expressly justified the obligation to provide non-financial reporting with the socio-political goal of enabling the transition to a sustainable global economy that combines the long-term profitability of companies with social justice and environmental protection.[9] Its core is the obligation for large public-interest companies with an average of more than 500 employees to issue a non-financial statement in their management report or in a separate non-financial report. The statement should contain the information necessary for understanding the course of business and should at least refer to social and environmental issues, employee issues, and human rights, as well as the fight against corruption. The NFRD is already in its second generation: the Corporate Sustainability Reporting Directive (CSRD) was adopted in 2022 and significantly expands and tightens the reporting requirements of the NFRD.[10] The CSRD develops non-financial reporting into sustainability reporting and expands its scope to include even small and medium-sized enterprises. Nevertheless, the underlying regulatory approach remains unchanged: just like the NFRD, the CSRD uses the instrument of information duties. Neither directive contains any obligations for managers to actively integrate sustainability aspects into corporate strategy.

Nevertheless, a transformative effect is achieved: through the use of transparency obligations, the European legislature activates market forces

7 Directive 2014/95/EU of the European Parliament and of the Council of 22 October 2014 amending Directive 2013/34/EU as regards disclosure of non-financial and diversity information by certain large undertakings and groups, OJ L 330/1 of 15.11.2014.

8 Directive 2013/34/EU of the European Parliament and of the Council of 26 June 2013 on the annual financial statements, consolidated financial statements and related reports of certain types of undertakings, amending Directive 2006/43/EC of the European Parliament and of the Council and repealing Council Directives 78/660/EEC and 83/349/EEC, OJ L 182/19 of 29.6.2013.

9 Directive 2014/95/EU of the European Parliament and of the Council of 22 October 2014 amending Directive 2013/34/EU as regards disclosure of non-financial and diversity information by certain large undertakings and groups, OJ L 330/1 of 15.11.2014, recital 3.

10 Directive (EU) 2022/2464 of the European Parliament and of the Council of 14 December 2022 amending Regulation (EU) No 537/2014, Directive 2004/109/EC, Directive 2006/43/EC and Directive 2013/34/EU, as regards corporate sustainability reporting, OJ L 322/15 of 16.12.2022.

and nudges companies to more sustainable behaviour, aligning the goals of profit maximisation and the protection of social and environmental interests.[11] Considering this purpose of the NFRD and CSRD, the European legislature could have used the instruments of company law to achieve their regulatory goal by addressing, for example, the duties of the board. As this was not done, the NFRD was referred to as a revolution of company law through the back door[12]: in order to report on compliance with human rights and environmental standards, boards had to make sure that the company engaged in these issues and complied. Thus, the reporting duties exerted – at least to some extent – a leverage effect on corporate behaviour.

The technique of regulating company law indirectly by creating information duties for market actors continued when sustainable finance entered the debate of corporate sustainability. In 2018, one year before the European Green Deal launched and put sustainability at the top of the agenda of the EU legislature,[13] the Commission published its ambitious Action Plan of Financing Sustainable Growth.[14] Shortly after that, the Taxonomy Regulation,[15] the Sustainable Finance Disclosure Regulation (SFDR),[16] and the new Benchmark Regulation[17] were adopted, forming the framework for the dynamic development of sustainable finance. Since August 2022, the delegated acts to MiFID II[18] and IDD[19] have required sustainability preferences to be included in investment and insurance advice. While the

11 Groundbreaking on the concept of nudging Thaler/Sunstein, 2009.

12 Bork/Kayser/Kebekus/Hommelhoff, p. 291.

13 European Commission, The European Green Deal, COM(2019) 640 final, December 11, 2019.

14 Communication from the Commission, Action Plan: Financing Sustainable Growth, COM(2018) 97 final of 8 March 2018.

15 Regulation (EU) 2020/852 of the European Parliament and of the Council of 18 June 2020 on the establishment of a framework to facilitate sustainable investment, and amending Regulation (EU) 2019/2088, OJ L 198/13 of 22.6.2020.

16 Regulation (EU) 2019/2088 of the European Parliament and of the Council of 27 November 2019 on sustainability-related disclosures in the financial services sector, OLJ L 317/1 of 9.12.2019.

17 Regulation (EU) 2019/2089 of the European Parliament and of the Council of 27 November 2019 amending Regulation (EU) 2016/1011 as regards EU Climate Transition Benchmarks, EU Paris-aligned Benchmarks and sustainability-related disclosures for benchmarks, OJ L 317/17 of 9.12.2019.

18 Directive 2014/65/EU of the European Parliament and of the Council of 15 May 2014 on markets in financial instruments and amending Directive 2002/92/EC and Directive 2011/61/EU, OJ L 173/349 of 12.6.2014.

19 Directive (EU) 2016/97 of the European Parliament and of the Council of 20 January 2016 on insurance distribution, OJ L 26/19 of 2.2.2016.

Taxonomy Regulation provides a framework for a definition of the concept of (ecological) sustainability, the SFDR again focuses on the instrument of information duties in order to reach the central goal of the Sustainable Finance Action Plan – to reorient capital flows towards sustainable investment to achieve sustainable and inclusive growth.[20] However, with the 2018 Action Plan, the Commission went one step further: Action 10 of the plan considers the possible need to require corporate boards to develop and disclose a sustainability strategy, including appropriate due diligence throughout the supply chain. It also considers a possible need to clarify the rules according to which directors are expected to act in the company's long-term interest.[21] This was not just about information duties; Action 10 of the 2018 Action Plan envisioned a direct obligation for boards to act. Crucially, this obligation extended beyond the financial sector and applied to companies in the real economy as well. In doing so, it created a conceptual and regulatory opening for a future European directive on sustainable company law.

C. The approach of the Sustainable Corporate Governance Initiative

The Commission's Sustainable Corporate Governance Initiative builds on Action 10 of the Sustainable Finance Action Plan and, for the first time, addresses company law directly. The Commission approached the issue in four steps, which it outlined in detail in a public consultation and put up for discussion of a company law directive. The consultation was divided into four sections accordingly:

Section 1: Need and objectives for EU intervention on sustainable corporate governance

Section 2: Directors' duty of care – considering stakeholder interests

Section 3: Due diligence duty; and

Section 4: Other elements of sustainable corporate governance, like better stakeholder engagement, remuneration of directors and enhancing sustainability expertise in the boards.

While the Commission did not question the need for action (section 1), it gradually abandoned the regulatory aspects outlined in Section 4 as the

20 Communication from the Commission, Action Plan: Financing Sustainable Growth, COM(2018) 97 final of 8 March 2018, p. 2.

21 Communication from the Commission, Action Plan: Financing Sustainable Growth, COM(2018) 97 final of 8 March 2018, p. 11.

initiative progressed. Sections 2 and 3 of the initiative thus remained highly relevant and formed the core of the initiative. In this vein, it is important to recognize that the CSDDD was never planned as a pure supply chain act. Instead, core company law – particularly in the form of a directors' duty of care embedded in the concept of the company's interest – was to be just as much a topic as the regulation of a corporate supply chain due diligence. From the outset, the Commission had the intention to link these two central approaches in a single piece of legislation. This twofold approach proved particularly challenging. During the legislative process, the CSDDD was ultimately reduced to a supply chain-focused instrument. The proposed duty of care for directors with regard to the considerations of sustainability aspects did not survive in the final version of the directive.

I. Directors' duty of care – Considering sustainability interests

In a first step, the Commission planned to harmonise the directors' duty of care. It emphasized the fact that the company law of all Member States required company directors to act in the interest of the company – this is the concept of the duty of care.[22] However, none of the national company laws clearly define what the interest of the company means. This lack of legal certainty, according to the Commission, contributes to short-termism and to a narrow interpretation of the duty of care that requires a focus predominantly on shareholders' financial interests. Conversely, the absence of such clarification may lead to a disregard of stakeholders' interests, which is not helpful in terms of sustainability, as these stakeholders may contribute to the long-term interest and the resilience of the company. To address this, the Commission initially intended to propose harmonising legislation concerning the company interest and, by extension, the directors' duty of care. The goal was to clarify that corporate directors should balance the interests of all stakeholders, rather than focusing solely on the short-term interests of the shareholders.

The Commission put this plan into action in the CSDDD proposal of February 2022: Art. 25 of the proposal stated in para. 1 that in fulfilling their duty to act in the best interest of the company, directors consider

22 It should be noted that the Commission's terminology "directors" is strongly influenced by the Anglo-American corporate governance discussion: the concept of directors does not have the same meaning in the legal tradition of continental Europe, where boards are the organs of a company.

the consequences of their decisions for sustainability matters. While in the beginning of the initiative the Commission had used the term "stakeholder interests", the draft CSDDD used the term "sustainability matters" and specified these as "including, where applicable, human rights, climate change and environmental consequences, including in the short, medium and long term". According to Art. 25(2) CSDDD proposal, Member States had to ensure that their rules on breaches of the duties of directors also applied to the determination of Art. 25(1) CSDDD and had to extend their sanction regimes to the duty to consider sustainability concerns.

In this respect, the proposal engaged with nothing less than the long-standing and well-known corporate governance debate concerning shareholder versus stakeholder interests as a guideline for the actions of a company's bodies and sought to resolve it in favour of the latter. The foundation of this discussion is found in economics.[23] Economic theories have, for decades, informed the legal debate on whose interests' corporate directors should prioritize when making decisions in the best interest of the company. The central underlying microeconomic theories play an essential role in the Anglo-American corporate governance discussion and lead to the paradigm that shareholders' interests should generally be prioritised in relation to the interests of other stakeholders (shareholder primacy). The diametrically opposed view prefers an interest-pluralistic stakeholder model that is based on the fundamental assumption that a company is generally managed in the interests of all stakeholders equally, without any abstract prioritisation of the shareholders or any other stakeholder group.[24] The dichotomy of the shareholder and stakeholder model has dominated corporate governance for many years not just in the US, but has been picked up in numerous other jurisdictions, including continental Europe, which has historically not focused on this dichotomy.[25] In the light of the

23 Fundamental from an economic perspective in particular Markowitz J. Finance 1952, 77; Fama J. Finance 1970, 383; Jensen/Meckling J. Financ. Econ. 1976, 305.

24 Freeman/Reed Cal. Mgmt. Rev. 1983, 88; Freeman Bus. Ethics Q. 1994, 409; Blair; Blair/Stout Va. L. Rev. 1999, 247; with fundamental considerations Alchian/Demsetz Am. Econ. Rev. 1972, 777, 779 et seqq., who also already use the term team production; in addition Dean Co. Law. 2001, 66, 69; Preston/Sapienza J. Behavioral Economics 1990, 361.

25 Hansmann/Kraakman Georgetown Law Journal 2001, 439, 441: "as a consequence of both logic and experience, there is convergence on a consensus that the best means to (...) the pursuit of aggregate social welfare is to make corporate managers strongly accountable to shareholders interests and, at least in direct terms, only to those inter-

growing demand for a more sustainable economy, the discussion has gained new momentum.

However, the Commission failed to capitalise on this momentum with Art. 25 of the draft CSDDD. Instead, Art. 25 and the harmonisation of the duty to act in the best interests of the company did not find political majority support. They were finally removed from the CSDDD final version. This was for several reasons.[26] First, the material scope and content of the sustainability-related topics that should be addressed by the board members had only been vaguely indicated. The expression "sustainability matters" was circumscribed by a narrow catalogue of examples, i.e., human rights, climate change, and environmental consequences. There was no direct definition or referral to a definition of these "matters" to be found in the CSDDD Proposal. Second, the CSDDD Proposal indistinctly stated that the board members' duty of care involved "taking into account" sustainability matters. Neither the CSDDD Proposal nor the Explanatory Memorandum provided guidance on how "taking into account" should be interpreted. It remained entirely unclear at what level of priority sustainability matters should be considered by the board members. And third, in light of this uncertainty, the liability risk was considered too high under Art. 25(2) of the draft CSDDD.

Ultimately, the idea of introducing a duty of care for company management to consider sustainability aspects through the CSDDD was not pursued further.

II. Due Diligence Duty

In a second step – the only one that made it from the early initiative into the final text of the CSDDD – the Commission planned to introduce a due diligence duty for companies of a certain size. This due diligence duty requires companies to establish and implement adequate processes to prevent, mitigate and account for human rights and environmental impacts, both in the company's own operation and in its supply chain. The idea of a due diligence duty originates from international standards like the UN Guiding Principles on Business and Human Rights (UNGPs) and the

---

ests"; for criticism see Sjåfjell/Richardson/Sjåfjell/Johnston/Anker-Sørensen/Millon, p. 79.

26 See in more detail Weber/Mittwoch RECol 2023, 143 (151).

OECD Guidelines for Multinational Enterprises. The due diligence aspect became the main component of the CSDDD, and the CSDDD officially entered into force in June 2024. In the beginning of the Sustainable Corporate Governance Initiative and in the draft CSDDD, the Commission used a broad concept of the term supply chain and included subsidiaries as well as suppliers and subcontractors. This went well beyond the understanding of national supply chain acts like the German LkSG[27] and recent actions under the current Omnibus Initiative,[28] which stipulate a due diligence duty only with regard to the company's direct contacts within the supply chain (the "Tier 1" approach).

In terms of the due diligence duty itself, the CSDDD today lays down compliance obligations for companies regarding actual and potential human rights adverse impacts and environmental adverse impacts, with respect to their own operations, the operations of their subsidiaries, and the operations carried out by their business partners in the chains of activities of those companies. According to Art. 7(1) CSDDD, Member States shall ensure that companies integrate due diligence into all their relevant policies and risk management systems and have a due diligence policy in place that ensures risk-based due diligence. Potential adverse impacts for human rights and the environment must be identified, prevented, and put to an end; where the latter is not possible, they must at least be adequately mitigated (Art. 8 CSDDD et seq.).

However, these obligations are not absolute. First, they are not spelled out as a duty to succeed or even a strict liability in such a way that every violation of human rights or environmental concerns in supply chains is stopped and compensated for but rather are designed as 'duties of effort'. The CSDDD refers to various international human rights and environmental agreements. Only with these in mind must companies conduct risk-based human rights and environmental due diligence as laid down in Articles 7 to 16 CSDDD. When fulfilling the due diligence duty, stakeholders must be involved in a meaningful way (Art. 13 CSDDD). Regular reports must be made on compliance with the due diligence duty (Art. 16 CSDDD). Enforcement is a melange of public and private enforcement, with national supervisory authorities that monitor compliance with due diligence obligations on the one hand (Art. 24 CSDDD) and a civil liability

27 Act on Corporate Due Diligence in Supply Chains (short LkSG) from 16. July 2021, BGBl. I 2021, p. 2959.

28 See the next paragraph (D).

in favour of victims of breaches of these duties on the other (Art. 29 CSDDD).

The due diligence duty laid down in the CSDDD thus follows a principle-based, not a sector-specific approach. The European legislator today combines this with additional sector-specific acts, namely the Conflict Minerals Regulation[29] and the Deforestation Regulation of 2023.[30]

Looking back to the origins of the Sustainable Corporate Governance Initiative, the idea of the due diligence duty is the only one that has prevailed, and it now forms the heart of the CSDDD. But even if the CSDDD does not develop the concept of the company's interest in the light of sustainability, this core company law concept is touched upon indirectly by the various elements of the CSDDD's due diligence duty. The many compliance obligations in the CSDDD's due diligence duty – i.e. integrating due diligence into the company's policies and risk management system, preventing and mitigating potential adverse impacts, carrying out meaningful engagement with stakeholders, and establishing and maintaining a notification mechanism and a complaints procedure – substantially change the tasks and behaviour of management. The resulting transformation effects have the potential to change our fundamental understanding of the company's interests in the future. For this reason, it is particularly important not to stop at an analysis of the specific compliance obligations of supply chain due diligence, but to observe and examine their effects on the fundamentals of company law – like the concept of the interest of the company.

D. The status quo: A challenged CSDDD in a jigsaw puzzle of sustainability

Even after more than five years of dynamic development, the saga surrounding the Commission's Sustainable Corporate Governance Initiative, and the CSDDD's principal outcome, is not yet concluded. The adoption

29 Regulation (EU) 2017/821 of the European Parliament and of the Council of 17 May 2017 laying down supply chain due diligence obligations for Union importers of tin, tantalum and tungsten, their ores, and gold originating from conflict-affected and high-risk areas, OJ L 130/1 of 19.5.2017.

30 Regulation (EU) 2023/1115 of the European Parliament and of the Council of 31 May 2023 on the making available on the Union market and the export from the Union of certain commodities and products associated with deforestation and forest degradation and repealing Regulation (EU) No 995/2010, OJ L150/206 of 9.6.2023.

of the CSDDD was a challenging process overall. The publication of the Commission's draft was already more complicated than usual, having previously been blocked twice by the Commission's Regulatory Scrutiny Board[31]. This weakened the CSDDD's provisions even before the first proposal was published in 2022, and the provisions were subsequently watered down further during the trilogue. Ultimately, the directive's adoption was almost prevented by the 'German vote': although the German federal government had supported the directive in the trilogue, it abstained in the final vote in the formal legislative procedure.

Even following its adoption in June 2024, discussion of the CSDDD remains on the political agenda. On 26 February 2025, the Commission made a U-turn and published the first proposal of its Omnibus Package for the revision and simplification of various sustainability-promoting legal acts.[32] Besides the CSRD and the Taxonomy Regulation, the CSDDD is centrally affected by this proposal. The Omnibus Package aims to reduce the bureaucratic burden on companies and to make the obligations to promote sustainability simpler and more coherent, in particular by reducing the burden on small and medium-sized enterprises. This development was announced in the Draghi report of September 2024[33] and a following Communication from the Commission of January 2025.[34] With regard to the CSDDD, the proposed amendments concern the scope of application and key regulatory concepts, specifically the scope of the activity chain, stakeholder participation, the climate protection plan, and civil liability of companies. In addition, the obligation to terminate business relationships under Art. 10(6) and Art. 11(7) CSDDD is to be abolished. Even if the basic concept of corporate due diligence for the protection of human rights and environmental concerns remains unchanged, the provisions of the CSDDD are thus being further watered down, even before companies have a chance to apply them in their daily practice. The future of sustainable corporate governance in the EU thus remains uncertain, but undoubtedly dynamic.

---

31 European Commission, Regulatory Scrutiny Board Opinion, 26.11.2021, SEC(2022) 95; in more detail Weber/Mittwoch RECol 2023, 143 (148 et seq.).

32 Proposal for a Directive of the European Parliament and of the Council amending Directives 2006/43/EC, 2013/34/EU, (EU) 2022/2464 and (EU) 2024/1760 as regards certain corporate sustainability reporting and due diligence requirements, COM(2025) 81 final, 2025/0045 (COD) of 26.2.2025.

33 The future of European competitiveness, 2024, Part A, A competitiveness strategy for Europe, p. 67–69; Part B. In-depth-analysis and recommendations, p. 161, 169.

34 Communication from the Commission, A Competitiveness Compass for the EU, COM(2025) 30 final of 29.1.2025.

E. The future of the company's interest as a vehicle for corporate sustainability

Although it seems unlikely given the current "ESG backlash", the shortcomings of Art. 25 draft CSDDD could certainly be remedied in the future. The adoption of a similar provision would represent a paradigm shift in company law and a milestone in the development of sustainable corporate governance. However, the most critical question in this respect remains unanswered. The Commission had explained that a board member's general duty of care for the company is present in the company law of all Member States and was only "being clarified" by the proposed Art. 25 draft CSDDD.[35] However, as far as can be determined, there is no comparative legal evidence for this assumption. On the contrary, the concept of the company's interest and its normative significance for corporate sustainability are evolving along divergent paths across the Member States.[36]

These developments are particularly relevant in light of the ongoing debate surrounding the concept of the company interest and its future evolution, as well as for the broader trajectory of corporate sustainability. The European legislature would be well advised to acquire a nuanced understanding of the realities of the economic sustainability transformation within the Member States. Only on this basis can a coherent legal framework for a sustainable European economy be established and practical acceptance by market actors be ensured. The second part of this book aims to help fill this gap. It analyses key developments across selected Member States, drawing conclusions as to how corporate sustainability can be further reinforced within European law.

References

Alchian, Armen/Demsetz, Harold, Production, Information Costs and Economic Organization, AER 1972, p. 777

Blair, Margaret M./Stout, Lynn A., A Team Production Theory of Corporate Law, VLR 1999, p. 247

Hommelhoff, Peter, Nichtfinanzielle Ziele in Unternehmen von öffentlichem Interesse – Die Revolution übers Bilanzrecht, in: Bork/Kayser/Kebekus (eds.), Festschrift für Bruno M. Kübler zum 70. Geburtstag, Berlin 2015, p. 291

35 Explanatory Memorandum 22 of the draft CSDDD.

36 For Germany and Poland see Weber/Mittwoch RECol 2023, 143.

Dean, Janice, Directing public companies: Company Law and the Stakeholder society, London 2001

Fama, Eugene F., Efficient Capital Markets. A Review of Theory and Empirical Work, The Journal of Finance 1970, p. 383

Freeman, Edward/Reed, David L., Stockholders and Shareholders: A New Perspective on Corporate Governance, CMR 1983, p. 88

Freeman, Edward, The Politics of Stakeholder Theory: Some Future Directions, BEQ 1994, p. 409

Hansmann, Henry/Kraakman, Reinier, The End of History for Corporate Law, GLJ 2001, p. 439

Jensen, Michael J./Meckling, William H., Theory of the Firm: Managerial Behavior, Agency Costs and Ownership Structure, JFE 1976, p. 305

Markowitz, Harry, The rand Corporation, The Journal of Finance 1952, p. 77

Preston, Lee E./Sapienza, Harry J., Stakeholder management and corporate performance, Jornal of Behavioral Economics 1990, 361

Sjåfjell, Beate/Johnston, Andrew/Anker-Sørensen, Linn/Millon, David, Shareholder Primacy: The Main Barrier to Sustainable Companies, in: Sjåfjell/Richardson (eds.), Cambridge 2015, p. 79

Thaler, Richard/Sunstein, Cass, Nudge: Improving Decisions About Health, Wealth and Happyness, New Haven, 2009

Weber, Anne-Marie/Mittwoch, Anne-Christin, Harmonizing duties of board members in the Anthropocene: When expectations meet reality, RECoL 2023, 143

5. A French Approach to the Company's Interest in the Context of Sustainability

Géraldine Goffaux Callebaut

The aim of this contribution is to assess company interest in relation to sustainability in French law, a concept that has long been a source of interest for French jurists. Changes in society and the economy make this a constantly-evolving concept, which is exciting for company law specialists. The proposed approach is also marked by reflections focused on ethics and norms that are central to the École d'Orléans.[1]

In France, company interest has been a fundamental issue of company law since the Cour de cassation recognized the legal personality of companies in an 1891 decision,[2] which distinguished the company as a legal entity distinct from its the shareholders. This distinguishment was made in various European countries around the same time, perhaps most notably is the UK's 1897 Salomon's Case.[3] What is interesting to note regarding the French case that distinguished the company as distinct from its shareholders is that it goes beyond the legal texts. Indeed, the Civil Code of the time did not contain any provision on legal personality. This can be explained by the Revolutionaries' distrust of intermediary bodies (such as corporations, for example) that formed a barrier between the State and citizens. In the 1891 decision, the judges considered that "it is of the essence of civil companies, as well as commercial companies, to create, for the benefit of the collective individuality, interests and rights that are specific and distinct from the interests and rights of each of its members". This solution is therefore a creation of judges who base the solution on what

---

1 The École d'Orléans is known in the French-speaking academic world for its work on norms and their evolution. Among the emblematic books, we can mention the *trilogy* led by Professor Catherine Thibierge: *La force normative – Naissance d'un concept*, LGDJ/Bruylant, 2009; *La densification normative – Découverte d'un processus*, mare & martin, 2014; La garantie normative – Exploration d'une notion-fonction, mare & martin, 2021.

2 Req. 23 février 1891, *DP* 1891. 1. 337, *S.* 1892. 1. 73, note E. Meynial.

3 Salomon v. A Salomon & Co Ltd [1897], AC 22. The development of a company's interest in the United Kingdom is analysed in detail by Andreas Rühmkorf in this volume.

they consider to be the reality of the situation and who extend a solution that existed for commercial companies. As we can see, this extension is based on the idea that a company has an interest distinct from that of its shareholders.

Legal personality of the company distinct from its shareholders has been further provided for in more modern law. In 1966, Section 1832 was added to the Civil Code, which, in its latest adopted version from 1978, specifies that the company is both a contract and an institution. A company's legal personality beings when it registers in the Trade and Companies Register, but the company's interest is still not defined by law. The PACTE Law of 2019 simply specified, in a new paragraph 2 of Section 1833 of the Civil Code, that "[t]he company is managed in its company's interest, taking into consideration the social and environmental issues of its activity." Thus, the law states how the directors and the judge must assess a company's interest, but it does not say what the company's interest *is*. This is what French law calls a "concept with variable content"; in other words, it is deliberately vague, leaving it up to the actors of company law (or the judge) to specify the interest on a case-by-case basis.

Determining the company's interest is important because reference to the company's interest is found in many provisions in French law: for example, abuse of voting rights (the abuse of majority, minority, or equality), where the shareholder uses their voting rights to vote in a way that is contrary to the company's interest and with the aim of harming the other partners, or in the civil charge for mismanagement (when the director takes a decision contrary to the company's interest), regardless of whether the company is *in bonis* or under insolvency law. Beyond that, reference to the company's interest is also found in criminal law, specifically in the offence of misuse of company assets, which consists, for a director of a commercial company, in knowingly using the company's assets, credit, or powers for personal purposes.

The dichotomy between the lack of a precise definition provided in law and the importance of defining company interest in many laws has been mobilizing French doctrine for more than a century. The development of the sustainability context[4] has reshuffled the cards and brought about other discussions. Some date the appearance of corporate social responsibility (CSR) in corporate law to the 2002 Earth Summit in Johannesburg. However, going back further, it must be noted that, in international law, the

4 See the contribution of Beate Sjafjell in this book.

Global Compact was mentioned as early as 1999 by the Secretary-General of the United Nations, and was subsequently put into practice in 2000. The aim of the Global Compact was to promote the values of the United Nations by inviting companies to adopt, support, and apply those values in their sphere of influence.

CSR is one of the ways that sustainable development for companies is handled. It addresses the three pillars of sustainable development: the environment, the economy, and social issues. More specifically, in 2002, the European Commission[5] defined CSR as "a concept whereby companies integrate social and environmental concerns in their business operations and in their interaction with their stakeholders on a voluntary basis". Since 2011, it has been accepted that CSR is no longer necessarily a voluntary approach but rather can be seen as a mandatory standard.[6] To that extent, it can be noted that, beyond the question of the company's interest, French doctrine has shown that certain legal tools (in civil law[7], consumer law[8] or financial law[9]) make it possible to transform responsibility into liability. In case law, the key example is the Erika case, which held oil company Total liable for failing to comply with their voluntary commitment to CSR on the basis of non-compliance with a voluntary commitment.[10] This finding is strengthened by a since-adopted law that provides for the duty of vigilance. The adoption of a law on the duty of vigilance now strengthens the legal

5 EU Communication, *Corporate Social Responsibility: A Business Contribution to Sustainable Development*, COM (2002) 347 final, 2 July 2002, p. 5.

6 See EC Communication "A New EU Strategy for 2011–2014 for Corporate Social Responsibility", 25 October 2011, COM (2011) 681 final.

7 See M. Mekki, « Le contrat, vecteur du devoir de vigilance », Dossier spécial *RSE et devoir de vigilance, Revue Lamy Droit des affaires*, mai 2015.

8 See G. Goffaux Callebaut, « La consommation responsable », in *Les enjeux de la réforme du droit de la consommation*, Actes du colloque du 27 mars 2014, LPA 27 juin 2014, p. 15 et seqq.; N. Sauphanor-Brouillaud, « Le consommateur », in Le droit économique, levier de la transition écologique, in A.-S. Epstein et M. Nioche (dir.), Larcier / Strada Lex, 2022, p. 137 et seqq.; P. Lequet, « Droit de la consommation durable : entre éthique environnementale et éthique des affaires », *in* J. Sohnle et C. Bouriau (dir.), *Éthique environnementale pour juristes*, mare & martin, 2024.

9 G. Goffaux Callebaut, « Densification et "dédensification" normatives en droit des sociétés », in *La densification normative – Naissance d'un processus, op. cit*, p. 797 et seqq., et « Garantie normative et responsabilité sociale des entreprises », in *La garantie normative, op. cit.*, p. 369 et seqq.

10 In this case, the questions were raised in both civil and criminal matters. Crim. 25 septembre 2012, n° 10–82.938, Bull. crim. n° 198.

arsenal. French law thus contains enforcement for sustainability tools, excluding a company's interest.

The link between a company's interest and CSR is best presented in two parts. First, this chapter will explain how the notion of company interest has mobilized doctrine and case law following the major company law of 1966 (A). Second, it will address more recent developments in CSR and how those developments have made it possible to revisit the definition of company interest (B).

A. The Evolution of the Notion of Company Interest in the Twentieth Century

The evolution of the notion of the company interest in the twentieth century will be considered, focusing on the latter part of the twentieth century, beginning with the 1966 Law which set the framework for modern company law in France. First, the evolution of company interest in the context of this law will be examined (I), and then the more specific context of the 1990s, which saw a significant liberal turn, will be looked at (II).

I. Company Interest in the Context of the 1966 Law

To better understand the evolution of company interest, we will first examine the doctrinal context of company interest (1) and then follow with the jurisprudential context (2).

1. The Doctrinal Context

The 1966 Law only mentions the notion of company interest in certain corporate policing tools, e.g. in the sanction for misuse of company assets, and thus is quite vague. In view of this vagueness, company interest has been widely discussed in order to determine its real ideology. These discussions are reflected in three major doctrinal currents.[11]

In the 1960s, the Ecole de Rennes defined company interest as "l'intérêt de l'*entreprise*", the interest of the *business*, which combines the different

11 For further details, refer to G. Goffaux Callebaut, « La définition de l'intérêt social », *RTDcom.* 2004, p. 35 et seqq.

interests involved. This meaning corresponded to the functionalist proposition of the 'company' as the legal *garment* of the business. Thus, the *business's* interest had to encompass not only the interest of the shareholders, but also that of the creditors, employees, and main partners of the company. This definition has been widely criticized in that "it makes the interest of the shareholders a component that is too negligible of the company's interest". However, this theory is relevant now, almost 60 years later, as it underpins the stakeholder theory by considering both employees and communities. However, given the era in which it was adopted, the 1966 law does not mention the environmental issues.

A more liberal doctrinal current suggests that a company's interest must be understood as the common interest of the shareholders of the company, which includes the sharing of company amongst shareholders. This vision of *shareholder primacy* is based on Section 1833 paragraph 1 of the Civil Code, which provides that "every company must [...] be constituted in the common interest of the shareholders". But this approach has also been criticised, first because the text refers to the *constitution* of the company and not its management, and second because it neglects the fact that the company must exist long-term.

Thus, a third understanding of a company's interest has emerged: it must ensure "an effective compromise between the real selfish or altruistic interests involved".[12] It must also be "a harmonious temporal synthesis of the interests of the members and that of the company".[13] Defined in this way, company interest is a compromise, a middle way.

2. The Case Law Context

The case law from 1960–2000 has also not provided much detail on the definition of a company's interest. Judges remained very pragmatic in their decisions and did not try to define company interest. However, there is one consistent thread in these judgments: company interest lies in the fact that it is destined to exist and to develop. This consensus results from situations where the directors or shareholders of a company committed acts that went against the company's interest, which led to the risk that

12 Y. Chaput, *Droit des sociétés*, PUF 1993, n° 717, p. 319.

13 J.-P. Bertrel, « Liberté contractuelle et sociétés », *RTD com.* 1996.595., spec. n° 52, p. 626.

the company would disappear.[14] This is the case, for example, if a majority of the shareholders of a company would decide to allow one shareholder to use the company's only asset, like a building, as collateral. In such an example, if the property were seized, the company would no longer have any assets or activities, and it would thus be dissolved.

It should be noted here that French law does not expressly recognize the Business Judgement Rule. However, judges do not sanction managers consistently across their decisions; the sanctions will vary depending on how serious the manager's misconduct is. Mismanagement, as a flexible concept, allows judges this discretion. Accordingly, the courts regularly grant a "right to make mistakes" to managers. In addition, as specified clearly in a law passed on 9 December 2016, insolvency law provides that simple negligence does not justify a director being liable for insufficient assets.[15] This makes it possible to integrate the Business Judgement Rule into French law.

A notable exception in case law should be mentioned: the *Fruehauf* judgment of 1965.[16] In this decision, the Paris Court of Appeal ruled that in order to define company interest, it was necessary to take into account not only the interests of the shareholders but also the interests of all persons who derive income or resources from the company's activity (including employees, suppliers, and subcontractors). The Ecole de Rennes relies on this decision to justify its position that company interest is defined as the interest of the *business*, but it should be noted that the *Freuhauf* decision did not come from the Cour de cassation, nor was it repeated.

By the end of the twentieth century, authors began to wonder whether legislative developments had made it possible to finally reconsider the definition of company interest.

14 See A. Vézinet, « La position des juges sur l'intérêt social », *Droit et patrimoine* avril 1997, p. 50 et seqq.

15 C.com., art. L. 651–2.

16 Paris 22 mai 1965, *JCP* 1965.II.14274 *bis*, concl. Nepveu; *RTD com.* 1965.619, obs. R. Rodière; *Rev. sociétés* 1965.288, *D.* 1968.147 and Chron. 45 (R. Contin, « L'arrêt Fruehauf et l'évolution du droit des sociétés »).

II. The Company's Interest and Laws of the Last Decade of the 20th Century

In France, the last decade of the 20th century saw the emergence of two major phenomena: the introduction of governance codes (1) and the creation of a company form marked by pronounced contractual freedom (2).

1. The introduction of governance codes

The 1990s were a period of important reflection for corporate governance issues. Like the Cadbury Committee in UK, France also tasked various commissions with reflecting on best practices. In 1995, the Viénot 1 Report noted that there was too great a concentration of power in favour of directors. The report insisted on the need for better information for shareholders, a more efficient organisation of boards, and strengthened checks and balances. Other proposals were then made by a Marini Report in 1996, and by a second Viénot Report in 1999. The reflections provided in all three reports were then integrated into the French governance codes. For example, the Afep-Medef Code, which is the reference code for large, listed companies,[17] refers to the "intérêt social de l'entreprise". This expression is surprising for the French jurist because it does not refer to any of the three doctrinal currents mentioned above, and it is questionable whether this adds any nuance to the definition of company interest. Curiously, the English translation only mentions the *company's interest.* The same can be said for the Middlenext Code, which is aimed at SMEs.[18] Thus, the governance codes did not directly specify what interest must be considered, but in this context, it is clear that the shareholders have a central place in the operation of the companies. Shareholders' interest, as providers of capital, was central to governance, even if these codes recognize the existence of other checks and balances.

17 https://afep.com/wp-content/uploads/2022/12/Afep_Medef_Code_revision_2022_version_EN_.pdf [last accessed Dec. 28 2024].

18 https://middlenext.com/IMG/pdf/code_middlenext_2021_-_version_en.pdf [last accessed Dec. 28 2024].

2. The creation of a contractual company

France also instituted a new type of company at the end of the 20th century: the simplified joint stock company (la société par actions simplifiée), which offered shareholders contractual collaboration.[19] In the articles of association of simplified joint stock companies, the partners are released from a number of public order rules that typically apply to the organisation of management or to the voting rules. This organizational structure allows the company to adapt to the needs of the shareholders.[20] However, the legislator has not addressed how the definition of company interest applies in this new type of company where the will of the shareholders is central.

Accordingly, the question has arisen as to whether the definition of company interest is possibly evolving towards a greater consideration of the interest of shareholders. However, the legislator has not taken this path, nor has the case law been modified, and the criteria for defining company interest has not changed. Thus, at the end of the 20th century, what appeared was a dual function of company interest, either as compass for directors and shareholders, or as an instrument for policing companies. This dual approach seems to be verified, or even reinforced, in the context of the development of sustainability.

B. The Evolution of the Notion of Company Interest in the Context of Sustainability

In France, the 2001 law on new economic regulations[21] took up some of the recommendations of the aforementioned reports. But soon, commentators noted that the French approach was slightly different from the Anglo-American approach, and there was talk of "French-style corporate governance". The French approach was undoubtedly European, as the European Action Plan for *Modernising Company Law and Enhancing Corporate Governance* of 2003 contained the same ideas. The European Action Plan focused

---

19 Loi n° 1994-1 du 4 janvier 1994 instituant la société par actions simplifiée, modified by Loi n° 1999-587 du 12 juillet 1999 sur l'innovation et la recherche which has further relaxed the rules for the incorporation of the SAS.

20 G. Goffaux Callebaut, *Du contrat en droit des sociétés – Essai sur le contrat instrument d'adaptation du droit des sociétés*, préf. J.-P. Gastaud, L'Harmattan, coll. Presses universitaires de Sceaux, 2008, spec. n° 136 et seqq.

21 Loi n° 2001-420 du 15 mai 2001 relative aux nouvelles régulations économiques.

not only on governance, and therefore by extension on directors and shareholders, but also on other checks and balances (in particular, from employees and consumers).[22] This demonstrates the first seeds of the shift from corporate governance to corporate social responsibility, and thus of the introduction of sustainability to company law.

In French law, CSR dates from the 2001 law on new economic regulations. More recently, in 2018, French law was impacted by a report on *The company, object of collective interest,*[23] which was partially adopted in the PACTE Law of 2019.[24] The general idea of the report, and the succeeding law, provides context to company law, freeing companies from having short-term profitability as their sole goal, and thus allowing companies to aim for sustainability.[25] In other words, even if the company does aim to make a profit, under the new regulation, it may also integrate other longer-term concerns into its strategy.

So how, considering the updated laws on CSR, has company interest changed? To answer this question, it is necessary to return to the conclusion of the first part, namely that company interest is both a compass for directors and shareholders (I) and an instrument for policing companies (II). It is from this dual point of view that conclusions will be drawn on the new contours of company interest.

22 See, in particular, G. Goffaux, « Le plan d'action de la Communauté européenne en droit des sociétés – Une approche française », *Bull. Joly Sociétés* 2003, § 213, p. 997 et seqq.

23 For further details, refer to: https://minefi.hosting.augure.com/Augure_Minefi/r/ContenuEnLigne/Download?id=FAA5CFBA-6EF5-4FDF-82D8-B46443BDB61B&filename=entreprise_objet_interet_collectif.pdf [last accessed Dec. 28 2024].

24 Loi n° 2019–486 du 22 mai 2019 relative à la croissance et à la transformation des entreprises (Law on the growth and transformation of companies, known as the PACTE Law).

25 The company is indeed intended to make profits, but its purpose also allows it to aim for another (sustainable) goal.

I. Company Interest Considered as a Compass for Directors and Shareholders

First, company interest serves as a compass[26] for company policy, which CSR necessarily has an impact on. The focus on ethics, social issues, and the environment is a general movement that affects the life of companies. Thus, the governance of companies is influenced by new values. In French law, this involves soft law instruments (1) and hard law instruments (2).

1. The Influence of Sustainability via Soft Law Instruments

The influence of CSR values on company interest is achieved through various soft law instruments.

First, corporate codes of ethics reflect the importance of CSR considerations. Today, many companies have adopted a code of ethics. These codes contain values, principles, and rules that guide directors in their obligations and influence their liabilities. Among the values put forward, there is systematic reference to protection of the environment, working conditions, or the interest of stakeholders.[27] In addition, these concerns are indirectly integrated by reference to international texts such as the United Nations Global Compact[28] or the OECD Guidelines for Multinational Enterprises.[29] Although a company's code of ethics is not a legally binding standard before court, it does serve a mandatory obligation internally. Thus, in court, "the code of ethics may [...] be used by the judge to measure behaviour

26 A. Pirovano, « La boussole de l'intérêt social – Intérêt commun, intérêt social, intérêt de l'entreprise? », *D.* 1997. chron. 189. See also M. Cozian, A. Viandier and F. Deboissy, *Droit des sociétés*, LexisNexis, coll. Manuel, 2017, 30ème éd., n° 555.

27 IDEP study on the codes of ethics of CAC 40 companies, supra. See the article by G. Gaède, « Panorama des sources d'inspiration des codes d'éthique », in *Les codes d'éthique – Prémices d'une gouvernance d'entreprise transnationale, Cahiers de droit de l'entreprise*, n° 4, juillet-août 2014, n° 20.

28 Known as *Global Compact*. See: https://pactemondial.org/ [last accessed Dec. 28 2024].

29 *OECD Guidelines for Multinational Enterprises* 2011. For a general view, refer to : M. Doucin, « La dimension internationale de la responsabilité sociale de l'entreprise », *in* L. Fonbaustier et V. Magnier (dir.), *Développement durable et entreprise*, Dalloz, coll. Thèmes et commentaires, 2013, p. 15 et seqq.

and give concrete expression to the assessment of a standard".[30] In addition, these values are sometimes reinforced such that they achieve the status of real norms and thus become binding on managers and employees.

In this way, companies integrate CSR considerations into the guidelines that directors must follow. Indeed, these *a priori* non-binding codes do in fact bind directors in the sense that their management must be in line with the concerns recognized by the entire company.

Second, management measurement tools now account for ethics as well. This illustrates the rise of CSR principles in the directions given to managers. Such management tools include the standardisation processes,[31] certifications, labelling, and ratings, and tend to incorporate sustainable values. These tools allow companies to specify their priorities, and, in practice, companies particularly emphasize social and environmental concerns, which again shows that the direction that companies set for themselves is indeed influenced by CSR issues. Among these tools is the ISO 26000 Social Responsibility standard[32] which focuses on the rights of stakeholders, the rights of employees, and human rights. As a tool without any binding force, the ISO 26000 standard is optional and lacks certification. The ISO 26000 works by providing recommendations that companies can choose from based on what they find appropriate.[33] However, being able to choose priorities makes it possible for companies adopt the steps taken in the

30 P. Deumier, « Appliquer, expliquer ou sanctionner? », in Dossier *Les codes d'éthique – Prémices d'une gouvernance d'entreprise transnationale, Cahiers de droit de l'entreprise*, juillet 2014, n° 25, p. 37–38.

31 "Standardisation is an activity of general interest which aims to provide reference documents developed by consensus by all interested parties, relating to rules, characteristics, recommendations or examples of good practice, relating to products, services, methods, processes or organisations". Décret n° 2009–697 du 16 juin 2009 sur la standardisation, Art. 1, paragraph 1. Paragraph 2 of this text adds that standardisation "aims to encourage economic development and innovation while taking into account sustainable development goals".

32 This standard was created in 2010 following a largely participatory process, with 436 experts and 195 observers from 94 ISO member countries and 42 international organizations. V. C. Ruwet, « ISO 26000 : vers une démocratisation de la procédure ISO? », *in* M. Capron, F. Quairel-Lanoizelée, M.-F. Turcotte (dir.), *ISO 26 000 : une norme « hors norme »? Vers une conception mondiale de la responsabilité sociétale*, Economica, coll. Recherche en Gestion, 2011, p. 69 et seqq.

33 Ph. Rozec, « La norme ISO 26000 : un nouveau souffle pour la responsabilité sociale des entreprises », *JCP S* n° 51, 21 décembre 2010, 1548.

societal and environmental fields.[34] Accordingly, company policy must also reflect these advancements.

In addition, labelling and rating incentives contribute to the way companies define their CSR objectives. The display of the labels or ratings obtained for CSR purposes reflects the commitment of companies to integrate ethics into their policies.

In addition to these global tools, there are two specific French tools (though similar instruments can be found in other jurisdictions) that were created by the PACTE Law of 2019.

The first is the *raison d'être* integrated into Section 1835 of the French Civil Code: "the articles of association may specify a *raison d'être*, consisting of the principles with which the company adopts itself and for the respect of which it intends to allocate resources in the performance of its activity". This is also incorporated into the law of public limited companies, in Section L. 225–35 of the French Commercial Code. *Raison d'être* should not be confused with corporate purpose, which is the program of activity that the company sets for itself and which, in turn, sets out the bounds of the company's legal capacity. In concrete terms, the *raison d'être* must allow the company to devote part of its human and financial resources to goals other than making a profit. In practice, many companies confuse *raison d'être* with an advertising slogan.

Since the implementation of the PACTE Law, shareholders can also decide to go further in the process and choose a specific status as a 'company with a mission'. This is not a new corporate form, but rather a type of label. In addition to choosing a *raison d'être*, companies 'with a mission' must also set social and environmental objectives and set up a monitoring committee to report on the procedures the company is implementing to achieve these objectives. These reports are subject to review by an independent third-party body. In the event of non-compliance with its commitments, the company may lose its 'company with a mission' label.[35]

Thus, these soft law tools, while not mandatory, do allow companies to specify how CSR issues are taken into account in their company policy, and

34 See, in particular, F. Laronze, « La norme ISO 26000, une source de droit en matière sociale? L'apport de la théorie du droit à la réflexion sur les normes RSO », *Droit social* 2013, p. 345 et seqq. However, since 2013, AFNOR has been offering, in support of the ISO 26000 standard, reference documents that offer methodological recommendations that make it possible to "objectify and demonstrate the relevance of the actions implemented".

35 C.com., art. L. 210–12.

consequently to specify how the company sees its own interest internally. Hard law tools also participate in this function.

2. The Influence of Sustainability via Hard Law Instruments

The influence of CSR on company interest also involves two hard law tools: non-financial reporting[36] and the duty of vigilance of parent companies through their subsidiaries.[37] Both tools are mandatory for some companies but are voluntary for others. Each tool has specific features.

French law has included an obligation to *report* on social and environmental matters since the 2001 law on new economic regulations. The Grenelle II Law of 2010 reinforced this system. For listed companies, the management report must include "information on the way in which the company takes into account the social and environmental consequences of its activity as well as on its societal commitments in favour of sustainable development and in favour of the fight against discrimination and the promotion of diversity".[38] The data that must be provided is specified by

36 See B. Petit, « « *Reporting* » RSE : un nouveau coup d'épée dans l'eau... », *Environnement*, Juillet 2014, étude 12; B. Rolland, « Le *reporting* social, sociétal et environnemental : regards critiques », *Bull. Joly Sociétés* 2014, p. 287 et seqq.; C. Malecki, « L'irrésistible montée en puissance de la RSE », *Bull. Joly Sociétés* 2013, p. 594 et seqq.

37 See P. Abadie and G. Goffaux Callebaut, « La responsabilité basée sur l'existence d'un risqué particulier », *in* Dossier *Responsabilité dans les groupes de sociétés*, *Actes pratiques et ingénierie sociétaire*, mai-juin 2017, p. 16 et seqq.

38 Art. 225-102-1, al. 5 C.com. The same type of obligation also exists in European law since the implementation of the Directive of 22 October 2014. Directive 2014/95/EU of 22 October 2014 amending Directive 2013/34/EU with regard to disclosure of non-financial and diversity information by certain large undertakings and groups. See C. Malecki, « Publication de la directive RSE ou comment faire confiance à la gouvernance d'entreprise durable », *Bull. Joly Sociétés*, déc. 2014, p. 732 et seqq.; B. Petit, art. above; B. Rolland, art. above; C. Malecki, « L'irrésistible montée en puissance de la RSE », art. above; I. Tchotourian, « Divulgation extra-financière des sociétés en Europe : Présentation et analyse du projet de la Commission européenne », *RTDeur.* 2014, p. 309 et seqq. *It makes* it mandatory to publish information on their environmental and company impacts, respect for human rights, and the fight against corruption, as well as on diversity policy in governance.

decree.[39] The 2014 Directive allowed the French Law of 2017[40] to strengthen the efficiency of this system. Since then, information provided in the reports must adhere to new criteria: specifically, they must identify the measure necessary to understand the company's situation, the evolution of the company's business, its economic and financial results, and the impact of the activity. The aim of these requirements is to integrate the "materiality matrix" into French law,[41] which is a tool borrowed from financial law that makes it possible to prioritise the strategic use of CSR issues for the company concerned. By carrying out this materiality analysis, the company will identify the subjects that potentially have a significant impact on its business.[42] For example, water consumption is *material* for a soft drink seller, but not necessarily for a communication company. This integration into positive law makes it possible to respond to one of the criticisms of the French financial markets supervisory body (AMF),[43] which noted

39 Three main types of indicators are targeted: company information, environmental information, and information relating to societal commitments in favour of sustainable development. See B. François, « Reporting RSE : commentaire du décret n° 2010–557 du 24 avril 2012 », *Rev. sociétés* 2012, p. 607 et seqq.

40 Ordonnance 2017–1180 du 19 juillet 2017 relative à la publication d'informations non financières par certaines grandes entreprises et certains groups d'entreprises (on the publication of non-financial information by certain large companies and certain groups of companies). See, in particular, M. Supiot, « Rapport de gestion : nouveau format de présentation des informations sur le gouvernement d'entreprise, réorganisation des obligations d'information, allégement et clarification des obligations pour les petites entreprises, nouveau dispositif de reporting extra-financier », *JCP E* n° 37, 14 septembre 2017, act. 636. See also Ordonnance n° 2017–1162 du 12 juillet 2017 portant diverses mesures de simplification et de clarification des obligations d'information à la charge des entreprises (on various measures to simplify and clarify the information obligations of companies). See also Décret n° 2017–1265 du 9 août 2017 pris pour l'application de l'ordonnance n° 2017–1180 du 19 juillet 2017 relative à la publication d'informations non financières par certaines grandes entreprises et certains groupes d'entreprises (adopted for the application of Ordonnance n° 2017–1180 du 19 juillet 2017 sur la publication des informations non financières par certaines grandes entreprises et certains goupes d'entreprises / on the publication of non-financial information by certain large companies and groups companies).

41 Which would be the translation of *materiality*, however a more appropriate term would be that of "relevance".

42 CSR actors have taken up this practice, in particular the *Global Reporting Initiative* (*GRI*) and the *International Integrated Reporting Council* (*IIRC*). For the GRI, "issues that have a direct or indirect impact on the organization's ability to create, preserve or erode value [...] for itself, for its stakeholders and company as a whole".

43 AMF Report on information published by listed companies on company, societal and environmental responsibility, 5 November 2013; C. Malecki, « Des chiffres et des

that while French companies have improved the structure of information and that the efforts made [...] in terms of CSR have been considerable",[44] "companies still needed to adopt a 'pragmatic' approach allowing them to identify and prioritise the information to be included in their strategy".[45]

But the question remains: does non-financial reporting have an influence on company interest? Non-financial reporting requires the company to specify the direction it intends to follow in terms of CSR in its management report submitted to the general meeting. Accordingly, non-financial reporting obligations allow non-financial objectives to be integrated into the mission of the directors. However, this influence of non-financial reporting is relative. First, the influence of *reporting* depends on the size of the company. Today, listed companies are only required to report if they meet certain thresholds.[46] SMEs and VSEs, as well as simplified joint-stock companies (SAS), which represent a significant proportion of companies, are thus *de facto* excluded from the scope of the text.[47] In addition, through the practice of *comply or explain* authorised by the decree, the company may exclude or mitigate certain CSR values.[48] Moreover, the influence of *reporting* is relative because of the sanctions attached to it. While the legal texts do not provide for a special sanction in the event of inaccuracy of non-financial information, sanctions for inaccurate reporting of non-financial information do exist in practice in the form of damage to reputation, which can lead to the end of contractual relations, the withdrawal of certain

---

lettres... de la noblesse du *reporting* non financier », *Bull. Joly Sociétés* 2013, p. 780 et seqq.

44 AMF Report above, p. 5.

45 *Ibid.*

46 The lowest thresholds are set at more than €20 million for the balance sheet, more than €40 million for the net amount of turnover, and more than 500 permanent employees. However, these thresholds are now assessed at the consolidated level when the company prepares consolidated accounts. Previously, thresholds were examined at the level of the parent company only.

47 The question of application to simplified joint-stock companies and in general to small businesses arises, since they represent a significant part of economic activity. Also, size criteria could replace the rating criterion. See the recommendations of the CSR Platform, http://www.actu-environnement.com/ae/news/ reporting-societal-recommendations-rse-platform-22120.php4 [last accessed Dec. 28 2024].

48 With regard to *comply or explain*, the AMF recommends that "companies include in their registration document a summary table of the information they do not publish, distinguishing between those that cannot be produced and those that do not appear relevant to them, as well as the related detailed explanations". See AMF Report above, p. 8.

shareholders, or the *boycott* of products by consumers.[49] In addition, the publication of inaccurate or misleading information falls within consumer law via the law of misleading commercial practices,[50] and also within financial criminal law, through the offence of false or misleading information.[51] However, tools based on company interest are not significantly impacted by this reporting obligation, except when it comes to the mismanagement of managers.

The duty of vigilance of parent companies also makes it possible to integrate CSR values into the compass of company interest. In France, the 2017 law[52] integrated this tool into the French Commercial Code. Under these regulations, companies must establish a vigilance plan that "includes reasonable due diligence measures to identify risks and prevent serious violations of human rights and fundamental freedoms, the health and safety of persons and the environment, resulting from the activities of the company and those of the companies it controls [...]".[53] Thus, a company's vigilance plan must include risk mapping, regular assessment procedures, actions to mitigate or prevent serious damage, an alert mechanism, and

49 See, in particular, G. Tusseau, « Vers un renversement du credo positiviste? L'éthique comme paradigme de nouvelles formes de juridicité », *Revue des juristes de Sciences Po*, n° 4, novembre 2011, p. 43 et seqq.; N. Cuzacq, "Le mécanisme du *Name and Shame* ou la sanction médiatique comme mode de régulation des entreprises", *RTD com.* 2017, p. 473 et seqq.; G. Goffaux Callebaut, "Garantie normative et responsabilité sociale des entreprises", *in* C. Thibierge (ed.), *La garantie normative – Exploration d'une notion-fonction*, *op. cit.*

50 Two years imprisonment and a fine of 300,000 euros (or a percentage of turnover), art. L. 121–1 C. conso.

51 Five years imprisonment and a fine of 100 million euros (up to a tenfold increase in the benefit derived from the offence), art. L. 465–2–1 CMF (amended by Loi n° 2016–819 du 21 juin 2016 réformant le système de repression des abus de marché / reforming the system for the repression of market abuse).

52 Loi n° 2017–399 du 27 mars 2017 relative au devoir de vigilance des sociétés mères et des entreprises donneuses d'ordre (on the duty of vigilance of parent companies and contracting companies). On the project, see in particular the dossier *Le Big Bang des devoirs de vigilance ESG : les nouveaux enjeux de RSE et droits de l'homme, RLDA* n° 104, mai 2015, p. 66 et seqq.; N. Cuzacq, « Le devoir de vigilance des sociétés mères et des entreprises donneuses d'ordre : Acte II, scène 1 », *D.* 2015, p. 1049 et seqq.; G. Goffaux Callebaut, « La responsabilité des sociétés mères et entreprises donneuses d'ordre », *Revue internationale de la compliance et de l'éthique des affaires*, juin 2015, comm. n° 65, p. 35 et seqq.; P. Abadie, « Le devoir de vigilance des sociétés mères : responsabilisation actuelle, responsabilités à venir », *Gaz. Pal.* HS, juin 2016, p. 65 et seqq.

53 C.com., art. L. 225–102–4-I.

a system for monitoring the implemented measures and evaluating their effectiveness. The company's CSR concerns must therefore be integrated into the management report, a public document that informs current and future shareholders and savers of the company's commitments, thus integrating these values into the compass of the company's interest. While the 2024 European Directive[54] will bring technical changes to this framework, no specific sanctions exist in the French tools using the criterion of company interest.

The influence of CSR values on company interest as a compass for the governance of companies therefore seems to be effective, even before the adoption of the PACTE Law, and even if the result is just internal effects within the company. But CSR concerns also involve instruments of positive law that are based on company interest, which leads us to consider the second function of company interest, namely as an instrument for policing companies.

II. Company Interest Considered as an Instrument for the Police of Companies

Company interest is also a necessary counterweight to power: it is an "instrument de police des sociétés".[55] Under French jurisdiction, company interest – as an instrument of company policing and enforcement – is used to implement certain mechanisms such as the abuse of voting rights or the appointment of a provisional administrator. In this context, does CSR really have an influence on the notion of the company's interest? Indeed, it is uncertain whether judges, tasked with implementing provisions on behalf of company interest, actually takes these new values into account when sanctioning certain behaviours. This question is fundamental in translating

54 Directive (EU) 2024/1760 of the European Parliament and of the Council of 13 June 2024 on corporate sustainability due diligence and amending Directive (EU) 2019/1937 and Regulation (EU) 2023/2859 (Text with EEA relevance).

55 S. Rousseau and I. Tchotourian, L'intérêt social en droit des sociétés – Regards canadiens", *Rev. Sociétés* 2009, p. 735 et seqq., spec. n° 4, quoting A. Constantin, « L'intérêt social : quel intérêt? », *Mélanges Mercadal*, éd. F. Lefebvre, 2002, p. 315 et seqq., spec. p. 320) and J. Schapira (« L'intérêt social et le fonctionnement de la société anonyme », RTD com. 1971, p. 95 et seqq.): "the company interest would thus have become the instrument of a corporate police".

CSR commitments made by companies into legally-binding obligations.[56] In this regard, some authors consider that "the company's interest appears to be an essential tool for integrating these new paradigms such as sustainable development, corporate social responsibility, or *stakeholder theory*, within the governance and legislative framework".[57] From this point of view, which is based on the idea of constraint, the influence of CSR considerations is less obvious (1). However, the PACTE Law has recently integrated company interest into the Civil Code and introduced a reference to social and environmental concerns (2).

1. The Weak Influence of CSR Concerns in Current Case Law

In French positive law, company interest is classically defined as the interest of the company to last and develop. Traditionally, case law is independent from doctrinal debate,[58] with a few exceptions.[59] However, given the importance of CSR, it is now debated whether case law should take into account a broader interest, integrating social and environmental concerns.

An analysis of case law shows that CSR data is not taken into consideration in determining company interest. This is evident for all the police measures of companies, whether they concern the limitation of the powers of directors,[60] the definition of control of one company by another,[61] or the definition of the misuse of company assets.[62] In no case did the analysis of the case law reveal that ethical data was considered in defining company interest.

Looking at a large number of decisions of the Cour de cassation, the definition of company interest has, up until now, always been the same: it is the interest of the legal person to develop and last.[63] Judges consider

56 For a general view, refer to : F.-G. Trébulle and O. Uzan (eds.), *La responsabilité sociale des entreprises – Regards croisés Droit et Gestion*, Economica, 2011.

57 S. Rousseau and I. Tchotourian, art. *supra*, spec. n° 1.

58 See A. Vézinet, « La position des juges sur l'intérêt social », *op.cit.*

59 Fruehauf Case, Paris 22 mai 1965, *supra.*

60 For civil partnerships, art. 1848 C.civ.: "in relations between partners, the manager may carry out all management acts in the interest of the company"; for the SNC, art. L. 221–4 C.com.; for SARLs, art. L. 223–18 C.com., referring to Section L. 221–4 C.com.

61 C.com., art. L. 233–3.

62 C.com., art. L. 242–6.

63 Here, a parallel with Slovenian law can be envisaged.

that an act likely to compromise the very existence of the company is contrary to the company's interest.[64] In this context, the integration of environmental considerations into company policy by the shareholders could not outweigh survival of the legal entity. Indeed, as specified by the Third Civil Chamber of the Cour de cassation's September 12, 2012 decision,[65] "the consent of the shareholders does not allow the validation of an act contrary to the company's interest".

However, environmental considerations may not necessarily call into question the continuity of company. For example, it is conceivable that a judge could recognize that a director has not respected the environmental goals that shareholders have required. But, so far, such a decision is just legal fiction; generally, CSR issues are just not considered.

How can this classic solution be justified?[66] The first reason is theoretical: company interest must not be confused with general interest.[67] Integrating social and environmental considerations into company interest moves away from the traditional function of the general interest of the company. CSR makes it possible to question "the very purpose of companies and their integration into a legal order that excludes neither the general interest nor public order".[68] But this means forgetting that a company follows a principle of specialty, both legal and statutory, which distances it from the general interest. Moreover, under French jurisdiction, when assessing a company's interest, a judge cannot interfere with the life of the company, which may prevent the judge from taking CSR issues into consideration. Another basis for the solution is judicial practice. Judges only answer the questions that are put to them. Thus, if shareholders or directors do not base their requests on aspects related to CSR, judges do not provide answers to these questions. However, the introduction of a class action in environmental matters may make it possible to change things.

That being said, traditional solutions may have to change. Five years ago, the legislator integrated the social and environmental considerations into company interest, which has brought to light certain difficulties.

---

64 Com. 23 septembre 2014, n° 13-17347, *Bull. civ.* IV, n° 142; Civ. 3, 27 avril 2017, pourvoi n° 16-12388.

65 Civ. 3, 12 septembre 2012, n° 11-17948, *Bull. civ.* III, n° 121.

66 For a general view, refer to: F.-G. Trébulle, « *Stakeholders Theory* et droit des sociétés », *Bull. Joly Sociétés* 2006, p. 1337 et seqq. et 2007, p. 7 et seqq.

67 V. M. Mekki, *L'intérêt général et le contrat – Contribution à une étude de la hiérarchie des intérêts en droit privé*, LGDJ, coll. Bib. Dr. privé, t. 411, n° 687 et seqq.

68 *Ibid.*

2. The Legislative Integration of CSR Concerns into Company Interest

The integration of social and environmental concerns into company interest was achieved by the PACTE Law, but this integration has also raised some difficulties.

Before the PACTE Law of 2019, paragraph 1 of Section 1833 of the Civil Code referred to the common interest of the shareholders (and not the company's interest) at the time of the incorporation of the company (not during its lifespan). Based on the Notat-Senard report,[69] the PACTE Law integrated company interest into the Civil Code by adding a second paragraph to Section 1833, which stipulates that "the company is managed in its company's interest, taking into consideration the social and environmental issues of its activity".[70] The text does not specifically define company interest[71] as such. Given this definition, previous case law of the Cour de Cassation becomes interesting. Simply, the text specifies that all companies must consider social and environmental issues, in addition to company interest, in their activities. These concerns, which are voluntarily integrated into company operation through their codes of ethics or the display of labels, are now also imposed on company directors, regardless of the size of the company in question. In addition to the Civil Code, this approach is also included in the Commercial Code as part of the missions of the boards of directors and the supervisory boards of public limited companies.

But integrating environmental concerns into company interest may be difficult for judges. Determining the higher interest of the company is already delicate. The rule adds the difficulty of articulating the company interest with the general economic, social, and environmental interests that underscore the consideration "of the social and environmental issues of one's activity", even if the text no longer mentions the term *"interest"* as in previous versions, but the term "*issues*". Judges therefore have to define company interest in cases themselves, balancing the various economic, social,

69 N. Notat and J.-D. Senard, *L'entreprise, objet d'intérêt collectif.* Report submitted on March 9, 2018. Online on the website of the Ministry of the Economy and Finance. For a critical reading of the report, see A. Couret, « La réforme de l'entreprise passe-t-elle nécessairement par une réécriture du Code civil? », *Rev. Sociétés* 2018, p. 639 et seqq.; J. Paillusseau, « Entreprise et société. Quels rapports? Quelle réforme », *D.* 2018, p. 1395 et seqq.

70 Art. 169 I, 1°, of the PACTE Law.

71 In this sense, refer to: D. Schmidt, « Loi PACTE: l'intérêt social », *JCP E*, n° 26, 27 juin 2019, 1318.

and environmental issues, while articulating both the company interest and the general interest, all without interfering with the management of the company. The exercise may be perilous in French jurisdiction,[72] even if the objective is laudable.

In conclusion, for the past ten years, French law has offered many possibilities for integrating CSR considerations into tools mobilizing company interest. Among these, the latest innovations of the PACTE Law are certainly the most promising when it comes to including sustainability in company law. Some of these tools could easily integrate European law, as has been done with extra-financial reporting or the duty of vigilance. Such integration at the EU level would enhance better corporate governance

References

Abadie, Pauline, « Le devoir de vigilance des sociétés mères: responsabilisation actuelle, responsabilités à venir », *Gaz. Pal.* 2016, p. 65.

Abadie, Pauline/Goffaux Callebaut, Géraldine, « La responsabilité basée sur l'existence d'un risque particulier », in Dossier: La responsabilité dans les groupes de sociétés, *Actes pratiques et ingénierie sociétaire* mai-juin 2017, p. 16.

Bertrel, Jean-Pierre, « Liberté contractuelle et sociétés », *RTDcom.* 1996, p. 595.

Chaput, Yves, *Droit des sociétés*, PUF Paris 1993.

Constantin, Alexis, « L'intérêt social: quel intérêt », in *Mélanges Barthélemy Mercadal*, Lefebvre Levallois-Perret 2002, p. 318.

Contin, Raphael, « L'arrêt Fruehauf et l'évolution du droit des sociétés », *Journal des sociétés* 1968, p. 363.

Couret, Alain, « La réforme de l'entreprise passe-t-elle nécessairement par une réécriture du code civil? », *Revue des Sociétés* 2018, p. 639.

Cozian, Maurice/Viandier, Alain/Deboissy, Florence, *Droit des sociétés*, 30. ed., Lexis Paris 2017.

Cuzacq, Nicolas, « Le devoir de vigilance des sociétés mères et des entreprises donneuses d'ordre: Acte II, scène 1 », *Recueil Dalloz* 2015, p. 1049.

Cuzacq, Nicolas, « Le mécanisme du Name and Shame ou la sanction médiatique comme mode de régulation des entreprises », *RTDcom.* 2017, p. 473.

Deumier, Pascal, « Appliquer, expliquer ou sanctionner? », in: Les codes d'éthique – Prémices d'une gouvernance d'entreprise transnationale, *Cahiers de droit de l'entreprise*, n° 4, juillet-août 2014, n° 25.

72 Even if the Spanish judge seems to do it: Supreme Court ruling from 2022 STS of 21 December 2022 (see Lola Melon's contribution).

Doucin, Michel, « La dimension internationale de la responsabilité sociale de l'entreprise », in: Fonbaustier/Magnier (eds.), Développement durable et entreprise, Dalloz Paris 2012, p. 15.

François, Bénédicte, « Reporting RSE : commentaire du décret n° 2012–557 du 24 avril 2012 », *Revue des Sociétés* 2012, p. 607.

Gaède, G., « Panorama des sources d'inspiration des codes d'éthique », in: Les codes d'éthique – Prémices d'une gouvernance d'entreprise transnationale, *Cahiers de droit de l'entreprise*, n° 4, juillet-août 2014, n° 20.

Goffaux Callebaut, Géraldine, « Densification et "dédensification" normatives en droit des sociétés », in: Thibierge (ed.), *La densification normative, découverte d'un processus*, mare & martin Paris 2013, p. 797.

Goffaux Callebaut, Géraldine, *Du contrat en droit des sociétés : essai sur le contrat instrument d'adaptation du droit des sociétés*, L'Harmattan Paris 2008.

Goffaux Callebaut, Géraldine, « Garantie normative et responsabilité sociale des entreprises », in: Thibierge (ed.), *La garantie normative, Exploration d'une notion-fonction*, mare & martin Paris 2021, p. 369.

Goffaux Callebaut, Géraldine, « La consommation responsable », in: Les enjeux de la réforme du droit de la consommation, Actes du colloque du 27 mars 2014, *Petites affiches* 2014, n° 128, 27 juin, p. 15.

Goffaux Callebaut, Géraldine, « La définition de l'intérêt social », *RTDcom.* 2004, p. 35.

Goffaux Callebaut, Géraldine, « La responsabilité des sociétés mères et entreprises donneuses d'ordre », *Revue internationale de la compliance et de l'éthique des affaires* juin 2015, p. 35.

Goffaux Callebaut, Géraldine, « Le plan d'action de la Communauté européenne en droit des sociétés – une approche française », *Bulletin Joly Sociétés* 2003, p. 997.

Laronze, Fleur, « La norme ISO 26000, une source de droit en matière sociale? L'apport de la théorie du droit à la réflexion sur les normes de la RSO », *Droit social* 2013, p. 345.

Lequet, Pierre, « Droit de la consommation durable : entre éthique environnementale et éthique des affaires », in: Sohnle/Bouriau (eds.), Éthique environnementale pour juristes, mare & martin Le Kremlin-Bicêtre 2024.

Malecki, Catherine, « Des chiffres et des lettres... de noblesse du reporting non financier », *Bulletin Joly Sociétés* 2013, p. 780.

Malecki, Catherine, « L'irrésistible montée en puissance de la RSE: les impulsions européennes et françaises de l'année 2013 », *Bulletin Joly Sociétés* 2013, p. 594.

Malecki, Catherine, « Publication de la directive RSE ou comment faire confiance à la gouvernance d'entreprise durable », *Bulletin Joly Sociétés* 2014, p. 732.

Mekki, Mustapha, « L'intérêt général et le contrat. Contribution à une étude de la hiérarchie des intérêts en droit privé », LGDJ Paris 2004.

Mekki, Mustapha, « Le contrat, vecteur du devoir de vigilance », Dossier spécial "RSE et devoir de vigilance", *Revue Lamy Droit des affaires*, mai 2015.

Notat, Nicole/Sénard, Jean-Dominique, *L'entreprise, objet d'intérêt collectif*, Rapport aux ministres de la Transition écologique et solidaire, de la Justice, de l'Économie et des Finances, du Travail, Paris 2018.

Paillusseau, Jean, « Entreprise et société. Quels rapports? Quelle réforme? », *Recueil Dalloz* 2018, p. 1395.

Petit, B., Reporting « RSE: un nouveau coup d'épée dans l'eau », *Revue Environnement* 2014, étude 12.

Pirovano, Antoine, « La "boussole" de la société, Intérêt commun, intérêt social, intérêt de l'entreprise? », *Recueil Dalloz* 1997, p. 189.

Rolland, Blandine, « Le reporting social, societal et environnemental: regards critiques », *Bulletin Joly Sociétés* 2014, p. 287.

Rousseau, Stéphane/Tchotourian, Ivan, « L' "intérêt social" en droit des sociétés : Regards canadiens », *Revue des sociétés* 2009, p. 735.

Rozec, Philippe, « La norme ISO 26000: un nouveau souffle pour la responsabilité sociale des entreprises? », *JCP S* 2010, 1548.

Ruwet, Coline, « ISO 26000 : vers une démocratisation de la procédure ISO? », in: Capron/Quairel-Lanoizelée/Turcotte (eds.), I*SO 26000 : une norme "hors norme"? Vers une conception mondiale de la responsabilité sociétale*, Paris 2011, p. 69.

Sauphanor-Brouillaud, Natacha, « Le consommateur », in: Epstein/Nioche (eds.), *Le droit économique, levier de la transition écologique?*, Larcier/Strada Lex Louvain la Neuve, p. 137.

Schapira, Jean, « L'intérêt social et le fonctionnement de la société anonyme », *RTD-Com.* 1971, p. 957.

Schmidt, D., « Loi PACTE: l'intérêt social », *JCP E* 2019, p. 1318.

Supiot, M., « Rapport de gestion : nouveau format de présentation des informations sur le gouvernement d'entrprise, réorganisation des obligations d'information, allégement et clarification des obligations pour les petites entreprises, nouveau dispositif de reporting extra-financier », *JCP E* 2017, act. 636.

Tchotourian, Ivan, « Divulgation extra-financière des sociétés en Europe, présentation et analyse du projet de la Commission européenne », *Revue trimestrelle de droit européen* 2014, p. 309.

Thibierge, Catherine (ed.), *La densification normative - Découverte d'un processus*, mare & martin, Paris 2014.

Thibierge, Catherine (ed.), *La force normative - Naissance d'un concept*, LGDJ/Bruylant, Paris 2009.

Thibierge, Catherine (ed.), *La garantie normative - Exploration d'une notion-fonction*, mare & martin, Paris 2021.

Trébulle, François Guy, « Stakeholders Theory et droit des sociétés », *Bulletin Joly Sociétés* 2006, p. 1337; 2007, p. 1.

Trébulle, François Guy/Uzan, Odile (eds.), *Responsabilité sociale des entreprises; regards croisés Droit et Gestion*, Dalloz Paris 2011.

Tusseau, Guillaume, « Vers un renversement du credo positiviste? L'éthique comme paradigme de nouvelles formes de juridicité », *Revue des juristes de Sciences Po* 2011, p. 43.

Vézinet, A., « La position des juges sur l'intérêt social », *Droit et patrimoine*, avril 1997, p. 50.

6. Navigating the Company's Interest in Italy: An Interplay of Legal Concepts

Diletta Lenzi

A. Understanding company's interest in the Italian legal framework

The Italian legal framework contains neither a single definition of company interest, nor a single definition of directors' fiduciary duties. Definitions for these concepts thus must be inferred through a systematic analysis of the current legal framework, which offers several insides.

Notably, the introduction of specific provisions regulating 'benefit' corporations and the updated version of the Corporate Governance Code for listed companies, which mentions corporate 'sustainable success', have revived the discussion surrounding company interest and sustainability.[1] While past debates questioned whether it was possible to distinguish a company's interest from that of its shareholders, the contemporary debate has shifted to how sustainability issues – and, in particular, environmental concerns – enter into corporate governance.[2] As will be further discussed, we are witnessing an increase in the factual and legal relevance of business risks to corporate stakeholders, such as the environment and local communities; and while until recently it was debatable whether corporate governance law should also address these issues (which were traditionally a matter of other branches of law, like administrative or environmental law), in the light of the current regulatory framework, it is now undeniable that

1 I use the concept of 'company interest' as a synonym for 'corporate purpose', while recognising that the two terms may carry distinct meanings in different jurisdictions. For the Italian legal debate on corporate purpose, see, among others: Busch/Ferrarini/Grünewald/Ferrarini 2021, p. 85; Ferrarini Riv. soc. 2023, 317; Tombari Riv. soc. 2021, 1; Spolidoro Riv. soc. 2022, 322. For an accurate analysis of the differences between the Italian concept of *interesse sociale* (company's interest) and *scopo sociale* (corporate purpose) see Angelici/Ferri Jr./Stella Richter Jr./Tombari 2025, 967.

2 See, among others, Angelici Giur. comm. 2011, 159; Angelici Riv. Soc. 2018, 3; Barcellona; Costi Banca impr. 2023, 503; Libertini Riv. soc. 2009, 1; Maugeri Riv. soc. 2019, 992.

the management of these risks is no longer just a matter of external business compliance.[3]

A further preliminary remark is also necessary. In Italy, as in many other jurisdictions,[4] the discussions surrounding company interest have primarily focused on large, limited liability companies. This is because a large, limited liability company's legal identity, the limited liability of its shareholders, and the complexity of its financial structure makes it a subject under the law that is clearly distinct from its shareholders, which raises questions as to whose interests should guide the management of the company. However, Italy's economic landscape, like many others in the European Union, is characterised by micro, small, and medium-sized enterprises (MSMEs), which are often family-owned. For such enterprises, the company's interest converges significantly with the interests of the main shareholders, who appoint the directors and can also dismiss them (in Italy, dismissal without cause is permitted; the only consequence is directors' rights to compensation for any damage incurred, according to Article 2383 of the Civil Code). Nevertheless, the need for more sustainable management of business activities also concerns MSMEs, which brings new challenges in corporate governance; in the Italian debate, these challenges are not so much rooted in the concept of a company's interest or the fiduciary duties of directors, but rather in directors' duty of care.[5]

Thus, in the discussion that follows, reference will be made to large corporations when dealing with company interest, whereas the considerations regarding directors' duty of care will concern – albeit with some differences – both partnerships and limited liability companies. Conversely, the following considerations do not apply to companies that operate in special business sectors such as banking, finance, or insurance, as they are subject to distinct and more detailed rules in terms of corporate purpose and of corporate sustainability.

This chapter will first examine a key legal provision, Article 2247 of the Italian Civil Code, which offers a definition of 'company' and delineates, among its core component, a 'profit purpose' (section B). The discussion will then explore what company interest is not (sections C and D). Subsequently, the analysis will address the Italian '*società benefit*' legislation (sec-

3 Cerrato/Lenzi, p. 233 (256 ff.).

4 For a comparative analysis, see Ferrarini (fn. 1).

5 Under the Italian legal system, directors are subject to two general duties: the duty to act in the best interest of the company (hereinafter, the 'fiduciary duty') and the duty to manage the company with due diligence and care (hereinafter, the 'duty of care').

tion E) and the recent developments in the Corporate Governance Code for listed companies (section F), to explore whether they can offer criteria to help build a definition of company interest. Lastly, some final remarks are offered on how corporate sustainability is affecting the governance of Italian companies and the duties of their directors (section G).

B. The company's interest in the Italian Civil Code: The definition of 'Company' under Article 2247

Article 2247 of the Civil Code[6] has always been a prime reference of the debate around company interest, as it provides that in a 'company contract', two or more parties (individuals or legal entities) provide goods or services for the joint exercise of an economic activity with the purpose of sharing profits.[7] This provision applies across various corporate forms, including partnerships (*società semplice*; *società in nome collettivo*; and *società in accomandita semplice*), limited liability companies (*società per azioni*; *società a responsabilità limitata*; and *società in accomandita per azioni*), and cooperatives (*società cooperativa*).

The rule seems to imply that companies must generate and distribute profits, but this statement necessitates at least two further clarifications. First, Italian scholars have long distinguished between two dimensions of the profit-making purpose. On the one hand, there is shareholders' right to profit (*lucro soggettivo*), and on the other, there is a company's commitment to generating profit (*lucro oggettivo*). Despite the text of the provision, Article 2247 of the Civil Code has been interpreted to refer exclusively to the latter, while lacking any enforceable right to profit distribution for individual shareholders at the end of the financial year.[8] Contrarily, shareholders are only entitled to be treated equitably regarding profit distribution.

Second, Article 2247 of the Civil Code includes for-profit companies *stricto sensu*, as well as cooperatives. Consequently, the profit-making requirement of the company's contract referenced in Article 2247 has been read in a broader way, to encompass the company's ability to generate

6 Royal Decree, 16 March 1942, No. 262.

7 Article 2247 of the Civil Code, original text: "*Con il contratto di società due o più persone conferiscono beni o servizi per l'esercizio in comune di una attività economica allo scopo di dividerne gli utili.*"

8 *Ex multis*, Ferrara/Corsi, 185.

an economic advantage capable of benefitting the members of the organisation, which includes savings in expenses (as in consumer cooperatives) or granting access to better job opportunities than those on the market (as in workers' cooperatives), etc.[9]

Given these two specifications regarding the definition of profit purpose, Article 2247 of the Civil Code seems to limit the use of companies (including cooperatives) by qualifying them as associative bodies that operate in order to achieve an economic result for the exclusive benefit of their members. This has long been the prevalent opinion of scholars: unless a specific exception to the profit purpose (in the interpretation described above) is legislated, profit-making remains the default purpose of Italian companies.[10] However, this does not make profit-making the *exclusive* corporate purpose. On the contrary, bylaws could *add* altruistic purposes as long as they do not overrule the profit-making purpose.[11] This incorporation of altruistic objectives in the bylaws serves as a constraint on the managerial and representative powers of corporate bodies.[12] At the same time, directors have the authority to undertake 'altruistic' actions, provided they serve as a means to achieve long-term profitability, such as by enhancing the company's market reputation. For example, the Italian Supreme Court decision of September 21, 2015, No. 18449 clarifies that a company's capacity to enter into a donation contract is not inherently restricted by its profit-driven nature or corporate purpose.

Fundamentally, companies remain self-interested entities, characterised by the institutional allocation of the economic benefits generated through business activity to their members (self-allocation). The Supreme Court has also reaffirmed that limited liability companies cannot abdicate their profit-making purpose in favour of a mutualistic agenda without formally

---

9 The main argument was a highly formal one: Article 2247 of the Civil Code is placed in the introductory section of the chapter regulating partnerships, limited liability companies, and cooperatives, making it applicable to all these models. Moreover, the provision is titled '*contratto di società*' (company's contract), and the Italian term '*società*' includes cooperatives as well.

10 Campobasso, p. 26. The reform on company law itself does not appear to have questioned the profit purpose, thus implicitly confirming it. See Oppo/Oppo, p. 346; Spada, p. 3886.

11 Colombo/Portale/Stella Richter Jr., p. 165 (242); Rossi ODC 2017, 6.

12 Corte di Cassazione, 21.09.2015 – 18449.

transforming themselves into cooperatives, thus assuming a difference in purpose between the two.[13]

However, since the late 20th century, a minority of Italian scholars, influenced by US models, have argued that companies – particularly limited liability companies – can operate under any lawful purpose. Challenging the prevailing scholarly consensus, these scholars contend that companies should be interpreted as 'purpose-neutral organisational structures',[14] freely available for private ordering. This perspective is based on the idea that the corporate model is inherently beneficial and thus deserving of legal protection, not primarily for profit-making, but rather for its ability to safeguard assets and establish a legal entity with an autonomous status.

This conclusion was reached via several arguments. First, Article 2332 of the Civil Code does *not* include the lack of profit-making purpose as a reason for the declaration of the nullity of the corporate constitutive act.[15] Second, consortium companies, namely companies with economic but *not* profit-making goals, do in fact exist. This thesis has been further supported by the argument that since individual entrepreneurs are not required by law to reveal the rationale behind their business activity, no rationale should be needed when the activity is run via a corporate structure.[16]

Another argument in favour of this interpretation is that it is neither uncommon to have companies whose members do not share the corporate purpose (whether profit-making or mutualistic), as in the case of financial investors in cooperatives, nor to have non-members who do share the corporate purpose, as in the case of holders of participatory financial instruments for limited liability companies under Article 2346, last paragraph, of the Civil Code. In light of all these arguments, the definition of company interest should be left to the contractual autonomy of the members.[17]

Finally, there are those who argue that companies should also be used for purposes other than profit-making, but believe that this result cannot be achieved by interpretation alone, given the wording of Article 2247 of the

13 Corte di Cassazione 12.04.2005 – 7536, and already Corte di Cassazione 14.10.1958 – No. 3251.

14 Santini Riv. dir. civ. 1973, 151; Perlingieri/Di Sabato, p. 45; Carrabba, p. 65. *Contra* Campobasso (fn. 10), 25.

15 Santini (fn. 14). *Contra* Campobasso (fn. 10), 28; Iudica/Zatti/Buonocore; Iudica/Zatti/Marasà; Spada Riv. dir. civ. 1985, 129.

16 Porzio Giur. comm. 2014, 661 (665). See also Bigiavi, 42.

17 Oppo/Oppo, 302.

Civil Code.[18] They therefore advocate *de iure condendo* for an amendment to Article 2247 to incorporate sustainability imperatives, redefining companies as 'functionally oriented' models. In line with this view, Article 2247 should be amended to allow shareholders to set the specific purpose of the company in the bylaws. The specific purpose could be: (i) an exclusively profit-making purpose; (ii) a hybrid purpose where shareholder value maximisation should be balanced with other interests as specified in the bylaws (in line with what is today legally required for Italian *società benefit* – see section E, below); or (iii) an exclusively non-profit purpose.[19]

C. The company's interest versus the shareholders' interest

Establishing the purpose for which a company is founded (see section B, above) is distinct from identifying the interests guiding its management by directors after incorporation. Considering the semantic complexities related to company interest, it is beneficial to approach this matter more pragmatically and a unified notion of 'company interest' should be rejected, in favour of the position of scholars who discuss company interest separately, with reference to the assessment of either the behaviour of shareholders or that of corporate directors.[20] While directors are required to manage the company in the company's interest (see section D, below), the shareholders participate in *shaping* that interest.[21] This is illustrated by Article 2484(6) of the Civil Code, which empowers shareholders to determine the continuation of the company's operations by voting on its liquidation. This indicates that directors lack the authority to independently decide whether the business can continue. On the contrary, directors have the duty of running the company and cannot determine its liquidation or undertake actions that make liquidation inevitable, within the limits dictated by bankruptcy law and creditors' protection.

Debates surrounding the shareholders' ability to define the company's interest tend to polarise around two predominant theories: the contract

18 Tombari.

19 Tombari (fn. 18), p. 94.

20 Angelici, p. 45; Angelici BBTC 2014, 25; Mengoni Riv. soc. 1956, 455; Minervini Riv. dir. civ. 1956, 332; Colombo/Portale/Preite, p. 9. See also Tribunale di Palermo Sezione imprese 15.10.2015; Tribunale di Palermo Sezione imprese 5.11.2015.

21 Cicu/Messineo/Angelici, p. 390; Angelici, p. 45.

theory (*contrattualismo*) and the institutional theory (*istituzionalismo*).[22] The contract theory identifies company interest as the common interest of shareholders in the exercise of a profit-making economic activity, in line with a narrow interpretation of Article 2247 of the Civil Code. This theory empowers shareholders by supporting greater shareholder freedom in defining the contents of the company's bylaws. The institutional theory, by contrast, holds that company interest extends beyond the common interests of shareholders to include third-party interests, such as those of employees, suppliers, and creditors. These diverse interests collectively shape the company's overarching interest, which emerges as an autonomous and distinct interest that directors must prioritise in their decision-making. 'Institutionalist' elements are given credence by the choice to exclusively assign the company's management to directors under Article 2380-*bis* of the Civil Code.

Both perspectives converge with the idea that the shareholders' interest is defined as the interest of shareholders as a *category* (with all the difficulties connected to its concrete definition) rather than individual shareholder gain. Article 2373 of the Civil Code reinforces this distinction by addressing conflicts of interest among shareholders in the shareholder general assembly, specifying that "*a decision taken with the deciding vote of those who have, on their own behalf or on behalf of third parties, an interest in conflict with that of the company may be challenged (...) if it may cause damage to the company*" (unofficial translation), thereby assuming a difference between the company's interest and the single shareholder interest.

Italian jurisprudence has not explicitly taken a position between these two doctrinal theses, but prevailing case law seems to lean toward the institutionalist view. See, for example, the decision of the Supreme Court, September 29, 2020, No. 20625, which establishes that the annulment of shareholder general meeting resolutions for abuse of majority power may also occur when the resolution lacks any justification in the company's interest, and the vote of the majority shareholders is driven by the pursuit of a personal interest contrary to that of the company.[23] This ruling reflects

22 Among the many, Mignoli Riv. soc. 1958, 725; Asquini, 221; Jaeger; D'Alessandro Foro It. 1988, 48; Jaeger Giur. comm. 2000, 795; Cottino Riv. soc. 2005, 693; Galgano, p. 154; Montalenti 81. See also the debate on the company's interest between Francesco Denozza and Mario Libertini in the law journal 'Giurisprudenza commerciale': Denozza Giur. comm. 2013, 480; Libertini Giur. comm. 2014, 669.

23 Corte di Cassazione 29.09.2020 – 20625.

an implicit recognition of a distinction between the company's interest and that of its shareholders, even in the case of the majority shareholder(s).

D. Directors' duties in limited liability companies: The company's interest versus the directors' interest

In the search of what company interest is *not*, a significant aspect is that it is distinct both from the shareholders' interest (as just discussed in section C) and from the directors' interest. Article 2391 of the Civil Code explicitly regulates the directors' duty of loyalty.[24] Under Article 2391, directors must disclose any interest they may have in a particular transaction or decision of the company, whether individually or through third parties, to the full board of directors and the company's internal supervisory board by specifying nature, conditions, origin, and extent of the interest. If the director is an executive director, he or she shall also refrain from carrying out the transaction and leave the decision to the board of directors. In the case of a company managed by a single director (thus with no board of directors), the director may adopt the decision, but should then inform the shareholders and the internal supervisory board. In any event, the decision must identify and specify the company's interest in the transaction: this implicitly recognises a difference between the company's interest and the interest of the directors.

However, to the extent that they do not allow their personal interests to interfere with their fiduciary duty, directors are the only ones in charge of managing the company. As mentioned above, in the case of limited liability companies, the company law reform of 2003–2004 has granted the 'exclusive' power to manage the company to the directors (according to Article 2380-*bis* of the Civil Code). In 2019, this provision was further strengthened by extending this 'exclusive' management power for directors to all companies (including partnerships).

In addition, the new version of Article 2086 of the Civil Code entrusts the collective entrepreneur, *ergo* its directors, with the task of setting up an organisational, administrative, and accounting structure *also* capable of detecting a corporate crisis in a timely manner, and of adopting the measures necessary to deal with such a crisis. Some scholars believe that the

24 Pacchi Giur. comm. 2004, 680; Spolidoro (fn. 1); Enriques; Jaeger, p. 13; Libonati/Stella Richter Jr., p. 281.

word 'also' implies that directors are allowed to set up an organisational, administrative, and accounting structure capable of doing things other than preventing and managing the company's financial crisis, such as considering the interests of stakeholders.[25] Under this interpretations, directors' discretion could be extended, and sustainability interests could be included in corporate governance considerations. In other words, directors could set up functional structures not only to prevent corporate financial crises, but also to take account of third-party interests such as environmental interests, within the limits that will be further discussed below (see section G).

E. The società benefit *legislation*

In 2015,[26] following the example of the United States, the Italian legislature introduced the *società benefit*, the Italian equivalent of benefit corporations.[27] Since 2016, partnerships, limited liability companies, and cooperatives[28] can qualify as '*società benefit*' by amending their bylaws to include

---

25 Cossu ODC 2023, 783 (792); Lucarelli/Santoni/Lenzi, p. 121 (133); Sanfilippo Riv. dir. civ. 2022, 993. Specifically on directors' management duties arising from sustainability disclosure obligations, see Rescigno ODC 2023, 630.

26 *Legge di stabilità* 2016 – Law 28 December 2015 No. 208.

27 Benefit corporations originated in the United States, driven by the non-profit organisation *B Lab*. Founded in 2006, *B Lab* was established to create an international community for certifying *B Corp* or *B Corporation* companies. This certification is granted to businesses that voluntarily commit to generating a positive social and environmental impact while adhering to specific standards of transparency, accountability, and sustainability. To obtain certification, companies must pass the *B Impact Assessment*. Notably, this certification is available to any company, regardless of whether it is legally structured as a benefit corporation or equivalent. Alongside its certification efforts, *B Lab* has been a key advocate for legislative initiatives on benefit corporations. It played a pivotal role in drafting the *Model Benefit Corporation Legislation*, which has influenced various state laws in the U.S.A., including Washington's *Social Purpose Corporation*, introduced in 2012. Since Maryland enacted the first benefit corporation law in 2010, nearly every U.S. state has adopted similar legislation, with minor variations, including differences in terminology. Italy's *società benefit* law seems to have drawn inspiration from B Lab's *Model Benefit Corporation Legislation*, with one notable distinction: the Italian definition of common benefit is broadly defined, resembling the 'general public benefit' concept found in Delaware's *Public Benefit Corporation* framework.

28 Pursuant to Article 1, Paragraph 377, of Law 208/2015, any company regulated under Book V, Titles V and VI of the Civil Code may qualify as a benefit company. The lack of an explicit restriction on single-shareholder *società per azioni* or *società a*

one or more common-benefit purposes. These purposes are defined as "*the pursuit, in the exercise of the economic activity of the benefit corporations, of one or more positive effects, or the reduction of negative effects, on one or more categories outlined in Paragraph 376*" (Paragraph 378, lett. a), Law No. 208/2015 – unofficial translation). These categories include "*persons, communities, territories and the environment, cultural and social goods and activities, bodies and associations and other stakeholders*" (Paragraphs 376, Law No. 208/2015 – unofficial translation), such as "*workers, customers, suppliers, lenders, creditors, public administration and civil society*" (Paragraphs 378, lett. b), Law No. 208/2015 – unofficial translation).[29] In other words, *società benefit* carry out economic activities not only for mutualistic or profit-making purposes (depending on whether they are cooperatives, partnerships, or limited liability companies), but also for one or more specific 'common benefit' objective(s). Further, *società benefit* are required to be managed in a responsible, sustainable, and transparent manner towards any corporate stakeholders (Paragraph 376, Law No. 208/2015).

Amending its bylaws to include 'common-benefit purposes' is a necessary and sufficient condition for an existing company to qualify as *società benefit*.[30] This decision must be made and executed in accordance with the rules governing the chosen corporate form, which always requires shareholder approval, whether by unanimous consent or majority vote.[31] Indeed, despite differences in the decision-making process, the choice to adopt the *società benefit* status ultimately lies with the shareholders. On the other hand, it is the directors' responsibility to fulfil the company's common-benefit purpose while balancing shareholder interests with the

responsabilità limitata suggests that these corporate forms are also eligible to adopt benefit company status.

29 Among others, see Assonime, La disciplina delle società benefit, Circolare No. 19, 20 June 2016; Calagna RDS 2016, 709; Corso NLCC 2016, 894; Lupoi Riv. not. 2016, 811; Ventura Contr. e impr. 2016, 1141.

30 A company that adopts common-benefit provisions in its bylaws may include, on a voluntary basis, the term 'benefit company' or the abbreviation 'SB' in its corporate name (Paragraph 379, Law No. 208/2015).

31 When an amendment to the bylaws is not adopted unanimously, the question arises as to whether a dissenting shareholder has the right to withdraw. Law No. 208/2015 does not explicitly address this issue, meaning that the rules governing the specific corporate form will apply. As a result, no universal solution can be established; instead, it must be assessed on a case-by-case basis whether the introduction of a common-benefit purpose constitutes valid grounds for withdrawal: Corso (fn. 29).

specific social or environmental goals outlined in the company's bylaws (Paragraph 380, Law No. 208/2015).[32]

The law requires these 'common-benefit' purposes to be *balanced* with the interests not just of shareholders, but of all relevant stakeholders, i.e., those affected by the company's activity (Paragraph 377, Law No. 208/2015). While the term 'balancing' might suggest conflicting priorities, the common benefit is not a distinct objective, but rather is an integral part of the company's purpose. Here, the obligation to pursue multiple objectives arises not from external legal imposition but instead from the shareholders' own decision. Shareholders of benefit corporations are therefore able to define the company's interest via a legal solution that strengthens contractual autonomy by allowing a self-imposed limitation on profit maximisation.

Given the broad scope of common-benefit purposes permitted by law, directors must navigate potential conflicting interests. Consequently, managerial discretion in benefit corporations may be broader than in conventional companies,[33] especially when the common benefit is only vaguely defined in the company's bylaws, as is often the case.[34]

Further, the legal provisions governing *società benefit* contain ambiguities, leading to interpretative challenges and scholarly debate over the meaning of 'balancing'. Different legal provisions support contrasting conclusions. One interpretation, based on Paragraph 376, suggests that profit remains the primary objective, and the common benefit is only legitimate if it serves long-term profitability. This opinion is strengthened by Article 2247 of the Civil Code, which remains applicable to benefit corporations since it is not explicitly overridden by Law No. 208/2015. Under this view, the company's core purpose remains unchanged, and the bylaws merely require that directors pursue the specific common benefit as long as it aligns with a profitable strategy.[35]

Conversely, another interpretation, which is supported by Paragraphs 377 and 380, considers the common benefit and profit-making to be equal-

32 For an analysis of the duties and liability of directors of benefit corporations see Denozza/Stabilini ODC 2017, 1; Lenzi Giur. comm. 2016, 894; Palmieri BIS 2017, 201; Prataviera Riv. soc. 2018, 919; Rossi (fn. 11).

33 Some have even proposed that, in the context of benefit corporations, the traditional *business judgment rule* should be reframed as a *benefit judgment rule*: Stella Richter Jr. Vita not. 2017, 953.

34 See, on this point, Denozza/Stabilini (fn. 32) and Tombari (fn. 18).

35 Palmieri (fn. 32) and Mosco AGE 2018, 81.

ly important. This view aligns with the legislative intent behind *società benefit*, which seeks to institutionalise 'dual-purpose companies'. Moreover, as previously noted, even prior to the introduction of the *società benefit* regulation, some Italian scholars had already acknowledged that companies could integrate social or environmental objectives alongside profit-making purpose, without compromising their inherently lucrative nature (see section B, above). Also, directors were acknowledged as having the discretion to undertake 'altruistic' actions as long as they contributed to long-term financial success, such as enhancing corporate reputation. For the *società benefit* legislation to represent true legal innovation, benefit corporations must be empowered to transcend the traditional corporate model. In particular, shareholders should have the authority to require that directors limit profit distribution and allocate a portion of the company's revenue to common-benefit objectives, provided that such allocations do not compromise the company's financial stability or solvency. Despite their benefit mission, indeed, *società benefit* remain fully subject to general corporate law, including obligations related to financial sustainability and capital preservation.[36]

Regardless of the preferred interpretative approach, according to Paragraphs 376 and 378 of Law No. 208/2015, the common benefit must be pursued as an integral part of the company's business activity. These provisions define *società benefit* as entities that carry out common-benefit objectives "*in the exercise of an economic activity*" (unofficial translation). Consequently, a company seeking to fulfil its common-benefit purpose exclusively through activities unrelated to its core business operations would likely fall outside the scope of the law.

Regarding directors' duty of care in *società benefit*, the introduction of common-benefit purposes serves as a benchmark for assessing directors' behaviours, while staying within the boundaries of the business judgment rule. Consequently, despite the silence of Law No. 208/2015 on the matter, failure to pursue the common benefit may constitute grounds for directors' removal without compensation.[37] However, it remains uncertain whether directors' failure to uphold this hybrid purpose – specifically, neglecting to pursue the common-benefit goal – can give rise to liability. Paragraph 381 of Law No. 208/2015 explicitly states that directors' liability will be determined by the regulatory framework established in the Civil Code for the chosen

36 Cordeiro Guerra/Lenzi Riv. tel. dir. trib. 2021, 1.
37 Lenzi (fn. 32) and De Donno/Ventura/Angelici, p. 19.

corporate form. This raises significant interpretative challenges, primarily because civil liability for directors generally requires the existence of economic harm. Under directors' civil liability rules, liability claims for failing to pursue the common benefit would be precluded unless the directors' conduct resulted in a measurable reduction in the company's asset value. Outside of scenarios involving reputational damage or loss of business opportunities, however, failing to pursue the common benefit may not cause quantifiable economic harm. Consequently, directors' civil liability for failing to pursue the common-benefit objective appears to be limited to exceptional circumstances. Furthermore, if, as mentioned, *società benefit* status extends directors' discretion, it likewise also extends the protective scope of the business judgment rule.

Finally, following the introduction of the *società benefit* model, some scholars questioned whether this new legal form effectively precludes traditional companies from considering altruistic objectives. Specifically, after 2016, could a company seeking to balance profit with social or environmental goals continue to operate under the conventional corporate structure, or would it be obligated to instead adopt the *società benefit* status? In short, the dominant scholarly consensus rejects the idea of an absolute restriction, asserting that non-benefit corporations remain capable of incorporating altruistic considerations into their governance frameworks.[38]

F. 'Sustainable success' in the Corporate Governance Code for listed companies

The evolving discourse on sustainability in corporate governance is also confirmed by the Corporate Governance Code for listed companies. The revised 2020 version introduces the concept of 'sustainable success' in Principle 1(I) on the 'Role of the board of directors'.[39] Principle 1(I) emphasises the role of the board of directors in guiding the company toward 'sustainable success', which is defined as the creation of long-term value for the

38 The main advantage of the benefit corporation "*appears to be on communication grounds, for the recourse to this form of company is a potent signal of the company's commitment to the care of stakeholder interests and social values, in addition to the pursuit of profit which remains a core component of corporate purpose also in benefit corporations*": Gilson/Isaksson/Lidman/Munck/Sjöman/Ferrarini/Zhu, p. 469 (486).

39 Callegari/Cerrato/Desana/Siri, p. 326.

benefit of the shareholders, taking into account the interests of other stakeholders relevant to the company. 'Sustainable success' must be embedded in the company's strategies, including those of any corporate group to which the company belongs.[40] Furthermore, according to Principle 1(IV), the board of directors is required to promote dialogue with shareholders and other stakeholders relevant to the company, "*in the most appropriate way*".

The Corporate Governance Code operates on a 'comply or explain' approach.[41] Principle 1 is meant to serve as a signal to capital markets, particularly to international investors who increasingly prioritise companies' ESG performances, indicating the company's awareness of sustainability-related matters.

Also, principle 1 aligns with the latest version of the *G20/OECD Principles of Corporate Governance* (2023), particularly with Chapter VI, which is dedicated to business sustainability and resilience, and it also follows the path set by foreign corporate governance traditions of 'enlightened shareholder value'.[42] The principle also aligns with the Italian constitutional framework; Article 41 of the Constitution safeguards business freedom while imposing limits to ensure compliance with social utility and the protection of the environment, as well as human health, security, and dignity.[43]

In the end, rather than altering the company's interest, the approach of Principle 1 of the Corporate Governance Code reshapes directors' duties by requiring a long-term perspective while granting them greater discretion in considering environmental and social factors. Directors of Italian listed companies then:

1) *May* consider the interests of stakeholders and support the associated costs when a cost-benefit analysis demonstrates that such actions will positively influence the company's long-term value (e.g., by enhancing its market reputation or making it more attractive to sustainability-con-

40 Among the earliest comments on the legislative amendment, see, *ex multis*, Alpa Contr. impr. 2020, 567 and Ventoruzzo Soc. 2020, 439.

41 *Ex multis*, Birkmose/Neville/Sørensen/Siri/Gargantini, p. 85.

42 The Principle, in particular, recalls the wording of Section 1 of the English Corporate Governance Code, as amended in 2018.

43 Assonime, Doveri degli amministratori e sostenibilità. Rapporto Assonime, Note e studi, No. 6, 18 March 2021. On Article 41, Italian Constitution and business sustainability see Cariello ODC 2022, 428 and Cerrato AGE 2022, 101.

scious investors),[44] and these decisions will be protected by the business judgment rule;

2) *Must* take sustainability factors into account when the risks of neglecting them could harm the company's value and its long-term profitability.

As a result, any lingering resistance to the compatibility between profit-making and sustainability concerns effectively fades.

G. Final remarks: Sustainability and directors' duty of care

An analysis of the ongoing debate regarding company interest in Italy shows that the legal framework allows for the consideration of sustainability concerns through two avenues. The first avenue is through shareholder decision. Shareholder decisions can introduce sustainability concerns as a company interest. This could be done in two main ways: either by establishing the company as a benefit corporation (*società benefit*), thereby integrating profit-oriented objectives with the pursuit of additional social or environmental goal(s), or by including altruistic elements in the bylaws of non-benefit companies; these altruistic elements orient the actions of directors but do not modify the company's fundamental purpose to be profit-driven.

The second avenue allows directors to consider sustainability concerns, even in the absence of a shareholder decision. Directors *can* indeed consider stakeholders' interests when pursuing the profit-making purpose of the company – which, as previously discussed, extends beyond shareholders' interests (and differs from that of the majority shareholders)[45] – whenever they determine that including sustainability efforts contributes to the profit-making ability or long-term value of the company. This aligns with the predominant institutionalist theories, which emphasise long-term value creation.

However, the latest debate on corporate sustainability has shifted attention from directors' fiduciary duty to their duty of care, and it becomes necessary to make some further considerations. First, despite potential slow-

44 Consequently, it increases directors' freedom in managing the company: Calvosa Riv. soc. 2022, 318; Tombari (fn.1), 14.

45 Cian Riv. soc. 2021, 449 (502).

downs due to the latest international political events, legislative attention to the socio-environmental impact of business activities is unlikely to be reversed. Instead, companies across the European Union are expected to face increased sustainability compliance requirements, particularly concerning environmental sustainability, which includes bans on production activities deemed harmful to ecosystems and the climate. Second, regardless of the regulatory landscape, environmental risks – especially climate-related risks – have become potential *financial* risks for companies even in a pure 'profit-centric' vision.[46] As a result, companies must account for environmental risks in terms of financial impact, irrespective of shareholders' or directors' ethical preferences.

Moreover, sustainability is gaining importance among consumers, employees, and investors. Even banks in the EU now consider climate risk when assessing company creditworthiness.[47] As a result, environmental sustainability has transcended mere regulatory compliance; it has become a strategic business imperative, not just in terms of economic opportunity, but also as a crucial element of risk management. The ecological transition and the effects of climate change represent today's exogenous risk factors that affect all businesses, with significant economic implications.[48] This is particularly relevant for companies operating in Italy, as it is a country that is increasingly vulnerable due to climate-related disasters such as floods and droughts.[49]

If environmental risks lead to cost increases, they must be incorporated into the corporate risk management function, which traditionally falls within the board's responsibility. Consequently, these risks should be addressed both in the company's internal management and control systems, as outlined in Article 2086 of the Civil Code,[50] and in organisational models for preventing environmental crimes under Legislative Decree No. 231/2001.[51] From this perspective, diligent directors can no longer ignore the environmental impact of business activities. At the very least, they must equip

46 Lucarelli/Santoni/Lenzi (fn. 25), p. 122.

47 In Italy, see Lener/Lucantoni BBTC 2023, 8; for an international perspective, amongst the most recent contributions, see Auzepy/Bannier.

48 Genovese.

49 CMCC Foundation, *Analisi del rischio. I cambiamenti climatici in Italia*, 2020, at https://www.cmcc.it/it/analisi-del-rischio-i-cambiamenti-climatici-in-italia.

50 Lucarelli/Santoni/Santoni, p. 107.

51 For environmental crimes, see Article 25-*undecies*, Legislative Decree No. 231/2001. See also, Maugeri ODC 2014, 1.

themselves to understand and assess the environmental profile of their specific business operations to make informed management decisions.

In conclusion, while company interest in Italy retains the traditional definition that companies will be profit-driven *stricto sensu* (or mutualistic in the case of cooperatives), the evolving legal framework – especially sustainability reporting obligations[52] – imposes new responsibilities on directors. They are now required to consider and act upon information that may influence the company's profitability, which includes 'material' sustainability information.

Furthermore, depending on the specific characteristics of the business, directors' duty of care requires to integrate sustainability considerations into strategic planning. For instance, in energy procurement strategies, the phase-out of fossil fuel-based energy sources represents a critical issue that directors of energy-intensive companies cannot afford to overlook. However, an unresolved question persists: are directors obligated to act today to address a foreseeable, yet not immediately urgent, issue? For non-listed companies, there is no direct equivalent of Principle 1 of the Corporate Governance Code, which mandates a long-term perspective. However, Article 2086 of the Civil Code and Article 2 of the new Bankruptcy Code[53] offers some guidance for non-listed companies. The new Bankruptcy Code calls for a 12-month financial sustainability outlook (Article 2), which also applies to corporate governance structures under Article 2086 of the Civil Code. This suggests that diligent directors must evaluate relevant risks and regulatory developments at least annually.[54] In conclusion, a director of any type of corporation must integrate (at least) environmental impact assessments into profit-driven decision-making. The intensity of this integration will vary depending on the type of activity carried out, the industrial sector, and other relevant factors in accordance with the risk management function. In conclusion, for all corporations besides *società benefit,* the ultimate goal remains profitability, albeit with a long-term horizon of at least twelve months.

---

52 See Legislative Decree 6 September 2024, No. 125 on corporate sustainability reporting obligations, implementing the Corporate Sustainability Reporting Directive (CSRD – Directive EU 2022/2464). Assonime, La nuova disciplina sugli obblighi di rendicontazione e informativa societaria in materia di sostenibilità, Circolare No. 21, 7 November 2024.

53 Legislative Decree 12 January 2019, No. 14.

54 Lucarelli/Santoni/Lenzi (fn. 25), p. 134.

References

Alpa, Il nuovo codice della "corporate governance" delle società quotate, Contr. e impr. 2020, 567

Angelici, Divagazioni sulla responsabilità sociale dell'impresa, Riv. Soc. 2018, 3

Angelici, La società per azioni e gli "altri", in L'interesse sociale tra valorizzazione del capitale e protezione degli stakeholders. In ricordo di Pier Giusto Jaeger, 1st ed., Milano 2010, p. 45

Angelici, La società per azioni: principi e problemi, in Cicu/Messineo (eds.) Trattato di diritto civile e commerciale, Milano 2012

Angelici, Note minime sull'interesse sociale, Banca borsa 2014, I, p. 25

Angelici, Responsabilità sociale dell'impresa, codici etici e autodisciplina, Giur. comm. 2011, I, 159

Angelici, Società benefit, in De Donno/Ventura (eds.), Dalla benefit corporation alla società benefit, Bari 2018, p. 19

Asquini, I battelli del Reno, in Scritti, III, Padova 1961

Assonime, Doveri degli amministratori e sostenibilità. Rapporto Assonime, Note e studi, No. 6, 18 March 2021, at https://www.assonime.it/attivita-editoriale/studi/Pagine/Note-e-Studi-6_2021.aspx (last accessed: 14 February 2025)

Assonime, La disciplina delle società benefit. Circolare No. 19, 20 June 2016, https://www.assonime.it/attivita-editoriale/circolari/Pagine/266544.aspx (last accessed: 14 February 2025)

Assonime, La nuova disciplina sugli obblighi di rendicontazione e informativa societaria in materia di sostenibilità, Circolare No. 21, 7 November 2024, at https://www.assonime.it/attivita-editoriale/circolari/Pagine/Circolare-21_2024.aspx (last accessed: 14 February 2025)

Auzepy/Bennier, Integrating Climate Risks in Bank Risk Management and Capital Requirements, 1st ed., Berlin, 2025

Barcellona, Shareholderism versus stakeholderism. La società per azioni contemporanea dinanzi al "profitto", 1st ed., Milano 2022

Bigiavi, Difesa dell'imprenditore commerciale occulto, Padova 1962

Buonocore, Le società, in Iudica/Zatti (eds.), Trattato di diritto privato, Milano, 2000

Calagna, La nuova disciplina della 'Società Benefit': profili normativi e incertezze applicative, RDS 2016, 709

Calvosa, La *governance* delle società quotate italiane nella transizione verso la sostenibilità e la digitalizzazione, Riv. soc. 2022, 318

Campobasso G.F., Diritto commerciale. II. Diritto delle società, 9th ed., Torino 2015

Cariello, Per un diritto costituzionale della sostenibilità (oltre la "sostenibilità ambientale"), ODC 2022, 428

Carrabba, Scopo di lucro e autonomia privata, 1st ed., Napoli 1994

Cerrato, Appunti per una "via italiana" all'ESG: l'impresa "costituzionalmente solidale" (anche alla luce dei nuovi artt. 9 e 41, comma 3, Cost.), AGE 2022, 101

Cian, Clausole statutarie per la sostenibilità dell'impresa: spazi, limiti e implicazioni, Riv. soc. 2021, 449

CMCC Foundation, Analisi del rischio. I cambiamenti climatici in Italia, 2020, at https://www.cmcc.it/it/analisi-del-rischio-i-cambiamenti-climatici-in-italia (last accessed: 14 February 2025)

Cordeiro Guerra/Lenzi, Il bilanciamento tra scopo lucrativo e beneficio comune nelle società benefit. Profili fiscali e societari, Riv. tel. dir. trib. 2021, 1

Corso, Le società benefit nell'ordinamento italiano: una nuova 'qualifica' tra profit e non-profit, NLCC 2016, 995

Cossu, *Stakeholders Theory*, obiettivi ESG e interesse sociale, ODC 2023, 783

Costi, Sostenibilità e scopo della società, Banca impr. 2023, 503

Cottino, Contrattualismo e istituzionalismo, Riv. soc. 2005, 693

D'Alessandro, Il diritto delle società da "i battelli del Reno" alle "navi vichinghe", Foro It. 1988, V, 48

Denozza, Quattro variazioni sul tema: "Contratto, impresa e società nel pensiero di Carlo Angelici", Giur. comm. 2013, I, 480

Denozza/Stabilini, La società benefit nell'era dell'*investor capitalism*, ODC 2017, 1

Di Sabato, Società in generale, in Perlingieri P. (ed.), Trattato di diritto civile del Consiglio Nazionale del Notariato, Napoli 2005

Enriques, Il conflitto d'interessi degli amministratori di società per azioni, 1st ed., Milano 2000

Ferrara/Corsi, Gli imprenditori e le società, 14th ed., Milano 2009

Ferrarini, Lo scopo delle società tra valore dell'impresa e valore sociale, Riv. soc. 2023, 317

Ferrarini, Redefining Corporate Purpose: Sustainability as a Game Changer, in Busch/Ferrarini/Grünewald (eds.), Sustainable Finance in Europe. Corporate Governance, Financial Stability and Financial Markets, Cham 2021, p. 85

Ferrarini/Zhu, Is There a Role for Benefit Corporations in the New Sustainable Governance Framework?, in Gilson/Isaksson/Lidman/Munck/Sjöman, *Festschrift for Rolf Skog*, Stockholm, 2021, p. 469

Galgano, Diritto commerciale. Le società, 16th ed., Bologna 2006

Genovese, La gestione ecosostenibile dell'impresa azionaria. Fra regole e contesto, 1st ed., Bologna 2023

Jaeger, Interesse sociale, 1st ed., Milano 1964

Jaeger, L'interesse sociale rivisitato (quarant'anni dopo), Giur. comm. 2000, I, 795

Lener/Lucantoni, Sostenibilità ESG e attività bancaria, Banca Borsa 2023, 8

Lenzi, La gestione del rischio di danno ambientale per le società di capitali, in Cerrato (ed.), Impresa e rischio. Profili giuridici del risk management, Torino 2019, p. 233

Lenzi, Rischio di danno ambientale e obbligo di diligenza nell'agire amministrativo, in Lucarelli/Santoni (eds.), Questione ambiente. Itinerari giuridici per l'impresa, vol. I, Pisa 2024, p. 121

Lenzi, Le società benefit, Giur. comm. 2016, I, 894

Lenzi, Sostenibilità delle imprese e dichiarazioni non finanziarie, Corp. Gov. 2022, 159

Libertini, Ancora in tema di contratto, impresa e società. Un commento a Francesco Denozza, in difesa dell'"istituzionalismo debole", Giur. comm. 2014, I, 669

Libertini, Impresa e finalità sociali. Riflessioni sulla teoria della responsabilità sociale di impresa, Riv. soc. 2009, 1

Lupoi, L'attività delle società benefit, in Riv. not. 2016, 811

Marasà, Società in generale, in Iudica/Zatti (eds.), Trattato di diritto privato, Milano 2000

Maugeri, Note in tema di doveri degli amministratori nel governo del rischio d'impresa (non bancaria), ODC 2014, 1

Maugeri, Informazione non finanziaria e interesse sociale, Riv. soc. 2019, 992

Mengoni, Appunti per una revisione della teoria del conflitto di interesse nelle deliberazioni dell'assemblea delle società per azioni, Riv. soc. 1956, 455

Mignoli, L'interesse sociale, Riv. soc. 1958, 725

Minervini, Sulla tutela dell'"interesse sociale" nella disciplina delle delibere assembleari e di consiglio, Riv. dir. civ. 1956, I, 332

Montalenti, Interesse sociale e amministratori, in L'interesse sociale tra valorizzazione del capitale e protezione degli stakeholders. In ricordo di Pier Giusto Jaeger, 1st ed., Milano 2010, p. 81

Mosco, Scopo e oggetto nell'impresa sociale e nella società benefit, AGE 2018, 81

Oppo, Pubblico e privato nelle società partecipate, in Oppo (ed.), Scritti giuridici, VII, Padova 2005, p. 346

Oppo, Sull'impatto sistematico della riforma del diritto societario, in Oppo (ed.), Scritti Giuridici, VII, Padova 2005, p. 302

Pacchi, Gli interessi degli amministratori e i limiti ai loro poteri, Giur. comm. 2004, I, 680

Palmieri, L'interesse sociale: dallo *shareholder value* alle società *benefit*, BIS 2017, 201

Porzio, ...Allo scopo di dividerne gli utili, Giur. comm 2014, I, 661

Prataviera, Società benefit e responsabilità degli amministratori, Riv. soc. 2018, 919

Preite, Abuso di maggioranza e conflitto di interessi del socio nelle società per azioni, in Colombo/Portale (eds.) Trattato delle società per azioni, III, Torino 1993, p. 9

Rescigno, L'evoluzione e il ruolo dell'informazione non finanziaria fra doveri informativi e obblighi gestori, ODC 2023, 630

Rossi, L'impegno *multistakeholders* della società *benefit*, ODC 2017, 6

Sanfilippo, Tutela dell'ambiente e "assetti adeguati" dell'impresa: *compliance*, autonomia ed *enforcement*, Riv. dir. civ. 2022, 993

Santini, Il tramonto dello scopo lucrativo nelle società di capitali, Riv. dir. civ. 1973, I, 151

Santoni, La prevenzione nelle strutture amministrative dell'impresa: la cura degli assetti organizzativi, in Lucarelli/Santoni (eds.), Questione ambiente. Itinerari giuridici per l'impresa, vol. I, Pisa 2024, p. 107

Siri, La sostenibilità nei codici di autodisciplina, in Callegari/Cerrato/Desana (eds.), Governance e mercati. Studi in onore di Paolo Montalenti, Torino 2022, p. 326

Siri/Gargantini, Corporate Governance Codes, in Birkmose/Neville/Sørensen (eds.), Instruments of EU Corporate Governance: Effecting Changes in the Management of Companies in a Changing World, Alphen aan den Rijn 2023, p. 85

Spada, Dalla nozione al tipo della società per azioni, Riv. dir. civ. 1985, I, 129

Spada, Dalla trasformazione delle società alla trasformazione degli enti e oltre, in Scritti in onore di Vincenzo Buonocore, III, Milano 2005, p. 3879

Spolidoro, Interesse, funzione e finalità. Per lo scioglimento dell'abbraccio tra interesse sociale e *Business Purpose*, Riv. soc. 2022, 322

Stella Richter Jr., Corporate social responsibility, social enterprise, benefit corporation: magic of words?, Vita not. 2017, 953

Stella Richter Jr., Forma e contenuto dell'atto costitutivo della società per azioni, in Colombo/Portale, Trattato, vol. 1, Torino 2004, p. 165

Stella Richter Jr., La collegialità del consiglio di amministrazione tra ponderazione dell'interesse sociale e composizione degli interessi sociali, in Libonati (ed), Amministrazione e amministratori di società per azioni, Milano 1995, p. 275

Tombari, Corporate Power and Conflicting Interests, 1st ed., Milano 2021

Tombari, *Corporate purpose* e diritto societario: dalla "supremazia degli interessi dei soci" alla libertà di scelta dello scopo sociale?, Riv. soc. 2021, 14

Tombari, *Scopo sociale*, in Angelici/Ferri Jr./Stella Richter Jr. (eds.), Enciclopedia del diritto. I Tematici: Società, IX-2025, p. 967

Ventoruzzo, Il nuovo Codice di Corporate Governance 2020: le principali novità, Soc. 2020, 439

Ventura, Benefit corporations and circulation of models: le 'società benefit', un transplant necessario?, Contr. impr. 2016, 1141

7. The Interest of the Company in Spain: Interés Social, Corporate Purpose, and EU Sustainability Law

Lela Mélon

A. Introduction

Corporate governance, broadly defined, refers to the ensemble of legal rules, institutional practices, and normative expectations that regulate the direction and control of corporations. Corporate governance's conceptual nucleus is the contested notion of the *interest of the company*, a legal standard that guides directors' fiduciary duties and the ultimate purpose of the company. In the Anglo-American context, this concept has traditionally been interpreted through the prism of shareholder primacy, situating the maximisation of shareholder value as the exclusive or dominant corporate objective. However, in continental Europe the picture is more complex. In many jurisdictions, company law and governance practice reflect stakeholder-oriented traditions that assign weight to employees, creditors, communities, and even broader public interests.

Spain occupies a distinct place within this debate. As a civil law jurisdiction, its corporate governance system is shaped by codified law rather than judge-made doctrine, with the *Ley de Sociedades de Capital*[1] ("LSC") providing the primary statutory framework. Within the LSC, the concept of the *interés social* – often translated as "company interest" – functions as the doctrinal anchor for corporate purpose. Yet unlike in some continental systems where the concept of the company's interest is explicitly defined, the Spanish legislature has maintained a degree of deliberate ambiguity, leaving its precise content to be fleshed out by doctrine, case law, and soft law codes of governance. Scholars have debated whether this *interés social* is equivalent to shareholder value maximisation or whether it allows –

1 Real Decreto Legislativo 1/2010, de 2 de julio, por el que se aprueba el texto refundido de la Ley de Sociedades de Capital. Boletín Oficial del Estado, 161, 58460–58665.

or even requires – consideration of collective, social, and environmental interests.[2]

This ambiguity in understanding the meaning of *interés social* has become particularly salient in the last two decades, as Spain has faced successive crises – corporate scandals in the early 2000s, the financial crisis of 2008 and its aftermath, and the sovereign debt crisis that reshaped the role of state and markets. These pressures brought questions of corporate legitimacy and responsibility to the forefront. Simultaneously, European Union directives – first on shareholder rights, then on non-financial reporting, and now on sustainability due diligence – have introduced new dimensions to the interpretation of company interest. Spanish law has had to reconcile the LSC's doctrinal framework with these supranational developments, resulting in a hybrid model in which sustainability imperatives are increasingly integrated into the core of corporate governance.

Recent doctrinal contributions exemplify the transformation that is underway. Fuentes Naharro and Megías López argue that Spain is experiencing a paradigm shift through the introduction of the *Sociedad de Beneficio e Interés Común* (SBIC), a new corporate form that legally recognises sustainability and common benefit as intrinsic to corporate purpose.[3] This innovation positions Spain among the few European jurisdictions that have moved beyond soft law CSR initiatives toward embedding sustainability in statute. Viscasillas similarly highlights how climate change has entered the corporate governance agenda, pushing Spanish boards to reconcile fiduciary duties with ecological obligations.[4] Together, these developments suggest that the Spanish concept of the company's interest is evolving from a narrow financial orientation toward a broader, sustainability-infused standard.

Empirical studies reinforce this evolution, albeit unevenly. Analysis of IBEX35 companies shows a steady increase in ESG reporting and compliance, though performance is often motivated by regulatory pressure rather than voluntary adoption. Gutiérrez-Ponce and Chamizo-González find that Spanish listed firms formally disclose environmental, social, and governance information but often treat such disclosures as compliance exercises

2 Fuentes Naharro, M., & Megías López, J. (2023). Sustainability in Spanish company law: State of the art and a special reference to the new SBIC (Sociedad de beneficio e interés común). *European Company Case Law (ECCL).*

3 Ibid.

4 Viscasillas, P. P. (2023). Climate change and corporate governance in Spain. ex/ante.

rather than substantive reorientations of the company's interest.[5] This compliance-driven view mirrors concerns across Europe: the challenge lies not in the presence of ESG language but rather in ensuring that sustainability is embedded in decision-making rather than relegated to peripheral reporting.

Spain is also notable for its ownership and governance structure, which complicates the sustainability debate. Corporate ownership is highly concentrated in Spain, with family-controlled firms, cross-shareholdings, and state-influenced entities dominating the landscape. Leech and Manjón demonstrated the enduring influence of blockholders in Spanish listed companies, the presence of which complicates the diffusion of shareholder primacy as an ideology.[6] Instead, with concentrated ownership, corporations often pursue long-term, relational strategies which theoretically can align with sustainability goals but also create risks of entrenchment and opacity. Family business governance in particular is central to the Spanish model, which shapes both the interpretation of the company's interest and the practice of corporate responsibility.[7]

The interplay of law, ownership structure, and European integration makes Spain a compelling case for examining the redefinition of the company's interest. Unlike Slovenia, where constitutional and historical legacies of self-management explain a stakeholder orientation, Spain's trajectory toward sustainability goals reflects a gradual adaptation of a shareholder-oriented legal structure influenced by EU law and domestic innovation. The *interés social* in Spain is thus a contest between competing logics: shareholder value, collective stakeholder responsibility, and the emerging framework of sustainability.

This chapter will explore the tension between these competing ideals in depth. Section 2 traces the historical evolution of Spanish corporate governance, highlighting the transition from Francoist corporatism to democratic codification and the role of family firms. Section 3 examines the legal framework of the LSC and associated soft law, focusing on how the

5 Gutiérrez-Ponce, H., & Chamizo-González, J. (2022). *Disclosure of environmental, social, and corporate governance information by Spanish companies: A compliance analysis.* Sustainability, 14(6), 3254.

6 Leech, D., & Manjón, M. (2002). Corporate governance in Spain (ownership and control in listed companies). Universidad Rovira i Virgili.

7 Lagos Cortés, D., & Botero, I. C. (2016). Corporate governance in family businesses from Latin America, Spain and Portugal: A review of the literature. *Academia Revista Latinoamericana de Administración, 29*(3), 231–254.

company's interest is defined and contested. Section 4 analyses ownership structures and empirical patterns of governance in crisis, drawing on studies of boards and performance. Section 5 situates Spain within the EU dimension, examining how EU sustainability directives reshape Spanish domestic law. Section 6 addresses the challenges of financialisation and political capture, particularly regarding the governance of banks and *cajas de ahorro*. Section 7 theorises Spain's juridical framework of sustainable governance, emphasising social, environmental, and institutional sustainability. Section 8 concludes by positioning Spain's model within broader European debates, arguing that the Spanish experience illustrates the possibilities and limits of integrating sustainability into company law in a system marked by concentrated ownership and soft law traditions.

By analysing the Spanish case, this chapter contributes to the comparative scholarship on the company's interest in Europe. It demonstrates that the "interest of the company" is neither static nor monolithic but evolves in response to crises, legal reforms, and supranational pressures. Spain, with its hybrid legal framework and distinctive ownership patterns, provides a laboratory for understanding how sustainability can be embedded in company law – not as an external appendage but as part of the very definition of the company's interest.

B. Historical Context: From Corporatism to Europeanisation

The historical development of corporate governance in Spain cannot be understood without reference to its broader political and economic transformations. Spanish corporate law evolved in tandem with the country's shift from authoritarianism to democracy, its transition from a protectionist to a market economy, and its integration into the European Union. These shifts shaped not only the structure of corporate ownership but also the legal and normative interpretation of the "interest of the company".

I. Corporatist Foundations under Francoism (1939–1975)

Under the Franco regime (1939–1975), a form of state-led corporatism was engrained in Spanish corporate law; private enterprises coexisted with significant government control over strategic sectors, tight regulatory oversight, and a paternalistic approach to labour. While private property remained formally recognized, the role of a corporation was seen as an instrument of national economic policy and social cohesion as opposed to that of a profit-generating vehicle.[8] As such, the idea of a company having a broader social function – *interés general* – predates the rise of sustainability discussions in Spain.

During this period, boards of directors often functioned more as extensions of political and familial networks than as professional managerial organs. Legal mechanisms for shareholder protection were underdeveloped and capital markets were weak.[9] The lack of a dynamic investor class allowed business elites to concentrate ownership and control across generations. This created a legacy of family-dominated governance and lack of transparency by boards that persists in many areas of Spanish corporate life today.[10]

II. Transition to Democracy and Legal Codification

Following Franco's death in 1975 and the adoption of the Spanish Constitution in 1978, Spain entered a period of rapid democratisation and economic liberalisation. The new constitutional order emphasized economic pluralism, property rights, and the social function of enterprise. Article 38 of the Constitution guarantees freedom of enterprise within the framework of a market economy, while Article 128 emphasizes the subordination of all economic activity to the general interest – a duality that continues to shape interpretations of the "interest of the company".[11]

In legal terms, gradual consolidation of corporate law through updates to the Commercial Code and the eventual promulgation of the *Ley de*

8 Foweraker, J. (1987). Corporatist strategies and the transition to democracy in Spain. *Comparative Politics, 20*(1), 57–72.

9 Guillén, M. F. (2000). Corporate governance and globalization: Is there convergence across countries? *Advances in International Comparative Management*, 13, 175–204.

10 Villanueva-Villar, M., Rivo-López, E., & Lago-Peñas, S. (2016). On the relationship between corporate governance and value creation in an economic crisis: Empirical evidence for the Spanish case. *Business Research Quarterly, 19*(4), 233–245.

11 Constitución Española, Boletín Oficial del Estado, núm. 311, 29 de diciembre de 1978 (Esp.).

Sociedades Anónimas (LSA)[12] and *Ley de Sociedades de Responsabilidad Limitada (LSRL)*[13] marked this period of transition. These two regimes coexisted until the enactment of the *Ley de Sociedades de Capital (LSC)* in 2010, which unified and modernised Spanish company law.[14] The LSC (Real Decreto Legislativo 1/2010) remains the cornerstone of corporate governance in Spain, codifying key provisions on director duties, shareholder rights, and the structure of corporate organs.

Importantly, the LSC reflects a hybrid model: it draws inspiration from the shareholder-centred Anglo-American model but operates within a civil law framework that allows broader doctrinal interpretation. The *interés social* (Article 225), while not explicitly defined, is widely interpreted as requiring loyalty to the company itself as a legal person, not merely to the shareholders.[15]

III. The Persistence of Family Business Governance

One of the defining characteristics of Spanish corporate life is the central role of family-owned firms. More than 85 % of Spanish businesses are family-owned, including many listed firms and companies of systemic importance.[16] This pattern is not merely a legacy of the Franco era, but a feature that is embedded in the structure of Spain's corporate economy.

Lagos Cortés and Botero describe the governance of Spanish family firms as combining formal legal mechanisms with informal social controls, such as family protocols, succession agreements, and intergenerational trust structures.[17] Although the boards of such firms often include both family members and external professionals, decision-making power typically remains concentrated within the family.

---

12 Ley 19/1989, de 25 de julio, de reforma parcial y adaptación de la legislación mercantil a las Directivas de la CEE en materia de sociedades (modifica la *Ley de Sociedades Anónimas*). BOE núm. 178, de 27 de julio de 1989, pp. 22797–22817 (España).

13 Ley 2/1995, de 23 de marzo, de Sociedades de Responsabilidad Limitada. Boletín Oficial del Estado, núm. 71, de 24 de marzo de 1995, pp. 8575–8599 (España).

14 Real Decreto Legislativo 1/2010, de 2 de julio, por el que se aprueba el texto refundido de la *Ley de Sociedades de Capital*, BOE núm. 161, de 3 de julio de 2010, pp. 58472–58594 (España).

15 Ibid.

16 Hoverd, L. (2025, July 9). The 10 largest family businesses in Madrid. Tharawat Magazine. Retrieved from https://www.tharawat-magazine.com/facts/largest-family-businesses-madrid/, last accessed on 01.09.2025.

17 Cortés and Botero (n7).

While this can foster long-term strategic thinking and social cohesion, it also raises challenges for minority shareholder protection, board independence, and accountability – especially in times of crisis or succession.[18]

The prevalence of family governance also influences the interpretation of the company's interest. In many cases, *interés social* is understood not in shareholder value terms, but as the long-term viability of the family firm, including its reputation, employment role, and intergenerational sustainability.[19] This culturally-embedded notion of fiduciary responsibility aligns in some respects with stakeholder theory, though it is not always consistent with transparency or regulatory compliance.[20]

IV. Post-Crisis Governance Reform and EU Harmonisation

Spain's experience with the 2008 financial crisis and subsequent sovereign debt crisis played a crucial role in reshaping the discourse surrounding corporate governance. Failures in the governance of *cajas de ahorro* (savings banks), excessive risk-taking in real estate-linked financial institutions, and cases of accounting manipulation (e.g., Bankia) exposed weaknesses in Spain's soft law approach to governance.[21] These events prompted the Spanish government and the CNMV (*Comisión Nacional del Mercado de Valores*) to strengthen corporate governance standards and align more closely with EU norms.

The 2014 revision of the Código de Buen Gobierno de las Sociedades Cotizadas (Good Governance Code for Listed Companies) emphasised board independence, diversity, and the role of audit and risk committees.[22] More significantly, Spain began transposing EU directives on non-financial

18 Ibid.

19 Schroeder, D., & Thomsen, S. (2022). *Foundation Ownership and Sustainability: International Evidence.* ECGI. Retrieved from the ECGI website: https://www.ecgi.global/sites/default/files/Paper%3A%20David%20Schroeder%2C%20Steen%20Thomsen.pdf.

20 La Porta, R., López-de-Silanes, F., & Shleifer, A. (1999). *Corporate ownership around the world. The Journal of Finance, 54*(2), 471–517.

21 International Monetary Fund. (2012). Spain: The reform of Spanish savings banks – Technical notes. IMF.

22 Comisión Nacional del Mercado de Valores. (2015). *Código de buen gobierno de las sociedades cotizadas.* Madrid: CNMV. Retrieved from https://www.cnmv.es/DocPortal/Publicaciones/CodigoGov/Codigo_buen_gobierno.pdf.

disclosure and shareholder rights into their national law, integrating sustainability concerns into mandatory reporting and board oversight.[23]

These reforms reflected not only a response to crisis, but also a broader process of Europeanisation. Spain, as an EU Member State, is bound by the Corporate Sustainability Reporting Directive (CSRD)[24] and the forthcoming Corporate Sustainability Due Diligence Directive (CSDDD),[25] as well as the EU Taxonomy.[26] As Martín and Fuentes Naharro & Megías López note, these directives have already begun to influence the interpretive scope of *interés social*, moving it beyond shareholder protection and toward environmental and social impact accountability.[27]

V. Doctrinal and Constitutional Ambiguity

While Spain has made significant strides toward modernising its governance framework, it retains a degree of doctrinal ambiguity regarding the company's interest. Unlike jurisdictions such as Germany or Slovenia,

23 European Union. (2014). *Directive 2014/95/EU of the European Parliament and of the Council of 22 October 2014 amending Directive 2013/34/EU as regards disclosure of non-financial and diversity information by certain large undertakings and groups. Official Journal of the European Union, L 330*, 1–9, https://eur-lex.europa.eu/legal-content/EN/TXT/?uri=CELEX%3A32014L0095; Gobierno de España. (2018). *Ley 11/2018, de 28 de diciembre, por la que se modifica el Código de Comercio, el texto refundido de la Ley de Sociedades de Capital aprobado por el Real Decreto Legislativo 1/2010, de 2 de julio, y la Ley 22/2015, de 20 de julio, de Auditoría de Cuentas, en materia de información no financiera y diversidad. Boletín Oficial del Estado, núm. 314*, de 29 de diciembre de 2018, 129168–129194. https://www.boe.es/buscar/doc.php?id=BOE-A-2018-17989.

24 Directive (EU) 2022/2464 of the European Parliament and of the Council of 14 December 2022 amending Regulation (EU) No 537/2014, Directive 2004/109/EC, Directive 2006/43/EC and Directive 2013/34/EU, as regards corporate sustainability reporting. Official Journal of the European Union, L 322, 16 December 2022, p. 15–43.

25 Corporate Sustainability Due Diligence Directive (CSDDD)
Directive (EU) 2024/1760 of the European Parliament and of the Council of 13 June 2024 on corporate sustainability due diligence and amending Directive (EU) 2019/1937 and Regulation (EU) 2023/2859. Official Journal of the European Union, L 168, 19 June 2024, p. 1–48.

26 Regulation (EU) 2020/852 of the European Parliament and of the Council of 18 June 2020 on the establishment of a framework to facilitate sustainable investment, and amending Regulation (EU) 2019/2088, Official Journal of the European Union, L 198, 22 June 2020, p. 13–43.

27 Fuentes Naharro and Megías López (n2); La Porta et al (n20).

where the country's constitutional or statutory frameworks explicitly define stakeholder rights, the Spanish system relies more heavily on judicial interpretation and soft law guidance.[28]

The Spanish Constitution provides a potential foundation for embedding sustainability within corporate governance. Article 45 enshrines the right to a healthy environment, while Article 33 recognises the social function of property.[29] However, these constitutional principles have not yet been interpreted in corporate case law to support a stakeholder-oriented understanding of the company's interest. Instead, sustainability has entered Spanish corporate law largely through EU directives and their transposition into national legislation,[30] rather than through domestic constitutional or doctrinal development.

This disconnect between constitutional potential and legislative practice creates both a vulnerability and an opportunity. On the one hand, the absence of a clear constitutional commitment to stakeholder governance allows space for short-termism and opportunistic behaviour. On the other hand, it opens the door for creative legal interpretation, judicial innovation, and academic advocacy to anchor sustainability more firmly within Spain's corporate law framework.[31]

C. The Legal Framework of Corporate Purpose: Interpreting Interés Social *in Spain's Statutory and Normative Framework*

I. Introduction

Following Spain's historical transition from state corporatism to European integration, the legal architecture of the company's interest has remained marked by ambiguity. Central to this framework is the concept of *interés social* – the statutory standard that guides director conduct under Article

28 Embid Irujo, J. M., & Del Val Talens, P. (2016). *La responsabilidad social corporativa y el Derecho de sociedades de capital: entre la regulación legislativa y el soft law*. Agencia Estatal Boletín Oficial del Estado.

29 España. Constitución Española de 1978, Boletín Oficial del Estado, núm. 311, 29 de diciembre de 1978. https://www.boe.es/eli/es/c/1978/12/27/(1).

30 Gutiérrez-Ponce et al (n5).

31 Fuentes Naharro and Megías López (n2).

225.2 of the Ley de Sociedades de Capital (LSC).[32] While the doctrinal significance of *interés social* is indisputable, its legal meaning is contestable.

This section examines how the Spanish legal system conceptualises and operationalises *interés social* in the absence of a precise statutory definition. Building on the historical and ownership context outlined in sections B and D, it argues that *interés social* operates as a legal placeholder, whose content is increasingly shaped by a layered legal framework. This framework is made up of codified ambiguity, interpretive doctrine, soft law guidance, and transposed EU obligations. The Spanish case, as we shall see, offers a unique instance of legal evolution – not through top-down redefinition, but through the gradual accrual of norms and through institutional experimentation.[33]

II. The LSC's Doctrinal Ambiguity: A Constructive Indeterminacy?

Article 225.2 LSC stipulates that directors must act "in the interest of the company", yet it offers no formal clarification as to what constitutes that interest.[34] This statutory silence has opened a doctrinal field characterized by competing theories:

- shareholder-oriented interpretations, influenced by Anglo-American models, define *interés social* as equivalent to shareholder value maximisation;[35]
- entity-based theories treat the company as a distinct legal subject, emphasising its integrity, solvency, and operational continuity;[36] and
- stakeholder-inclusive interpretations, increasingly present in academic commentary and policy discourse, include social, environmental, and governance considerations in directors' duties.[37]

Rather than resolving this ambiguity, Spanish lawmakers have preserved it as a form of constructive indeterminacy, enabling *interés social* to evolve

32 *See* n14.

33 Fuentes Naharro and Megías López (n2).

34 *See* n14.

35 Alfaro Águila-Real, J. (2016). *El interés social y los deberes de lealtad de los administradores. Anuario de la Facultad de Derecho de la UAM, 20,* 213–236.

36 Embid Irujo and Del Val Talens (n28).

37 Apalategui, J. M. C. (2024). *La indeterminación intencional en el derecho.* Revista de la Facultad de Derecho de la Universidad de Deusto, (27).

in line with external pressures and evolving norms. This differs notably from the German model, where the company's interest is interpreted through statutory frameworks and institutionalised stakeholder representation via co-determination, and from Slovenia, where post-socialist legal development has produced more explicit constitutional orientation toward stakeholder governance.[38]

III. The Evolving Legal Content of *Interés Social*: Sectoral Reforms and Sustainability Mandates

The doctrinal vacuum of the LSC has gradually been filled by sector-specific legislation that indirectly redefines what constitutes lawful and legitimate corporate behaviour, such as the following:

- the Ley de Economía Sostenible (2011) links corporate activity to environmental and social objectives;[39]
- the Ley de Sociedades Laborales y Participadas (2015) embeds worker participation in corporate governance;[40]
- the Ley de Cambio Climático y Transición Energética (2021) mandates business alignment with climate goals;[41] and
- the Ley de Transparencia (2013) broadens the scope of disclosure beyond financial information and shareholder accountability.[42]

Although these statutes do not directly redefine *interés social*, they expand its content by linking the company's interest to social utility, environmental alignment, and participatory governance. As Martín argues, these developments reflect a growing normative convergence between sustainability and fiduciary responsibility. Compared to jurisdictions like the UK, where Section 172 of the Companies Act of 2006 introduces "enlightened shareholder

38 Djokić, D. (2009). *The Corporate Governance Statement and Audit Committee in the European Union and Republic of Slovenia.* CYELP, 5, 283–289.

39 España. Ley 2/2011, de 4 de marzo, de Economía Sostenible. *Boletín Oficial del Estado,* núm. 55, de 5 de marzo de 2011, pp. 25033–25235.

40 España. Ley 44/2015, de 14 de octubre, de Sociedades Laborales y Participadas. *Boletín Oficial del Estado,* núm. 247, de 15 de octubre de 2015, pp. 95086–95104.

41 España. Ley 7/2021, de 20 de mayo, de Cambio Climático y Transición Energética. *Boletín Oficial del Estado,* núm. 121, de 21 de mayo de 2021, pp. 62072–62120.

42 España. Ley 19/2013, de 9 de diciembre, de Transparencia, Acceso a la Información Pública y Buen Gobierno. *Boletín Oficial del Estado,* núm. 295, de 10 de diciembre de 2013, pp. 97922–97952.

value" but remains tethered to shareholder benefit,[43] the Spanish approach offers more interpretive elasticity, while still retaining the codified core of civil law.

IV. Soft Law as Normative Glue: The Role of the CNMV

In the absence of statutory reform, the Código de Buen Gobierno de las Sociedades Cotizadas (CNMV, 2020)[44] has emerged as a pivotal interpretive tool for *interés social.* Revised in 2020, the Code introduces guidelines on long-term value creation, board independence, ESG oversight, and risk control structures. Although the Code operates on a "comply or explain" basis, empirical studies suggest that listed firms increasingly treat these norms as de facto obligations.[45]

Soft law bridges the gaps between these norms: it reconciles the LSC's formal ambiguity with emerging investor, societal, and EU expectations. This mirrors governance developments in Germany, where the *Deutscher Corporate Governance Kodex* plays a similar role,[46] albeit within a more rigid institutional architecture, and in the UK, where the UK Corporate Governance Code exerts pressure primarily through investor relations.

In Spain, however, soft law is more doctrinally significant because it fills interpretive gaps left by the LSC; soft law effectively functions as a "living commentary" on the meaning of *interés social.*

V. Institutional Innovation and the Codification of Purpose: The SBIC

The establishment of the *Sociedad de Beneficio e Interés Común* (SBIC) in 2022 marks a significant departure from the previous soft-law approach to corporate sustainability, which relied on voluntary compliance with

43 United Kingdom. Companies Act 2006, c. 46, §172. *An Act to reform company law and restate the greater part of the enactments relating to companies.* London: The Stationery Office.

44 *See* n22.

45 Gutiérrez-Ponce et al (n5).

46 Regierungskommission Deutscher Corporate Governance Kodex. (2022). *Deutscher Corporate Governance Kodex [German Corporate Governance Code].* Berlin: Regierungskommission. Retrieved from https://www.dcgk.de.

non-binding principles and reporting guidelines.[47] SBICs must incorporate social and environmental purpose into their statutes and deliver annual public reporting on their impact.[48] This statutory form mirrors international experiments such as the US Benefit Corporation[49] or France's Société à mission.[50]

Unlike traditional companies under the LSC, SBICs legally define their purpose beyond profit. This innovation positions Spain as a leader in institutionalising sustainability within corporate law, going beyond CSR rhetoric to bind companies to plural objectives. However, the effectiveness of the SBIC model will depend on uptake, enforcement, and integration into broader governance norms – a challenge also observed in countries with similar legal frameworks.[51]

VI. Conclusion: A Juridical Field in Motion

The Spanish legal framework for the company's interest presents no single authoritative doctrine. Rather, *interés social* serves as a dynamic legal construct, shaped by constitutional principles, sectoral statutes, soft law codes, and transnational norms.

This layered juridical architecture allows for gradual transformation without the disruption of holistic statutory overhaul. Yet this same flexibility invites institutional ambiguity and requires judicial, doctrinal, and governance actors to play interpretive roles. In this respect, Spain's model may offer a hybrid approach to integrating sustainability goals in the corporate governance framework, situated between the rigid codification of the German model and the voluntary compliance of Anglo-Saxon jurisdictions.

As European directives on sustainability due diligence and ESG integration deepen, the Spanish framework – with its civil law roots, high

47 España. Ley 18/2022, de 28 de septiembre, de creación y crecimiento de empresas. *Boletín Oficial del Estado,* núm. 234, de 29 de septiembre de 2022, pp. 125893–125952.

48 Fuentes Naharro and Megías López (n2).

49 United States. Model Benefit Corporation Legislation. (2016). *Benefit Corporation White Paper.* B Lab. Retrieved from https://benefitcorp.net/for-legal-professionals/model-legislation.

50 France. Loi n° 2019–486 du 22 mai 2019 relative à la croissance et la transformation des entreprises (Loi PACTE). *Journal Officiel de la République Française,* 23 mai 2019.

51 Martínez, B., & Fontrodona, J. (2024). *Benefit corporations y sociedades de beneficio e interés colectivo: un movimiento en auge* (Cuaderno n.º 59). Cátedra CaixaBank de Sostenibilidad e Impacto Social, IESE Business School.

ownership concentration, and plural legal instruments – provides fertile ground for observing how sustainability as a goal becomes codified, not merely an aspect of business to be reported on. Whether *interés social* will evolve into a truly stakeholder-oriented legal standard remains to be seen, but the direction of reform is increasingly clear: the company's interest in Spain is being redefined not through revolution, but through layered legal evolution.

D. Ownership, Control, and Crisis: The Company's Interest in the Shadow of Concentrated Power

In the doctrinal architecture of Spanish company law, *interés social* is flexible: ambiguous enough to absorb evolving sustainability imperatives but stable enough to anchor director duties in formal legality. Yet, as the preceding sections suggest, legal doctrine alone does not determine the actual trajectory of the company's interest. Ownership structures function as a deeper juridical infrastructure – shaping not only the substance of corporate governance reforms but also their capacity to evolve and take root in practice.

In Spain, corporate ownership is deeply concentrated. Whether in public firms dominated by family groups, in state-linked strategic sectors, or in the shadow of the *cajas de ahorro* collapse, concentrated control continues to shape how the company's interest is defined. This chapter contends that Spain's governance model is not merely *civil law with concentrated ownership* – but a structurally-distinct system in which legal ambiguity interacts with informal power and institutional disinterest.

To understand the limits – and the possibilities – of embedding sustainability into the actual corporate law doctrine in Spain, we must examine how concentrated ownership influences legal interpretation, board dynamics, and resistance to reform. Drawing on comparative examples from Germany and Anglo-Saxon jurisdictions, the following chapter situates Spain's tradition of corporate control as both a barrier and a potential vehicle for transformation.

I. Ownership as Infrastructure: Beyond Share Concentration

Ownership in Spain is not simply a matter of who holds how many shares – it is a socio-legal infrastructure that organises access to control, constrains the diffusion of countervailing interests, and perpetuates elite governance logics. According to Leech and Manjón, more than half of IBEX35 companies have ownership structures where a single blockholder controls over 30 % of voting rights, often through pyramid or crossholding arrangements.[52]

This is not a transitional condition on the way to dispersed Anglo-American capitalism – it is manufactured equilibrium. Spanish company law, while formally enabling shareholder equality and board independence, rarely disrupts these control configurations. Minority shareholder protections exist, but they are weakly enforced, and institutional investors have historically played a minimal role in challenging dominant blocs. The result is what scholars have called *insider governance* – a model where dominant families, state-linked entities, or crossholding conglomerates control strategic decisions through social, rather than competitive, mechanisms.[53]

II. Family Capitalism and the Temporal Logic of Purpose

Family firms represent the core of Spanish corporate culture. More than 85 % of companies are family-owned, including many listed firms.[54] But their significance lies not only in numbers but in their *temporal logic*. Family ownership often brings about long-term strategy for the firm, intergenerational planning, and embedding the firm in the local community, all of which *could* align with sustainability imperatives.

Yet this alignment is conditional. Governance in family firms frequently involves informal institutions – succession protocols, family councils, cross-generational mentorships – that exist outside of formal legal channels. While these practices can foster stability and loyalty, they can also obscure

52 Leech and Manjón (n6).

53 Aguilera, R. V., & Cuervo-Cazurra, A. (2004). Codes of good governance worldwide: What is the trigger? *Organization Studies*, 25(3), 415–443.

54 Instituto de la Empresa Familiar. (2015). *The Family Business in Spain 2015*. Madrid: IEF.

decision-making, limit board independence, and shield controlling interests from public accountability.[55]

Succession moments offer a rare opening: as Lagos Cortés and Botero show, sustainability commitments tend to increase when generational transfer occurs to heirs educated in international business ethics and ESG principles.[56] Yet this is uneven across sectors and highly dependent on external reputational incentives, not legal mandates.

III. Blockholder Logic and ESG Absorption

A key tension lies in the strategic logic of dominant shareholders. Blockholders in Spain – be they family owners or industrial conglomerates – are not inherently opposed to sustainability. But their ESG commitments tend to be instrumental, reputational, or defensive, not transformative.

Gutiérrez-Ponce and Chamizo-González demonstrate that while ESG disclosure among Spanish firms has risen, particularly in response to EU directives, such disclosures are often shallow, aimed at meeting regulatory expectations without altering internal governance priorities.[57] The ESG function is isolated, detached from strategic decision-making, and is rarely reflected in executive incentives or board mandates.

Such concerns are also raised across Europe, but the Spanish context amplifies them. Without pressure from dispersed shareholders or codified co-determination (as in Germany), dominant insiders face little structural incentive to integrate sustainability as a *purpose-defining* obligation.

IV. The Case of the Cajas: Governance Without Accountability

The collapse of the *cajas de ahorro* system after 2008 reveals how stakeholder governance in form can mask profound governance failure in substance. *Cajas* were structured as non-profit entities, regionally rooted and stakeholder focused. But their boards were often populated by political ap-

---

55 Amato, S., Minichilli, A., & Corbetta, G. (2023). Family firms amid the global financial crisis: Territory-embedded and employment-protective behaviors in Spain. *Journal of Business Ethics, 183*(2), 459–477. https://doi.org/10.1007/s10551-021-04930-0.

56 Cortés and Botero (n7).

57 Gutiérrez-Ponce et al (n5).

pointees who lacked financial expertise and operated with minimal external oversight.[58]

The Bankia case exposed how political interference and weak supervision frameworks permitted reckless lending, especially in the real estate sector, to spiral into a systemic crisis. The failure here was not stakeholder governance – it was the absence of legally-enforceable fiduciary standards that would balance stakeholder aims with prudential control.

Unlike Germany, where worker participation is legally mandated on corporate boards, Spain lacked binding stakeholder governance mechanisms. The *cajas* demonstrate that "plural purpose" in rhetoric, without institutional checks, can facilitate capture rather than accountability.

V. Path Dependency and the Limits of Post-Crisis Reform

In the aftermath of the crisis, Spain implemented a series of reforms – strengthening the CNMV's supervisory powers, updating the Good Governance Code, and transposing EU directives such as the Non-Financial Reporting Directive (NFRD) and the Corporate Sustainability Reporting Directive (CSRD) into domestic law. Yet these reforms operate largely through soft law, transparency obligations, and reputational mechanisms.

This contrasts sharply with Germany, where co-determination law mandates employee board representation, or with France, where *Sociétés à mission* are backed by audit and certification regimes. In Spain, the newly introduced *Sociedad de Beneficio e Interés Común* (SBIC) remains low in uptake and lacks integration into mainstream corporate governance.[59]

The path dependency of insider control limits the effectiveness of these reforms. Board diversity quotas are met formally, but decision-making remains centralised. ESG functions exist but they are isolated. Sustainability is reported but rarely governs decision-making.

58 Cuñat, V., & Garicano, L. (2010). Did good cajas extend bad loans? Governance, human capital and loan portfolios. *FEDEA Working Paper 2010-04.* Fundación de Estudios de Economía Aplicada.

59 Hopt, K. J. (2011). Comparative corporate governance: The state of the art and international regulation. *American Journal of Comparative Law, 59*(1), 1–73; Segrestin, B., Hatchuel, A., & Levillain, K. (2021). When the law distinguishes between the enterprise and the corporation: The case of the new French law on corporate purpose. *Journal of Business Ethics, 171*(1), 1–13.

VI. Comparative Reflections: Spain Between Models

Spain occupies a distinct place in the European corporate governance landscape. Unlike Germany, it lacks institutionalised stakeholder governance. Unlike Slovenia, it has no constitutional memory of self-management. Unlike the UK or the US, it does not rely on active capital markets to discipline management.

Instead, Spain's governance regime is a hybrid of legal ambiguity, network-based control, and high ownership concentration. While this configuration enables stability, it also allows for inequality of voices on the board. The regime absorbs sustainability mandates procedurally but resists substantive doctrinal transformation.

If Spain is to transition toward adopting a definition of the company's interest that takes the obligations of ecological and social sustainability seriously, it must address the deep-seeded structure of control. For Spain to address these structural issues, it must do more than transposing EU directives – it requires aligning fiduciary duties with plural purpose, democratising board structures, and recognizing that ownership *is* governance.

VII. Conclusion: Reimagining Purpose Through Control

Ownership concentration in Spain is not simply a fact – it is a system of power that defines how the company's interest is constructed, contested, and constrained. Legal doctrine may open the door for a concrete legal framework for sustainability. Nonetheless, in Spain, it is who controls the company that ultimately determines whether that space is used for transformation or co-optation.

Until the architecture of control shifts – from opaque relational blocs to accountable, plural governance – efforts to redefine the *interés social* will remain structurally constrained. In this context, sustainability becomes not a question of regulatory compliance, but of political economy.

E. The EU Dimension and Sustainability: Transposing Supranational Purpose into Spanish Corporate Law

As corporate governance frameworks across Europe undergo transformation, the EU has emerged as both a regulatory engine and a legal architect in redefining the company's interest. Through an increasingly ambitious suite of directives – ranging from non-financial disclosure and sustainable finance to mandatory human rights and environmental due diligence – the EU is not merely regulating corporate behaviour but actively reconstituting the conceptual boundaries of the business corporation.[60] In this evolving landscape, the function of the company no longer equates to private wealth generation; rather, it is being juridically recast as a socio-economic institution embedded within broader ecological and human rights frameworks.[61]

Spain stands at a critical intersection of this transformation. As a civil law jurisdiction with a legacy of concentrated ownership and path-dependent governance institutions,[62] it faces the dual challenge of complying with EU mandates while navigating the ambiguities of its own doctrinal constructs – chiefly, the open-textured nature of *interés social*.[63] The transposition of EU sustainability law into Spain's corporate legal order is not a mere technical exercise in compliance. It constitutes a deeper realignment of norms, in which previously peripheral considerations – such as environmental stewardship, stakeholder engagement, and intergenerational equity – begin to migrate toward the centre of the company's interest.[64]

This section examines how Spain is internalising the EU's sustainability turn, both legally and institutionally. It considers the evolution from the 2014 Non-Financial Reporting Directive (NFRD) to the more demanding 2022 Corporate Sustainability Reporting Directive (CSRD), as well as the emergent Corporate Sustainability Due Diligence Directive (CSDDD).[65] These instruments are analysed not only in terms of their formal implementation but also through their effects on corporate governance practices, legal interpretation, and the practical meaning of *interés social*. Spain pro-

---

60 Sjåfjell, B., & Wiesbrock, A. (Eds.). (2015). *The greening of European business under EU law: Taking article 11 TFEU seriously*. Routledge.

61 Directive (EU) 2024/1760 of the European Parliament and of the Council of 13 June 2024 on corporate sustainability due diligence and amending Directive (EU) 2019/1937 and Regulation (EU) 2023/2859 PE/9/2024/REV/1, OJ L, 2024/1760.

62 Leech and Manjón (n6).

63 Viscasillas (n4).

64 Sequeira Martín, A. (2021). *El desarrollo de la responsabilidad social corporativa versus sostenibilidad, y su relación con el gobierno corporativo en las directivas comunitarias y en el derecho español de sociedades cotizadas. Revista de Derecho de Sociedades*, (61), 39–8.

65 Consolidated text: Directive (EU) 2022/2464 of the European Parliament and of the Council of 14 December 2022 amending Regulation (EU) No 537/2014, Directive 2004/109/EC, Directive 2006/43/EC and Directive 2013/34/EU, as regards corporate sustainability reporting, ELI: http://data.europa.eu/eli/dir/2022/2464/2025-04-17.

vides a rich ground for observing the frictions and possibilities of aligning national company law with supranational regulatory ambitions.

I. From Reporting to Purpose: The Trajectory of EU Sustainability Law

The trajectory of EU corporate sustainability law has shifted decisively from transparency to transformation. Early legislative efforts, such as the Non-Financial Reporting Directive (2014/95/EU), were framed primarily as disclosure obligations, requiring certain large undertakings to report on ESG issues.[66] While this approach was significant in prompting corporations to consider non-financial dimensions of performance, it maintained a clear separation between ESG reporting and the core of the company's interest.

This separation is now eroding. The Corporate Sustainability Reporting Directive (CSRD), which entered into force in January 2023, redefines the normative foundations of corporate reporting. The CSRD expands both the scope and the depth of ESG obligations: it applies to a wider range of companies (including listed SMEs from 2026), mandates alignment with the EU Taxonomy for Sustainable Activities,[67] and requires disclosures to be integrated into management reports and verified by independent assurance providers.

For Spain, this regulatory transformation carries both technical and doctrinal implications. On the technical side, companies must adapt internal governance systems to comply with the European Sustainability Reporting Standards (ESRS).[68] But on the doctrinal level, the CSRD catalyses a shift in how *interés social* – the statutory corporate purpose under Article 225 of the Ley de Sociedades de Capital – is interpreted. No longer merely a reference to shareholder welfare or corporate solvency, *interés social* increasingly

66 Directive 2014/95/EU of the European Parliament and of the Council of 22 October 2014 amending Directive 2013/34/EU as regards disclosure of non-financial and diversity information by certain large undertakings and groups, OJ L 330, 15.11.2014.

67 Regulation (EU) 2020/852 of the European Parliament and of the Council of 18 June 2020 on the establishment of a framework to facilitate sustainable investment (EU Taxonomy), OJ L 198, 22.6.2020.

68 European Financial Reporting Advisory Group (EFRAG). (2023). *European Sustainability Reporting Standards (ESRS) Set 1.* Brussels: EFRAG.

encompasses environmental risks, social impacts, and long-term sustainability objectives as material concerns for directors' fiduciary duties.[69]

This shift builds upon Spain's earlier transposition of the NFRD through Ley 11/2018, de 28 de diciembre, which introduced binding obligations for large public-interest entities to disclose information relating to environmental matters, employee-related issues, respect for human rights, anti-corruption, and board diversity.[70] Crucially, the law required this information to be included in the management report, reinforcing the integration of ESG concerns into core corporate oversight mechanisms. Spain's relatively robust implementation positioned it among the more assertive EU Member States in embedding sustainability within its corporate governance frameworks.[71]

The CSRD extends this trajectory by reframing sustainability not merely as a reporting issue but as a governance imperative. It challenges Spanish corporate boards to reconsider their obligations under the ambiguous standard of *interés social.* Whereas historically *interés social* accommodated both shareholder-oriented and entity-based interpretations, the CSRD introduces a new regulatory logic: sustainability is no longer reputational but fiduciary.

Comparatively, Spain's path contrasts that of other EU systems. Unlike Germany, where the codetermination regime enshrines stakeholder involvement through institutional channels,[72] Spain operates without formalised worker representation in governance. At the same time, Spain has avoided the pitfalls of the UK's Section 172 "enlightened shareholder value" model, which remains legally vague and weakly enforced.[73] Instead, Spain's evolution has followed a distinct trajectory of compliance-induced convergence: the progressive juridification of sustainability via EU law in a civil law context with high ownership concentration.

---

69 Fuentes Naharro and Megías López (n2).

70 Ley 11/2018, de 28 de diciembre, por la que se modifica el Código de Comercio, el texto refundido de la Ley de Sociedades de Capital aprobado por el Real Decreto Legislativo 1/2010, de 2 de julio, y la Ley 22/2015, de Auditoría de Cuentas, en materia de información no financiera y diversidad. *Boletín Oficial del Estado*, 314, 29 de diciembre de 2018.

71 Sequeira Martín (n64).

72 Hopt, K. J., & Leyens, P. C. (2004). Board models in Europe – Recent developments of internal corporate governance structures in Germany, the United Kingdom, France, and Italy. *European Company and Financial Law Review*, 1(2), 135–168.

73 Keay, A. (2013). The enlightened shareholder value principle and corporate governance. *Company Lawyer*, 26(10), 307–314.

The CSRD thus becomes more than a compliance mechanism: it acts as a catalyst for doctrinal transformation. It pushes the meaning of *interés social* toward a pluralistic, forward-looking understanding of the company's interest – one that reflects not only fiduciary loyalty to the firm but also accountability to environmental thresholds, societal expectations, and intergenerational equity. Whether this reinterpretation can take hold in corporate practice depends on enforcement, judicial uptake, and cultural transformation – but the legal direction is now unmistakable.

II. From Voluntary Responsibility to Legal Obligation: The CSDDD and the Hardening of Corporate Duty

The Corporate Sustainability Due Diligence Directive (CSDDD) represents a watershed moment in the European Union's effort to embed sustainability into the legal architecture of corporate governance. While earlier EU instruments focused on transparency and reporting, the CSDDD imposes affirmative duties on companies to identify, prevent, mitigate, and account for adverse impacts on human rights and the environment throughout their value chains.[74] This shift from disclosure to legal obligation is not merely technical – it signals a redefinition of the company's interest within the EU legal order, and a recalibration of directors' fiduciary duties.

In contrast to prior soft-law approaches, the CSDDD applies extraterritorially, covers both upstream and downstream operations, and includes enforcement mechanisms via administrative sanctions and civil liability. It thus solidifies expectations that were previously voluntary as binding legal norms.[75] Spain, as a Member State, will be required to transpose the directive within two years of its entry into force, compelling significant adjustments to domestic company law, particularly the interpretation and operationalisation of *interés social.*

At the core of the CSDDD is the imposition of due diligence duties not merely as compliance mechanisms, but as expressions of fiduciary respon-

74 European Union. (2024). *Directive (EU) 2024/1760 of the European Parliament and of the Council of 13 June 2024 on corporate sustainability due diligence and amending Directive (EU) 2019/1937 and Regulation (EU) 2023/2859. Official Journal of the European Union, L 1760,* 5 July 2024.

75 De Schutter, O., Ramasastry, A., Taylor, M. B., & Thompson, R. (2020). Human rights due diligence: The role of states. *International Journal of Human Rights,* 24(10), 1471–1491.

sibility. Article 25 of the directive requires Member States to ensure that directors "take into account the human rights, climate and environmental consequences of their decisions". This provision effectively reconfigures the scope of director loyalty, compelling a pluralistic orientation that includes non-shareholder interests.[76] Such a requirement marks a radical departure from classic corporate law paradigms, particularly in jurisdictions like Spain where *interés social* has traditionally accommodated multiple interpretations but lacked enforceable stakeholder protection.[77]

Spain's transposition of the directive is likely to intersect with ongoing debates over the scope of directors' duties under Article 225.2 of the Ley de Sociedades de Capital. As Martín notes, Spanish corporate law has so far permitted – but not mandated – a stakeholder-sensitive reading of fiduciary obligations.[78] The CSDDD may resolve this ambiguity by introducing minimum sustainability duties that redefine what directors must consider when acting "in the interest of the company".

This shift also raises questions about enforcement. While Spain has made strides in integrating ESG into governance codes and reporting obligations, enforcement remains weak, particularly in firms with concentrated ownership and low investor oversight.[79] The CSDDD introduces national supervisory authorities that are empowered to investigate breaches and impose sanctions. This may help address the enforcement deficit observed under Ley 11/2018 and the CSRD, aligning legal theory with governance in practice.

Comparatively, Spain may be better prepared for this transition than some peers. Its prior experience with Sociedades de Beneficio e Interés Común (SBICs) has already created a statutory form in which social and environmental purpose are legally embedded.[80] While still marginal in number, SBICs provide a conceptual template for operationalising the CSDDD's principles in company statutes, board procedures, and performance metrics.

Yet challenges remain. Spanish firms – especially SMEs and family-controlled entities – may struggle to implement robust due diligence processes

76 European Parliament. (2023). *Explanatory Memorandum for the Proposal for a Corporate Sustainability Due Diligence Directive*. COM(2022) 71 final.
77 Viscasillas (n4).
78 Sequeira Martín (n64).
79 Gutiérrez-Ponce et al (n5).
80 Fuentes Naharro and Megías López (n2).

across complex supply chains. Furthermore, the cultural norm of informal governance and reliance on soft law may delay full compliance.[81] Bridging this gap will require not only regulatory clarity, but institutional support from the CNMV, judicial engagement, and active stakeholder pressure.

In sum, the CSDDD represents a paradigmatic evolution: from permissive stakeholder orientation to obligatory sustainability governance. Its implementation will likely mark a turning point for *interés social* in Spain – not by replacing the concept, but by supplying it with normative content and enforceable duties. If Spain embraces this shift, it may not only comply with EU law but also catalyse a deeper transformation in the meaning of corporate purpose.

III. ESG as Governance: The CNMV's Evolving Role

In Spain's journey from shareholder-centred governance toward sustainability-oriented regulation, the Comisión Nacional del Mercado de Valores (CNMV) occupies a strategic yet paradoxical position. As the national securities regulator, the CNMV has played a critical role in transposing European Union sustainability mandates into Spanish governance practice. Its main mechanism for doing so has been the Código de Buen Gobierno de las Sociedades Cotizadas, the voluntary governance code applicable to listed companies. Since its revision in 2020, the Code has elevated ESG considerations from peripheral concerns to normative benchmarks of board performance and corporate legitimacy.[82]

Among the Code's most significant updates are provisions that encourage boards to integrate long-term ESG risks into their oversight functions, establish specific ESG committees, and link variable remuneration to sustainability metrics.[83] These guidelines – though formally "soft law" – carry quasi-regulatory weight due to the "comply or explain" mechanism enforced through public reporting and investor scrutiny. As empirical studies indicate, firms on the IBEX 35 index increasingly treat CNMV recom-

81 Lagos Cortés and Botero (n7).

82 CNMV. (2020). *Código de Buen Gobierno de las Sociedades Cotizadas*. Madrid: Comisión Nacional del Mercado de Valores.

83 Gutiérrez-Ponce et al (n5).

mendations as *de facto* obligations, particularly in areas related to board diversity, climate risk, and ESG disclosure.[84]

This evolution positions the CNMV as a norm entrepreneur – a domestic institutional actor capable of translating EU legal innovations (such as the CSRD and forthcoming CSDDD) into the lived governance practices of Spanish firms. By embedding ESG into the fiduciary routines of corporate boards, the CNMV bridges the doctrinal gap between the abstract notion of *interés social* and its operational meaning in boardroom decision-making.

Yet, the CNMV's impact is structurally constrained. Its jurisdiction is limited to listed companies – just a fraction of the Spanish corporate ecosystem, which is overwhelmingly composed of family-controlled, unlisted firms and SMEs.[85] These firms often lack both the institutional incentives and the internal capacity to adopt ESG governance frameworks, which results in a two-sided system: sophisticated ESG compliance among large, listed firms versus regulatory evasion or inertia among smaller entities.[86]

Moreover, the CNMV lacks coercive enforcement power; its recommendations rely on reputational pressure rather than legal obligation. In contexts where ownership is concentrated and external accountability is weak – as is common in Spain's relational capitalism – such pressure may prove insufficient. ESG commitments risk becoming ornamental, embedded in corporate communications rather than in core strategy.[87]

Addressing these limitations will require multi-level coordination. First, the Spanish legislature could expand ESG-related obligations beyond listed entities, especially in high-impact sectors. Second, the CNMV could strengthen its monitoring function through ESG benchmarking and enhanced disclosure audits. Finally, institutional investors – particularly public pension funds and EU-based asset managers – must align their stewardship policies with the trajectory of EU sustainability law.[88]

In sum, the CNMV is no longer merely a market supervisor but a governance architect, responsible for domesticating EU sustainability norms and redefining the company's interest through ESG oversight. Its evolving role illustrates the potential – and the limits – of soft law in transforming

84 Garnacho Cabanillas, L. (2020). *Revisión del código de buen gobierno de las sociedades cotizadas. Revista de Derecho de Sociedades*, (60), 257–292.

85 Lagos Cortés and Botero (n7).

86 Sequeira Martín (n64).

87 Fuentes Naharro and Megías López (n2).

88 European Commission. (2023). *Guidelines on the involvement of asset managers in sustainable corporate governance.* Brussels: DG FISMA.

entrenched governance cultures. In the Spanish context, where doctrinal ambiguity persists and ownership remains concentrated, the CNMV's soft law instruments serve as both catalyst and constraint: capable of directing firms toward sustainability, yet dependent on a broader legal and institutional ecosystem to ensure durability and diffusion.

IV. Spain's Interpretive Convergence: From Compliance to Conceptual Change?

In the transposition of EU sustainability directives, Member States often prioritise formal compliance over substantive conceptual realignment. This dynamic – characteristic of harmonisation processes in European company law – risks neutralising the transformative ambitions of EU-level sustainability initiatives by confining them to the procedural margins of corporate reporting. Yet in Spain, the interaction between EU law and domestic company interest reveals signs of a deeper interpretive recalibration: a shift from compliance as obligation to compliance as doctrinal opportunity.[89]

Recent scholarship suggests that the evolving EU sustainability architecture – particularly the Corporate Sustainability Reporting Directive (CSRD) and the Corporate Sustainability Due Diligence Directive (CSDDD) – is gradually altering the meaning of *interés social.* Traditionally underdefined in the Ley de Sociedades de Capital, *interés social* functioned as a doctrinal vessel for diverse, often contradictory interpretations: shareholder value, corporate continuity, managerial discretion. However, as Martín and Fuentes Naharro and Megías López observe, EU sustainability law is beginning to fill this vessel with content, reconfiguring *interés social* as an anchor for long-term environmental stewardship, social inclusion, and intergenerational equity.[90]

This evolution is not guaranteed. It depends on a complex web of legal considerations: the judiciary's willingness to interpret fiduciary duties in light of EU environmental and human rights obligations; the academic community's capacity to articulate coherent doctrinal syntheses; and the responsiveness of corporate boards to the emerging governance logic of sustainability. Instruments such as double materiality, value chain responsi-

89 Aguilera, R. V., & Jackson, G. (2003). *The cross-national diversity of corporate governance: Dimensions and determinants.* Academy of Management Review, 28(3), 447–465.

90 Sequeira Martín (n64); Fuentes Naharro and Megías López (n2).

bility, and stakeholder engagement – far from being technical novelties – constitute conceptual levers for reshaping the legal imagination of what a company is for.

Indeed, Spain's case demonstrates that sustainability governance is not merely a functional overlay on traditional corporate form, but a site of a shift in the foundation of norms. As EU law migrates from the regulatory periphery into the core architecture of the company's interest, the role of national legal cultures becomes critical: not only to translate obligations into local practice, but to embed new values into the doctrinal DNA of corporate law. In this process, compliance ceases to be a mere threshold – it becomes a catalyst for conceptual transformation.

V. Comparative Insight: A European Laboratory?

Spain's reception of EU sustainability law makes it a revealing site for comparative corporate governance analysis – a legal "laboratory" where supranational norms confront national traditions of ownership, governance, and doctrinal ambiguity. Unlike jurisdictions with deeply entrenched models of stakeholder governance (Germany) or investor-led ESG compliance (United Kingdom), Spain offers a hybrid configuration: one where civil law formality coexists with concentrated ownership, weak institutional voice mechanisms, and evolving soft law instruments.[91]

In Germany, the architecture of *Mitbestimmung* (co-determination) places employee interests directly in the boardroom through parity representation, institutionalising a pluralist vision of the *Gesellschaftszweck* (company interest). ESG objectives are not externally imposed but embedded within governance structures that balance labour, capital, and environmental concerns. In contrast, the United Kingdom continues to rely primarily on market-based mechanisms: Section 172 of the Companies Act of 2006 encourages directors to consider stakeholder interests but remains anchored to the primacy of shareholder benefit.[92] ESG in the UK is increasingly shaped by investor expectations, stewardship codes, and reputational calculus.

Spain occupies an intermediate position. It lacks co-determination and doctrinal clarity but compensates through a dynamic interplay between

91 Aguilera and Jackson (n89).
92 Keay (n73).

EU directives, evolving soft law (e.g., CNMV Codes), and recent statutory innovations such as the *Sociedad de Beneficio e Interés Común* (SBIC). These developments allow Spain to operate as a "transitional jurisdiction": its legal system remains rooted in traditional civil law architecture, yet its responsiveness to EU mandates and normative pluralism opens the door for governance experimentation.[93]

This hybridity is both an advantage and a vulnerability. On one hand, it enables flexibility and innovation without the need for statutory reform. Spain can integrate EU sustainability principles through interpretive layering, soft law, and sectoral legislation, avoiding the political and legal inertia often seen in more rigid systems. On the other hand, the absence of institutionalised stakeholder mechanisms and the dominance of blockholder governance constrain the reach of sustainability reforms. Without deeper reforms in board composition, fiduciary standards, and enforcement mechanisms, ESG risks remain at the periphery of the company's interest – cosmetic rather than constitutive.

In this sense, Spain offers a cautionary and instructive case. It demonstrates how EU law can catalyse national governance transformation through juridical diffusion and soft power. But it also illustrates the limits of top-down convergence: unless the structural foundations of corporate control – particularly ownership concentration and political capture – are addressed, sustainability remains a compliance variable rather than a guiding purpose.

VI. Conclusion: European Law as a Vector of Normative Realignment

The evolving body of EU corporate sustainability law – rooted in the CSRD, the forthcoming Corporate Sustainability Due Diligence Directive (CSDDD), and the EU Taxonomy – has become more than a regulatory framework. It realigning norms, gradually reconfiguring what company interest means across Member States. In Spain, this shift is particularly resonant, not because of statutory clarity or constitutional overhaul, but because the legal ambiguity around *interés social* is grounds for interpretive innovation.

EU directives are not simply overlaid upon the Spanish system – they seep into its doctrinal gaps, activating a redefinition of fiduciary duties,

93 Fuentes Naharro and Megías López (n2).

board obligations, and reporting practices. As these norms migrate from the periphery of compliance toward the core of governance logic, they demand a deeper recalibration of legal, institutional, and business practices. The *interés social* – once a doctrinal placeholder – is increasingly reframed to include ecological risk, social cohesion, and long-term sustainability as integral components of corporate legitimacy.

Yet this transformation is precarious. Without stronger enforcement mechanisms, clearer stakeholder representation, and structural reform of Spain's ownership concentration, EU sustainability law will likely remain performative rather than transformative. ESG, under these conditions, does not become a central aspect of decision-making.

Nonetheless, Spain's evolving governance remains a dynamic site of legal and normative experimentation. The combination of soft law guidance, EU alignment, and institutional innovation – such as the *Sociedad de Beneficio e Interés Común* – suggests that change is not just possible, it is already underway. If doctrinal development continues to align *interés social* with the EU's sustainability imperatives, Spain could emerge as a prototype for gradual but substantive integration of stakeholder values into company law.

In this light, European law is not merely harmonising reporting obligations – it is reframing the interest of the company. Spain, through its adaptive legal frameworks and interpretive flexibility, demonstrates how a Member State can absorb, reinterpret, and project supranational norms into national corporate governance. Whether this realignment becomes embedded in institutional DNA or remains a surface-level adaptation will depend on the next phase: judicial uptake, enforcement rigor, and a cultural shift in corporate decision-making.

F. Financialisation, Political Capture, and the Governance of Spanish Capital

As European corporate governance realigns through the growing force of sustainability directives, Spain confronts a deeply entrenched barrier: the structural inertia of financial capital. While *interés social* evolves in legal doctrine and EU instruments urge a reorientation toward dynamic corporate purposes, the Spanish financial sector remains anchored to a legacy architecture shaped by financialisation without democratisation – and by stakeholder rhetoric devoid of enforceable accountability.

This section argues that the promise of EU-driven reform cannot be realized without reckoning with the persistent influence of elite relational networks, institutional opacity, and risk-externalising financial logics. Spain's experience reveals a critical insight: that sustainability cannot be retrofitted onto governance systems deliberately designed to concentrate power, obscure responsibility, and resist transformation. Unless these dynamics are addressed, sustainability risks becoming a procedural facade – absorbed in compliance routines but excluded from the strategic core of financial governance.

I. Financialisation Without Market Discipline

Unlike the Anglo-American model of financial capitalism – where dispersed ownership and liquid capital markets provide external checks on managerial discretion – Spain's financial system is defined by ownership concentration, institutional entrenchment, and nearly-absent shareholder activism.[94] The post-2008 consolidation of the banking sector did not democratise governance; rather, it engrained oligopolistic structures, producing a financial architecture in which discipline is internal, strategic, and often unaccountable.[95]

Flagship institutions such as Santander, BBVA, and CaixaBank exemplify this model. Their public adherence to ESG frameworks, sustainability indices, and EU reporting standards masks an internal governance logic still dominated by short-term financial metrics, capital efficiency, and shareholder return.[96] ESG units exist – often well-resourced and externally visible – but they remain structurally decoupled from strategic decision-making, with little influence over credit allocation, investment priorities, or executive compensation schemes.

The Spanish case thus reveals the paradox of financialised sustainability: where ESG metrics proliferate in reporting cycles, but the underlying financial calculus remains extractive, speculative, and ecologically disembedded. Compliance is abundant; transformation is absent. The result is a

94 Deeg, R., & Hardie, I. (2016). What is patient capital and who supplies it? Socio-Economic Review, 14(4), 627–645.

95 Hardie, I., & Howarth, D. (2013). Market-based banking and the international financial crisis. Oxford University Press.

96 Gutiérrez-Ponce et al (n5); CNMV. (2023). Informe Anual sobre Gobierno Corporativo de las Entidades Cotizadas. Madrid: Comisión Nacional del Mercado de Valores.

system where sustainability is not a constraint on capital, but a language through which capital justifies itself.

II. The Political Economy of the *Cajas*: Stakeholder Rhetoric and Elite Capture

The collapse of the *cajas de ahorro* in the aftermath of the 2008 financial crisis stands as one of the clearest indictments of Spain's stakeholder governance architecture – an architecture that operated in form but failed in function.[97] These savings banks, historically rooted in regional development and social cohesion, were designed as stakeholder-oriented entities. Their governance structures included representatives from municipalities, depositors, employees, and civil society organizations.[98] Yet in practice, these multi-stakeholder boards became sites of political patronage, opacity, and financial imprudence.

Rather than serving as bulwarks against short-termism, many *cajas* became vehicles for politically driven credit expansion – especially in the real estate sector – underwritten by weak risk controls and minimal supervisory scrutiny.[99] The absence of formal shareholder pressure was not replaced by participatory accountability, but by elite entrenchment. The democratic potential of stakeholder governance was hollowed out by the instrumentalisation of public and civic seats for partisan gain.

The case of Bankia – created through the forced merger of several failing *cajas* and later nationalized following a massive bailout – reveals how stakeholder rhetoric can mask institutional capture.[100] Bankia's board, populated by political appointees with little banking expertise, approved

97 Fernández, R., & Aalbers, M. B. (2016). Financialization and housing in Spain: A crisis on the Southern periphery of neoliberal capitalism. *Housing Policy Debate*, 26(4–5), 1–25.

98 Martínez-Ferrero, J., Vaquero-Cacho, L.-A., Cuadrado-Ballesteros, B., & García-Sánchez, I.-M. (2015). El gobierno corporativo y la responsabilidad social corporativa en el sector bancario: el papel del consejo de administración. *Investigaciones Europeas de Dirección y Economía de la Empresa, 21*(3), 129–138.

99 Luque-Vílchez, M., & Larrinaga, C. (2016). Reporting models do not translate well: Failing to regulate CSR reporting in Spain. *Social and Environmental Accountability Journal, 36*(1), 56–75.

100 Rodríguez-Gutiérrez, P., Fuentes-García, F. J., & Sánchez-Cañizares, S. M. (2013). Transparency in social disclosure in financial institutions through Spanish CSR reports in the context of crisis. *Universia Business Review*, Segunda época, 18, 85–106.

reckless strategies with limited dissent, shielded by an accountability vacuum. The failure was not of stakeholder governance *per se*, but of a model in which stakeholder representation lacked the legal teeth, fiduciary clarity, and external checks necessary for meaningful constraint.

This experience continues to cast a long shadow over Spanish corporate governance reform. Efforts to embed sustainability or pluralistic purpose into board structures now confront scepticism rooted in the *cajas'* collapse. For stakeholder governance to regain legitimacy in Spain, it must not only articulate inclusive ideals but also institutionalise enforceable standards – combining plural representation with technical competence, transparency, and independent oversight.

III. Governance Reform and the Limits of Institutional Memory

In the aftermath of the *cajas* crisis, Spain undertook a series of institutional reforms designed to restore financial stability and align banking governance with EU regulatory expectations. These included the consolidation of savings banks into commercial entities, increased capital requirements under the CRR/CRD IV framework, and the partial privatisation of state-rescued banks overseen by the FROB (Fund for Orderly Bank Restructuring).[101] On paper, these reforms marked a transition from politicised stakeholder governance toward market-based professionalism. In practice, however, they left the core architecture of elite control largely intact.

One key limitation lies in the absence of robust institutional memory. The crisis was treated not as a systemic failure of governance culture, but as a technical failure of risk management.[102] As a result, reform focused on financial ratios and supervisory oversight rather than on restructuring board composition, conflict-of-interest rules, or mechanisms of political insulation. Former political figures continued to occupy board seats in key financial entities, and the revolving door between public office and bank directorships remained largely unregulated.

101 Bank of Spain. (2021). *Informe anual 2021: Evolución del sistema bancario español.* Madrid: Banco de España; European Parliament and Council. (2013). *Capital Requirements Directive IV (CRD IV)* and *Capital Requirements Regulation (CRR).* Official Journal of the European Union, L176.

102 Castillero-Ostio, E., Moreno-Cabanillas, A., & Castillo-Esparcia, A. (2023). *Transparencia y gobierno: puertas giratorias en España. Revista Española de la Transparencia,* (18), 201–229. https://doi.org/10.51915/ret.295.

Moreover, governance reform failed to address the broader question of the company's interest within financial institutions.[103] While EU law increasingly requires financial actors to align with climate transition goals and human rights frameworks, Spanish banking governance has not structurally internalised these imperatives. ESG functions exist, but they are often marginal, focused on reporting without strategic integration. Climate risk remains decoupled from core credit risk assessments, and few institutions embed double materiality into their decision-making processes.

The result is a form of regulatory adaptation without normative transformation. Spain's financial sector now complies more effectively with external rules, but the underlying governance logic continues to prioritise shareholder return, political influence, and institutional self-preservation over sustainability or stakeholder accountability. Without deeper reforms – especially in board appointment processes, fiduciary standards, and supervisory enforcement – financial governance risks replicating past failures under the guise of ESG alignment.

IV. The Persistence of Capture: Relational Capital and Soft Power

Despite reforms to enhance transparency, accountability, and risk governance in Spain's financial sector, the deeper architecture of influence remains largely intact. Political capture and elite entrenchment persist not through overt illegality, but through the informal economies of relational capital: revolving doors between regulatory agencies and financial institutions, networked appointments to bank boards, and the soft power of institutional proximity.[104]

These mechanisms, while subtle, exert profound influence over how governance norms – especially those relating to sustainability – are interpreted, prioritised, or deferred. Regulatory bodies such as the Bank of Spain and the CNMV have historically maintained permeable boundaries with the financial institutions they supervise. Former ministers, regulators, and central bank officials frequently assume post-retirement roles on the boards

103 Álvarez-Román, L., Mayordomo, S., Vergara-Alert, C., & Vives, X. (2024). *Climate risk, soft information and credit supply* (Banco de España Working Paper No. 2406).

104 Juste de Ancos, R. (2023). *La gran transformación del poder económico: puertas giratorias, capital y consejeros en la red de empresas españolas cotizadas. Revista Española de Sociología, 32*(2), a157. https://doi.org/10.22325/fes/res.2023.157.

of major banks or their philanthropic foundations, reinforcing a shared cognitive and normative framework that resists adversarial oversight.[105]

This relational ecosystem is not unique to Spain, but its density and cultural normalisation distinguish it within the European context. Unlike jurisdictions with strong civic counterweights or judicial activism in corporate governance (e.g. Germany or the Netherlands), Spain lacks robust institutional channels through which stakeholder or public interest claims can effectively challenge deep-seated corporate-financial alliances.[106] Even EU-mandated sustainability obligations – such as those under the CSRD or forthcoming CSDDD – risk dilution when filtered through institutional cultures oriented toward consensus, continuity, and elite coordination.

Moreover, the technocratic rhetoric of ESG often obscures these power dynamics. Sustainability, framed as a matter of data, ratings, and KPIs, can become a discursive shield behind which business-as-usual persists. The shift toward sustainability is thus not simply a question of legal transposition or board training – it requires confronting with the normative legitimacy of relational governance itself.

In this light, Spain's financial governance landscape demonstrates that the barriers to sustainable company interests are not just legal or structural, but epistemic and relational. The persistence of capture ensures that sustainability remains vulnerable to instrumentalisation, and that *interés social* may be rhetorically expanded but strategically hollowed out.

V. Reclaiming Financial Governance: Toward a Sustainable Political Economy of Capital

If sustainability is to function as more than regulatory rhetoric in Spain's financial sector, a deeper reconfiguration is needed – one that moves beyond green branding and ESG disclosure toward democratised financial governance.[107] The core argument of this section is that without structural transformation of how capital is governed, allocated, and contested, sus-

105 Pons-Hernández, M. (2022). *Power(ful) connections: Exploring the revolving doors phenomenon as a form of state-corporate crime. Critical Criminology, 30*(2), 305–320. https://doi.org/10.1007/s10612-022-09626-z.

106 Colonnello, S., Koetter, M., Sclip, A., & Wagner, K. (2023). *The reverse revolving door in the supervision of European banks.* (Working paper). SSRN. https://doi.org/10.2139/ssrn.3997731.

107 Rubio Nieto, C. (2025). *Social Activity in Spanish Banking Foundations. Sociology Journal,* 14(3), 166.

tainability in Spanish finance will remain performative, rather than substantive.

This transformation requires confronting the legacy of elite entrenchment, especially in the governance of Spain's major financial institutions. The revolving doors between political elites and bank leadership, the role of economic ministries in appointing regulators, and the informal coalitions between large corporate groups and public financial agencies form a dense web of relational power. These networks are not anomalies – they are systemic features of Spain's financialised capitalism. They enable the externalisation of risk, insulation from accountability, and resistance to reform that sustainability governance seeks to overcome.[108]

In parallel, Spain lacks institutionalised mechanisms of stakeholder voice in financial decision-making. Unlike Germany, where labour representatives sit on supervisory boards, or Scandinavian countries with public ownership models, Spanish banks operate without meaningful democratic input, even in publicly-significant sectors like housing, energy, and infrastructure. Community impact, environmental thresholds, and intergenerational justice remain marginal concerns – unless translated into reputational or legal risk.

A genuinely sustainable financial governance model would require several strategic shifts:[109]

- embedding planetary boundaries into financial supervision via the Banco de España and the CNMV, including mandatory stress testing for climate and biodiversity-related risks;
- aligning fiduciary duties with long-term ecological and social value, revising definitions of prudence, loyalty, and care in banking law;
- expanding stakeholder representation, particularly from affected communities and labour, in oversight structures of public and quasi-public financial entities; and
- restructuring incentives, so that executive pay and investment decisions reflect real-world sustainability outcomes, not just ESG metrics or short-term returns.

108 López, I., & Rodríguez, E. (2011). *The Spanish model. New Left Review*, 69, 5–29.
109 Sullivan, R., Martindale, W., Feller, E., & Bordon, A. (2015). *Fiduciary Duty in the 21st Century.* UNEP FI, PRI, UNEP Inquiry, and The Generation Foundation.

These proposals may appear radical in the current Spanish context, but they are not utopian. Across Europe, similar initiatives are gaining traction: the European Central Bank has begun integrating climate risks into its prudential frameworks,[110] the Netherlands has explored legal duties to divest from unsustainable assets, and France has introduced obligations for institutional investors to disclose climate goal alignment.[111]

In Spain, however, the political economy of financial governance remains resistant. Banks wield outsized influence over economic policy, media, and political parties. Regulatory institutions lack sufficient independence or mandate to challenge entrenched interests. And civil society mobilisation around financial reform remains limited in comparison to environmental or labour movements.

Nonetheless, the sustainability transition will not succeed without finance, and finance will not be sustainable without democratisation. Reclaiming financial governance is not merely a question of technical reform, it is a political project – one that confronts power, redistributes voice, and redefines legitimacy in a world where ecological thresholds are non-negotiable.

Spain has the legal tools, policy levers, and constitutional values to lead this shift. What is lacking is the political will to challenge the structural impunity of financial capital, and the articulation of a vision of finance that serves society – not the other way around.

G. Toward a Juridical Framework for Sustainable Governance in Spain

Spain's encounter with EU-driven sustainability regulation has catalysed a reconfiguration of its corporate governance discourse. What began as compliance with supranational reporting standards is maturing into a broader normative project: the gradual emergence of a juridical framework for sustainable governance. This framework does not denote a new code or singular statute, but a set of evolving legal, institutional, and cultural logics

110 Martínez-Ferrero, J., & García-Sánchez, I. M. (2017). Sustainability performance and stakeholder engagement: The role of institutional investors in Spain. *Corporate Social Responsibility and Environmental Management, 24*(1), 28–43.

111 European Central Bank. (2025). *ECB to introduce 'climate factor' into lending operations.* Reuters; European Central Bank. (2025). *European banks have progressed on climate risk, but more still needs to be done.* Green Central Banking.

through which sustainability becomes juridified – not merely in form, but in function.

This section maps the juridical framework across three interdependent aspects: social sustainability (via family firms and employment embeddedness), environmental sustainability (via EU-aligned CSR and climate law), and institutional sustainability (via the resilience-building function of EU legal integration). Together, these dimensions demonstrate how Spain is becoming a "laboratory" for reconciling path-dependent ownership structures with supranational norms of company interest.

I. Social Sustainability: Family Firms and Employment

In the Spanish context, social sustainability is not an abstract policy ideal but a lived corporate logic, deeply rooted in the structure of its business landscape. With over 85 % of Spanish companies classified as family-owned – including some of the country's most significant corporate actors – the company's interest is often embedded in long-term relational capital, employment continuity, and regional anchoring.[112]

This ownership configuration has both regressive and progressive implications. On one hand, concentrated control and succession opaqueness poses challenges for board independence, stakeholder participation, and gender diversity. On the other hand, family firms often display a temporal logic aligned with intergenerational responsibility – an element that EU sustainability law now recognises as essential to fiduciary transformation.

Indeed, Spain's social sustainability trajectory hinges on whether these firms can operationalise ESG mandates as intrinsic components of their continuity strategies as opposed to external constraints. Emerging practices – such as ESG-driven succession planning, purpose-led governance charters, and stakeholder-inclusive governance protocols – suggest that this transformation is already underway, albeit unevenly.[113]

112 Sánchez-Famoso, V., Cano-Rubio, M., & Fuentes-Lombardo, G. (2025). *Relational capital's contribution to international success: Evidence from family-owned wineries and olive oil mills in Spain. Research in International Business and Finance, 74.*

113 Cabaleiro-Cerviño, G., & Mendi, P. (2024). *ESG-driven innovation strategy and firm performance.* Eurasian Business Review, 14(1), 137–185.

II. Environmental Sustainability: The Juridification of Climate and CSR

Spain's legislative transposition of CSR norms – initially through Ley 11/2018 and more recently through the CSRD – has initiated a shift in how environmental sustainability is framed within corporate governance. While earlier frameworks encouraged transparency through "non-financial" disclosures, the CSRD, EU Taxonomy, and forthcoming CSDDD compel firms to integrate environmental risks into core governance processes.[114]

Environmental sustainability is now embedded into the operational language of director duties, risk reporting, and board accountability. Article 225.2 of the LSC, though still doctrinally indeterminate, is being reinterpreted by scholars and regulators to include climate risks as material to the long-term interest of the company. This is a significant development: it reframes environmental concerns not as reputational liabilities but as fiduciary obligations.

Spain's Ley de Cambio Climático y Transición Energética (2021) reinforces this evolution, mandating climate alignment in corporate and sectoral planning. Yet, enforcement remains weak, and ESG considerations often take the form of fragmented compliance rather than systemic transformation. Bridging this gap requires embedding environmental governance in internal corporate structures – via ESG committees, board-level responsibility, and integration with remuneration policies.[115]

III. Spain as a Laboratory: Between Ownership Path Dependency and Legal Innovation

Spain's corporate governance model – marked by high ownership concentration, soft law governance, and civil law elasticity – presents a paradox. On one hand, it is structurally conservative: relational capitalism, elite control, and weak external accountability persist. On the other hand, it is

---

114 Grant Thornton (2023). *Corporate Sustainability Reporting Directive (CSRD): Double materiality and corporate governance.* Grant Thornton Spain.

115 *España. Ley 7/2021, de 20 de mayo, de cambio climático y transición energética.* Boletín Oficial del Estado, 21 May 2021; *Proyecto de Real Decreto sobre informes de riesgo financiero por riesgos climáticos.* April 2023; *Real Decreto 214/2025*, de 12 de abril, sobre huella de carbono y reducción de emisiones de gases de efecto invernadero; López Ramón, F. (2021). *Notas sobre la Ley 7/2021 de cambio climático y transición energética. Actualidad Jurídica Ambiental*, n.º 114.

institutionally innovative, absorbing EU norms through soft law, doctrinal commentary, and sectoral statutes.

This paradox positions Spain as a laboratory for testing how sustainability governance can emerge through interpretive and institutional layering instead of through wholesale statutory reform. Its hybridity is not a weakness, but a site of experimentation: a mid-point between institutional rigidity and liberal market voluntarism.

The question that remains is whether Spain's juridical framework can stabilize into a durable legal paradigm. This will require sustained judicial engagement, stronger enforcement of ESG norms across ownership structures, and integration of stakeholder voice into governance processes. But the trajectory is visible: sustainability is no longer peripheral to Spanish corporate law – it is moving toward the centre.

H. Conclusion: Redefining Corporate Purpose in Spain through Layered Legal Evolution

Spain's corporate governance order is undergoing a transformation that is neither loud nor abrupt but is no less profound for its subtlety. The elusive concept of *interés social*, still formally undefined in the Ley de Sociedades de Capital, has become a vessel for reinterpretation. Its content is being reconstructed not by statute but through a multilayered legal process: doctrinal innovation by scholars, incremental adaptation by institutions, harmonising pressures from EU law, and the steady accumulation of regulatory codes.[116] What emerges is not new corporate statute, but a *juridical framework* – a flexible idiom that can integrate environmental, social, and institutional sustainability into the very heart of the company's interest.

Sustainability in Spain has not entered corporate law by way of constitutional rupture or revolutionary legislation. Rather, it has seeped across the fabric of governance: through non-financial disclosure laws, corporate governance codes, judicial interpretation, and supranational directives.[117] The result is a hybrid model – still marked by concentrated ownership and the weight of family capitalism, yet increasingly receptive to European legal principles of sustainability and stakeholder engagement.

116 Embid Irujo and Del Val Talens (n28).
117 Ibid.

Spain's trajectory differs markedly from other European jurisdictions. In Germany, stakeholder rights are structurally entrenched through *Mitbestimmung* (co-determination). In Slovenia, post-socialist constitutional legacies of self-management embed a stakeholder logic in law.[118] Spain lacks such institutional anchors. Yet what appears as weakness doubles as flexibility: the ambiguity of *interés social* allows Spanish corporate law to absorb new normative content without legislative rupture.

Seen from this angle, Spain becomes a laboratory for company interest in post-transitional economies. It shows how civil law systems with path-dependent ownership structures can nevertheless evolve toward stakeholder-oriented governance by leveraging soft law innovation, EU alignment, and doctrinal reinterpretation. The statutory creation of the *Sociedad de Beneficio e Interés Común* (SBIC) in 2022, however embryonic, exemplifies a willingness to experiment with weaving sustainability into the corporate fabric through codification.

Still, the risks are evident. Without addressing structural constraints – concentrated ownership, weak enforcement, and regulatory asymmetries – sustainability may remain cosmetic, a gloss on prevailing logics of financial control. Banks, family firms, and politically-connected conglomerates continue to dominate strategic sectors, often without embedding ESG into governance beyond compliance. Courts, meanwhile, have been slow to embrace expanded readings of *interés social*.

Yet the trajectory of change is unmistakably pointing forward. Spain is shifting from shareholder primacy by default to sustainability by design – not by abandoning its legal tradition, but by stretching it. Here, EU law acts not as an external imposition but as a normative catalyst, urging domestic actors to reimagine the corporation in light of planetary limits, social cohesion, and intergenerational justice. In doing so, Spain lends its voice to the wider European debate about firms in the 21st century: not as a mere profit machine, but as a civic institution bound by the grammar of public purpose, ecological boundaries, and shared value.

118 Spain's trajectory differs markedly from other European jurisdictions. In Germany, stakeholder rights are structurally entrenched through *Mitbestimmung* (co-determination). In Slovenia, post-socialist constitutional legacies of self-management embed a stakeholder logic in law.

References

Legal Texts & Legislation (Spain):

España. (1978). *Constitución Española* [Spanish Constitution]. *Boletín Oficial del Estado*, núm. 311, 29 de diciembre de 1978. https://www.boe.es/eli/es/c/1978/12/27/(1)

España. (1978). Constitución Española [Spanish Constitution]. Boletín Oficial del Estado, núm. 311, 29 de diciembre de 1978. https://www.boe.es/eli/es/c/1978/12/27/(1)

España. (1989). Ley 19/1989, de 25 de julio, de reforma parcial y adaptación de la legislación mercantil a las Directivas de la CEE en materia de sociedades. Boletín Oficial del Estado, núm. 178, 27 de julio, 22797–22817.

España. (1995). Ley 2/1995, de 23 de marzo, de Sociedades de Responsabilidad Limitada. Boletín Oficial del Estado, núm. 71, 24 de marzo, 8575–8599.

España. (2010). Real Decreto Legislativo 1/2010, de 2 de julio, por el que se aprueba el texto refundido de la Ley de Sociedades de Capital. Boletín Oficial del Estado, núm. 161, 3 de julio, 58460–58665.

España. (2011). Ley 2/2011, de 4 de marzo, de Economía Sostenible. Boletín Oficial del Estado, núm. 55, 5 de marzo, 25033–25235.

España. (2013). Ley 19/2013, de 9 de diciembre, de Transparencia, Acceso a la Información Pública y Buen Gobierno. Boletín Oficial del Estado, núm. 295, 10 de diciembre, 97922–97952.

España. (2015). Ley 44/2015, de 14 de octubre, de Sociedades Laborales y Participadas. Boletín Oficial del Estado, núm. 247, 15 de octubre, 95086–95104.

España. (2018). Ley 11/2018, de 28 de diciembre, sobre información no financiera y diversidad. Boletín Oficial del Estado, núm. 314, 29 de diciembre, 129168–129194. https://www.boe.es/buscar/doc.php?id=BOE-A-2018-17989

España. (2021). Ley 7/2021, de 20 de mayo, de Cambio Climático y Transición Energética. Boletín Oficial del Estado, núm. 121, 21 de mayo, 62072–62120.

España. (2022). Ley 18/2022, de 28 de septiembre, de creación y crecimiento de empresas. Boletín Oficial del Estado, núm. 234, 29 de septiembre, 125893–125952.

European Union Directives & Regulations:

Directive 2014/95/EU of the European Parliament and of the Council. (2014). Disclosure of non-financial and diversity information by certain large undertakings and groups. Official Journal of the European Union, L 330, 1–9. https://eur-lex.europa.eu/legal-content/EN/TXT/?uri=CELEX%3A32014L0095

Directive (EU) 2022/2464 of the European Parliament and of the Council. (2022). Corporate sustainability reporting. Official Journal of the European Union, L 322, 15–43.

Directive (EU) 2024/1760 of the European Parliament and of the Council. (2024). Corporate Sustainability Due Diligence Directive (CSDDD). Official Journal of the European Union, L 168, 1–48.

Regulation (EU) 2020/852 of the European Parliament and of the Council. (2020). Establishing a framework to facilitate sustainable investment. Official Journal of the European Union, L 198, 13–43.

Academic and Institutional Sources:

Aguilera, R. V., & Cuervo-Cazurra, A. (2004). Codes of good governance worldwide: What is the trigger? Organization Studies, 25(3), 415–443.

Aguilera, R. V., & Jackson, G. (2003). The cross-national diversity of corporate governance: Dimensions and determinants. Academy of Management Review, 28(3), 447–465.

Alfaro Águila-Real, J. (2016). El interés social y los deberes de lealtad de los administradores. Anuario de la Facultad de Derecho de la UAM, 20, 213–236.

Amato, S., Minichilli, A., & Corbetta, G. (2023). Family firms amid the global financial crisis: Territory-embedded and employment-protective behaviors in Spain. Journal of Business Ethics, 183(2), 459–477. https://doi.org/10.1007/s10551-021-04930-0

Apalategui, J. M. C. (2024). La indeterminación intencional en el derecho. Revista de la Facultad de Derecho de la Universidad de Deusto, (27).

Comisión Nacional del Mercado de Valores. (2015). Código de buen gobierno de las sociedades cotizadas. https://www.cnmv.es/DocPortal/Publicaciones/CodigoGov/Codigo_buen_gobierno.pdf

Djokić, D. (2009). The corporate governance statement and audit committee in the European Union and Republic of Slovenia. Croatian Yearbook of European Law & Policy, 5, 283–289.

Embid Irujo, J. M., & Del Val Talens, P. (2016). La responsabilidad social corporativa y el Derecho de sociedades de capital: Entre la regulación legislativa y el soft law. Agencia Estatal Boletín Oficial del Estado.

Foweraker, J. (1987). Corporatist strategies and the transition to democracy in Spain. Comparative Politics, 20(1), 57–72.

Fuentes Naharro, M., & Megías López, J. (2023). Sustainability in Spanish company law: State of the art and a special reference to the new SBIC (Sociedad de beneficio e interés común). European Company Case Law.

Gutiérrez-Ponce, H., & Chamizo-González, J. (2022). Disclosure of environmental, social, and corporate governance information by Spanish companies: A compliance analysis. Sustainability, 14(6), 3254. https://doi.org/10.3390/su14063254

Hoverd, L. (2025, July 9). The 10 largest family businesses in Madrid. Tharawat Magazine. https://www.tharawat-magazine.com/facts/largest-family-businesses-madrid/

La Porta, R., López de Silanes, F., & Shleifer, A. (1999). Corporate ownership around the world. The Journal of Finance, 54(2), 471–517.

Lagos Cortés, D., & Botero, I. C. (2016). Corporate governance in family businesses from Latin America, Spain and Portugal: A review of the literature. Academia Revista Latinoamericana de Administración, 29(3), 231–254.

Leech, D., & Manjón, M. (2002). Corporate governance in Spain (ownership and control in listed companies). Universidad Rovira i Virgili.

Martínez, B., & Fontrodona, J. (2024). Benefit corporations y sociedades de beneficio e interés colectivo: un movimiento en auge (Cuaderno n.º 59). Cátedra CaixaBank de Sostenibilidad e Impacto Social, IESE Business School.

Schroeder, D., & Thomsen, S. (2022). Foundation ownership and sustainability: International evidence. European Corporate Governance Institute (ECGI). https://www.ecgi.global/sites/default/files/Paper%3A%20David%20Schroeder%2C%20Steen%20Thomsen.pdf

Sequeira Martín, A. (2021). El desarrollo de la responsabilidad social corporativa versus sostenibilidad, y su relación con el gobierno corporativo en las directivas comunitarias y en el derecho español de sociedades cotizadas. Revista de Derecho de Sociedades, (61), 39–83.

Villanueva-Villar, M., Rivo-López, E., & Lago-Peñas, S. (2016). On the relationship between corporate governance and value creation in an economic crisis: Empirical evidence for the Spanish case. Business Research Quarterly, 19(4), 233–245.

Viscasillas, P. P. (2023). Climate change and corporate governance in Spain. ex/ante.

8. The Interest of the Company in Slovenia: Corporate Purpose in a Post-Transitional Economy

Lela Mélon

A. Introduction

Corporate governance refers to the system of rules, practices, and processes that direct and control companies. At its core, corporate governance is about the distribution of power and responsibility among boards, managers, shareholders, employees, creditors, and wider stakeholders.[1] The concept of the "interest of the company" lies at the heart of the corporate governance framework, but its meaning has evolved over time.[2] Once narrowly equated with shareholder primacy in Anglo-American jurisdictions, the interest of the company is increasingly interpreted in stakeholder-oriented terms, acknowledging that long-term corporate success requires balancing profitability with sustainability, employee engagement, and broader societal welfare.[3]

Slovenia offers a compelling and distinctive case for examining the nature and purpose of corporate governance. Unlike many post-socialist states, Slovenia inherited a self-management model from Yugoslavia that embedded participation and stakeholder logics at the firm level. From the 1950s onward, Yugoslav enterprises, including those in Slovenia, were governed not by shareholders or state bureaucrats, but rather by workers' councils that exercised significant decision-making power.[4] As Koyama has shown, the Yugoslav self-management model rejected centralized Sovi-

1 Bezo, Y., Brahimi, A., & Dibra, R. (2015). *Corporate governance in transition countries.* CORE.

2 See *Sjåfjell, B., & Bruner, C. M. (Eds.). (2020). The Cambridge handbook of corporate law, corporate governance and sustainability. Cambridge University Press.*

3 Bohinc, R. (2001). Corporate governance in post-privatized Slovenia. American Journal of Comparative Law, 49(1), 49–74; Mayer, C. (2018). *Prosperity: Better business makes the greater good.* Oxford University Press.

4 Prasnikar, J. (1997). *Behavior of a Slovenian firm in transition.* University of Michigan Working Paper. https://deepblue.lib.umich.edu/bitstream/handle/2027.42/39416/wp26.pdf.

et-style socialism and resisted wholesale imitation of Western shareholder governance, creating a hybrid model in which corporate entities were conceived as social institutions with multiple purposes, not merely as vehicles for capital accumulation.[5]

This legacy shaped Slovenia's transition following its independence in 1991. Unlike many of its post-socialist peers who embraced "shock therapy," Slovenia adopted a gradualist path, prioritizing institutional stability and social cohesion over rapid liberalisation.[6] Privatisation was designed to preserve insider and employee ownership, reinforcing stakeholder participation even as market mechanisms were introduced. As Mygind et al. note, Slovenia's model diverged significantly from that of Russia or Hungary, where concentrated ownership and foreign takeovers quickly consolidated shareholder primacy.[7]

The evolution of Slovenia's corporate governance was further structured by its accession to the European Union in 2004, which required the adoption of EU directives on company law, capital markets, and shareholder rights.[8] Yet Slovenia's incorporation of EU law occurred through its own constitutional and institutional filters. The Companies Act (ZGD-1), first enacted in 1993 and substantially revised thereafter, underpins the corporate governance framework. Article 263 of ZGD-1 is especially significant: directors are legally mandated to act "in the best interest of the company," a formulation that has been **interpreted** as extending fiduciary duty beyond shareholders to include employees, creditors, and the broader community.[9] This statutory language reflects Slovenia's distinctive orientation, embedding stakeholderism not as soft ethics but as binding corporate law.

Empirical evidence confirms the persistence of embedding stakeholderism as binding corporate law. Stubelj et al. surveyed Slovenian managers and found that a majority explicitly rejected shareholder primacy, instead prioritizing balanced responsibility that included employees, com-

5 Koyama, Y. (2013). *Self-management in Yugoslavia and after.* Gdansk University.

6 Mrak, M., Rojec, M., & Silva-Jáuregui, C. (2004). *Slovenia: From Yugoslavia to the European Union.* World Bank.

7 Mygind, N., Demina, N., Gregorič, A., & Kapelyushnikov, R. (2004). Corporate governance cycles.

8 Mrak et al. (n6).

9 Companies Act (ZGD-1). *Uradni list RS*, št. 42/2006 (with amendments).

munities, and sustainability goals.[10] Rozman likewise observed that corporate governance practices in Slovenian enterprises remain shaped by the ethos of participation and internal consensus, rather than pure financial maximization.[11]

Taken together, these historical, legal, and empirical factors make Slovenia a laboratory for rethinking corporate purpose in small post-transitional economies. Its governmental framework challenges the assumption prevalent in Anglo-American theory that shareholder value maximization is inevitable or universal. Instead, Slovenia demonstrates that the "interest of the company" can be constructed as a pluralist fiduciary duty, grounded in law, culture, and constitutional principles. As European corporate governance increasingly turns toward ESG and sustainability, Slovenia's model provides a powerful example of how stakeholder orientation can be constitutionalized and embedded in practice.

The interplay of law, ownership structures, and Slovenia's socialist past makes the country a compelling case for examining stakeholder-oriented corporate governance. Unlike Spain, where legal frameworks gradually adapted from shareholder-oriented structures to sustainability imperatives, Slovenia's constitutional and historical traditions of self-management and social ownership provide the foundation for an inherently stakeholder-focused orientation. The concept of *interes družbe* (interest of the company) in Slovenia thus serves as a basis for negotiation between labour, community, state, and shareholder claims, reflecting enduring tensions between collective responsibility and market-oriented pressures.

This chapter explores these dynamics in detail. Section B traces the historical evolution of Slovenian corporate governance, highlighting the legacies of Yugoslav self-management and the transition to a market-oriented system. Section C examines the legal framework that governs companies, including the Companies Act and associated soft law instruments, focusing on how the "interest of the company" is defined and effectuated. Section D analyses ownership structures, emphasising the persistence of employee, state, and family ownership in shaping governance practices and corporate responses to crises. Section E provides comparative analysis, situating Slovenia within European and global debates on corporate governance. It

10 Stubelj, I., Dolenc, P., Biloslavo, R., Nahtigal, M., & Laporšek, S. (2017). Corporate purpose in a small post-transitional economy: The case of Slovenia. *Economic Research – Ekonomska Istraživanja, 30*(1), 818–835.

11 Bohinc (n3).

examines three dimensions – historical legacies, institutional design, and stakeholder practices – to highlight what is distinctive about Slovenia and what can be learned from its experience in a broader context. Section F addresses challenges of privatisation, financialisaton, and political influence, particularly in banking and strategic industries. Section G theorises Slovenia's juridical framework of stakeholder governance, highlighting social, environmental, and institutional sustainability embedded in corporate decision-making. Section H concludes by situating Slovenia's experience in comparative European debates, demonstrating how historical legacies and hybrid ownership models shape the possibilities and limits of embedding sustainability in corporate law.

By analysing Slovenia as a case study, this chapter contributes to the broader literature on corporate purpose and governance. It shows that the "interest of the company" in Slovenia is neither fixed nor solely shareholder-driven, but emerges from a complex interplay of legal norms, historical legacies, and stakeholder pressures. Slovenia's model offers valuable insights into how collective responsibility, social ownership, and participatory governance can coexist with market imperatives in shaping sustainable corporate purpose.

B. Historical Context: Self-Management and Transition

Understanding Slovenia's corporate governance model requires tracing its origins to Yugoslavia's experiment with worker self-management. Starting in the 1950s, Yugoslavia created an alternative to centralised socialism and Western capitalism, where decision-making power was embedded in workers' councils rather than state bureaucracies or private shareholders. In Slovenia, this participatory model had lasting institutional effects on both enterprise structure and legal culture.[12]

As Koyama explains, Yugoslav firms were not "owned" in the Western capitalist sense; they were operated under a system of delegated social ownership, where formal control was exercised by employee-elected management boards.[13] Firms had quasi-autonomous status and were expected to serve not just economic goals but also broader social purpose. This hybrid

12 Uvalić, M. (1992). Investment and property rights in Yugoslavia: The long transition to a market economy. Cambridge University Press.

13 Koyama (n5).

structure produced a corporate logic distinct from shareholder primacy, prioritizing internal consensus-building and community welfare.[14]

Upon declaring independence in 1991, Slovenia resisted the "shock therapy" route taken by many other post-socialist economies. Instead, it pursued a gradual transition marked by institutional stability and phased legal reform.[15] This gradual transition allowed for many features of the self-management model to be retained: internal ownership dominated privatisation, and employee participation remained a central norm in corporate life.[16] This institutional continuity preserved a stakeholder-oriented mindset, even as market mechanisms were introduced.

Scholars note that Slovenia's path-dependent evolution is visible not only in governance norms but also in ownership structure and managerial attitudes. Lahovnik (2019), for instance, argues that many Slovenian firms still demonstrate a soft form of stakeholder capitalism in which social and relational objectives coexist alongside commercial imperatives.[17] Similarly, Stubelj et al. (2017) found in a national survey that managers prioritise employee well-being and community engagement over profit maximisation for shareholders.[18] The institutional legacy of self-management, reinforced by Slovenia's legal and cultural choices during transition, has thus embedded a model of corporate governance where the "interest of the company" is interpreted through a broader stakeholder lens – one that continues to distinguish Slovenia in the European context.

C. Contemporary Legal Framework in Slovenia

Slovenia's approach to corporate governance is shaped by the layered interaction of post-socialist legal continuity, EU legal harmonisation, and an embedded commitment to stakeholder values. The contemporary legal framework governing corporate entities is not confined to a single statute but consists of an interconnected matrix of laws, codes, and administrative

14 Estrin, S. (1991). Yugoslavia: The case of self-managing market socialism. Journal of Economic Perspectives, 5(4), 187–194. https://doi.org/10.1257/jep.5.4.187.

15 Mrak et al. (n6).

16 Bohinc, R., & Bainbridge, S. M. (2001). Corporate governance in post-socialist countries: Slovenia in comparative perspective. Columbia Journal of East European Law, 7(2), 119–146.

17 Lahovnik, M. (2019). Corporate governance following the Slovenian transition: From success story to failed case. Economic and Business Review, 21(1), 5–20.

18 Stubelj et al. (n10).

practices. These collectively define what it means to act in the "interest of the company" – a phrase that, in the Slovenian context, is understood to include employees, creditors, the environment, and broader society.

I. The Companies Act: Core Legal Definition of Purpose

At the centre of Slovenia's corporate governance structure is the Companies Act (Zakon o gospodarskih družbah, "ZGD-1"), adopted in 2006 and amended regularly to reflect evolving EU directives and domestic legal interpretations. Article 263 of ZGD-1 is critical: it requires directors and management boards to act in the best interest of the company, with the standard of care of "a conscientious and honest businessperson".[19]

Notably, ZGD-1 does not define the "interest of the company" solely in terms of shareholder value. Instead, Slovenian courts and doctrine interpret the interest of the company as a multi-stakeholder duty.[20]

Scholars such as Bohinc and Bainbridge (2001) argue that the Slovenian model blends civil law formalism with socially-rooted substance, particularly in its recognition that long-term corporate health is tied to relationships with employees, creditors, customers, and communities.[21]

Further, ZGD-1 makes dual-board governance structures as the default for public companies and large firms, mandating institutional separation between management and oversight, which promotes accountability and deliberation – two critical mechanisms for embedding stakeholder voice into governance structures.

II. Labor Relations Act: Embedding Employee Stakeholding

The Labor Relations Act (Zakon o delovnih razmerjih, "ZDR-1") reinforces stakeholder logic by framing employment as not just a contractual relationship but a mutual social partnership. ZDR-1 implements equal treatment,

19 Zakon o gospodarskih družbah (ZGD-1). *Uradni list RS*, št. 42/2006.

20 Petrović, T. J. (2012). *Directors' Responsibility to Creditors in Company Law. Annals Fac. L. Belgrade Int'l Ed.*, 2012, 89–108.

21 Bohinc, R., & Bainbridge, S. M. (2001). Corporate governance in post-privatized Slovenia. *American Journal of Comparative Law* 49.

human dignity, and participatory mechanisms in workplace governance[22] as follows:

- Article 6 enshrines respect for human dignity;
- Articles 9–11 regulate collective bargaining and consultation rights; and
- Articles 44–47 extend employer obligations beyond wages – employers must actively ensure safe and dignified working conditions and enable employees to express and participate in matters affecting their well-being.

While ZDR-1 is formally aligned with EU labour directives, its spirit is rooted in Slovenia's legacy of worker self-management, where employment relations were historically conceived as cooperative rather than hierarchical.[23]

III. Worker Participation in Management Act

A unique feature of Slovenia's legal framework is the Zakon o sodelovanju delavcev pri upravljanju ("ZSDU"), which mandates employee representation in company supervisory boards. In firms with over 50 employees, at least one-third of board seats must be filled by employee-elected representatives.[24]

This provision incorporates employees at the heart of corporate decision-making and is a statutory institutionalisation of stakeholder governance. Employee representatives have full voting rights and participate in decisions on corporate strategy, remuneration, mergers, and more. Their presence not only diversifies perspectives but ensures that labour-related risks and opportunities are considered in board deliberations.

This is a rare legal feature in global corporate governance and a point of divergence from shareholder-centric regimes.

22 Zakon o delovnih razmerjih (ZDR-1). *Uradni list RS*, št. 21/2013.
23 Uvalić (n12).
24 Zakon o sodelovanju delavcev pri upravljanju (ZSDU). *Uradni list RS*, št. 42/1993.

IV. Competition Protection Act: Corporate Ethics and Market Fairness

Slovenia's Competition Protection Act ("ZVK") aligns with EU competition law (Article 101 and 102 TFEU) but integrates principles of market fairness and social responsibility more explicitly. Article 6 of ZVK prohibits anti-competitive agreements and the abuse of dominant positions in ways that may harm consumers, competitors, or market integrity.[25]

ZVK positions corporate actors not just as profit-seekers but as participants in a socially-governed market, reinforcing that the "interest of the company" cannot involve behaviours that distort competition or exploit economic power.

The Slovenian Competition Protection Agency ("AVK") plays a pivotal role in monitoring compliance and sanctioning firms whose actions undermine ethical market behaviour.

V. Anti-Money Laundering and Terrorist Financing Act: Ethical Oversight as Governance Duty

The Anti-Money Laundering and Terrorist Financing Act ("ZPPDFT-1") imposes obligations on legal persons, particularly financial and commercial entities, to implement compliance programs, conduct risk assessments, and provide beneficial ownership transparency.[26]

While not traditionally viewed as part of corporate purpose, this law signals a shift: ethical and legal compliance is central, not peripheral, to fiduciary duties. Corporate leaders are expected to maintain systems of internal control and reputational oversight, elevating the ethical component of corporate governance.

---

25 Zakon o preprečevanju omejevanja konkurence (ZVK). *Uradni list RS*, št. 36/2008.

26 Zakon o preprečevanju pranja denarja in financiranja terorizma (ZPPDFT-1). *Uradni list RS*, št. 68/2016.

VI. Integrity and Prevention of Corruption Act: Purpose as Integrity

The Zakon o integriteti in preprečevanju korupcije ("ZIntPK") governs both public and private entities and requires that conflicts of interest be disclosed and corruption risks be mitigated through organisational policies.[27]

The law's relevance to corporate purpose lies in its assertion that personal enrichment and company interests may diverge, and that boards and executives have a duty to act in ways that preserve integrity, legality, and public trust.

The act's enforcement body, the Commission for the Prevention of Corruption ("KPK"), has issued guidelines for private companies, reinforcing the relationship between ethical conduct and legitimate governance.

VII. Financial Operations and Insolvency Act: Purpose in Times of Distress

The Financial Operations, Insolvency Proceedings, and Compulsory Dissolution Act ("ZFPPIPP") reinforces Slovenia's stakeholder model by clarifying the hierarchy of obligations during financial instability.[28] While Slovenian company law generally recognises a multi-stakeholder conception of corporate purpose, the ZFPPIPP establishes specific fiduciary obligations for company management to act in the interests of creditors and contractual partners when the company becomes financially distressed.

In particular, the Act obligates directors to:

- monitor solvency proactively;
- avoid delay in initiating insolvency proceedings;
- prioritize creditor protection once insolvency risk is imminent; and
- prevent asset-stripping or preferential treatment to insiders.[29]

This does not represent a shift from shareholder primacy to creditor focus, but rather a recalibration within an already stakeholder-oriented regime, where the legal priority of interests evolves based on the firm's situation.

ZFPPIPP thus confirms the dynamic nature of corporate purpose in Slovenia: directors are expected to balance stakeholder interests in ordinary

27 Zakon o integriteti in preprečevanju korupcije (ZIntPK). *Uradni list RS*, št. 45/2010.

28 Zakon o finančnem poslovanju, postopkih zaradi insolventnosti in prisilnem prenehanju (ZFPPIPP). *Uradni list RS*, št. 13/2014.

29 See Articles 33–35 and 38 of the Financial Operations, Insolvency Proceedings, and Compulsory Dissolution Act (ZFPPIPP), *Uradni list RS*, št. 13/2014.

circumstances, but during insolvency, interests must shift toward legal obligations that protect the financial system and ensure fair treatment of creditors. This aligns with broader EU insolvency standards but retains Slovenia's emphasis on governance as responsible stewardship.

VIII. Environmental Protection Act: Legalizing Sustainability

The 2022 revision of Slovenia's Environmental Protection Act ("ZVO-2") represents a paradigm shift in how corporate purpose is defined in legal and governance terms.[30] It moves beyond environmental compliance to integrate sustainability into the core responsibilities of corporate governance.

Under ZVO-2, medium and large companies must:

- conduct regular environmental risk assessments;
- monitor and disclose environmental impacts;
- integrate sustainable development principles into corporate strategy; and
- implement internal environmental management systems.

This legal architecture is not merely procedural; it institutionalises a broader rethinking of the corporate entity's societal obligations. ZVO-2 explicitly aligns Slovenian law with the EU Green Deal and the Taxonomy Regulation, effectively enshrining long-term planetary health as part of the "interest of the company".

In this framework, the environment becomes a legal stakeholder – not metaphorically, but functionally. Firms must anticipate, mitigate, and report on their ecological impacts as a matter of fiduciary and statutory obligation.

Scholars have noted that such laws mark a significant development in stakeholder theory, expanding its scope to non-human actors and intergenerational interests.[31] Sustainability, once framed as voluntary corporate social responsibility, is now part of the legal definition of the interest of the company, reinforcing Slovenia's distinct model of stakeholder capitalism.

30 Zakon o varstvu okolja (ZVO-2). *Uradni list RS*, št. 44/2022.
31 Raworth, K. (2017). *Doughnut Economics: Seven Ways to Think Like a 21st-Century Economist.* Chelsea Green Publishing.

IX. Soft Law: The Corporate Governance Code for Listed Companies (2016)

Although not legally binding, the Corporate Governance Code for Listed Companies (revised in 2016 by the Ljubljana Stock Exchange in collaboration with the Slovenian Directors' Association and the Securities Market Agency)[32] plays a crucial role in shaping corporate behaviour in Slovenia. As a form of soft law, the Code provides a framework of voluntary best practices that complements statutory obligations under the Companies Act (ZGD-1) and related legislation.

The Code sets out a series of governance principles that reflect both international standards and the distinct institutional identity of Slovenian corporate culture. These principles include:

- transparency in board operations and remuneration;
- the independence and professional qualification of supervisory boards;
- engagement with stakeholders through structured dialogue; and
- promotion of environmental, social, and governance (ESG) practices.

Although compliance with these principles is voluntary, listed companies are required to follow the "comply or explain" principle – publicly stating whether they follow the Code and justifying any deviations. This mechanism establishes a system of accountability that encourages alignment with the Code's principles without relying on coercive enforcement.

Oversight of auditing practices is carried out by the Agency for Public Oversight of Auditing, which assesses auditors' compliance with professional standards and publishes public reports on audit quality. In the area of corporate governance reporting, compliance with the "comply or explain" principles is generally monitored by the Ljubljana Stock Exchange and the Securities Market Agency (ATVP). Companies that deviate from recommended principles without sufficient justification risk reputational damage and reduced investor confidence.

Importantly, the Code reflects the stakeholder-oriented ethos that permeates Slovenian governance. It frames corporate purpose not solely in terms of shareholder return, but in terms of long-term sustainability, social legitimacy, and inclusive governance. In doing so, the Code reinforces

32 Ljubljana Stock Exchange. (2016). *Corporate Governance Code for Listed Companies*. Retrieved from https://ljse.si/en/non-financial/for-issuers/corporate-governance/code.

the legal culture where corporate accountability extends beyond capital to include employees, communities, and the environment.

In essence, the Code functions not as a supplement to the law but as an anchor, institutionalising a multi-dimensional understanding of performance and responsibility that is central to Slovenia's corporate governance identity.

X. Constitutional Foundations of Stakeholder Governance in Slovenia

While the specific provisions governing corporate governance and fiduciary duties are found in sectoral legislation, the broader normative infrastructure is anchored in the Constitution of the Republic of Slovenia[33], which provides clear support for a stakeholder-oriented understanding of the company's interest.

Several constitutional provisions articulate a vision of economic life that goes beyond individual property rights or market autonomy:

- Article 67 mandates that property serve not only private interests but also its economic, social, and environmental function – effectively subordinating corporate rights to the broader public good;
- Article 74 protects economic freedom but explicitly limits enterprise activity that is "contrary to the public interest", legitimizing regulatory interventions aligned with societal goals;
- Article 72 grants all persons the right to a healthy environment, requiring the state to regulate economic activity to prevent environmental harm – a foundation for environmental stakeholder duties codified in acts such as ZVO-2; and
- Article 76 guarantees workers' rights to participate in enterprise governance, embedding co-determination into the constitutional order and reinforcing the legitimacy of employee-elected board representation under the ZSDU.

These provisions collectively illustrate that Slovenia's model of corporate governance is not a product of political fashion or policy trend but rather reflects a deeply-embedded constitutional vision – one that sees economic

33 Republic of Slovenia. (1991). *Constitution of the Republic of Slovenia* (Ustava Republike Slovenije), Official Gazette of the Republic of Slovenia No. 33/91-I with amendments.

actors as social agents governed by principles of inclusion, responsibility, and intergenerational equity.

In this light, the company's interest in Slovenia is shaped not just by legislative drafting or EU harmonisation, but by a constitutional culture that assigns companies a public role within a democratic and sustainable economy.

The Slovenian legal framework therefore does not merely allow for a stakeholder interpretation of the company's interest – it actively demands it. Through a combination of mandatory employee governance, ethical compliance, environmental reporting, and insolvency duties, Slovenia's corporate law constructs a vision of the company as a social institution.

The "interest of the company" in Slovenia is not an empty legal phrase but a dynamic legal standard, deeply embedded in a constitutional culture of inclusion, responsibility, and long-term interests. As pressures from globalisation and financialisation grow, this legal architecture offers both a shield and a compass – protecting foundational values while guiding firms through modern governance challenges.

D. Governance in Practice: Empirical Realities of the Company's Interest in Slovenia

While Slovenia's corporate legal framework firmly endorses a stakeholder approach to the company's interest, it is in actual governance practice that this orientation is either confirmed or challenged. Empirical studies reveal that Slovenian corporate behaviour is not only structured by formal legal obligations but also shaped by institutional memory, ownership patterns, and managerial culture that collectively resist shareholder-dominant models. This section evaluates the expression of the company's interest in Slovenia's enterprise governance, focusing on ownership, board structure, managerial ideology, and adaptive responses to economic shocks.

I. Ownership Structure and Institutional Continuity

Slovenia's post-socialist ownership structure continues to reflect a deliberate rejection of radical liberalisation. During the 1990s, the country adopted a gradualist privatisation model centred on insider ownership, avoiding mass selloffs to foreign investors or state-managed voucher schemes. The outcome was a dispersed but domestically-rooted ownership base, largely composed of managers, employees, and domestic institutional actors such as KAD (Pension Fund) and SOD (Development Fund).[34]

This structure promoted long-term planning and institutional continuity, emphasising established relationships over speculative interests. As Lahovnik notes, this insider model also helped preserve a degree of firm-level autonomy and participatory culture, linking economic control to social legitimacy.[35] Unlike post-socialist states that shifted rapidly to market governance, Slovenia's model remained organisationally patient, reinforcing stakeholder-oriented governance logics.

II. Board Composition and Employee Participation

The legal architecture of corporate governance in Slovenia embeds stakeholder logic into the boardroom itself. Under the Workers' Participation in Management Act (ZSDU), large and medium-sized enterprises must reserve one-third of supervisory board seats for employee-elected representatives.[36]

This co-determination framework is not a symbolic holdover – it meaningfully shapes governance outcomes. Stubelj et al. point out that worker representatives are not passive; they actively participate in discussions concerning firm strategy, investment decisions, and sustainability practices.[37] This two-tier board structure, required under Slovenian law, facilitates oversight and management that embeds non-capital voices into strategic deliberation.

These features align Slovenia more closely with Rhine-style stakeholder capitalism (as seen in Germany or Austria) than with Anglo-American shareholder governance.[38] The presence of employees on supervisory boards provides an institutional channel for employee interests, internal accountability, and long-term interests.

34 Koyama (n5).
35 Lahovnik (n17).
36 Zakon o sodelovanju delavcev pri upravljanju (ZSDU), *Uradni list RS*, št. 42/1993.
37 Stubelj et al. (n10).
38 Cioffi, J. W. (2006). Corporate governance reform, regulatory politics, and the foundations of finance capitalism in the United States and Germany. *German Law Journal, 7*(6), 533–562.

III. Managerial Conceptions of Corporate Purpose

Empirical studies of managerial culture further affirm Slovenia's divergence from shareholder primacy. In a national survey by Stubelj et al., most Slovenian managers expressed a multi-dimensional concept of corporate purpose.[39] Managers' stated priorities included:

- maintaining stable employment and high employee morale;
- ensuring financial sustainability (rather than profit maximization);
- supporting community development and social trust; and
- promoting environmental responsibility.

This stakeholder orientation of managers' priorities reflects both normative beliefs and strategic realism. In a small, open economy, firms often rely on local social capital and public legitimacy as much as they do on market-based indicators of performance. The persistence of these managerial values suggests that managerial decision-making in Slovenia is habitually aligned with constitutional and legal mandates that prioritise inclusiveness and responsibility.

IV. Resilience under Pressure: Financial Crises and Market Forces

Despite this institutional logic, Slovenian firms are not insulated from global market dynamics. As Villanueva-Villar et al. show, periods of macroeconomic stress – particularly during the 2008 financial crisis – moved some firms to temporarily prioritize liquidity and investor reassurance over stakeholder investment.[40] However, even under financial duress, most firms retained their commitment to employee protection and environmental stewardship, demonstrating a level of governance resilience uncommon in market-driven systems.

This resilience stems not only from regulatory compliance, but also from Slovenia's long-standing governance practice – participatory practices, insider ownership, and employee representation have shaped managerial routines and expectations. Coupled with constitutional principles that pri-

39 Stubelj et al. (n10).

40 Villanueva-Villar, M., Rivo-López, E., & Lago-Peñas, S. (2020). On the relationship between corporate governance and value creation in an economic crisis: Empirical evidence for Slovenia. Economic Research – Ekonomska Istraživanja, 33(1), 1576–1595. https://doi.org/10.1080/1331677X.2020.1748506.

oritize social and environmental responsibility, these features provide firms with a normative and institutional anchor. As a result, even under economic stress, Slovenian firms rarely abandon stakeholder commitments or collapse into short-term, shareholder-driven behaviour.

All in all, the empirical landscape of corporate governance in Slovenia demonstrates that the country's stakeholder-oriented legal framework is not a legal fiction but a functional and resilient institutional reality. Ownership structures remain domestically-rooted and focused on long-term interests, avoiding the volatility of capital mobility. The mandatory inclusion of employee representatives on supervisory boards ensures that labour concerns are structurally embedded in governance processes. Managerial ideologies reflect a widespread rejection of shareholder primacy in favour of a pluralistic conception of the company's interest.

Moreover, Slovenia's corporate sector has shown resilience in the face of external shocks. Even during financial crises, stakeholder commitments – particularly to employees and environmental standards – have largely endured. This resilience is not cultural or accidental, but institutionally-produced by legal mandates, historical legacies, and constitutional norms that collectively configure firms as socially embedded entities.

Thus, Slovenian corporate governance should not be seen as an anomaly or a remnant of socialism, but as an example of path-dependent institutional evolution, offering a compelling counterpoint to shareholder-centric models dominant elsewhere in Europe.

This sets the stage for the next section, which will contrast the Slovenian model with other legal and economic regimes, and explore the implications for EU harmonisation, global ESG frameworks, and the future of the company's interest in small market economies.

E. Comparative Analysis: Slovenia in European and Global Perspective

Slovenia's corporate governance model acquires sharper analytical clarity when viewed from a comparative or theoretical perspective. Four aspects are particularly enlightening: its similarities with the Germanic co-determination tradition, its divergence from the Anglo-American shareholder-primacy regime, its contrast with other post-socialist economies, and its partial affinities with the Nordic stakeholder model. These comparisons situate Slovenia within broader debates on the company's interest, varieties of capitalism, and the institutional embedding of economic life.

I. Germany and the Coordinated Market Economy Tradition

Slovenia is frequently located within the "coordinated market economy" (CME) family, as described by Hall and Soskice in the *Varieties of Capitalism* framework.[41] Like Germany, Slovenia employs a two-tier board structure, which institutionalises co-determination, and emphasises long-term, relational contracting.[42]

However, co-determination in Slovenia is less formalised: while German firms over a certain size grant employees parity (50 %) on supervisory boards, Slovenian law only mandates one-third representation for employees on supervisory boards.[43] This difference reflects Slovenia's hybrid heritage: a blend of Yugoslav self-management, which emphasised worker councils, and German-style co-determination imported during EU legal harmonisation.

However, both systems share a constitutional foundation. The German Basic Law requires that property serve the public good (Art. 14 GG), while the Slovenian Constitution mandates that property fulfil its "economic, social, and environmental function" (Art. 67).[44] These parallels illustrate how Slovenia belongs to the European tradition of constitutionalised stakeholder capitalism.

II. The Anglo-American Shareholder Primacy Model

The Anglo-American corporate governance regime has a different legal and theoretical foundation. As Hansmann and Kraakman famously argued, the "end of history for corporate law" was expected to establish shareholder wealth maximisation as the standard objective for corporations globally.[45] In this tradition, fiduciary duties are owed almost exclusively to shareholders, with stakeholders framed as externalities.

---

41 Hall, P. A., & Soskice, D. (2001). *Varieties of Capitalism: The Institutional Foundations of Comparative Advantage*. Oxford University Press.

42 Bohinc, R. (2016). Corporate governance following the Slovenian transition: From success story to failed case. *Acta Oeconomica, 66*(2), 303–323.

43 Mitbestimmungsgesetz [Co-determination Act], BGBl. I S. 1153, 1976 (Germany).

44 Constitution of the Republic of Slovenia, *Uradni list RS*, No. 33/91-I; Basic Law for the Federal Republic of Germany, BGBl. 1949 I, 1.

45 Hansmann, H., & Kraakman, R. (2001). The end of history for corporate law. *Georgetown Law Journal, 89*(2), 439–468.

UK law illustrates the limits of stakeholderism under the Anglo-American model: Section 172 of the Companies Act of 2006 requires directors to "have regard" to employees, customers, and the environment, through the lens of promoting the success of the company for the benefit of shareholders. In the U.S., Delaware jurisprudence has often been interpreted as enshrining shareholder primacy (commonly citing *Dodge v. Ford Motor Co.*)[46], yet contemporary scholarship challenges this interpretation. For example, Mélon demonstrates that shareholder primacy is less a doctrinal necessity than an, reinforced by corporate governance codes, transnational regulation, and financial market logics.[47] Thus, what distinguishes the Anglo-American model is not an absolute legal mandate but ideological export a regulatory and cultural ecosystem that elevates shareholder interests above stakeholder claims.

In contrast, Slovenia shows a persistent rejection of shareholder primacy in favour of multi-constituency purpose.[48] In theoretical terms, Slovenia challenges the inevitability of Hansmann & Kraakman's "end of history" thesis, demonstrating the viability of alternative corporate governance logics in small, open economies.

III. Post-Socialist Divergences

Slovenia also differs sharply from its regional peers. The privatisation pathways of Poland, Hungary, and the Czech Republic were characterized by rapid liberalisation, often under IMF/World Bank pressure, leading to foreign-dominated ownership structures and weak employee voice.[49] In these countries, EU legal harmonisation accelerated convergence towards shareholder models, with stakeholder provisions often left underdeveloped or weakly enforced.

46 *Dodge v. Ford Motor Co.*, 170 N.W. 668 (Mich. 1919); Companies Act 2006, s. 172 (UK).

47 Mélon, L. (2019). *Shareholder Primacy and Global Corporate Governance: A Critical Perspective.* Routledge.

48 Stubelj et al. (n10).

49 Estrin, S., Hanousek, J., Kocenda, E., & Svejnar, J. (2009). The effects of privatization and ownership in transition economies. *Journal of Economic Literature, 47*(3), 699–728.

By contrast, Slovenia's gradual transition preserved insider ownership, state stakes in strategic sectors, and mandatory worker participation.[50] As a result, Slovenia retained institutional features of its self-management legacy, whereas many post-socialist states converged on liberal shareholder capitalism. This divergence demonstrates the importance of path dependency and political choices in shaping post-transition governance models.

IV. Nordic Models: Foundations and Trust-Based Stakeholderism

Slovenia also shares similarities with the Nordic model, particularly Sweden and Denmark, where long-term oriented ownership structures (e.g. family-controlled and foundation-owned firms) and robust welfare states foster a stakeholder-oriented governance equilibrium.[51] Nordic firms often operate under consensual industrial relations, strong unions, and high trust environments, which mirror Slovenia's community-embedded corporate culture.

Yet, there are differences: Nordic stakeholderism is defined by macro-institutional welfare and labour market policies, whereas Slovenia relies more on firm-level governance mechanisms (e.g., worker board representation). Nonetheless, both cases illustrate that stakeholder capitalism is institutionally viable outside of large, coordinated economies like Germany, offering comparative legitimacy to Slovenia's path.

V. EU Harmonization and ESG Convergence

The European Union has become the most ambitious supranational actor in embedding environmental, social, and governance (ESG) principles in corporate law. Directives on takeovers (2004/25/EC), shareholder rights (2007/36/EC), and non-financial disclosure (2014/95/EU) have gradually extended both transparency and investor rights across Member States, while recent initiatives such as the Corporate Sustainability Reporting Directive (CSRD) and the proposed Corporate Sustainability Due Diligence

---

50 Mrak et al. (n6).

51 Thomsen, S., & Rose, C. (2004). Foundation ownership and financial performance: Do companies need owners? *European Journal of Law and Economics, 18*(3), 343–364.

Directive (CSDDD) aim to turn sustainability objectives from a voluntary commitment to a binding duty.[52]

For many Member States – particularly those with liberal or post-socialist governance models – this represents a profound recalibration of the company's interest. In Slovenia, however, ESG harmonization lands differently. Since Slovenia's legal order already constitutionalises the social and environmental function of property (Art. 67) and the right to a healthy environment (Art. 72), the incorporation of ESG standards does not displace an entrenched shareholder model but rather reinforces a pre-existing stakeholder conception of the company's interest.[53]

The 2022 revision of the Environmental Protection Act (ZVO-2) exemplifies this synergy. ZVO-2 requires firms to conduct environmental risk assessments, implement internal sustainability controls, and disclose ecological impacts – obligations that mirror EU ESG directives but acquire deeper normative force in Slovenia.[54] They are not framed as external compliance costs, but as constitutionalised fiduciary responsibilities toward society and nature. In effect, Slovenian law recognizes the environment as a stakeholder whose interests directors must safeguard alongside those of employees, creditors, and communities.

From this perspective, Slovenia should not be seen merely as a laboratory of ESG integration but as a proof of concept for the EU's broader ambitions: a demonstration that ESG obligations can be internalized within governance as part of a constitutional framework of corporate responsibility. Where other Member States must reorient entrenched shareholder doctrines, Slovenia is a case of supranational ESG norms converging seamlessly with domestic traditions of participatory governance and constitutional stakeholderism.

---

52 Directive 2004/25/EC of the European Parliament and of the Council of 21 April 2004 on takeover bids; Directive 2007/36/EC of the European Parliament and of the Council of 11 July 2007 on the exercise of certain rights of shareholders in listed companies; Directive 2014/95/EU of the European Parliament and of the Council of 22 October 2014 amending Directive 2013/34/EU as regards disclosure of non-financial and diversity information by certain large undertakings and groups; Directive (EU) 2022/2464 of the European Parliament and of the Council of 14 December 2022 on corporate sustainability reporting (CSRD); Proposal for a Directive of the European Parliament and of the Council on corporate sustainability due diligence and amending Directive (EU) 2019/1937 (CSDDD), COM(2022) 71 final.

53 Constitution of the Republic of Slovenia, *Uradni list RS*, No. 33/91-I.

54 Zakon o varstvu okolja (ZVO-2). *Uradni list RS*, št. 44/2022.

F. Challenges and Future Directions

Slovenia's corporate governance framework represents one of the most distinctive articulations of the company's interest as stakeholder-oriented in Europe. Its normative depth is anchored in the legacy of self-management, its gradualist transition strategy, and its constitutional embedding of social and environmental duties. Yet this model, however robust, is not immune to pressure. As Slovenia becomes more integrated into global markets, European Union policy frameworks, and transnational governance debates, it faces challenges that will determine whether its stakeholder model will endure, adapt, or erode.

The following subsections outline the principal challenges confronting Slovenian corporate governance. These challenges are not merely technical or economic; they are constitutional and normative. They revolve around the tension between embedded stakeholder logics and external pressures of financialisation, political capture, and global ESG standardisation. The section concludes by sketching possible trajectories for Slovenia's governance model, including its potential role as a European norm entrepreneur in defining the company's interest.

I. Financialisation and Capital Market Pressures

One of the defining global trends of the past four decades has been the financialisation of corporate governance. Financialisation refers to the growing dominance of financial logics, actors, and instruments over productive economic activity.[55] In corporate law, this manifests in prioritising shareholder returns and quarterly earnings, and maximising stock price. For small open economies, financialisation often arrives through external capital flows, foreign direct investment, and cross-border financial institutions.

Slovenia has, until recently, remained relatively insulated from financialisation. Its insider privatisation model of the 1990s produced firms with dispersed, domestic ownership, dominated by employees, managers, and state-controlled funds. This ownership structure shielded Slovenian firms from hostile takeovers, activist investors, and the pressure of shareholder

55 Krippner, G. R. (2005). The financialization of the American economy. *Socio-Economic Review*, 3(2), 173–208.

value maximisation.[56] The constitutional duty for property to serve social and environmental functions further legitimised stakeholder priorities.

However, as Slovenia deepens its integration into global financial markets, foreign ownership of listed companies has increased and international institutional investors play a growing role.[57] These actors are often driven by short-term performance metrics and standardised ESG ratings, rather than Slovenia's constitutionalised stakeholder logics. This raises the risk of creeping toward shareholder primacy – not by explicit legal reform, but through market practice and investor expectations.

Comparisons are instructive. Ireland, another small EU economy, embraced financialisation aggressively, attracting multinational corporations and financial institutions by deregulating corporate law and taxation.[58] The result was rapid growth, but also vulnerability to global capital flows, as seen in the 2008 financial crisis. Slovenia's institutional path is different, but the lesson is clear: unless stakeholder duties are continually reinforced, financialisation can erode stakeholder commitments gradually and silently.

II. State-Owned Enterprises and Political Capture

State-owned enterprises (SOEs) remain a pillar of Slovenia's corporate landscape. In sectors such as energy, finance, telecommunications, and infrastructure, the state retains significant ownership stakes.[59] On paper, this could serve as a bulwark of stakeholder governance, ensuring that firms act in the public interest and align with constitutional principles. In practice, however, SOEs have been a double-edged sword.

The key problem lies in political capture. SOEs in Slovenia are managed through the Slovenian Sovereign Holding (SSH), which centralises state ownership. Although the SSH was designed to professionalise governance, it is frequently criticised for its susceptibility to political appointments and short-term electoral considerations.[60] This creates a paradox: the state, as shareholder, is constitutionally mandated to safeguard the public interest,

---

56 Lahovnik (n17).

57 Cernat, L. (2004). The emerging European corporate governance model: Anglo-Saxon, Continental, or still the century of diversity? *Journal of European Public Policy, 11*(1), 147–166.

58 Hardiman, N. (2012). *The Irish tiger: Economic crisis and the politics of austerity.* Palgrave Macmillan.

59 Lahovnik (n17).

60 Slovenian Sovereign Holding (SSH). (2023). *Annual Report.* Ljubljana.

yet in practice SOEs are vulnerable to patronage, clientelism, and government scandals.

The most notorious case of this happening is the TEŠ6 power plant project, where cost overruns, opaque contracts, and political interference resulted in massive financial losses and public distrust.[61] Instead of embodying stakeholder governance, in this case, the SOE became a vehicle for rent-seeking and elite capture. Such instances risk undermining the legitimacy of Slovenia's stakeholder model, reinforcing narratives that stakeholderism equates to inefficiency and corruption.

The challenge, then, is not whether SOEs should exist – they are constitutionally and economically justified – but how they are governed. Without stronger safeguards against political interference, SOEs may become the Achilles' heel of Slovenia's corporate governance system.

III. Generational Change and Managerial Mindsets

A striking feature of Slovenian firms is that managers overwhelmingly reject shareholder primacy. Stubelj et al. found that Slovenian executives see the company's interest in multi-dimensional terms, balancing financial sustainability with employee well-being, community engagement, and environmental stewardship.[62]

Yet managerial culture is not static. As Slovenia globalises, new generations of managers are increasingly trained abroad in Anglo-American business schools or recruited by multinational corporations. These institutions often socialise managers into favouring the shareholder value approach, emphasizing return on equity, stock options, and financial metrics. This raises the prospect of a cultural shift in Slovenia, where Slovenia's stakeholder ethos is gradually replaced by imported managerial ideologies.

Moreover, Slovenia faces a brain drain problem: talented young professionals often leave for careers abroad, further weakening the domestic managerial pool.[63] If the managers who remain are disproportionately shaped

61 Rep, M. (2016). *Zero tolerance of corruption? The act of systemic investigations of projects of national importance.* In Criminal Justice and Security in Central and Eastern Europe: Safety, Security and Social Control in Local Communities (pp. 442–454). Ljubljana: University of Maribor Press.

62 Stubelj et al. (n10).

63 Mrak et al. (n6).

by multinational logics, the normative content of Slovenia's corporate governance model may erode, even without formal legal reform.

From the perspective of corporate constitutionalism, this represents a potential breakdown in the "constitutional memory" of self-management and participation.[64] The law may mandate stakeholder duties, but if managers interpret these duties through a shareholder lens, the constitutional spirit of the Slovenian model risks dilution. The challenge, therefore, is to embed stakeholder values not just in statutes, but in managerial identity and education.

IV. ESG: Between Substantive Duty and Market Capture

The rise of ESG (environmental, social, and governance) frameworks offers Slovenia both opportunities and risks. On one hand, ESG aligns closely with Slovenia's constitutional ethos: Article 72 guarantees the right to a healthy environment, while the ZVO-2 explicitly embeds environmental responsibilities into corporate operations.[65] This positions Slovenia as a leader in what might be called constitutional ESG – where sustainability is not a voluntary commitment but a fiduciary duty.

On the other hand, the globalisation of ESG has generated risks of financialisation and capture. ESG performance is increasingly assessed through ratings agencies, benchmarks, and indices. Scholars warn that this process risks reducing sustainability to quantitative proxies, favouring disclosure over substance.[66] In such a scenario, Slovenia's deep stakeholder commitments could be hollowed out into box-ticking exercises, eroding their normative force.

Comparisons with other EU jurisdictions highlight the stakes. France's *loi PACTE* (2019) introduced "purpose" clauses for firms, but enforcement was weak. Germany's Lieferkettengesetz (2021) mandates supply chain due diligence but has been criticized for its limited scope. Slovenia's ZVO-2, by contrast, has constitutional backing, but it will require strong enforcement to avoid the fate of formalistic ESG regimes elsewhere.

---

64 Teubner, G. (2011). *Constitutional fragments: Societal constitutionalism and globalization.* Oxford University Press.

65 Zakon o varstvu okolja (ZVO-2). *Uradni list RS*, št. 44/2022.

66 Crane, A., Henriques, I., Husted, B. W., & Matten, D. (2022). *Measuring Corporate Sustainability: Towards Integrating Qualitative and Quantitative Assessment.* Journal of Business Ethics, 179(1), 15–32.

V. Geopolitical and EU Integration Pressures

Slovenia's integration into the European Union raises the question of convergence versus distinctiveness. EU directives on shareholder rights and corporate transparency often reflect a liberal-market orientation, emphasising capital mobility and investor protection.[67] For post-socialist states, these directives have accelerated convergence toward shareholder models. Slovenia, however, incorporated EU law within its stakeholder framework, illustrating the possibility of hybridisation.

The challenge is whether this hybridisation can be sustained. As EU law evolves through the CSRD and CSDDD, Slovenia will face pressure to conform to standardised ESG models that may dilute its constitutional specificity. At the same time, this opens opportunities for Slovenia to act as a norm entrepreneur, shaping EU debates by offering a concrete example of stakeholder constitutionalism.[68] Slovenia's small-state status, often framed as a vulnerability, may thus become a source of normative influence.

VI. Normative Futures: Scenarios for Slovenian Governance

Looking forward, Slovenia's governance model faces three plausible futures:

1. Resilient Stakeholder Model: Slovenia doubles down on constitutional ESG, professionalises SOE governance, and embeds the stakeholder value approach in managerial education. Its model becomes a reference point in EU debates, contributing to the Europeanisation of stakeholder capitalism.
2. Hybrid Convergence: Slovenia retains formal stakeholder provisions, but under pressure from financialisation and EU harmonisation, these provisions are gradually hollowed. Firms perform stakeholder duties as compliance exercises, while managers adopt a shareholder value approach in practice.

67 Directive 2007/36/EC on shareholder rights; Directive 2014/95/EU on non-financial disclosure.

68 Katzenstein, P. (1985). *Small states in world markets: Industrial policy in Europe.* Cornell University Press; Finnemore, M., & Sikkink, K. (1998). International norm dynamics and political change. *International Organization, 52*(4), 887–917.

3. Erosion Scenario: Political capture of SOEs, brain drain, and ESG financialisation combine to erode stakeholder governance. Slovenia converges with liberal models, losing its distinct identity.

Which future prevails will depend not only on legal reform, but on constitutional interpretation, managerial culture, and Slovenia's capacity to act as a norm entrepreneur within the EU.

G. Conclusion: Slovenia and the Constitutionalisation of Sustainable Corporate Purpose

This chapter has traced the historical, legal, and empirical dimensions of corporate governance in Slovenia, demonstrating how the concept of the "interest of the company" has been constructed in ways that defy the dominant shareholder-oriented narrative of corporate law. By situating Slovenia within its unique trajectory – from the Yugoslav system of self-management, through a gradual post-socialist transition, to EU integration – it becomes clear that Slovenia has forged an alternative understanding of the company's interest: one that is explicitly stakeholder-oriented, constitutionally grounded, and sustainability-driven.

The significance of this model cannot be overstated. In comparative scholarship, small post-socialist states are often treated as transitional anomalies, destined either to converge toward Anglo-American shareholder primacy or to replicate the continental co-determination structures of larger European states. Slovenia's case demonstrates that another destiny is possible. It shows that corporate governance can evolve into a distinctive constitutional form, one that embeds social and environmental sustainability not as discretionary add-ons but as core fiduciary duties.

I. Social Sustainability: Companies as Social Institutions

Slovenia's most enduring contribution lies in its treatment of companies as social institutions. This is not merely rhetoric but an institutional design principle that flows directly from the Yugoslav legacy of worker self-management. Even after the dismantling of socialist councils, Slovenia retained a culture, and accompanying structure, of participation. Employee representation on supervisory boards institutionalises the voice of labour within governance. State ownership of strategic firms – though imperfect in its execution – reflects a constitutional recognition that companies are vehicles of collective goods, not merely instruments of private capital.

This approach embeds social sustainability within corporate law. Whereas liberal shareholder regimes often confront crises of legitimacy, Slovenia maintains a framework in which firms are expected to balance profitability with fairness, inclusion, and social cohesion. Stubelj et al. confirm this: Slovenian managers consistently reject the idea that shareholder value alone defines corporate success. Instead, they understand the "interest of the company" as a multi-constituency responsibility that binds together employees, communities, and broader societal interests.

In this sense, Slovenia operationalises corporate social sustainability by ensuring that companies maintain a social license to operate, one grounded in legal duties rather than soft codes. This is a crucial insight for sustainability debates: legitimacy and inclusion are not afterthoughts but conditions of long-term viability.

II. Environmental Sustainability: Nature as a Constitutional Stakeholder

Equally significant is Slovenia's pioneering recognition of environmental sustainability as a core component of company interest. The Slovenian Constitution goes further than most European counterparts by explicitly embedding ecological responsibility in its provisions: Article 72 guarantees the right to a healthy environment and Article 67 mandates that property must serve social, environmental, and economic functions.

This constitutional grounding is reinforced by statutory law. The ZVO-2 requires firms to conduct environmental risk assessments and integrate sustainability into governance practices. This effectively elevates environmental stewardship into the realm of fiduciary obligation: directors are not free to ignore ecological impacts because these impacts form part of the company's legally-defined purpose.

The ZVO-2 positions Slovenia at the forefront of what might be called corporate ecological constitutionalism. Whereas other jurisdictions are only beginning to contend with how to integrate environmental concerns into corporate law – through voluntary ESG disclosures or soft governance codes – Slovenia has already constitutionalised the environment as a stakeholder. This implication is profound: the natural environment is not an "externality" but a co-constituent of a firm's legal purpose.

III. Institutional Sustainability: Path Dependence and Resilience

Slovenia's governance framework also demonstrates a unique form of institutional sustainability. Its post-independence trajectory was marked by gradual transition: rather than pursuing shock therapy or wholesale privatisation, Slovenia deliberately preserved continuity in its governance structures. This path dependence has had long-term consequences.

Namely, it produced a corporate landscape dominated by insider ownership, state participation, and managerial cultures infused with the ethos of participation. At the same time, EU integration required Slovenia to adopt directives on shareholder rights, transparency, and reporting. Unlike other post-socialist states, Slovenia embedded these EU norms within its own constitutional culture, preventing convergence toward shareholder primacy.

This resilience shows that corporate governance systems are not fragile by default. When designed with constitutional anchoring and cultural legitimacy, they can absorb external pressures – such as financialisation and ESG standardisation – without losing their unique identity.

IV. Theoretical Implications: Corporate Purpose as Constitutional Choice

Slovenia's system has major implications for corporate governance theory. Slovenia's system has major implications for corporate governance theory. Hansmann and Kraakman's influential "end of history" thesis claimed that shareholder value maximisation would inevitably become the global model. Slovenia demonstrates the opposite: that the company's interest is not a functional inevitability but a constitutional choice. As Mélon has argued, shareholder primacy is not doctrinally necessary but an ideological export. Slovenia resists this export by embedding stakeholder duties into its constitution and statutes. The result is a governance system that not only survives within the EU's liberalising framework but actively contributes to its sustainability agenda.

At the same time, as discussed in Section F, this achievement is not immune to erosion. The global financialisation of ESG and the growing dominance of quantitative rating systems risk hollowing out Slovenia's stakeholder commitments into formal compliance, undermining their normative substance. This tension forces a rethinking of corporate governance theory: efficiency cannot be the sole criterion of evaluation. Legitimacy, inclusion, and ecological stewardship must be treated as constitutional goods, on par with profitability. Slovenia thus provides both a model and a warning – showing that small economies can constitutionalise corporate sustainability, but that maintaining its substance requires vigilance against global pressures toward homogenisation.

As Mélon has argued, shareholder primacy is not doctrinally necessary but is an ideological export. Slovenia resists this export by embedding stakeholder duties into its constitution and statutes. The result is a governance system that not only survives within the EU's liberalising framework but actively contributes to its sustainability agenda.

This forces a rethinking of corporate governance theory. Efficiency cannot be the sole criterion of evaluation. Legitimacy, inclusion, and ecological stewardship must be treated as constitutional goods, on par with profitability. Slovenia provides the empirical evidence for this claim, demonstrating that small economies can constitutionalise corporate sustainability without sacrificing integration into global markets.

V. Toward a Juridical Framework of Sustainable Capitalism

Perhaps the most groundbreaking insight from Slovenia is that it offers a juridical framework for sustainable corporate governance. This framework consists of three interlinked dimensions:

- social sustainability: mandatory employee participation, stakeholder fiduciary duties, and a managerial culture resistant to shareholder primacy;
- environmental sustainability: constitutional provisions and statutory duties that elevate ecological protection to the level of fiduciary obligation; and
- institutional sustainability: a gradual, path-dependent approach that is a hybridisation of EU norms and domestic constitutional traditions, ensuring resilience against convergence pressures.

Together, these dimensions amount to a vision of corporate purpose that is both distinctive and transferable. Slovenia demonstrates that corporate law can be written to sustain not only financial returns but also social legitimacy and ecological balance.

VI. Closing Reflection: Shareholder Primacy is Not Destiny

The final lesson is that shareholder primacy is not destiny. Slovenia's experience proves that corporate governance can be designed otherwise – that firms can be constituted as social and ecological institutions, with fiduciary obligations extending beyond investors to communities, employees, and nature itself.

This is not a utopian abstraction but an institutional reality that has taken root within a small, open European economy. While the future of Slovenia's model remains contingent, several factors suggest that its stakeholder orientation is likely to endure: the constitutional embedding of social and environmental duties, the resilience of cooperative and public ownership structures, and the growing alignment between EU policy frameworks and sustainability-oriented governance.

Slovenia thus illustrates that constitutional sustainability in corporate governance is not only possible but politically and institutionally resilient – though its preservation depends on continued resistance to the financialisation and standardisation pressures that threaten to erode its normative foundations.

For scholars, this challenges us to reconceptualise corporate law as a field of constitutional design, not mere efficiency. For policymakers, it provides a model of how sustainability can be embedded in company law, not as an external burden but as a core purpose. For practitioners, it demonstrates that firms can thrive within a legal framework that treats stakeholders and the environment as integral to long-term success.

In an era of ecological collapse, legitimacy crises, and rising inequality, Slovenia offers more than a case study. It offers a proof of concept that the company's interest can be constitutionalised in the service of sustainability. Its story is not marginal but pioneering, not transitional but transformative. Slovenia stands as evidence that the future of corporate governance lies not in the triumph of shareholder primacy but in the constitutional embedding of social and environmental sustainability as the very definition of the company's interest.

References

Legal Sources

Companies Act (ZGD-1). (2006). *Uradni list RS*, št. 42/2006 (with amendments).

Constitution of the Republic of Slovenia. (1991). *Uradni list RS*, No. 33/91-I.

Directive 2004/25/EC of the European Parliament and of the Council of 21 April 2004 on takeover bids.

Directive 2007/36/EC of the European Parliament and of the Council of 11 July 2007 on the exercise of certain rights of shareholders in listed companies.

Directive 2014/95/EU of the European Parliament and of the Council of 22 October 2014 amending Directive 2013/34/EU as regards disclosure of non-financial and diversity information.

Directive (EU) 2022/2464 of the European Parliament and of the Council of 14 December 2022 as regards corporate sustainability reporting (CSRD).

Slovenian Sovereign Holding (SSH). (2020). *Annual report.* Ljubljana.

Zakon o varstvu okolja (ZVO-2). (2022). *Uradni list RS*, št. 44/2022.

Academic References

Bezo, Y., Brahimi, A., & Dibra, R. (2015). *Corporate governance in transition countries.* CORE. https://core.ac.uk/download/pdf/234630519.pdf

Bohle, D., & Greskovits, B. (2012). *Capitalist diversity on Europe's periphery.* Cornell University Press.

Bohinc, R. (2001). Corporate governance in post-privatized Slovenia. *American Journal of Comparative Law, 49*(1), 49–74.

Bohinc, R. (2016). Corporate governance following the Slovenian transition: From success story to failed case. *Acta Oeconomica, 66*(2), 303–323. https://doi.org/10.1556/032.2016.66.2.6

Crane, A., Henriques, I., Husted, B. W., & Matten, D. (2022). *Measuring Corporate Sustainability: Towards Integrating Qualitative and Quantitative Assessment.* Journal of Business Ethics, 179(1), 15–32.

Crane, A., Matten, D., & Spence, L. J. (2022). *Corporate social responsibility: Readings and cases in a global context* (4th ed.). Routledge.

Eman, K., & Hacin, R. (2015). A discourse on the gray economy. In K. Eman, T. Furdi, & B. Dobovšek (Eds.), *Corruption, fraud, organized crime, and the shadow economy* (pp. 167–186). CRC Press.

Estrin, S., Hanousek, J., Kocenda, E., & Svejnar, J. (2009). The effects of privatization and ownership in transition economies. *Journal of Economic Literature, 47*(3), 699–728. https://doi.org/10.1257/jel.47.3.699

Finnemore, M., & Sikkink, K. (1998). International norm dynamics and political change. *International Organization, 52*(4), 887–917. https://doi.org/10.1162/002081898550789

Gregorič, A., Prašnikar, J., & Ribnikar, I. (2000). Corporate governance in Slovenia: An international perspective. *Slovenian Economic Review, 51*(1), 27–52.

Hansmann, H., & Kraakman, R. (2001). The end of history for corporate law. *Georgetown Law Journal, 89*(2), 439–468.

Hardiman, N. (2012). *The Irish tiger: Economic crisis and the politics of austerity.* Palgrave Macmillan.

Katzenstein, P. J. (1985). *Small states in world markets: Industrial policy in Europe.* Cornell University Press.

Koyama, Y. (2013). *Self-management in Yugoslavia and after.* Gdansk University.

Krippner, G. R. (2005). The financialization of the American economy. *Socio-Economic Review, 3*(2), 173–208. https://doi.org/10.1093/SER/mwi008

Lahovnik, M. (2019). Corporate governance in post-privatization Slovenia: Patterns of control and sustainability. *Acta Oeconomica, 69*(2), 253–271.

Mayer, C. (2018). *Prosperity: Better business makes the greater good.* Oxford University Press.

Mélon, L. (2019). *Shareholder primacy and global corporate governance: A critical perspective.* Routledge.

Mrak, M., Rojec, M., & Silva-Jáuregui, C. (2004). *Slovenia: From Yugoslavia to the European Union.* World Bank.

Mygind, N., Demina, N., Gregorič, A., & Kapelyushnikov, R. (2004). Corporate governance cycles during transition: A comparison of Russia and Slovenia. Copenhagen Business School Working Paper.

Prašnikar, J., & Gregorič, A. (2002). The influence of workers' participation on the power of management in transitional countries: The case of Slovenia. *Annals of Public and Cooperative Economics, 73*(2), 269–297. https://doi.org/10.1111/1467-8292.00163

Rep, M. (2016). Zero tolerance of corruption? The act of systemic investigations of projects of national importance. In *Criminal justice and security in Central and Eastern Europe: Safety, security and social control in local communities* (pp. 442–454). University of Maribor Press.

Sjåfjell, B., & Bruner, C. M. (Eds.). (2020). *The Cambridge handbook of corporate law, corporate governance and sustainability.* Cambridge University Press.

Stubelj, I., Dolenc, P., Biloslavo, R., Nahtigal, M., & Laporšek, S. (2017). Corporate purpose in a small post-transitional economy: The case of Slovenia. *Economic Research – Ekonomska Istraživanja, 30*(1), 818–835. https://doi.org/10.1080/1331677X.2017.1311230

Teubner, G. (2011). *Constitutional fragments: Societal constitutionalism and globalization.* Oxford University Press.

9. The Understanding of the Company's Interest in Lithuania and its Receptiveness to Sustainability Imperatives

Lina Mikaloniene

A. Introduction

After the restoration of Lithuania's independence on 11 March 1990, the country developed a new civil law system to reflect the new political and economic circumstances. This transformation of the Lithuanian civil law system was inevitable, as during the nearly 50-years that Lithuania was occupied and annexed by the Soviet Union, civil law was based on socialist ideology, which essentially denied private ownership and freedom of economic activity and initiative.[1] In the Soviet era, the main emphasis was on legal persons that belonged to the state; these legal persons, as institutions, were used to carry out functions set by the Soviet authorities, and for-profit legal persons were ignored.[2] In its legal reform, Lithuania had to validate the freedom of economic activity of natural and legal persons; accordingly, reforming the institution of a corporate personality was as important as restoring the institution of private ownership.[3]

In 1990, Lithuania adopted the Law on Undertakings, which provided a general framework for business organizations to operate as undertakings and listed the types of business undertakings (*inter alia,* stock companies – a public limited liability company and a private limited liability company) that were to be regulated by specific laws.[4] The law also provided a guarantee that undertakings would be autonomous and would not be bound to perform tasks assigned by state authorities (Art 14(1)). This law served as the foundation for the further development of the legal framework for

1 Sagatys/Pakalniškis, p. 13 (14, 16); Sinkevičius/Jakulevičienė/Drukteinienė/Jurkevičius, p. 280.

2 Sinkevičius/Jakulevičienė/Bitė, p. 311 (318, 320–322, 338); an important group of legal entities consisted of agricultural and fishermen collective farms and cooperatives.

3 Mesonis/Pakalniškis/Tikniūtė, p. 575 (577).

4 Law on Undertakings of the Republic of Lithuania No. I-196, Lietuvos aidas, 1990, No. 3–0, which came into force on 1 July 1990.

companies.[5] Soon after, the law governing stock companies was adopted: the 1990 Law on Stock Companies governed both public limited liability companies and private limited liability companies.[6]

After transitioning to a market economy, the Lithuanian Law on Stock Companies, which set out a legal framework for public limited liability companies (*akcinė bendrovė, AB,* "public company") and private limited liability companies (*uždaroji akcinė bendrovė, UAB,* "private company") (hereafter both together referred as "companies" or "company") was reworked three times, in 1990, 1994,[7] and 2000,[8] with each iteration being further amended and supplemented.[9] The new Civil Code ("CC") of 2000[10] established a general framework for legal persons, but it did not codify different types of undertakings; thus, companies continued to be governed by the Law on Stock Companies.

All three versions of the Law on Stock Companies (1990, 1994, 2000) defined a company as both an undertaking and a legal entity. However, a hard law rule on whose interests a company should pursue,[11] for whom the company is managed,[12] or who the ultimate beneficiaries of corporate activities should be[13] (hereafter "company's interest") – as it currently stands in the Law on Stock Companies, was not adopted from the start.

---

5 Mesonis/Pakalniškis/Tikniūtė, p. 575 (578); Birštonas/Žilys, p.13 (52–57).

6 Law on Stock Companies of the Republic of Lithuania No. I-425, Lietuvos aidas, 1990, No. 57–0, which came into force on 1 August 1990.

7 Law on Stock Companies of the Republic of Lithuania No. I-528, VZ, 1994, 55–1046, which came into force on 20 July 1994.

8 Law on Stock Companies of the Republic of Lithuania No. VIII-1835, VZ, 2000, 64–1914, which came into force on 1 July 2001 (with further amendments and supplements) ("LSC").

9 For a historical evolution of the Law on Stock Companies since 1990: Birštonas/Bitė, p. 150 (150–180); Sinkevičius/Jakulevičienė/Bitė, p. 311 (322–338).

10 Civil Code of the Republic of Lithuania No. VIII-1864, VZ, 2000, No. 74–2262, which came into force on 1 July 2001, safe to certain exceptions (with further amendments and supplements).

11 Ferrarini, Corporate Purpose and Sustainability, 2020, https://ssrn.com/abstract=3753594, p. 6.

12 Hopt, Corporate Purpose and Stakeholder Value – Historical, Economic and Comparative Law Remarks on the Current Debate, Legislative Options and Enforcement Problems, 2023, https://ssrn.com/abstract=4390119, p. 2, 41; Rock, For Whom is the Corporation Managed in 2020?: The Debate over Corporate Purpose, 2020, https://ssrn.com/abstract=3589951, p. 7–16.

13 Kershaw/Schuster, The Purposive Transformation of Corporate Law, 2019, https://ssrn.com/abstract=3363267, p. 1, 54. For different meanings of a corporate purpose also see: Fleischer, Corporate Purpose: A Management Concept and its Implications

The normative terms "*objectives of the activities of the legal person*" and "*objectives of the legal person*" must be considered to understand a company's interest. In a narrow sense, these terms reflect the company's types of business activities, while in a broader sense, they encompass the general characteristics of the particular class of a legal person.

The first version of the Law on Stock Companies (1990) required that the articles of association of a company list commercial activities (types of products, works and services), but it did not contain an obligation to include broader objectives of the company in the articles of association, nor did it deal with a company's interest in a direct and specific manner.

The second version of the Law on Stock Companies (1994) required that the articles of association of a company include both the objectives of the company's activities and the types of business activities the company performs (Art. 7(2)-3).[14] In addition, it imposed a duty on corporate management bodies to act in accordance with the objectives of the company's activities as set out in the articles of association. According to Article 18(6):

> *[t]he management bodies of the company shall not be entitled to take any decisions or perform other actions that are in breaches of the company's articles of association or contrary to the objectives of the company's activities as set out in the articles of association, that are manifestly in excess of the normal production-business risks, that are manifestly loss-making (purchase of goods, services or works at prices higher than, or sale below market prices, wasting of the company's assets), or that are manifestly not economically viable.*

It was proposed that, rather than having a complicated regulation that listed possible abuses that could be committed by a company's management, an all-inclusive general norm that places a duty on management bodies to "act solely in the interests of the company" should be used. Specifically, Article 18(6) of the Law on Stock Companies (1994) could be amended as follows:

> *[t]he company's supervisory council, board and administration shall not be entitled to take any decisions or take any other actions that are in breaches of the articles of association of the company or that are contrary to the*

---

for Company Law, 2021, https://ssrn.com/abstract=3770656; EMCA, 2017, https://ssrn.com/abstract=2929348, p. 34–36, 50–51, 257–258.

14 Law amending and supplementing Law on Stock Companies of the Republic of Lithuania No. VIII-666, VZ, 1998, No. 36–961, which came into force on 17 April 1998.

objectives of the company's activities as set out in the articles of association, and shall be obliged to act solely in the interests of the company.[15]

However, this proposed amendment to the Law on Stock Companies (1994) was not adopted.

According to the third version of the Law on Stock Companies (2000), articles of association of a company must specify the objectives of the company's activities, as well as the nature of its business activities (Art. 5(2)-3). Since 2004, aiming to harmonize the legislation with the EU *acquis communautaire,* the Law on Stock Companies has been amended, requiring the articles of association of a company to include "*objectives of the company's activities, indicating the object of a company's activities*" (Art. 4(2)-4).[16]

Unlike the first two versions of the Law on Stock Companies that did not deal with a company's interest in a direct and specific way, the third version of the Law on Stock Companies (2000) required corporate management bodies to act for the benefit of the company and its shareholders, as follows:

- Between 1 July 2001 until 31 December 2003, Article 22(8) of the Law on Stock Companies stated the following : *[t]he management bodies of the company must act solely for the benefit of the company and its shareholders. The management bodies of the company shall not be entitled to take any decisions or perform other actions that are in breaches of the company's articles of association or contrary to the objectives of the company's activities set out in the articles of association, that are manifestly in excess of the normal production-business risks, that are manifestly loss-making (purchase of goods, services or works at prices higher than, or sale below market prices, wasting of the company's assets), or that are manifestly not economically viable.*

15 Explanatory Note No. P-1498 of 14 December 1998 regarding draft Law amending and supplementing Law on Stock Companies.

16 According to Directive (EU) 2017/1132 of the European Parliament and of the Council of 14 June 2017 relating to certain aspects of company law ((codification) (Text with EEA relevance), OJ L 169, 30.6.2017, p. 46–127, ELI: http://data.europa.eu/eli/dir/2017/1132/2022-08-12), the statutes or the instrument of incorporation of a public company have to state its objects (Art. 3(b)). Further, for both a public and private company, its objects play a vital role in addressing the *ultra vires* doctrine (Art. 9) as well as in applying the company's nullity (Art. 11). In the Lithuanian version of Arts. 3(b), 9 and 11 of the directive (EU) 2017/1132 the term "*the objects of the company*" is translated as "*bendrovės veiklos objektas*" which, read literally, could be understood as "*the object of the company's activities*".

- From 1 January 2004[17]until the present, Article 19(8) of the Law on Stock Companies sets forth the following: *[t]he management bodies of the company must act for the benefit of the company and its shareholders, comply with laws and other legal acts and follow the company's articles of association.*

The first version of the Law on Stock Companies (1990)[18] introduced mandatory rules on employee co-determination, however, subsequently the other versions of the Law on Stock Companies (1994, 2000) did not retain such rules.

Therefore, since 1990, the concept of a company has been linked to that of an undertaking and an entity, and it was not until the third version of the Law on Stock Companies (2000) ("LSC") that a specific rule as to the company's interest was introduced. On 1 July 2001, the hard law rule on a company's interest came into force, along with the new CC which, *inter alia,* laid out a binary classification of legal persons based on the difference in founding interests between legal persons pursuing social goals and those pursuing private interests.

A company's interest as the central concept in corporate governance attracted considerable attention from foreign scholars. In short, there are two prevailing theories that are established either as a hard law rule or as a social norm as to how a company's interest is defined, where boundaries are designed for corporate management bodies in their direction and control of the companies.[19] First is the shareholder primacy theory, which aims to promote shareholder value. The enlightened shareholder value approach when other stakeholder interests are considered while maintaining the interest of shareholders will become the shareholder primacy theory. Second is the stakeholder theory, which focuses on a pluralistic governance

17 A new wording of the Law on Stock Companies of the Republic of Lithuania No. IX-1889, VZ, 2003, No. 123–5574.

18 1/3 of members of the supervisory council had to be elected by an employees' meeting of the company, however, save to private companies with 200 or less employees (Arts. 17 and 23(2)).

19 E.g. Hopt, Corporate Purpose and Stakeholder Value – Historical, Economic and Comparative Law Remarks on the Current Debate, Legislative Options and Enforcement Problems, 2023, https://ssrn.com/abstract=4390119; Fleischer, Corporate Purpose: A Management Concept and its Implications for Company Law, 2021, https://ssrn.com/abstract=3770656; Ferrarini, Corporate Purpose and Sustainability, 2020, https://ssrn.com/abstract=3753594. Bebchuk/Tallarita, Will Corporations Deliver Value to All Stakeholders? 2021, https://ssrn.com/abstract=3899421.

model. In both theories, the company's interest helps to define what duties the company management has.

Corporate strategies and business models, as well as the decisions and practices of companies that integrate economic, social, and environmental issues (all three together being dimensions of sustainability) are essential in achieving more sustainable development. One could argue that a company's interest as a core concept of corporate governance should be broad, encompassing various stakeholders' interests (pluralistic governance model).[20] A broad concept of stakeholders' interests would help define the sustainability-related duties of a company's management.

Lithuanian scholars share different doctrinal views as to which theory of defining company's interest is actually embedded in the national legal framework and thus, which definition is applicable. Unlike in the international arena, where sustainable corporate governance has recently been a heated topic of debate among legal scholars, in Lithuanian legal doctrine, the research on the relationship between sustainable corporate governance and company's interest did not attract much attention.

Lithuanian case law shows that courts have typically examined the correlation between company's interest and the behaviour of corporate actors (corporate management bodies and shareholders of the company) when there is an internal dispute (a company-management dispute, a company-shareholder dispute, or a shareholders' dispute) or when interests of the creditors of the company are at stake. However, case law provides little guidance in interpreting what the company's interest is for sustainability matters.

20 Sjåfjell, Sustainable Value Creation Within Planetary Boundaries – Reforming Corporate Purpose and Duties of the Corporate Board, 2020, https://ssrn.com/abstract=3666952; Petrin, Beyond Shareholder Value: Exploring Justifications for a Broader Corporate Purpose, 2020, https://ssrn.com/abstract=3722836; Sjåfjell/Mähönen, 2023, p. 315-322.

This chapter explores the concept of company's interest[21] for both public and private companies[22] from the perspective of Lithuanian company law.[23] It also examines whether a definition of company's interest is open to the sustainability imperatives in light of societal developments that focus on fostering a better transition to sustainable corporate governance.

B. Conceptual features of a company

To determine a company's interest, it is first necessary to examine how a company is defined under the binary classification of legal persons by considering the concept of a company as a commercial enterprise and the relevance of the status of a legal person.

I. Conventional understanding of a company

Principally, legal persons are classified in two fundamentally different groups based on which interests are pursued by the entity: private interests or public interests (Art. 2.34 of the CC).[24] Private legal persons aimed at

21 The article neither addresses issues for a company to become a social enterprise, nor other peculiarities in terms of, e.g. specific business sectors, regulated activities, group of companies, insolvency, etc.

22 Statistics Lithuania, Official Statistics Portal – Number of enterprises in operation a by legal form and personnel group at the beginning of the year, 2025 https://osp.stat.gov.lt/statistiniu-rodikliu-analize?hash=4c919020-9559-4fcd-a7ab-8f6e68e1cd9e#/; Number of undertakings in operation at the beginning of the year https://osp.stat.gov.lt/statistiniu-rodikliu-analize?hash=47d2396f-9242-4cb7-937c-defd27cc1504#/; Number of small and medium undertakings in operation at the beginning of the year https://osp.stat.gov.lt/statistiniu-rodikliu-analize?hash=47d2396f-9242-4cb7-937c-defd27cc1504#/; At the beginning of 2024, there were 119,944 SMEs and a total of 120,412 undertakings in operation. At the beginning of 2025, there were more than 82,5 thous. private companies and 237 public companies (those can be listed or non-listed) in operation in Lithuania. There was only one operating European Company, hence a SE is not included into the scope of the analysis.

23 The chapter analysis the concept of the company's interest under Lithuanian law of 1 January 2025.

24 The legal underpinning in terms of classification of legal entities into two fundamentally different groups and application of the related rules is not, however, always certain. For example, the Constitutional Court concluded that Art. 2.34(5) of the CC, in so far as it excludes public establishments, as public legal persons, from the application of Chapter IX of Book II of the CC, is not contrary to Art. 23 and

pursuing private interests possess general legal capacity; while public legal persons that pursue public interests and seek benefit for the society act on the basis of the *ultra vires* doctrine.[25] Both a public company and a private company are considered private legal persons.

The objective of a company, as a business undertaking, is to engage in commercial activities and make profit (Art. 2(1) of the LSC; Art. 1.110(1) and 2.33 of the CC)[26].[27] A company, as a private for-profit legal entity, pursues private interests (Art. 2(1),(2) of the LSC, Art. 2.34 (3) of the CC). A public legal person is an entity established by a state or municipality, their institutions, or others who do not seek personal benefits from such entity and pursue public interests (state and municipal undertakings, statutory and municipal institutions, public establishments, religious communities, etc.). Unlike in case of public legal persons, the CC does not disclose the addressees of the private interests that have to be pursued by a private legal person. Nevertheless, from the opposite interpretation of Art. 2.34 (2),(3) of the CC, it can be deduced that founders (members) of the private legal person are such addressees and they may seek personal benefits out of the incorporation of a legal person.

The doctrine which analyses the conceptual understanding of a private legal entity describes the private interests by linking them to the material benefits of the founders (members) of the legal entity through the distribu-

---

Art. 46(3) of the Constitution and the constitutional principle of the rule of law. Chapter IX lays down legal regulations for a forced sale of the membership of those members whose actions are contrary to the objectives of the legal person and where it is not reasonable to assume that those actions will change in the future. The Supreme Court has interpreted the ruling of the Constitutional Court as permitting Art. 2.34(5) of the CC to be applied *mutatis mutandis* to public establishments (Constitutional Court 13.12.2022 – KT149-N15/2022, TAR, 2022, No. 25400, para. 2.3, 5.2, 11; Supreme Court 06.04.2023 – e3K-3–158–403/2023, para. 50; 22.12.2021 – e3K-3–260–403/2021).

25 Mesonis/ Pakalniškis/Tikniūtė p. 575 (586–588).

26 Art. 1.110(1) of the CC: an undertaking, as a complex of assets, property, and non-property rights as well as debts and other duties, belonging to the person who is engaged in business (seeking profit), may be the object of civil rights. The Law on Undertakings in force between 1 July 1990 and 1 January 2004 has listed the types of undertakings permitted to engage in regular commercial activities seeking to make profits, and it has included among them private limited liability companies and public limited liability companies (Art. 1, Art. 6(4), Art. 10).

27 A concept of an undertaking encompasses the triple meaning – as an object of civil rights, a subject of civil relations, and a legal business form (Sagatys/Jakutytė-Sungailienė, p. 129 (132–133); Mikelėnas, in: Abramavičius/Mikelėnas, p. 256–258.

tion of the entity's profits, earned capital gains, increasing services, and opportunities.[28] To note, the LSC sets forth a list of shareholder's standard financial rights, which includes, *inter alia,* a right to receive dividends during the course of the company's operations and a right to receive net assets when a company is liquidated (Art. 15(1)). Shareholders, as owners of the shares, can derive private benefits from disposal of their shares.

It follows from the jurisprudence of the Constitutional Court of the Republic of Lithuania ("Constitutional Court") that members of a private legal person generally seek material benefits from the activities of the legal person for themselves and other members, and that a private legal person has the objective of serving the private interests of their members.[29]

A conventional understanding of a company is also underlined in the jurisprudence of the Supreme Court of Lithuania ("Supreme Court"). The Supreme Court has stated that although the specific objectives of the company's activities are set out in the articles of association of a company, the general objective of private legal persons is to satisfy private interests, and pursuit of profit is one of the ways of satisfying private interests.[30] The Supreme Court also held that a decision of the corporate body is considered unlawful if it is, *inter alia*, contrary to the objectives of the company's activities as stated in the company's articles of association – in the case in question, to achieve economic benefits – and this objective has to be pursued by both the shareholders and the management of the company.[31] The Supreme Court also emphasised that by contributing capital to the company, shareholders seek both to preserve their investments and to benefit from the investments (receive profit); in this way, the objective of the shareholders becomes the objective of the legal person.[32]

In conclusion, a conventional understanding of the company, as a commercial enterprise and a private for-profit legal entity, encompasses two aspects: (i) doing business to earn a profit by a company and (ii) generating economic benefits for shareholders of the company.

This concept of a company as a commercial vehicle for doing business must be further explored, in conjunction with the concept of corporate

---

28 Bartkus, in: Mikelėnas/Bartkus/Mizaras/Keserauskas, p. 98–99, 119. Kiršienė, in: Kiršienė/Pakalniškis/Ruškytė/Vitkevičius, p. 208–209.

29 Constitutional Court 13.12.2022 – KT149-N15/2022, TAR, 2022, No. 25400.

30 Supreme Court 16.12.2011 – 3K-3–511/2011.

31 Supreme Court 14.07.2008 – 3K-3–287/2008.

32 Supreme Court 06.09.2021- e3K-3–215–378/2021, para. 41, 51; 01.07.2020 – e3K-3–214–219/2020, para. 26, 27.

personality of the company, to identify whether the legal form of corporate personality is relevant such that a company that serves the private interests of its shareholders may nevertheless have its own interest.

II. Corporate personality of a company

In the context of the analysis, a separate corporate personality for a company has the following important consequences –

First, a legal person acts in its own name: it assumes rights and duties in its own name, and also may act as a plaintiff and a defendant in court (Art. 2.33(1) of the CC). There must be at least two corporate bodies within a private company – a general shareholders' meeting and a company manager who is a single-member management body of the company. Public companies must have these two corporate bodies as well, but in addition must have at least one additional collective corporate body – a supervisory council or board (Art. 19(1)(2) of the LSC). The company manager is responsible for organising the company's activities and implementation of the company's objectives (Art. 37(12)-1 of the LSC). *Second*, unless modified in the company's articles of association, the default rule is that a company is established for an indefinite period of time, which in turn indicates that there is long-term perspective for the company as a legal entity (Art. 4(2)-14 of the LSC). *Third*, it follows from the wording of Article 19(8) of the LSC, which obliges both single-member and collective corporate management bodies to act for the benefit of the company and its shareholders, that priority is given to the interests of the company over the interests of the company's shareholders.

The Supreme Court held that a private company, as one of the forms of organisation for business activities, has a corporate personality guaranteed by law that is employed through special organisational structures – a management body (collegial, single) and a members' meeting. The company's management bodies have to act solely in the company's interest, i.e. to ensure its stable, efficient, and competitive operations as a market player.[33]

The Supreme Court has emphasised the role of corporate governance for a going-concern company, as a legal entity, and for the company's long-term concerns. For example, when assessing if the shareholders have

33 Supreme Court 14.02.2019 – 3K-3–35–469/2019, para. 39; 25.11.2016 – 3K-3–485–421/2016, para. 36; 19.04.2013 – 3K-3–234/2013.

acted contrary to the company's interest in the situation of a shareholder deadlock in a private company, the Court stressed that the company is an employer and a tax payer and therefore, in the event of a corporate governance crisis, public interest also requires that the generation of profits by the company's members is reconciled with the prospect of long-term operation and development of the company.[34]

Legal doctrine recognises that a company, as a legal entity, has an autonomous will which is separate from the will of its shareholders or other stakeholders,[35] and that the interests of a private legal person, as an autonomous person, and its members diverge.[36]

Similarly, both in civil proceedings involving protection of interests of creditors of the company and in the course of internal corporate disputes, the courts have stressed that the interests of members of a legal person do not always have to coincide with the interests of the legal person itself.[37] Over the last years, courts have consistently ruled that a company's manager has a duty to the company itself as an autonomous legal entity[38] and also must act *ex officio* and exclusively in the company's interest.[39]

Furthermore, the legislative goal to consider the company's interest on its own is implied by legal regulations that provide for shareholders' remedies and are primarily aimed at protecting the interest of the company as a separate going-concern legal entity. Such remedies only have a derivative effect on the shareholder of the company who makes use of the remedy (e.g. initiating corporate inquiry proceedings concerning investigation into corporate governance issues and the company's activities, challenging

34 Supreme Court 23.12.2013 – 3K-3–681/2013; In addition, the criterion of the protection of the public interest was strengthen, taking into account of the status of the company as a social enterprise for the employment of the disabled persons which has obtained subsidies for its activities.
Court of Appeal of Lithuania ("Court of Appeal") 30.12.2019- e2A-620–781/2019, para. 28.

35 Kiršienė, in: Kiršienė/Pakalniškis/Ruškytė/Vitkevičius, p. 220.

36 Bartkus, in: Mikelėnas/Bartkus/Mizaras/Keserauskas, p. 98, 119.

37 Supreme Court 25.11.2016 – 3K-3–485–421/2016, para. 50; 11.12.2015 – 3K-3–665–969/2015; 23.12.2013 – 3K-3–681/2013.

38 Supreme Court 21.09.2018 – 3K-3-326-1075/2018, para. 46; 16.10.2017 – 3K-7–177–701/2017, para. 27.

39 Supreme Court 26.05.2021 – e3K-7-30-969/2021, para. 47; 20.11.2009 – 3K-7–444/2009.

a company's *ultra vires* transaction, pursuing a derivative damage claim against the company's management).[40]

In cases where a company's interest is at stake, it is not unusual for courts to assess whether a behaviour of the corporate actors – members of the management bodies or shareholders of the company – contradicts interests of the company as a legal entity as such.[41] For example, the Supreme Court held in a civil litigation claim concerning a shareholder deadlock that a specific shareholder's behaviour was contrary to the interests of the company and breached the principles of reasonableness and good faith.[42] The Supreme Court reasoned that the shareholder's behaviour was exclusively aimed at personal gain and thus neglected the common objective of the members of the legal person: improving the performance of the company in order to ensure the satisfaction of the private interest of each shareholder.[43] A shareholder's pursuit of dividends must be balanced as far as possible with the company's long-term commercial interests.[44]

In conclusion, the corporate personality of a company plays a special role in determining a going-concern company's own interest, separate and distinct from the interests of the company's shareholders.

C. Concept of the interest of a company as such

Now that it is clear that a company as a legal entity has its own interest, what that interest *is* must be determined in legal terms by identifying for whom the company should be managed.

I. Scholars on a company's interest

In Lithuania, scholars have differing views as to the theory that underpins the company's interest.

Given that the function of a legal entity is to align collective interests, some scholars opine that the stakeholder theory should prevail, even

40 Mikalonienė, p. 70–81.
41 Supreme Court 06.09.2021 – e3K-3–215–378/2021, para. 51, 53; 20.11.2013 – 3K-3–548/2013; 23.12.2013 – 3K-3–681/2013.
42 Supreme Court 01.07.2020 – e3K-3–214–219/2020, para. 33.
43 Ibid.
44 Ibid, para. 37.

though there is no clear endorsement of this particular theory as the definition for a private legal entity's interest by the national legislature.[45] A company manager does not express the shareholders' will, but must act in the interests of all stakeholders of a legal entity – shareholders, employees, and even creditors.[46]

Some scholars support the shareholder primacy theory, stating that a private legal person is established to pursue private interests, and this is its main and exclusive purpose of such a company, even though a private legal person must take into account the legitimate expectations of various stakeholders (creditors, employees, clients, local society, etc.) and comply with the standards of justice, reasonableness, and good faith.[47] Through systemic interpretation of the legal framework, others conclude that a company's interest is increasing shareholder ownership or seeking profits, and thus, that the legal framework can be considered as more restrictive to or not encouraging the voluntary implementation of corporate social responsibility principles by a company's management bodies.[48] Some scholars argue that decisions taken by members of management bodies of the company should be assessed by considering whether these decisions are consistent with the objective of maximising shareholder benefit (company value).[49] Accordingly, as the company's interest is to create value for the shareholders as a whole, business decisions taken by the company manager must be consistent with the interests of the company and its shareholders, i.e. be profit-oriented, and that management bodies will satisfy the interests of all interest groups (including creditors) by acting in the best interests of the company.[50] Others argue that there is no established prevailing theory on the definition of a company's interest in either doctrine or case law, and thus endorse the enlightened shareholder value approach. These scholars propose that the long-term interests of the company's shareholders should prevail and be considered as an ultimate and the main purpose of the company, and the short-term interests of the shareholders should be weighed less than the interests of other stakeholders of the company, all while ensuring that the activities of the company are successful and that the

45 Mizaras/Bosaitė/Butov, p. 222–223; Greičius, p. 83–84.
46 Sagatys/Tikniūtė/ Jurkevičius, p. 359 (390–391).
47 Bartkus, in: Mikelėnas/Bartkus/Mizaras/Keserauskas, p. 119, 180, 193.
48 Lauraitytė, p. 115, 132–133, 201.
49 Jakuntavičiūtė, p. 10, 111–113.
50 Ibid.

long-term interests of the shareholders are secure.[51] There are also scholars who emphasise that the company and the company manager acting in the interests of the shareholders must also comply with the mandatory restrictions for the company's activities that prevent from overriding the interests of the shareholders or placing them at odds with the interests of the society as a whole.[52]

Finally, according to some authors, a unity of the interests of various groups of stakeholders (shareholders, employees, clients, etc.) should be considered as the interest of the legal person, and priorities among the interests should be set *ad hoc*.[53]

II. A company's interest in case law

In a number of cases that compared the interests of a solvent company with those of an insolvent company, the Supreme Court stressed that when a company is going-concern, the company manager's primary duty is to serve the interests of the equity providers, i.e. its shareholders. Further, the Supreme Court specified that the company manager's fiduciary duties that are to take into account also the interests of creditors (the interests of the company's providers of debt capital) in making decisions relating to the company's business, only arises when the company's financial situation deteriorates; in the event that the company becomes insolvent, the interests of the creditors then take precedence.[54]

In earlier jurisprudence, the Supreme Court highlighted profit-maximisation for shareholders, and lower courts of general jurisdiction have followed a similar path in recent decisions as well. Regarding civil liability of members of management bodies for a private for-profit legal person, the case law emphasised that such a legal person is established to implement a particular business model and to obtain economic benefits, i.e. making a

51 Miliauskas, in: Mikalonienė/Mikelėnas/Miliauskas/Mitkevičius/Tikniūtė, p. 138–139, 247.

52 Mikelėnas, in: Abramavičius/Mikelėnas, p. 259–261.

53 Kiršienė, in: Kiršienė/Pakalniškis/Ruškytė/Vitkevičius, p. 162.

54 Supreme Court 12.12.2023 – e3K-3–315–421/2023, para. 23; 04.05.2022 – e3K-3–107–403/2022, para. 32; 11.04.2022 – e3K-3–79–469/2022, para. 36; 03.12.2021 – e3K-3–307–421/2021, para. 65, 68; 14.02.2019 – 3K-3–35–469/2019, para. 40; 21.12.2018 – e3K-3–526–219/2018, para. 29; 08.02.2018 – e3K-3–105–421/2018, para. 51; 29.05.2015 – 3K-3–331–695/2015; 01.02.2012 – 3K-3–19/2012.

profit for the members of the legal person. Accordingly, the management bodies' have to ensure that the legal person derives the greatest possible economic benefit from its business activities, and the management bodies must not cause harm to the entity.[55]

The Supreme Court held that appropriate legal tools to ensure good corporate governance may be applied as long as corporate transactions are not manifestly loss-making, but this behaviour may be considered uneconomic or inefficient if the actions of the management body are favourable to a single shareholder rather than the company itself, and provided that such activities of the management body are, or are likely to be, detrimental to the company and thus jeopardise the shareholders' proprietary interest in obtaining the best possible return on their investments.[56] Lower courts stressed that as long as the company does not face solvency problems, the management bodies are considered to have acted in the interests of the shareholders, and thus also serving the interests of creditors and employees of the company.[57]

The Supreme Court has also stated that a company manager must adhere to laws, the company's articles of association, and internal rules. This includes balancing the interests of all stakeholders of the legal person (shareholders, employees, and also creditors, when the company faces insolvency).[58] There is established case law regarding the distinction between the interests of two groups of company stakeholders – shareholders and creditors. However, there is no clear consensus in legal rulings on how the interests of employees should be considered or balanced with those of other stakeholders by the company's management.

In managing a conflict between the interests of the employees-creditors and the company's other creditors, normal commercial risk, business failure, and continuation of the company's activities are considered when solvency of the company is at stake. For example, in one Supreme Court

55 Supreme Court 19.04.2013 – 3K-3–234/2013; Court of Appeal 14.06.2023 – e2A-380–330/2023, para. 30; Vilnius Regional Court 03.10.2022 – e2–1060–661/2022, para. 49 and 30.06.2020 – e2A-1375–933/2020, para. 25.

56 Supreme Court 11.02.2008 – 3K-3–73/2008.

57 Vilnius Regional Court 03.10.2022 – e2–1060–661/2022, para. 49 and 30.06.2020 – e2A-1375–933/2020, para. 25.

58 Supreme Court 03.12.2021 – e3K-3–307–421/2021, para. 63; 23.09.2020 – e3K-3–235–421/2020, para. 26; 05.07.2019 – e3K-3–247–684/2019, para. 42; 22.09.2015 – 3K-3–470–969/2015; 12.09.2014 – 3K-3–389/2014.

case,[59] the State Tax Inspection, a creditor of the company involved in the dispute, pursued a direct claim against the former company manager of the private company. The claimant asked for damages for a breach of the order of creditor payments; specifically, undue preference was given to other lower-ranking creditors of the company, leaving the company with no funds to pay the outstanding taxes. The court found no basis for the company manager's civil liability since the company manager gave preference to other creditors – suppliers, landlords, and employees – because the company's future activity was dependent on these creditors. Further, the company manager had not committed any criminal actions, the company was not fraudulently bankrupt, and the company manager's dishonest acts were not directed at the claimant-creditor. In another case,[60] employees of a private company had not been paid on time, as the employer paid out less than their full salaries, declaring that this was a rational decision for the company since the company lacked funds to settle with its employees, and if employees were dismissed under the collective agreement the company would have had to pay much larger amounts than the calculated late payment interest. The court ruled against the company manager, taking into consideration that the company manager violated mandatory preference rules to settle with the employees when making payments to other creditors and did not address the employees' dismissal in due time despite the company being unable to provide employees with work, and it also rejected the argument regarding the collective agreement as unfounded. The company's bankruptcy was declared fraudulent, and it was established that the company manager's failure to ensure the timely payment of remuneration to the employees was not related to normal commercial risks, business failure, or the like.

Case law in civil proceedings regarding assessment of the performance of the company manager's duties in the ordinary course of business suggests that reconciliation between the employees' and shareholders' interests is set *ad hoc*.[61]

Some scholars argue that, despite a small number of cases dealing with the interests of the company's employees that make it difficult to reach

59 Supreme Court 30.09.2020 – e3K-3-241-421/2020.

60 Supreme Court 21.09.2018 – 3K-3-326-1075/2018; Court of Appeal 26.11.2019 – 2A-368-790/2019.

61 Supreme Court 14.03.2019 – e3K-3-98-684/2019; 09.01.2014 – 3K-7-124/2014; 28.05.2012 – 3K-3-252/2012.

the overall conclusions, case law nonetheless imposes a duty to reconcile interests of shareholders and employees of the company on the company manager; however, the interests of the company's employees are not on equal footing with the interests of shareholders and creditors of the company.[62]

There is also case law where the Supreme Court has referred to an indefinite group of stakeholders of the company; the Supreme Court has stated that the company must take into account interests of all relevant stakeholders, including creditors, and the company's manager has a duty to reconcile and balance these interests.[63] Further, in civil proceedings concerning civil liability of the company manager in both solvent and insolvent companies, the Supreme Court stressed that both the company and corporate management bodies must comply with the laws governing companies, and the company's interest cannot be put at odds with the interest of the society.[64]

Jurisprudence stating that interests of all relevant stakeholders of the company must be considered may suggest that the interests of all stakeholders should be placed on equal footing when determining the company's interest. The Supreme Court's position that members of the management bodies may not put the company's interest at odds with the interest of society may indicate for a broader interpretation of the company's interest.[65] Having said that it has to be noted that case law has viewed this position as either directed at the specific groups of stakeholders – mainly the company's creditors but on some occasions employees of the company – or mentioned more generally in the abstract. Legal doctrine states that courts have applied the theory to determining a company's interest without any methodological underpinning and in some cases, referral to the stakeholders' theory was theoretical and not substantiated by the factual circumstances of the case.[66] Some scholars contend that, given the specific circumstances of individual cases, the management body's duty to balance

62 Lauraityte, 153–161.

63 Supreme Court 28.11.2013 – 3K-3–624/2013; 20.11.2013 – 3K-3–581/2013; 01.02.2012 – 3K-3–19/2012.

64 Supreme Court 11.05.2018 – 3K-3–177–248/2018, para. 39; 28.11.2013 – 3K-3–624/2013; 20.11.2013 – 3K-3–581/2013; 01.03.2013 – 3K-3–64/2013; 16.11.2012 – 3K-3–493/2012; 01.02.2012 – 3K-3–19/2012; 25.03.2011 – 3K-3–130/2011; 12.06.2006 – 3K-3–298/2006; 25.05.2006 – 3K-7–266/2006.

65 Lauraitytė/Miliauskas, p. 14, 19.

66 Miliauskas, in: Mikalonienė/Mikelėnas/Miliauskas/Mitkevičius/Tikniūtė, p. 134.

the interests of various stakeholders should be interpreted narrowly – as a duty to consider and not prejudice the interests of the company's creditors – rather than as a mandate to pursue broader social objectives or to account for public interest concerns.[67]

In the aforementioned case law that supposes a broader audience, where the court observed a duty of the company manager to balance the interest of all concerned stakeholders, the interests of stakeholders as opposed to shareholders, creditors, or employees of the company was not clarified, and therefore those observations are not necessarily *obiter dictum*. Lithuanian case law thus provides little guidance in interpreting the company's interest for sustainability-related matters.

III. A company's interest and the regulatory framework

Given that Lithuanian scholars have different views as to which theory for defining a company's interest is actually embedded in the national legal framework and there is no sufficient guidance in case law on how interests of all of the company's stakeholders should be taken into account (except for a demarcation between interests of two groups of stakeholders of the company – shareholders and creditors), in light of societal developments it is necessary to re-visit the concept of the company's interest within the current regulatory framework.

A linguistic interpretation of Article 19(8) of the LSC, which requires management bodies of both a public and a private company to act for the benefit of the company and its shareholders and thus highlights a single group's (shareholders') interests, suggests that Article 19(8) LSC is consistent with the shareholder primacy theory, i.e. promoting shareholder value. In 1998, a proposed amendment to the LSC provided that the management bodies must "act solely in the interests of the company", which would suggest a pluralistic approach, placing interests of all stakeholders of the company on equal footing. However, this amendment was not adopted.

The view that the LSC is worded to reflect the shareholder primacy theory is systematically supported by Article 2.87 of the CC, which sets out the key duties of the members of the management body of a legal person. A member of the management body has a duty of loyalty to the legal person.

67 Lauraitytė, p. 145–146, 154–161.

While a duty to act in good faith and reasonably is imposed on a member of the management body not only towards the legal person itself, but also to other members of bodies of the legal person (and a general shareholders' meeting is a corporate body of the company). Further, it is at the discretion of the general shareholders' meeting, a corporate body which appointed the company manager, to remove the company manager from the term without regard to the manager's fault or any other conditions.[68]

Considering that Article 19(8) of the LSC sets forth a priority of interests of a single group of stakeholders (the company's shareholders over those of the other stakeholders of the company), it is important to note that, in contrast to the version that was in force from 1 July 2001 until 31 December 2003, the current wording does not contain the requirement for the management bodies to act "solely" for the benefit of the company and its shareholders. The LSC imposes a duty on the company's management bodies to comply with laws and follow the company's articles of association. Those other provisions of the LSC limit the shareholders' primacy theory to some degree.

Regarding internal corporate governance, there are certain statutory tools that safeguard a group of interests broader than just shareholders' interests or give a preference to the interests of other stakeholders rather than the shareholders of the company. Some examples of these safeguards are as follows:

- When there are outstanding taxes not paid in due course, the company cannot pay out dividends to the shareholders or bonuses to employees (Art. 59(8) of the LSC).
- The doctrine on legal capital limits distributions of corporate assets to shareholders at the expense of creditors of the company (Art. 59(6)-3 of the LSC).
- To defend the public interest, a prosecutor may initiate a corporate investigation through the civil judicial proceedings when activities of the legal entity, its corporate management bodies or their members are in contradiction with the public interest (Art. 2.125(2) of the CC).
- A prejudiced creditor of the company has a right to challenge the decision of corporate organ (Art. 2.82(4) of the CC, Art. 19(10) of the LSC).
- There is a mechanism for employee participation in the company's share capital (Arts. 43, $45^{2,}$ and 47^{1} of the LSC).

68 Supreme Court 06.01.2021 – 3K-3–169–248/2021, para. 26; 28.05.2012 – 3K-3–252/2012.

- A statutory distribution of functions and competencies between the corporate bodies set up limits for the shareholders', as members, participation in the day-to-day company's management (Art. 19(3)–(5) and 20(2) of the LSC).

Although these types of rules somewhat dilute the shareholder primacy theory, they do not modify the existing hard law rule embedded in Article 19(8) of the LSC regarding the company's interest, nor do they establish a general proactive duty of a management body to promote interests of other stakeholders of the company over shareholders; the interests of the other relevant stakeholders just are not on an equal footing with the interests of the company's shareholders.

Further, the shareholders' primacy theory is watered-down by specific laws aimed at regulating activities of the companies that impose statutory duties on companies. These laws specify that management bodies must have regard the interests of other stakeholders in a particular way (in tax law, labour law, environmental law, antitrust law, anti-money laundering law, insolvency law, etc.). This regulatory approach must be seen in the context of the Constitutional Court's jurisprudence concerning constitutional protection of private ownership, freedom of economic activity, and the regulation of economic activity by the state. The Constitutional Court[69] has repeatedly stated that the state, when regulating economic activity, must balance the interests of the private person (the subject of the economic activity) with the interests of society and strive not for the welfare of the particular persons, but rather for the general welfare of the nation as a whole. The Constitutional Court stated that the interests of society must not be opposed to the legitimate interests of the entity which activity is subject to the regulation, or to the persons who established or manage that economic entity; and that the content of the concept of "general welfare of the nation" is defined on a case-by-case basis, taking into account economic, social, and other important factors.

Finally, all companies must follow the general standards of justice, reasonableness, and good faith (Arts. 1.5(1) and 1.137 of the CC), standards that change in light of societal developments.

Given these principles, along with the fact that (1) the LSC has established a priority for the interests of the company as a going-concern legal entity over those of its shareholders, and (2) that the legal framework

69 Constitutional Court 13.12.2022 – KT149-N15/2022, TAR, 2022, No. 254, para. 10.3 with further references to its jurisprudence.

reduces the shareholder primacy theory in order to account for various interests, – when acting in the company's interest, management bodies of the company must act for the benefit of the shareholders as a whole, while at the same time taking into account interests of the other relevant stakeholders of the company.

For listed companies, it seems that the Corporate Governance Code for the companies listed on Nasdaq Vilnius of 2019,[70] which is applicable under the "comply and explain" approach,[71] has taken a similar path. The principle that "*the overriding objective of a company should be to operate in common interests of all the shareholders by optimizing over time shareholder value*" (Principle 1 "Basic provisions") is no longer included in the Code, nor is the explanation that "*a company's supervisory and management bodies should act in close co-operation in order to attain maximum benefit for the company and its shareholders*", as embedded in the Code's previous version. Nevertheless, an overall analysis of the Code suggests that the Code's primary focus is on the company's shareholders: the corporate governance framework has to protect the rights of shareholders and recognise the rights of stakeholders (investors, employees, creditors, suppliers, clients, local community, and other persons having certain interests in the that company) entrenched in the laws or mutual agreements.[72]

Accordingly, it can be assumed that the current regulatory framework essentially places the concept of the company's interest under the enlightened shareholder value approach.

D. Receptiveness of the company's interest to sustainability imperatives

In addition to responsible business conduct pursued voluntarily by companies themselves, there are statutory sustainability-related duties imposed on companies by specific laws aimed at fostering better transition to sustainable corporate governance. These laws are, in principle, national

70 AB Nasdaq Vilnius, Corporate Governance Code for the Companies Listed on Nasdaq Vilnius, 2019, https://www.nasdaqbaltic.com/files/vilnius/teisesaktai/Nasdaq%20Vilnius%20bendroviu%20valdysenos%20kodeksas%20(galioja%20nuo%20%202019_01_15)%20EN.pdf; It was introduced in 2006 and then revised in 2009 and 2019 accordingly.

71 Law of Securities of the Republic of Lithuania No. X-1023 (VZ, 2007, No. 17–626 (with further amendments and supplements), Art. 12(3).

72 E.g. Principles 1–3 and 8.

transposition measures of EU directives (e.g. corporate sustainability reporting directive,[73] directive on gender-balanced boards,[74] amendments to the shareholders' rights directive aimed to encourage more long-term engagement of shareholders[75]).

For example, for better linking directors' remuneration to sustainability targets in listed companies, a shareholders' general meeting must approve the remuneration policy. The remuneration policy must, at a minimum, be addressed to the company manager, members of the board, and the supervisory council, and, *inter alia,* detail how it reflects the company's business strategy, long-term goals, and interests, and include financial and non-financial performance criteria, including, where appropriate, criteria relating to corporate social responsibility (Art. 37^3 of the LSC). Further, an annual management report of a listed company must contain information about remuneration to individual members of the management body with explanation, *inter alia,* as to how the remuneration is in line with the approved remuneration policy and how performance criteria have been applied.[76]

Another example is the new rules on sustainability reporting for large undertakings (which, *inter alia,* includes public and private companies) and listed companies (except micro-companies) enacted on 1 July 2024.[77] Sustainability reporting covers environmental, social, and human rights,

73 Directive (EU) 2022/2464 of the European Parliament and of the Council of 14 December 2022 amending Regulation (EU) No 537/2014, Directive 2004/109/EC, Directive 2006/43/EC and Directive 2013/34/EU, as regards corporate sustainability reporting (Text with EEA relevance), OJ L 322, 16.12.2022, p. 15–80, http://data.europa.eu/eli/dir/2022/2464/oj.

74 Directive (EU) 2022/2381 of the European Parliament and of the Council of 23 November 2022 on improving the gender balance among directors of listed companies and related measures (Text with EEA relevance), OJ L 315, 7.12.2022, p. 44–59, http://data.europa.eu/eli/dir/2022/2381/oj.

75 Directive 2007/36/EC of the European Parliament and of the Council of 11 July 2007 on the exercise of certain rights of shareholders in listed companies (consolidated text), http://data.europa.eu/eli/dir/2007/36/2024-01-09, Arts. 9a and 9b.

76 Law on reporting of undertakings and groups of undertakings of the Republic of Lithuania No. XIV-2811, TAR, 2024, No. 12134, which entered into force on 1 July 2024 ("Law on Reporting") and repealed Law on reporting of undertakings of the Republic of Lithuania as well as Law on consolidated reporting of groups of undertakings of the Republic of Lithuania; Art. 10(1)-3, Art.19, Art. 25.

77 Arts. 4 and 19 of Law on Reporting. There is also a requirement to ensure a public accessibility to the third-country company's sustainability report at a consolidated level to be applied for their 2028 activities (Arts. 26 and 41(21)).

and governance factors; it contains information about the company's own operations, its group, and its value chain (Art. 3(30), Art. 21 of the Law on Reporting). In consideration of short-, medium-, and long-term indicators, sustainability reporting, as an integral component of the annual management report, should encompass, *inter alia*, a description of the company's business model and strategy, its policies relating to sustainability matters, relevant sustainability-related targets, and describe the role of corporate bodies in relation to sustainability matters. The report should also include an overview of the corporate sustainability due diligence process, as well as an assessment of the impact of corporate activities on individuals and the environment, by outlining principal actual or potential adverse impact associated with both the company's own operations, its group and its value chain. Furthermore, it should detail actions undertaken to prevent, mitigate, remediate, or eliminate such adverse impact, along with the outcomes of these measures.[78] Sustainability reporting prepared according to the European standards and accompanied by an assurance opinion from an independent expert (auditor, assurance services provider) must be submitted to the business register and disclosed on a website of the listed company (Art. 22(1), Art. 34, Art. 36(1), Art 37(1) of the Law on Reporting).

To fulfil the sustainability reporting duty, undertakings likely will have to adapt their information systems, define policies and strategies, and review their business model.[79] The Law on Reporting is gradually applied in terms of its personal scope; it sets forth that large public-interest entities with more than 500 employees on average per annum and parent undertakings of large groups with more than 500 employees in the group have to start reporting on their 2024 activities, while other large undertakings beginning reporting with their 2025 activities, and listed small and medium-sized undertakings beginning with their 2026 activities (with an opt-out for their activities until 1 January 2028) (Art. 41).[80]

78 Law on Reporting provides for certain exceptions for simplified sustainability reporting, e.g. for listed SMEs (Art 21 (9)).

79 Explanatory note No. XIVP-3684 of 25 April 2024 to the draft laws No. XIVP-3675 – XIVP-3690.

80 The repealed legislation has already required large public-interest companies with more than 500 employees to prepare a corporate social responsibility report as part of an annual corporate reporting, (Art. 23(5), Art. 23^2 of Law on reporting of undertakings of the Republic of Lithuania No. IX-575, VZ, 2001, No. 99–3516, with further amendments and supplements).

The amendments to the Law on Equal Opportunity for Men and Women at the end of 2024, that are aimed at enhancing gender diversity at boards of large undertakings, is another example of measures taken in pursuance of sustainable corporate governance.[81] It was stressed in *travaux prepatories* of the amendments to the Law on Equal Opportunity for Men and Women that the proportion of women on the boards of the largest listed companies in Lithuania is below the EU average.[82] The progress in Lithuania has been slow: over the last 7 years, the number of women on the boards of medium and large Lithuanian companies increased by only 3 percent, and only 1 percent for company manager positions.[83] As this rate, it would take more than three decades to achieve full gender balance on corporate boards.[84]

For selection procedures starting from 1 December 2024, large companies with boards and/or supervisory councils must take necessary measures to ensure that persons of the underrepresented gender occupy at least 33 percent (but not more than 49 percent) of the positions of company manager, board members, and members of supervisory council by 30 June 2026. Large companies must determine the relevant requirements and criteria for occupying such positions. Candidates to the positions of company manager, board members, and members of supervisory council of a large company must be selected based on a comparative assessment of the qualifications of each candidate. When candidates are equally qualified, priority must be given to the candidate of the underrepresented gender, with a few exceptions. Large companies must inform their shareholders who vote to elect the company manager, members of management, and supervisory bodies about the rules on gender-balanced boards.

The Law on Reporting[85] requires that, for large listed companies with boards and/or supervisory councils, the management report on corporate governance, which is submitted on a yearly basis to the business register and published on the company's website, must include: statistical infor-

81 Law on equal opportunities for women and men of the Republic of Lithuania No. VIII-947, VZ, 1998, No. 112–3100 (with further amendments and supplements); Law No. XIV-3011 amending Law on equal opportunities for women and men of the Republic of Lithuania, TAR, 2024, No. 17776, which came into force on 1 December 2024, save to a few exceptions; Art 2 ($1^{1)}$-(1^2), Art. 6^1, Art. 11^1, Art. 20.

82 Explanatory note No. XIVP-4002 of 27 June 2024 to the proposed amendments to the Law on Reporting.

83 Ibid.

84 Ibid.

85 Art. 24(2); Law No. XIV-3012 amending Law on Reporting, TAR, 2024, No. 17777, which came into force on 1 December 2024; Art. 24(1)-12.

mation on gender representation in the company's management and supervisory bodies (percentage of representation by gender); details of the measures the company has already taken or intends to take to ensure that the persons of the underrepresented gender occupy at least 33 percent (but not more than 49 percent) of the positions of company manager, board members, and members of supervisory council; and, in the event that the threshold has not been met, the reasons why this proportion has not been achieved. Other large non-listed companies must report on gender balance on their management and supervisory bodies on a yearly basis by submitting a gender equality report to the Office of the Equal Opportunities Ombudsman.

In addition to the above sustainability-related duties – reporting and formation of gender-balanced corporate boards as imposed on certain types of companies by specific laws, in the sustainability context it is worth mentioning a general duty not to cause harm to others which is embedded in the CC.

Every person has a duty to follow the rules of such behaviour so as not to harm another person with their actions (acts, omissions) (Art. 6.263(1) of the CC). Civil liability may arise from a failure to fulfil not only a duty established by law or contract (wrongful omission) or from the performance of acts prohibited by law or contract (wrongful act), but also from a breach of a general duty to act carefully and diligently (Art. 6.246(1) of the CC). A person is at fault if, taking into account the essence of the obligation and other circumstances, she/he was not as careful and prudent as was necessary under the relevant circumstances (Art. 6.248(3) of the CC). If the above sustainability-related specific duties are imposed only on large and/or listed companies, a general duty of care not to cause harm to others concerns all companies in their activities. Accordingly, all companies, in complying with their general duty of care not to cause harm to others, have to act prudently in order to manage sustainability risks.

Nonetheless, given that sustainability is predominantly about the manner in which the company pursues its corporate purpose, the duty of care of the corporate management could better reflect the move towards sustainability.[86] For example, according to the Corporate Governance Code for the companies listed on Nasdaq Vilnius, the management board should take into account the needs of the company and of its shareholders, employees,

86 Bianchini/Palmiter/Mikalonienė, p. 161 (169).

and other stakeholders when implementing the company's strategy and exercising good corporate governance by striving to build sustainable business (3.1.2 in relation to Principle 3). However, the Corporate Governance Code, last revised in 2019, does not yet take into account the 2023 updated guidance on corporate sustainability set out in the OECD Principles of Corporate Governance,[87] nor does it account for other comparative modern Corporate Governance Codes that reflect the move towards sustainability with regard to listed companies.

E. Conclusion

In Lithuania, both going-concern public and private companies have their own interests that are separate and distinct from the interests of shareholders and other stakeholders of the company. The conventional understanding of a company as a commercial undertaking and a private for-profit legal entity, which was introduced during the transformation from socialism to a market economy, plays an essential role in determining the company's interest. The legal framework essentially puts the concept of the company's interest under the enlightened shareholder value approach, which means that management bodies acting in the interests of the company must act for the benefit of the company's shareholders as a whole, while at the same time taking into account the interests of other relevant stakeholders.

To balance various interests that are linked to the companies' activities and to respond to societal developments, the regulatory approach in fostering better transition to sustainable corporate governance is to not redefine the company's interest, a central concept of corporate governance, nor to repeal the priority of shareholders' interests in a favour of a pluralistic approach and not to put the interests of other stakeholders of the company on the same footing as shareholders. Instead, the legislature uses a different technique – *first*, establishing the general standards of justice, reasonableness, and good faith, and a general duty of care not to cause harm to others that concern all companies in their activities, and *second*, imposing statutory sustainability-related duties on companies that limit the private autonomy of the companies that must comply with those legal duties and restricting the discretion of the corporate management in a business decision-making.

87 OECD, G20/OECD Principles of Corporate Governance 2023, OECD Publishing, Paris, https://doi.org/10.1787/ed750b30-en.

Regarding sustainability-related duties in the corporate governance context, the regulatory approach is to focus on large and/or listed companies by prescribing statutory corporate duties that originate from EU directives into Lithuanian law. It is likely that societal change will be integrated into the corporate governance of the (non-listed) SMEs that dominate in Lithuania through voluntary responsible action and prudent behavior on not-to-harm basis. SMEs will also be better able to contribute to sustainable development through their business relationships with partners who must comply with corporate sustainability reporting and due diligence obligations.

References

AB Nasdaq Vilnius, Corporate Governance Code for the Companies Listed on Nasdaq Vilnius, 2019, https://www.nasdaqbaltic.com/files/vilnius/teisesaktai/Nasdaq%20Vilnius%20bendroviu%20valdysenos%20kodeksas%20(galioja%20nuo%20%202019_01_15)%20EN.pdf (last accessed 27 December 2024)

Abramavičius, Armanas/Mikelėnas, Valentinas, Įmonių vadovų teisinė atsakomybė, 2-as leid., Vilnius 1999

Andersen, Paul Krüger/Andersson, Jan Bertil/Bartkus, Gintautas/Baums, Theodor/Clarke, Blanaid J./Conac, Pierre-Henri/Corbisier, Isabelle/Daskalov, Waltschin/Engrácia Antunes, José/Fuentes, Mónica/Giudici, Paolo/Hannigan, Brenda/Kalss, Susanne/Kisfaludi, Andras/de Kluiver, H. J./ Opalski, Adam/ Patakyova, Maria/Perakis, Evanghelos Emm/Porkona, Jarmila/Roest, Joti/Sillanpää, Matti J./Soltysinski, Stanislaw/Teichmann, Christoph/Urbain-Parleani, Isabelle/Vutt, Andres/Sørensen, Karsten Engsig/Winner, Martin/De Wulf, Hans, European Model Company Act (EMCA) (September 1, 2017), Nordic & European Company Law Working Paper No. 16–26, https://ssrn.com/abstract=2929348 (last accessed 9 January 2025)

Bebchuk, Lucian A. B/Tallarita, Roberto, Will Corporations Deliver Value to All Stakeholders? (August 4, 2021), forthcoming in Vanderbilt Law Review, Vol. 75 (May 2022), https://ssrn.com/abstract=3899421 (last accessed 9 January 2025)

Bitė, Virginijus, Uždarosios akcinės bendrovės teisinis reglamentavimas: sukūrimas, raida ir šių dienų tendencijos, in Birštonas (ed.), Privatinės teisės doktrina ir praktika: Liber Amicorum Vytautui Pakalniškiui. Mykolo Romerio universitetas, Vilnius 2014, p. 150–180

Bosaitė, Akvilė/Butov, Sergej, Juridiniai asmenys kaip civilinės teisės subjektai, in Mizaras (ed.), *Civilinė* teisė. Bendroji dalis: vadovėlis, Vilniaus universitetas, Vilnius 2009, p. 211–316

Drukteinienė, Simona/Jurkevičius, Vaidas/Mikelėnas,Valentinas/Bitė, Virginijus-Pakalniškis, Vytautas, Civilinės teisės ir jos pošakių bei institutų raida 1918–2018 m., in Sinkevičius/Jakulevičienė (eds.), Lietuvos teisė 1918 – 2018 m.: šimtmečio patirtis ir perspektyvos, Mykolo Romerio universitetas, Vilnius 2018, p. 280–338

Ferrarini, Guido, Corporate Purpose and Sustainability (December 7, 2020). European Corporate Governance Institute – Law Working Paper #559/2020, An edited version of this paper will be published as a chapter in Danny Busch, Guido Ferrarini and Seraina Grünewald (eds.), Sustainable Finance, Palgrave MacMillan (forthcoming), SSRN: https://ssrn.com/abstract=3753594 (last accessed 9 January 2025)

Fleischer, Holger, Corporate Purpose: A Management Concept and its Implications for Company Law (January 21, 2021). European Corporate Governance Institute – Law Working Paper No. 561/2021, https://ssrn.com/abstract=3770656 (last accessed 11 December 2024)

Greičius, Rimgaudas, Privataus juridinio asmens vadovo fiduciarinės pareigos, Vilnius 2007

Hopt, Klaus J., Corporate Purpose and Stakeholder Value – Historical, Economic and Comparative Law Remarks on the Current Debate, Legislative Options and Enforcement Problems – (March 15, 2023). European Corporate Governance Institute – Law Working Paper No. 690/2023, https://ssrn.com/abstract=4390119 (last accessed 9 January 2025)

Jakuntavičiūtė, Gintarė, Civil liability of the members of management bodies of the legal entities, Doctoral dissertation, Mykolo Romerio University, Vilnius 2012

Jakutytė-Sungailienė, Asta, Įmonė – *sui generis* civilinių teisių objektas, in Sagatys (ed.), Lietuvos Respublikos civilinis kodeksas: pirmieji dešimt galiojimo metų, Mykolo Romerio universitetas, Vilnius 2013, p. 129–159

Kershaw, David/Schuster, Edmund-Philipp, The Purposive Transformation of Corporate Law (March 31, 2019). LSE Legal Studies Working Paper No. 4/2019, Forthcoming, American Journal of Comparative Law, European Corporate Governance Institute – Law Working Paper No. 616/2021, https://ssrn.com/abstract=3363267, (last accessed 11 December 2024)

Kiršienė, Julija/Pakalniškis, Vytautas/Ruškytė, Ramutė/Vitkevičius, Pranciškus, in Pakalniškis (ed.), Civilinė teisė. Bendoji dalis, T.1, Lietuvos teisės universitetas, Vilnius 2004

Lauraitytė, Eglė, Corporate social responsibility – company law aspects., Doctoral dissertation, Vilnius University, Vilnius 2016

Lauraityte, Eglė/Miliauskas, Paulius, Sustainable Companies under the Lithuanian Company Law (April 11, 2013). University of Oslo Faculty of Law Research Paper No. 2013–10, https://ssrn.com/abstract=2248591 (last accessed 9 January 2025)

Mikalonienė, Lina. Sustainability Concept in Company Law and Corporate Governance: Why, How and Who, in Bianchini/Palmiter (eds.), The Emerging Law of Sustainable Corporations: Chronicles from a Course, a Colloquium, and a Symposium, Padova University Press, Padova, 2022, p. 161–176 https://www.padovauniversitypress.it/en/publications/9788869383335

Mikalonienė, Lina, Uždarosios akcinės bendrovės akcininko teisės ir jų gynimo būdai, Vilnius 2015

Mikalonienė, Lina/Mikelėnas, Valentinas/Miliauskas, Paulius/Mitkevičius, Vilius/Tikniūtė, Agnė, The convergence and divergence of legal forms of enterprises: is Lithuanian legal regulation attractive in international context? Vilnius university, Vilnius 2017, https://www.tf.vu.lt/publications/imoniu-teisiniu-formu-konvergencija-ir-divergencija-ar-lietuvos-teisinis-reglamentavimas-yra-patrauklus-tarptautiniame-kontekste-2017/

Mikelėnas, Valentinas/Bartkus, Gintautas/Mizaras, Vytautas/ Keserauskas, Šarūnas, Lietuvos Respublikos civilinio kodekso komentaras. Antroji knyga. Asmenys, Vilnius 2002

OECD, G20/OECD Principles of Corporate Governance 2023, OECD Publishing, Paris, https://doi.org/10.1787/ed750b30-en (last accessed 27 December 2024)

Pakalniškis, Vytautas, Pirmasis Lietuvos Respublikos civilinis kodeksas – modernios valstybės kūrimo priemonė, in Sagatys (ed.), Lietuvos Respublikos civilinis kodeksas: pirmieji dešimt galiojimo metų, Mykolo Romerio universitetas, Vilnius 2013, p. 13–32

Pakalniškis, Vytautas/Tikniūtė, Agnė, Juridinio asmens instituto raidos bruožai šiuolaikinėje Lietuvos privatinėje teisėje, in Mesonis (ed.), Regnum est: 1990 m. Kovo 11-osios Nepriklausomybės Aktui – 20. Liber Amicorum Vytautui Landsbergiui. Mykolo Romerio universitetas, Vilnius 2010, p. 575–593

Petrin, Martin, Beyond Shareholder Value: Exploring Justifications for a Broader Corporate Purpose (November 1, 2020). Research Handbook on Corporate Purpose and Personhood (Elizabeth Pollman & Robert B. Thompson, eds, Edward Elgar Publishing) (Forthcoming), https://ssrn.com/abstract=3722836 (last accessed 9 January 2025)

Rock, Edward B., For Whom is the Corporation Managed in 2020?: The Debate over Corporate Purpose (May 1, 2020). European Corporate Governance Institute – Law Working Paper No. 515/2020, NYU School of Law, Public Law Research Paper No. 20–16, NYU Law and Economics Research Paper, https://ssrn.com/abstract=3589951 (last accessed 9 January 2025)

Sjåfjell, Beate K./Mähönen, Jukka, The future of Nordic company law, in Sjåfjell, Beate K./Mähönen, Jukka (eds.), Nordic Company Law: Broadening the Horizon. Scandinavian University Press 2023, p. 305-322

Sjåfjell, Beate, Sustainable Value Creation Within Planetary Boundaries – Reforming Corporate Purpose and Duties of the Corporate Board (August 4, 2020). Sustainability 2020, 12, 6245, University of Oslo Faculty of Law Research Paper No. 2020–20, Nordic & European Company Law Working Paper No. 21–04, https://ssrn.com/abstract=3666952 (last accessed 11 December 2024)

Tikniūtė, Agnė/Jurkevičius, Vaidas. Atstovo samprata Lietuvos civilinėje teisėje, in Sagatys (ed.), Lietuvos Respublikos civilinis kodeksas: pirmieji dešimt galiojimo metų, Mykolo Romerio universitetas, Vilnius 2013, p. 359–393

Žilys, Juozas, Visavertės nuosavybės teisės ir ūkio sistemos konstitucinių pagrindų genezė. Teisiniai tekstai ir kontekstai, in Birštonas (ed.), Privatinės teisės doktrina ir praktika: Liber Amicorum Vytautui Pakalniškiui. Mykolo Romerio universitetas, Vilnius 2014, p. 13–78

10. Enlightened Shareholder Value: UK Company Law and Corporate Governance

Andreas Rühmkorf

A. Introduction

Shareholder primacy has long been the dominant theory of company law and corporate governance in the United Kingdom. Initially, shareholder primacy developed from increasingly dispersed share ownership and the separation of ownership and control. A shareholder-oriented understanding of companies was strengthened by the fiduciary duty for directors to act *bona fide* in the best interest of the company, which was interpreted to mean the interest of shareholders as a group. After its landslide victory in the 1997 UK General Election, the New Labour government started a comprehensive review of the scope of company law in the UK. This review devoted a significant amount of time to corporate theory and considered three different options: shareholder value, a pluralist approach, and the enlightened shareholder value theory. The latter was finally adopted and has since been the dominant theory of UK company law and corporate governance.

This chapter traces the historical origins of shareholder primacy in the UK and then critically assesses the implementation of the enlightened shareholder value theory through the UK Companies Act 2006, specifically the duty to promote the success of the company located in section 172 (1), as well as nonfinancial information disclosure duties. Moreover, the chapter situates the doctrinal legal analysis in the institutional context that favours shareholder primacy, such as the market for corporate control and the preference for a soft law approach to corporate governance, particularly through the UK Corporate Governance Code. The final part of this chapter discusses to what extent the UK aligns with, or deviates from, current European approaches to corporate sustainability post-Brexit.

Overall, the chapter shows that shareholder primacy is deeply enshrined in the UK's system of company law and corporate governance – both as a legal norm and as a social norm. The dominance of the shareholder primacy theory in the UK has significant practical impact due to the extensive use of the public limited company as a form of business organisation.

Regarding terminology, the chapter often refers to 'stakeholder value' and the 'pluralist approach', particularly in relation to the Companies Act of 2006. However, considering the final part of the chapter – which discusses convergence or divergence of the UK with the recent European regulations designed to achieve greater corporate sustainability – reference in this chapter is also frequently made to the term 'sustainability'.[1] The chapter adopts the definition of Griggs et al., who define sustainability as 'development that meets the needs of the present while safeguarding Earth's life-support system, on which the welfare of current and future generations depends'.[2] This understanding requires amending the three-pillar model of economic, environmental, and social sustainable development as an interlocked concept.

B. Historical perspective: The evolution of shareholder primacy in the United Kingdom

The chapter starts by analysing the reasons why the shareholder primacy theory gained such a strong position in UK company law. This section will examine four different grounds: first, the historic debate about corporate theory and its strong push for shareholder value; second, the common law duty for directors to act *bona fide* in the best interest of the company; third, the existence of a market for corporate control with hostile takeovers; and fourth, the strong preference for a soft law approach to corporate governance.

I. The historic debate about corporate theory

The theory of shareholder primacy (also referred to as 'shareholder value' in this chapter) has long been the dominant theory of UK company law

1 In fact, the terms 'sustainability' and 'sustainable development' are often used interchangeably. See A Rühmkorf (ed) Nachhaltige Entwicklung im deutschen Recht: Möglichkeiten und Grenzen der Förderung, (Nomos 2018), p. 9.

2 Griggs et al. Nature 2013, 496.

and corporate governance;[3] shareholder primacy has dominated corporate law in the United Kingdom since the 1980s.[4] However, the theoretical aspect of the shareholder primacy theory was developed earlier than the 1980s, and this background helped the theory gain a strong grip on the general thinking about the aims and objectives of companies.

As the owners of shares, shareholders were historically equated with the company; focus on shareholders evolved from 19th century partnership law.[5] The best point to start from is the Companies Act of 1844, which facilitated the formation of companies. However, for quite a while, the idea of limited liability was not included in the general thinking regarding company law, and the idea of the company being a separate legal entity from its shareholders was not a universally-accepted fact. However, this changed with the realisation that investors needed security, which could only be offered through limited liability.[6] The concept of the company being a separate legal entity was finally settled in 1897 with the landmark decision of *Salomon v. Salomon*.[7]

A significant development for the discussion on shareholder paradigm was the 'separation of ownership and control', a phrase coined by Berle and Means in the 1930s.[8] Specifically, Berle and Means stated that managers and shareholders had become divided. In the UK, the exact timing of this separation of ownership and control is controversial.[9] The traditional view is that families remained in control of companies for the first half of the 20th century.[10] However, it has been argued that, insofar as listed companies in the UK are concerned, the separation of ownership occurred in the early 20th century with increasingly dispersed shareholding.[11] Berle and Means base their observation on the fact that shareholders lacked the ability or knowledge to control the corporation, and accordingly, that the shareholders had delegated this role to management. Consequently, the managers (directors) effectively controlled the company, unlike the share-

3 Chiu Law and Financial Markets Review 2016, 173.
4 Keay ECFR 2010, 369 (370).
5 Ireland MLR 1999, 32.
6 Gamble/Kelly Corporate Governance 2001, 110 (111).
7 [1897] AC 22.
8 Berle/Means, The Modern Corporation and Private Property (Transaction Publishers 1991, originally published in 1932).
9 See for a detailed discussion: Johnston/Segrestin/Hatchuel Legal Studies 2019, 75.
10 Chandler, 288 et seq.
11 See Hannah Business History 2007, 404 (417).

holders. This situation led to the evolution of professional management in the UK.[12] Managerialism describes the power of professional managers.[13] An information asymmetry developed between the increasingly dispersed shareholders and the managers – heightened by the increasing size and complexity of companies.

This 'separation of ownership and control' is closely linked to one of the main lines of theoretical support for shareholder primacy. The 'agency theory' stems from this separation: it views directors as the agents of shareholders (as the owners of the shares and providers of the capital who are the principals).[14] Moreover, the agency theory argues that management should be accountable to shareholders, maximising the shareholders' investments.[15] This approach would prevent managers from acting in a self-serving way, which is one of the dangers of the information asymmetry between managers and shareholders.[16] As shareholders purchase shares, they are seen as the owners of the company, or at least of the business, which helps classify them as 'principals' in this theory.[17]

A more recent line of support for shareholder value came via the 'nexus of contracts theory', which has further influenced thinking about company law in the Anglo-American world, including the United Kingdom.[18] This theory treats the corporate entity as a 'legal fiction' based on explicit and implicit private contracts. All constituents of the corporate entity have contracts with it.[19] However, the only constituents whose claim is not fixed are the shareholders. Other constituents, such as employees, creditors, suppliers, or customers, all have a fixed claim, i.e. the contract determines what they can claim from the corporate entity. In contrast, the shareholders claims are not fixed; shareholders only receive what is left once all other (fixed) claims have been met through dividends (the 'residual earnings').[20] Arguably, this situation would be unjustified, given that the shareholders provide the capital. In turn, the nexus of contracts theory leads to the

12 Johnston/Segrestin/Hatchuel Legal Studies 2019, 75 (77).
13 Johnston, EBOLR 2006, 817 (818).
14 Easterbrook/Fischel, p. 37.
15 Sheikh/Rees; *Hutton v West Cork Railway Co. Ltd.* [1883] 23 Ch. D. 654, 673.
16 Hansmann/Kraakman Geo.L.J. 2001, 439 (448).
17 See Hansmann, Journal of Law, Economics and Organisation 1988, 267.
18 See for the ‚nexus of contracts theory': Easterbrook/Fischel, p. 12.
19 ibid, p. 37.
20 ibid, p. 25.

argument that directors must prioritise the interest of shareholders and focus on maximising return on shareholders' investment.[21]

These different theoretical debates cumulatively lend strong support to the idea that directors must work in the interest of shareholders and maximise shareholder value. The shareholder value theory provides a clear means of measuring the performance of directors.[22] Thus, the shareholder value theory helps to address the issues identified by both the agency theory and the nexus of contracts theory. As mentioned, these debates about the role of the company are similar in the USA and the UK and have had a significant impact on corporate doctrine in the UK.

Based on the theoretical justifications of the shareholder value theory, Friedman argued that a director who acts in a socially responsible manner would impose taxes on shareholders when, in fact, he would be an 'employee of a private enterprise'.[23] The consequence of these arguments is a significantly limited scope for directors to pursue goals other than those that maximise shareholder value. In turn, there is only scope to pursue the interests of other stakeholders – including sustainability – when those interests further the business, i.e. when it is done as a 'business case'.

These theoretical debates have shaped the approach to company law in much of the 20th century. However, other developments such as the common law duty to act *bona fide* in the best interest of the company, the market for corporate control, and the soft law approach to corporate government as evidenced by several self-regulatory codes, particularly the UK Corporate Governance Code, helped entrench shareholder value in the UK during the 20th century. Each of these factors will be addressed in the following parts.

II. The common law duty to act bona fide in the best interest of the company

Prior to the UK Companies Act of 2006, directors' duties were not codified. The Companies Act of 1985 covered most aspects of the formation and running of companies, but it continued to leave the development of directors' duties up to case law. This is possible in common law jurisdictions as both

21 Hansmann/Kraakman, Geo.L.J. 2001, 439 (449).
22 See for a discussion of this point: Keay, 18 et seq.
23 M Friedman, 'The Social Responsibility of Business is to Increase its Profits' New York Times (New York 13 September 1970) § 6 Magazine.

statutes and cases are primary sources of law. However, Parliament can always decide to intervene and make laws that replace common law.

Pre-2006, the shareholder value focus of UK company law was found in the fiduciary duty for directors to act *bona fide* in what they considered to be in the best interests of the company.[24] The phrase 'interests of the company' was equated with 'shareholders as a general body', which led to the interpretation of this duty as being focused on shareholder interests.[25] Consequently, common law effectively required directors to pursue shareholder value.

In the Companies Act of 2006, directors' duties were codified. The legislature was careful to find the right balance between the 'old' and the 'new' when codifying the duties. Section 170 (3) Companies Act 2006 stipulates that the general duties for directors in the Companies Act of 2006 are based on certain common law rules and equitable principles as they apply in relation to directors, and that the Companies Act of 2006 has effect in place of those rules and principles regarding the duties owed to a company by a director. Second, section 170 (4) Companies Act 2006 adds that the general duties must be interpreted and applied in the same way as common law rules or equitable principles, and regard shall be given to the corresponding common law rules and equitable principles in interpreting and applying the general duties. This point in section 170 (4) Companies Act 2006 is important for the doctrinal analysis of the new duty in section 172 (1) Companies Act 2006 to promote the success of the company, as analysis of section 172 (1) refers to the common law where relevant.

III. The market for corporate control

The third important historical reason for the firm grip that the shareholder value theory has on UK company law is its reliance on the market for corporate control. Takeovers (both hostile and voluntary) became an important tool to hold directors accountable for promoting the interests of shareholders.[26] The first wave of hostile takeovers in the UK occurred in the

24 See only *Re Smith and Fawcett Ltd* [1942] Ch [304].

25 See *Re Smith & Facett Ltd* [1942] Ch [304], [306]; *Hutton v West Cork Railway Company* (1883) 23 Ch. D. 654; *Parke v Daily News Ltd* [1962] Ch. 927.

26 See Gamble/Kelly, Corporate Governance 2001, 110 (112).

early 1950s.[27] Hostile takeovers play an important role in the shareholder primacy theory as they serve as a means for controlling the efficiency of boards of directors.[28] If boards are underperforming, it is reflected in the share price. This situation attracts outside investors who may be interested in taking over the company by purchasing a majority of the shares. The existing shareholders are then offered more for their shares than current market value.[29] The theoretical assumption is that inefficient boards are then replaced by efficient ones and that, consequently, the company will be managed better. This scenario means that the threat of a hostile takeover exercises control over a board and, thus, according to the shareholder value theory, this control over boards benefits society by making companies more efficient.

Regulation of takeovers in the UK is found in different sources, including Part 28 of the Companies Act of 2006 and the City Code on Takeovers and Mergers (referred to as the 'City Code').[30] The City Code is issued and administered by the Panel on Takeover and Mergers (referred to as the 'Panel') whose membership is comprised of practitioners and regulatory organisations in the City of London.[31] It would go beyond the scope of this chapter to fully analyse the rules of the UK Takeover Code, but two points are significant for the analysis here. First, the Panel has overseen takeover regulation in the UK since 1968, the year the City Code was first issued. This means that takeovers have been subject to self-regulation in the UK since 1968. Second, the Code prioritises the interests of shareholders and takes a strict approach towards defensive measures against hostile takeovers through the 'no frustration rule'. General Principle 3 states that

> [t]he board of directors of an offeree company must act in the interests of the company as a whole and must not deny the holders of securities the opportunity to decide on the merits of the takeover bid.

Building on General Principle 3, Rule 21 ('Restrictions on Frustrating Action') of the Code stipulates that the board of directors must not take,

27 See Johnston/Segrestin/Hatchuel Legal Studies 2019, 75 (91).

28 Armour/Deakin/Konzelmann, British Journal of Industrial Relations 2003, 531 (534).

29 See generally on takeovers: Davies, p. 107 et seqq.

30 See for a detailed historical account: Johnston Cambridge Law Journal 2007, 422.

31 The Panel comprises up to 34 members, representing a spread of expertise in takeovers, securities markets, industry and commerce, see: The Takeover Panel, Panel membership, available at: https://www.thetakeoverpanel.org.uk/structure/panel-membership (last accessed: 15 February 2025).

or agree to take, any restricted action or any other action which could result in the frustration of any offer or *bona fide* possible offer unless it has the approval of shareholders in general meeting or the consent of the Panel. With its strict approach towards defensive measures, the UK Takeover Code helps bidders by pushing directors to pursue shareholder value in order to increase share price and dividends.[32] Deakin argues that shareholder primacy as a cultural and social norm in the UK originated in the rise of hostile takeovers in Britain during the 1970s and 1980s[33] which illustrates the significance of the UK's approach towards the market for corporate control in the context of shareholder primacy.

IV. The soft law approach to corporate governance

The fourth historic reason for shareholder primacy in the UK is its preference for a corporate governance system that is based on self-regulation and soft law. The composition of a company's board of directors is largely untouched by the Companies Act of 2006. The modern corporate governance debate in the UK started in the early 1990s and led to a series of corporate governance reports (Cadbury, Greenbury and Hampel reports). In the absence of statutory rules on board composition, these reports, *inter alia*, often addressed the role of non-executive directors to enhance the 'control' of companies. The 'Cadbury Code' of 1992 was the basis for what is now the 'UK Corporate Governance Code'.[34] The hallmark of the UK Corporate Governance Code is the 'comply or explain' approach, which means that the code contains a set of recommendations, but companies are given the flexibility to deviate from those recommendations if they 'explain' why they have chosen to do so.[35] By the start of the 2000s, corporate governance in the UK was entrenched in shareholder value.[36]

More recently, the UK Corporate Governance Code has started to reflect a slightly broader understanding of the company and is no longer exclusively focused on shareholders. The introduction of the latest version of the

32 See Davies, p. 117.

33 See Deakin Corporate Governance 2005, p. 11 et seqq.

34 As with takeover regulation, it would go beyond the scope of this chapter to fully address the composition and structure of the UK's regulation of corporate governance. See for an overview: Davies, p. 36 et seqq.

35 See for an overview: P Davies, p. 36 et seqq.

36 See Sjåfjell/Bruner/Johnston, p. 204 (207).

UK Corporate Governance Code of 2024 notes that 'companies do not exist in isolation'. It also states that companies 'will need to build and maintain successful relationships with a wide range of stakeholders' in order 'to succeed in the long-term'. The tone in the Principles of the Code mirrors this broader conception of companies – evidenced, for example, by Principle 1 of the Code, which states that it is the role of the board 'to promote the long-term sustainable success of the company, generating value for shareholders and contributing to wider society'. While the language still expressly mentions shareholder value, it also includes other factors; in fact, it resembles the language of the enlightened shareholder value theory that underpins the Companies Act of 2006.[37] The current version of the Code is therefore not a radical shift, but rather a continuation of the legal reality since the Companies Act of 2006.

C. UK Companies Act of 2006: The impact of the enlightened shareholder value theory in practice

This section will critically review the impact of the enlightened shareholder value theory on the Companies Act of 2006. It will start with the Company Law Review process, which considered different corporate theories before adopting the enlightened shareholder value theory. This review of the theoretical foundation of the Companies Act will be followed by a doctrinal assessment of both the duty for directors to promote the success of the company (section 172 Companies Act 2006) and the various nonfinancial information duties in the Act, such as strategic reports and nonfinancial statements.

I. Background: The Company Law Review process leading to the UK Companies Act 2006

The best starting point for understanding both the past and present position of corporate theory in UK company law and corporate governance is the Company Law Review process, which commenced in 1998 and ultimately led to the UK Companies Act of 2006, which is still in force

37 See below for a full analysis of this theory in the context of the UK Companies Act 2006.

today. This Company Law Review process was initiated by the New Labour government after it won the General Election in 1997. As part of its general modernisation agenda, New Labour also aimed to reform UK Company Law and equip it for the 21st century.

In 1998, the Department of Trade and Industry (DTI) launched a process for reviewing Company Law. The Company Law Review was made up of a Steering Group whose membership was comprised of lawyers, businessmen, and academics.[38] One of the central objectives of the Company Law Review process was assessing the question of corporate theory.[39]

The Company Law Review Steering Group addressed the question of whether company law should be reorientated and adopt a corporate theory other than shareholder value. The reason for raising this question was that British companies were often criticised in the 1980s and 1990s for being too short-term fixated.[40] For example, in 1999, a study by the Institute of Directors showed that many directors thought they were legally required to maximise short-term shareholder benefits to the detriment of long-term profit.[41]

In its document, *Modern Company Law for a Competitive Economy: The Strategic Framework*, the Company Law Review Steering Group set out its objective of identifying the scope of company law, i.e. in whose interest companies should be run. Determining which interest should be the objective was paramount to being able to develop a firm theoretical framework for the new Companies Act. It is against this background that the Company Law Review Steering Group comprehensively reviewed corporate theory.

II. The three different theoretical approaches

In reviewing corporate theory, the Company Law Review Steering Group compared the shareholder value theory to the pluralist approach and a third approach, the 'inclusive approach'.

---

38 See for an overview of the company law reform process: Keay, p. 14.

39 See for a review of the Company Law Review discussion of corporate theory: A Rühmkorf, p. 32 et seqq.

40 See, for example, Commission on Public Policy and British Business, Promoting Prosperity: A Business Agenda for Britain (Vintage 1997).

41 Institute of Directors, Good Boardroom Practice (IOD 1999).

1. The shareholder value approach

The Company Law Review Steering Committee acknowledged that the shareholder value approach had been in operation in the UK before.[42] As outlined above, Anglo-American corporate governance historically was widely considered to follow the theory of shareholder value and, at least since the 1980s, this theory has dominated corporate law in the UK.[43] However, prior to the Companies Act of 2006, shareholder primacy was not legally imposed on companies through statutory law. In common law, the shareholder value focus of UK company law was found in the fiduciary duty for directors to act *bona fide* in what they considered to be in the best interests of the company.[44] The phrase 'interests of the company' was equated with 'shareholders as a general body', which led to the interpretation of this duty as being focused on shareholder interests.

At the outset of the review process, the Company Law Review noted that shareholders are given rights of control over management by law in return for their investment through the purchase of shares.[45] The shareholders' rights over the management should ensure that the company is run in the shareholders' interest and that the value of their investments will increase.[46] Given that the theoretical foundations of the shareholder value theory are outlined above, they will not be replicated here. Instead, the next parts will address the two other approaches that the Company Law Review Steering Group considered as alternative frameworks.

2. The pluralist (stakeholder) approach

The Company Law Review Steering Group compared the shareholder primacy approach with the pluralist understanding of the corporation. The pluralist approach is also referred to as 'stakeholder value' or the 'produc-

42 See Company Law Review, Modern Company Law for a Competitive Economy: The Strategic Framework (DTI 1999) paras 5.1.4.-5.1.7.

43 Keay ECFR 2010, 369 (370); Gamble/Kelly Corporate Governance 2001, 110.

44 See only *Re Smith and Fawcett Ltd* [1942] Ch [304].

45 See Company Law Review, Modern Company Law for a Competitive Economy: The Strategic Framework (DTI 1999) paras 5.1.4.-5.1.7.

46 ibid, para 5.1.5.

tive coalition model'.[47] The understanding of the term 'stakeholder' is not settled. Freeman defines this term as 'any group or individual who can affect or is affected by the achievement of the organisation's objectives'.[48] The Company Law Review Steering Group noted that, under the pluralist approach, directors must pursue the interests of all stakeholders of the company and not automatically prioritise shareholders.[49] Consequently, it is the role of directors to maximise the total creation of wealth in the company as opposed to just profit.[50]

One strong justification for this approach can be found Blair and Stout's 'productive coalition model'. Blair and Stout see the public corporation as 'a team of people who enter into a complex agreement to work together for their mutual gain'.[51] In contrast to the theoretical foundations of the shareholder value theory, they argue that no member of the team takes precedent over other members as all members of the team have agreed to give up control rights.[52] The board of directors is central to this model, as it is given the control rights over the company. The directors are 'mediating hierarchs' who balance the competing interests of the various members of the team.[53] As 'trustees for the corporation itself', the board of directors ensures the functioning of the productive coalition.

The pluralist approach takes a very different theoretical approach than the shareholder value theory towards understanding the firm. The pluralist approach emphasises that individuals owe obligations to each other as a community, independently of contractual obligations.[54] This argument differs from that of the 'nexus of contracts' theory, outlined above. Proponents of the pluralist approach question whether shareholders are the only constituents that deserve prioritisation. First, shareholders are not the only constituents who invest in the firm and have a stake in it: employees often

47 Blair/Stout Virginia Law Review 1999, 247. See for a discussion of the stakeholder theory: Keay The Enlightened Shareholder Value Principle and Corporate Governance Richmond Law Journal of Global Law & Business 2010, 249.

48 See: Freeman, p. 246. See for an overview of the discussion: Keay, p. 47.

49 Company Law Review, Modern Company Law for a Competitive Economy: The Strategic Framework (DTI 1999) para 5.1.13.

50 J Kay and A Silberston, 'Corporate governance', available at: http://www.johnkay.com (last accessed: 15th February 2025).

51 Blair/Stout Virginia Law Review 1999, 247 (278).

52 ibid, 277.

53 ibid, 281.

54 Millon Wash. & Lee L.Rev. 1993, 1373 (1382).

invest in firm-specific training.[55] Second, the claim that shareholders are the owners of the company is disputed. Shareholders acquire a title to the shares that they purchase, but not to the company.[56] Other points of criticisms regarding the shareholder value theory include that: (i) it results in short-termism; and (ii) it disregards the fact that shareholders' interests can diverge.[57] It would go beyond the scope of this chapter to address all the criticisms of the shareholder value theory in detail.

Regarding the issue of sustainability, the pluralist approach provides directors with significant discretion that they could use to promote aspects of sustainability. At the very least, the pluralist approach does not require directors to place all other issues below shareholder value and therefore enables them to decide on a case-by-case basis what is in the best interest of the company. Blair and Stout further support this view by referring to the business judgment rule and the discretion it gives to the board.[58]

However, following a consultation, the Company Law Review Steering Group decided not to adopt the pluralist approach. It cited several reasons for this decision, including concern that this approach would move directors from their core role as managers of the business towards moral, political, and economic arbiters.[59] Moreover, it was held that the external benefits of the pluralist approach would be better achieved by specific legislation on issues such as environmental matters.[60] In practical terms, a concern was that directors would find it difficult to decide which interest to prioritise in the event of a conflict.[61]

---

55 Kelly/Parkinson CfiLR 1998, 174 (188).

56 Ireland MLR 1999, 32.

57 See for a more detailed overview: Keay ECFR 2010, p. 369 et seqq.

58 Blair/Stout Virginia Law Review 1999, 247 (320). The business judgment rule is explained in the following way: '...directors of a corporation...are clothed with [the] presumption, which the law accords to them, of being [motivated] in their conduct by a bona fide regard for the interests of the corporation whose affairs the stockholders have committed to their charge...', see: *Gimbel v. Signal Cos.*, 316 A.2d 599, 608 (Del. Ch. 1974).

59 See Company Law Review, Developing the Framework (2000), para 2.21.

60 Company Law Review, Strategic Framework, paras 5.1.25 – 5.1.29.

61 Company Law Review, Completing the Structure (2000) para 3.5.

3. The inclusive approach (enlightened shareholder value)

Finally, the third approach that was finally adopted by the Company Law Review was called the 'inclusive approach'. The government's White Paper settled on using the inclusive approach.[62] The inclusive approach was later labelled 'enlightened shareholder value' (abbreviated as 'ESV') which is the fundamental corporate theory used in the UK Companies Act of 2006, as it embodies the duty for directors to promote the success of the company (section 172 Companies Act 2006).[63]

As was a common approach of the New Labour government at that time, the inclusive approach was a 'third way', i.e. an alternative to the dichotomy between traditional shareholder value and the pluralist approach.[64] The starting point for this approach is that company law should move away from one of its main critique points, short-termism.[65] Enlightened shareholder value therefore posits that directors should pursue long-term profit maximisation which would require cooperative relationships with the various non-shareholder stakeholders.[66] Section 172 of the Companies Act of 2006, which employs this theory in the directors' duties, requires directors to take 'other factors into account' and to consider the interests of other stakeholders such as employees, suppliers, the community, or the environment.[67] Theoretically, the inclusive approach aims to achieve not just long-termism, but also better relationships with the company's various stakeholders.

However, as the name 'enlightened shareholder value' more explicitly suggests as compared to the name 'inclusive approach', this theory ultimately promotes shareholder value.[68] At the end of the day, directors must act in the collective best interest of shareholders.[69] This situation raises the question as to how shareholder value should be 'enlightened' in practice. This point will be addressed in the next section in the legal analysis of the

---

62 Company Law Review, The White Paper: Modernising Company Law (DTI 2002, Cm 5553-I and Cm 5553-II) para 3.3. See for an overview of the background to the adoption of the enlightened shareholder value theory: Keay, chapter 3.

63 See for a detailed analysis of the enlightened shareholder value theory: Keay.

64 Vasudev/Watson/Millon, p. 69.

65 ibid.

66 Roach Company Lawyer 2005, 98 (99).

67 See below for a full analysis of section 172 Companies Act 2006.

68 Keay Company Lawyer 2007, 106 (107).

69 Company Law Review, Modern Company Law for a Competitive Economy: Developing the Framework (DTI 2000) para 2.22.

duty of directors to promote the success of the company under section 172 (1) Companies Act of 2006. Legal analysis of that section will determine whether the scope of the inclusive approach includes promoting sustainability or whether it is simply the shareholder value theory in disguise.

In practical terms, the enlightened shareholder value theory was implemented in the Companies Act of 2006 in two ways: first, in the duty for directors in section 172 (1) Companies Act 2006 and second, in the duty to issue a non-financial report.

III. Directors' duties: the duty to promote the success of the company, section 172 (1) Companies Act of 2006

In this part, the duty to promote the success of the company will be doctrinally assessed to determine what it requires from directors, how it operates, and what enlightened shareholder value means for directors in the context of this duty.

For the doctrinal assessment of section 172 (1) Companies Act 2006, it is important to note that section 170 of the Act stipulates two important rules regarding the relationship between the now-codified directors' duties and the previous common law duties. First, the statutory duties of directors have effect in place of the common law duties;[70] second, the statutory duties must be interpreted and applied in the same way as common law rules or equitable principles, and regard must be given to the corresponding common law rules and equitable principles in interpreting and applying the general duties.[71] The second provision is the basis for the reference to common law decisions in the interpretation of the section 172 (1) Companies Act 2006 duty below.

1. The duty to promote the success of the company

First, the duty to promote the success of the company will be assessed in order to examine enlightened shareholder value theory means in practice.[72] Section 172 (1) Companies Act of 2006 reads as follows:

70 Companies Act 2006, s170 (3).
71 Companies Act 2006, s170 (4).
72 See also Rühmkorf, p. 39 et seqq.

172 Duty to promote the success of the company

(1) A director of a company must act in the way he considers, in good faith, would be most likely to promote the success of the company for the benefit of its members as a whole, and in doing so have regard (amongst other matters) to
  (a) the likely consequences of any decision in the long term,
  (b) the interests of the company's employees,
  (c) the need to foster the company's business relationships with suppliers, customers and others,
  (d) the impact of the company's operations on the community and the environment,
  (e) the desirability of the company maintaining a reputation for high standards of business conduct, and
  (f) the need to act fairly as between members of the company.
(2) Where or to the extent that the purposes of the company consist of or include purposes other than the benefit of its members, subsection (1) has effect as if the reference to promoting the success of the company for the benefit of its members were to achieving those purposes.
(3) The duty imposed by this section has effect subject to any enactment or rule of law requiring directors, in certain circumstances, to consider or act in the interests of creditors of the company.

Initially, this duty can give the impression that it is closely linked to stakeholder interests due to the number of different factors that are mentioned. In fact, these different factors overlap with the different dimensions of sustainability as they range from the employees (b) to the environment (d) and the long-term consequences of any decision (a).

The following section will critically assess the meaning of the different conditions of section 172 (1) to determine the extent to which this duty provides scope for directors to pursue sustainability. Specifically, the requirements to act in the way: (i) the director considers, in good faith; (ii) is most likely to promote the success of the company; and (iii) having regard to the list of factors provided in the section.

a) Good faith

The starting point for the doctrinal analysis of the duty to promote the success of the company is that the wording of the law refers to the director's 'good faith'.

Section 172 (1) first notes that 'a director of a company must act in the way he considers, in good faith...'. This wording raises the question as to what standard is expected of directors. The phrases 'he considers' and 'in good faith' place the emphasis on the subjective view of the director. Combined, these two phrases give directors a lot of discretion when making decisions in accordance with section 172 (1). Consequently, judges do not have much power to second-guess business decisions.

Considering the corresponding common law rules,[73] it is likely that courts would consider relevant case law in determining the meaning of 'good faith' in this section.[74] Under the common law,[75] the traditional test was that directors must act '...bona fide in what they consider – not what a court may consider – is in the interest of the company, and not for any collateral purpose'.[76] This test focuses on the director's 'state of mind'.[77]

After the enactment of the Companies Act of 2006, it was noted in *Cobden Investments Ltd v. RWM Langport Ltd*[78] that

> [t]he perhaps old-fashioned phrase acting 'bona fide in the interests of the company' is reflected in the statutory words acting 'in good faith in a way most likely to promote the success of the company for the benefit of the members as a whole'. They come to the same thing with the modern formulation giving a more readily understood definition of the scope of the duty.[79]

This point was also made in *Iesini v. Westrip Holdings Ltd.*[80] In *Iesini*, the court held that it was not in the best position to make judgments about the weight of the considerations in section 172 and would only be able to

73 See Companies Act 2006, s170 (4).
74 See Keay Company Lawyer 2011, p- 138 et seqq.
75 see *Smith and Fawcett Ltd* [1942] Ch 304 [306].
76 ibid.
77 See *Regentcrest plc v Cohen* [2001] 2 BCLC 80 [105].
78 [2008] EWHC 2810 (Ch) [52].
79 *Cobden Investments Ltd v RWM Langport Ltd, Southern Counties Fresh Foods Limited, Romford Wholesale Meats Limited* [2008] EWHC 2810 (Ch [52].
80 [2009] EWHC 2526.

make such a judgment if the case were very clear. Otherwise, priority would be given to the directors' subjective judgments. Good faith in section 172 is therefore seen as a continuation of the previous phrase 'bona fide', which was called an 'perhaps old-fashioned phrase' which 'comes to the same thing'.[81]

In essence, directors are given significant discretion when deciding what is in the best interest of the company. It is not for the courts to second-guess these decisions, unless there are very rare exceptions. The focus is therefore on the subjective view of directors.

The assessment of 'good faith' as the first constituting element of section 172 therefore indicates that the 'new' duty to promote the success of the company places great emphasis on the subjective view of directors.

b) Success of the company

The second constituting element of section 172 (1) Companies Act 2006 is the phrase 'success of the company for the benefit of the members as a whole'. The term 'success' is not defined in this section.

The Guidance on Key Clauses in the Company Law Reform Bill notes the following about the phrase 'success of the company':

> The decision as to what will promote success, and what constitutes such success, is one for the directors' good faith judgment. This ensures that business decisions on, for example, strategy and tactics are for the directors and not subject to decisions by the courts, subject to good faith.[82]

The wording emphasises that success must be 'for the benefit of the members as a whole'. This clearly indicates the way in which interpretation of 'success' is headed. Again, the common law duty to act *bona fide* in the best interest of the company helps with the interpretation of the statutory wording here: the common law duty to act *bona fide* in the best interest of the company was interpreted as meaning the shareholders collectively,

81 See *Cobden Investments Ltd v RWM Langport Ltd, Southern Counties Fresh Foods Limited, Romford Wholesale Meats Limited* [2008] EWHC 2810 (Ch [52].

82 DTI, Guidance on Key Clauses to the Company Law Reform Bill (2005) para 63.

i.e. as a general body, which effectively required the directors to pursue shareholder value.[83]

A similar approach can be taken to the meaning of 'success' in the context of section 172 (1). The 'success' must be 'for the members as a whole'. Section 112 Companies Act 2006 defines members as shareholders. The expression 'members as a whole' is understood by courts as 'present and future shareholders'.[84] The Company Law Review Steering Group interpreted this phrase in a similar way; they included the phrase 'members as a whole' to emphasise that directors must work for the collective interests of shareholders and not for one individual member.[85]

c) Having regard to the list of factors

The third constituting element of section 172 (1) Companies Act 2006 is that directors must 'have regard to' a list of stakeholder-oriented factors. The factors cover a broad range of stakeholders and issues. First, the list is non-exhaustive. This is indicated by the wording that a director must have regard to the list of factors 'amongst other matters'. Second, as mentioned above, the listed factors in section 172 (1) Companies Act 2006 overlap with the different dimensions of sustainability as, for example, reference is made to the long-term consequences of decisions. Such long-term consequences of decisions refer to, in turn, all aspects of sustainability: the economic dimension, the environment, and the social (by referencing employees).

At least in theory, the enumeration of these factors allows directors to pursue sustainability in their decision-making. However, in practice, the scope for sustainability is much more limited than a first glance of section 172 might indicate. This is for two main reasons. First, directors must 'have regard to' the list of factors when they act, in good faith, for the benefit of the members as a whole, i.e. the shareholders. One can 'have regard to' those factors in various ways. Irrespective of how much regard a director has for these factors – and it is not specified by the law how much regard is required – they are ultimately only secondary issues to shareholder value

83 See *Re Smith & Facett Ltd* [1942] Ch [304], [306]; *Hutton v West Cork Railway Company* (1883) 23 Ch. D. 654; *Parke v Daily News Ltd* [1962] Ch. 927.

84 See *Gaiman v National Association for Mental Health* (1971) Ch [317].

85 The Company Law Review, Modern Company Law for a Competitive Economy: Developing the Framework (DTI 2000) para 3–51.

being pursued. The wording of the section indicates a hierarchy between promoting the success of the company for the benefit of the members (which means that directors must effectively pursue shareholder value) and the regard that they must have for the stakeholder interests in the list of factors.[86]

The second reason for this cautious view as to the impact of 'the list of factors' for sustainability is that there is no clarity as to what directors must *do*. Unanswered questions are, for example, the extent to which they need to consider stakeholder interests and how they can balance competing stakeholder interests (e.g. a decision benefits employees, but not the environment or vice versa).[87] While these questions, which are important from a sustainability point of view, have been left open, directors have clarity on two other points: (i) they must ultimately strive to promote shareholder value;[88] and (ii) they have considerable discretion to do so, as the focus is on the directors' subjective view. As directors may only consider these factors within the constraints of shareholder value, the wording 'have regard to' can be seen as an educational matter, clarifying for directors that they can take other interests into account. From a more theoretical perspective, the combination of prioritising shareholder interests and taking those other factors into account indicates the theory of enlightened shareholder value as the underlying approach for the Companies Act of 2006.

The question of 'having regard to' the list of factors was considered in the case *R. (on the application of People & Planet) v. HM Treasury*.[89] Here, the case was brought against the government because it had purchased roughly 84 % of the shares of the Royal Bank of Scotland (RBS) during the financial crisis. Activists of the student network, People & Planet, brought the case on the grounds that RBS was a significant provider of the energy sector. In People & Planet's view, the directors had breached their section 172 (1) Companies Act 2006 duty as they did not have sufficient regard for environmental issues, per factor (d) of the list of factors. People & Planet argued that the government was in breach of section 172 as it had agreed to a policy document outlining the way RBS should be run through a limited company, UK Financial Investments (Ltd).

86 See Rühmkorf, p. 47.
87 See for the conflict between two or more of the factors: Hannigan, p. 10 et seqq.
88 See for this point: Loughrey/Keay, p. 50 (74).
89 [2009] EWHC 3020 (Admin) QBD (Admin).

In essence, the government stated in this policy document that it would not intervene with the legal duty of boards to run the company in the interests of all their shareholders.[90] The court took a cautious view of the extent to which shareholders (such as here the limited company) could influence the directors' decision-making, noting that shareholders that seek to influence the decisions of the board could only do so within the constraints of the duty to promote the success of the company for benefit of the members as a whole (i.e. shareholders). Any attempt by the government to impose its own policy on climate change on the board of the private company that ran RBS would 'cut across the duties of the board as set out in section 172 (1)'.[91]

Despite being a somewhat different set of facts, since the judicial review in People & Planet's case was based on the ownership of RBS, the key aspect of the judgment is that shareholder interests prevail in the courts' understanding of section 172 (1) Companies Act 2006. This decision further reaffirms the view taken in this section that the 'list of factors' are secondary to the interests of shareholders.

d) Enforceability

The final remaining question regarding the extent to which section 172 (1) Companies Act 2006 can promote sustainability depends on the enforceability of the duty to promote the success of the company. The above analysis has demonstrated the strong focus of the duty on (i) the shareholder interests and (ii) the director's good faith. These two aspects already significantly limit the scope for any legal actions based on an alleged breach of this duty.

If any action were to be taken, then the proper claimant would be the company (so-called 'proper plaintiff rule').[92] The board of directors therefore decides whether any action should be pursued against a director who has breached their duty. Additionally, shareholders are given the right to bring a derivative action pursuant to sections 260 Companies Act of 2006, provided that certain conditions for such an action are met. The different

90 *R. (on the Application of People and Planet) v HM Treasury* [2009] EWHC 320 (Admin), [13e.].

91 ibid, at para 34.

92 *Foss v Harbottle* (1843) 2 Hare 461.

stakeholders listed in section 172 (1), such as the employees, are omitted from the groups who have legal standing. The two groups that do have legal standing – the directors and, if certain conditions are met, the shareholders – are those that are primarily interested in financial considerations. This situation significantly restricts the practical effect of including the different sustainability-related factors in section 172 (1). This duty has therefore been called 'a right without a remedy'.[93]

2. Sustainability and section 172 (1) Companies Act: All talk, but no walk?

Overall, the doctrinal assessment of section 172 (1) Companies Act 2006 provides a rather bleak perspective for the promotion of sustainable development. There is, at least in theory, some scope for directors to consider the different dimensions of sustainability in the form of long-termism, environmental issues, and social aspects. Yet, in practice, shareholder value trumps any attempts to significantly open up boardroom decisions. In the end, the wording of section 172 (1) leaves little room for anything else other than the pursuit of shareholder value. The express inclusion of the list of factors was supposed to 'enlighten' shareholder value, but it appears as if this 'new' duty is not so new after all. In many ways, it is rather a continuation of the common law case law from the pre-Companies Act of 2006 era that required directors to act *bona fide* in the best interest of the company, i.e. in the best interest of the shareholders.[94]

In sum, the only effect of the wording of the duty to promote the success of the company in section 172 (1) is that it prevents a completely narrow understanding of shareholder value that would not allow directors to take anything else into account. Apart from that, the duty leaves much to be desired and little room for any significant promotion of sustainable development.

93 Loughrey/Keay, p. 50.
94 See *Re Smith and Fawcett Ltd* [1942] Ch 304 [306].

IV. Non-financial reporting: from the business review to the non-financial statement

As the enlightened shareholder value is based on two limbs of the Companies Act of 2006, section 172 and the duty to issue non-financial reporting, this section will now turn to non-financial reporting.[95] Again, due to space constraints, it is only possible to give a brief overview and assess how the different reporting duties impact corporate theory and the promotion of sustainability in the UK. In addition to the narrative reporting requirements outlined by the Company Law reform for the 2006 Companies Act, the UK has also implemented other relevant disclosure regimes. This chapter will therefore briefly address these regimes, such as, the 'transparency in supply chains clause' included in the UK Modern Slavery Act 2015. Generally, the UK is a system that favours nonfinancial information disclosure in its corporate governance system; it relies on information disclosure to steer companies towards promoting sustainability.[96] These laws are also referred to as 'narrative reporting'. Such laws are intended to enable directors to explain the company's performance without numbers and to indicate the future direction of the company's business.[97]

Originally, the Company Law Review Steering Group had planned to include an Operating and Financial Review (OFR) in the Companies Act, which would have required companies to disclose information about their relationships with stakeholders, including employees, and their projects and programmes insofar as the information was 'material'.[98] Such a report would have helped hold directors accountable for the company's performance.[99] To that end, directors would have been required to provide 'more qualitative and forward-looking reporting, in addition to information that is quantitative'.[100] The OFR was eventually abolished in 2005 by Chancellor Gordon Brown, who justified this decision as reducing the burden on companies.[101] Johnston criticises this decision, stating that it had 'startling corporate governance implications' as, from that point onwards, sharehold-

95 See Keay, p. 14.
96 See B Sjåfjell/Bruner/Johnston, p. 204 et seqq.
97 See generally: Villiers, p. 85 et seqq.
98 See for a full account of the OFR: Johnston EBOR 2006, 817 (829).
99 See Modernising Company Law, Cm 5553, July 2002, para 2.37.
100 See Keay, p. 147 et seqq.
101 See McBarnet/Voiculescu/Campbell/Campbell/Vick, p. 257 et seq.

er value was 'enshrined as the default purpose of UK company law' without the information that was supposed to 'enlighten' it.[102]

1. Business review

Instead of the OFR, the Companies Act of 2006 employed 'business review',[103] a significantly slimmed-down version of the OFR. This reporting duty required directors to inform members about how they had discharged their duty to promote the success of the company, including the list of factors contained in section 172 (1) Companies Act 2006. The main weakness of the business review approach was that it gave significant discretion to companies as to what they wanted to report, leaving the companies with the freedom to leave out nonfinancial information such as information related to sustainability issues. Research consequently demonstrated the flaws of this reporting regime. For example, Villiers and Aiyegbayo showed that, based on semi-structured interviews with key corporate governance actors like investor relations managers and corporate governance directors from institutional investment firms, the business review approach made little difference to the quality of reports compared to the reports that companies published prior to the Companies Act of 2006.

2. Strategic report

Following considerable criticism of the original version and a consultation, the business review approach was replaced by the 'strategic report' in 2013 which was intended to complement the financial statements.[104] The strategic report is now found in Chapter 4A of the Companies Act. Under the strategic reporting requirement, directors must prepare a strategic report for each financial year of the company[105] unless they are subject to a small company exemption[106]. The strategic report for each financial year of the company must include a 'section 172(1) statement'[107] that describes how the

---

102 Johnston EBOR 2006, 817 (832).
103 This reporting duty was found in s415 (1) CA before it was abolished and replaced by the 'strategic report'.
104 See Financial Reporting Council, Guidance on the strategic report (2014).
105 Companies Act 2006, s414A.
106 Companies Act 2006, s414B.
107 Companies Act 2006, s414 CZA.

directors have regarded the matters set out in section 172(1)(a) to (f) when performing their duty.

Additionally, in the case of a quoted company, the strategic report must also include information about environmental matters (including the impact of the company on the environment), the company's employees, and social, community, and human rights issues. The report must include information about any policies of the company in relation to those matters and the effectiveness of those policies. However, the important caveat for this reporting provision is that these points must only be included 'to the extent necessary for an understanding of the development, performance or position of the company's business'.[108] If the report does not contain information about these issues, then it must at least state which of these kinds of information it does not contain.[109]

While the strategic report is a further development of the business review, it is also a rather 'light touch' regulatory tool. Effectively, the strategic report allows companies to choose whether to report on sustainability issues as these can be left out as long as the company discloses this in its report. The strategic report is therefore a rather soft disclosure provision that does not make much of a difference compared to voluntary reporting by companies.

3.Section 172 (1) statement

Although the purpose of the strategic report is to inform members of the company and help them assess how the directors have performed their duty under section 172 (1) Companies Act, a separate statement on s172 (1) is required from companies within the large company accounts regime. The 'section 172 (1) statement' in the Companies Act was introduced in 2019.[110] This amendment was part of a transition from the discussion about the scope of s172 (1) to its practical impact.[111]

Affected companies are required to include a statement in their strategic report for a financial year that describes how the directors have had regard to the matters set out in section 172(1)(a) to (f) when performing their

108 Companies Act 2006, s414C (7).

109 Companies Act 2006, s414C (8).

110 This section was introduced through the Companies (Miscellaneous Reporting) Regulations of 2018 (the "Miscellaneous Reporting Regulations").

111 see Hannigan, para 10–35.

duty under section 172. In its guidance on this reporting duty, the Financial Reporting Council notes that the information contained in this statement will depend on the individual circumstances of each company. However, it points out that companies will probably want to include information on some or all of the following: (i) the issues, factors, and stakeholders the directors consider relevant in complying with section 172(1)(a) to (f) of the Companies Act and how they have formed that opinion; (ii) the main methods the directors have used to engage with stakeholders and understand the issues to which they must have regard; and (iii) information on the effect of that regard on the company's decisions and strategies during the financial year.[112]

Moreover, the Guidance states that section 172 (1) statements should focus on the matters that are of strategic importance to the company and that the information in the statement should be commensurate with the size and complexity of the company.[113] While principally, specific reporting for section 172 (1) is a positive step forward, it just toys with the existing framework instead than reforming what is ultimately a duty for directors to pursue shareholder value.

4. Non-financial and sustainability information statement

The UK's narrative reporting framework contains further reporting duties. First, prior to Brexit, the UK implemented the EU's nonfinancial information disclosure in the Companies Act, which covered large public-interest companies (i.e. listed companies, banks, insurances) with more than 500 employees.[114] Since the UK kept this reporting duty after it exited the European Union, the provision is very similar to those known in EU member states. Companies that fall under this provision are required to issue a 'non-financial statement'. This duty was subsequently amended; since 2022, companies are now required to issue a 'non-financial and sustainability

112 Financial Reporting Council, Section 172 statements: How to make them more useful (2020).

113 ibid.

114 see Companies Act of 2006, 414 CA and 414 CB. The UK transposed the Directive through the Companies, Partnerships and Groups (Accounts and Non-Financial Reporting) Regulations of 2016, which came into force in mid-December 2016.

information statement'.[115] The non-financial and sustainability information statement must contain climate-related financial disclosures of the company.[116]

The climate-related financial disclosures in this statement, introduced by the amendment, require companies to report on several matters related to climate. These include: a description of how the company identifies, assesses, and manages climate-related risks and opportunities and how these are integrated into the company's overall risk management process; a description of the principal climate-related risks and opportunities arising in connection with the company's operations; an analysis of the resilience of the company's business model and strategy, taking into consideration different climate-related scenarios; and a description of the targets used by the company to manage climate-related risks and to realise climate-related opportunities as well as performance against those targets.[117]

While this reporting on the climate-related impact of the company is novel and a positive step forward for sustainability, the provision has limitations that are comparable to those of the strategic report: directors can choose not to make these reports where they 'reasonably believe' that disclosure would not be necessary for an understanding of the company's business. In this case, they must provide a clear and reasoned explanation of their reasonable belief.[118]

5. Slavery and human trafficking statement

Furthermore, the UK introduced a duty to report about human trafficking and modern slavery through the UK Modern Slavery Act of 2015. Section 54 of the UK Modern Slavery Act requires every organisation operating a business in the UK with a total annual turnover of £36 million or more to produce a slavery and human trafficking statement for each financial year of the organisation.[119]

115 This amendment was introduced through the Companies (Strategic Report) (Climate-related Financial Disclosure) Regulations 2022.
116 Companies Act 2006, s414CB.
117 Companies Act 2006, s414CB (2A).
118 Companies Act 2006, s414 CB (4A), (4B).
119 UK Modern Slavery Act 2015, s54 (1).

This slavery and human trafficking statement is

(a) a statement of the steps the organisation has taken during the financial year to ensure that slavery and human trafficking is not taking place –
    (i) in any of its supply chains, and
    (ii) in any part of its own business, or
(b) a statement that the organisation has taken no such steps.[120]

At the time when it was introduced, this reporting duty was rather novel as it imposed a duty on companies to report about specific human rights issues in their supply chain (i.e. human trafficking and forced labour). However, it has become apparent that this duty gives too much discretion to companies: the companies can effectively decide the 'if' and 'how' of any steps, i.e. whether they take any steps in the first place and, if so, what steps they take. Finally, the companies may also decide what information they choose to include in their statement. Literature has extensively discussed the weaknesses of this clause[121] and has shown that it has little impact on corporate practices[122].

Overall, this section has demonstrated that the UK's strong focus and reliance on disclosure laws is an instrument to 'enlighten' shareholder value. However, while disclosure laws can vary in terms of scope and stringency, they are generally a softer form of regulation that is not 'heavily interventionist'.[123] They are a 'communicative-based tool'.[124] Recent amendments to UK corporate governance that were intended to promote more sustainability have tended to take the form of disclosure laws, such as the recent statement on section 172 (1) Companies Act 2006 and the inclusion of climate aspects in the non-financial statements. Despite the (still increasing) quantity of non-financial information disclosure duties, its quality and reliability continue to be weak.[125]

120 UK Modern Slavery Act 2015, s54 (4).
121 Iqbal Company Lawyer 2018, 3; Okoye, International Company and Commercial Law Review 2017, 196.
122 see LeBaron/Rühmkorf, Global Policy 2017, 15.
123 Baldwin/Cave, p. 49.
124 Morgan/Yeung, p. 96.
125 see, for example, Sjåfjell/Bruner/Johnston, p. 217.

D. After Brexit: convergence or divergence with European developments towards more sustainable companies?

This section will shift focus to the relationship of the UK with the recent European trend towards promoting greater corporate sustainability. This question is particularly interesting in the case of the UK given its exit from the European Union and the recent wave of European directives and regulations as part of the 'European Green Deal'.

First, post-Brexit, the UK is under no obligation to implement any of the regulations that are part of the Green Deal. The non-financial statement in section 414 of the Companies Act, discussed above, is a reminder of the UK's membership of the European Union as it was implemented when the UK was still an EU member. In fact, the UK is now free to diverge from this obligation which means that in addition to not following any new pieces of EU legislation, it can also decide to remove or amend existing regulations that it implemented in its national law during EU membership.

Therefore, the recent significant developments at the EU level concerning sustainability, including the Corporate Sustainability Reporting Directive (CSRD), the Corporate Sustainability Due Diligence Directive (CSDDD), and the Taxonomy Regulation do not directly affect the UK. However, some of these regulations can apply to UK companies; for example, the CSDDD also applies to non-EU companies with a turnover of at least €450 million in the EU.[126] Other regulations will indirectly affect UK companies: UK companies may be suppliers to EU companies, and these EU companies may then ask their suppliers to adhere to certain contractual assurances on sustainability as part of their own compliance with EU laws. Accordingly, it is incorrect to assume that these European developments have no impact on the UK whatsoever, though the impact now is less direct than it would have been pre-Brexit.

Notwithstanding these general points on the EU-UK relationship, this chapter has shown that the scope for sustainability in the UK was already narrow before Brexit. Even though the enlightened shareholder value, as the approach underlying the Companies Act of 2006, intended to broaden considerations, the theory and practice of company law in the UK remains deeply entrenched in shareholder value. The duty to promote the success of the company in section 172 (1) Companies Act 2006 has had little impact in

---

126 Directive (EU) 2024/1760 of the European Parliament and of the Council of 13 June 2024 on corporate sustainability due diligence, 5.7.2024, Article 2 (2).

practice and the various forms of non-financial information disclosure laws in the UK continue to tinker with problems rather than solve them.

There are proposals on the table as to how UK company law could be made more sustainable.[127] For example, a meaningful reform of section 172 (1) could end the prioritisation of shareholder value and instead rely on directors to balance competing stakeholder interests on a case-by-case basis while operating within the planetary boundaries.[128] Such a move would end the legal norm of shareholder value. However, to reform the social norm of shareholder value, it would be necessary to address its wider institutional entrenchment in the UK, including the *laissez fair* approach to business regulation, the soft law approach to corporate governance, and the incentive structures that the market for corporate control sets.

In addition to these points, the UK has fallen behind other European countries in sustainability-related laws, and not just because of Brexit. Despite its weaknesses, when the UK Modern Slavery Act of 2015 was enacted, its reporting duty in section 54 was one of the first attempts to address human rights abuses in global supply chains. However, since then, the political and legal developments in sustainability have moved on, with other countries such as France and Germany passing laws that impose mandatory human rights due diligence on companies. The UK has not followed this trend but rather has continued with its preference for information disclosure. This is evidenced by the lack of amendments to the Modern Slavery Act of 2015, coupled with the introduction of climate-related financial disclosures in the non-financial statement. Moreover, rather than significantly reforming section 172 (1) itself, the UK introduced a separate statement requirement for large companies. This fact alone exemplifies the reluctance of the UK to intervene with business and its continued preference for self-regulation.

For that reason, there are significant doubts as to whether the UK is ready for any significant change. The quantity of disclosure laws that were analysed in this chapter show the strong preference the UK has for this legislative tool. In the words of Andrew Johnston, any significant change would require 'experimentation in corporate governance' rather than 'the tried (and failed) prescription of more information disclosure'.[129]

127 Johnston European Company Law 2014, 63.
128 Sjåfjell Sustainability 2020, 6245.
129 Sjåfjell/Bruner/Johnston, p. 217.

E. Conclusion

This chapter has shown that, both historically and presently, the UK is firmly entrenched in the shareholder value theory. Prior to the Companies Act of 2006, shareholder value was largely a social norm.[130] The practical importance of shareholder value in company law and corporate governance was supported by the common law duty to act *bona fide* in the best interest of the company, and it has become enshrined in the UK through the market for corporate control (via hostile takeovers) and the soft law approach to corporate governance.

The Company Law Review process devoted significant time to considering corporate doctrine for the Companies Act of 2006. It reviewed three different approaches: shareholder value, a pluralist approach, and an inclusive approach (which was termed 'enlightened shareholder value'). The Act eventually adopted the enlightened shareholder value theory as a 'third way', which would overcome the dichotomy between pure shareholder value and stakeholder value. The idea of a 'third way' was reflective of what the New Labour government often did at that time. However, the doctrinal analysis of the present state of UK company law and corporate governance in this chapter has shown that there is very little that is enlightened. Rather, the two main limbs of the enlightened shareholder value theory do very little to promote considerations other than those of shareholders.

The duty to promote the success of the company in section 172 (1) Companies Act 2006 legally imposes shareholder value on directors by requiring them to work for the benefit of the 'members as a whole' (i.e. the shareholders); they only need to 'have regard to' other factors with little specification as to how this should be done. The second limb, nonfinancial reporting duties, appear to be a popular legislative choice in the UK when it comes to addressing the impacts of companies on sustainability issues. However, while there is a high quantity of reporting, there is little quality. The disclosure regime in the Companies Act implemented by the strategic report (the nonfinancial and sustainability statement and the section 172 statement) was shown to be weak and ineffective. Further, nonfinancial reporting duties outside of the Companies Act, like the 'human trafficking and modern slavery statement' (required by the UK Modern Slavery Act of 2015), adds to the list of 'light touch' regulation that does little to improve the sustainability record of companies.

130 See Sjåfjell/Richardson/Sjåfjell/Johnston/Anker-Sorensen/Millon, p. 95 et seqq.

After Brexit, the outlook is somewhat bleak, as the UK is no longer subject to European requirements. Therefore, the UK is not directly affected by the European Green Deal and its range of different new directives and regulations, including the Corporate Sustainability Reporting Directive and the Corporate Sustainability Due Diligence Directive. While some of these regulations might be slimmed down via the 'Omnibus package', they are still a step in the right direction that the UK is not subject to. It remains to be seen whether the UK will follow any of these European developments towards more sustainable corporate governance, or if instead, it will continue to follow a soft-touch regulatory approach based on shareholder value and disclosure laws.

References

Armour, John/Deakin, Simon and Konzelmann, Suzanne J., Shareholder Primacy and the Trajectory of UK Corporate Governance, British Journal of Industrial Relations 2003, 531

Baldwin, Robert/Cave, Martin, Understanding regulation: theory, strategy and practice, Oxford 1999

Berle, Adolf/Means, Gardiner, The Modern Corporation and Private Property, Piscataway 1991 (originally published in 1932)

Blair, Margaret/Stout, Lynn, A Team Production Theory of Corporate Law, Virginia Law Review 1999, 85

Campbell, Kevin/Vick, Douglas, Disclosure law and the market for corporate social responsibility, in McBarnet/Voiculescu/Campbell (eds.), The New Corporate Accountability: Corporate Social Responsibility and the Law, Cambridge 2007, p. 241

Chandler, Alfred, Scale and Scope: The Dynamics of Industrial Capitalism, Cambridge, Massachusetts, 1990

Chiu, Iris H-Y Chiu, Operationalising a stakeholder conception in company law, Law and Financial Markets Review 2016, 173

Davies, Paul, Introduction to Company Law, 3rd edn, Oxford 2020

Deakin, Simon, The coming transformation of shareholder value, Corporate Governance 2005, 11

Easterbrook, Frank/Fischel, Daniel, The Economic Structure of Corporate Law, Cambridge, Massachusetts 1991

Freeman, Robert, Strategic management: A stakeholder approach, Boston 1984

Gamble, Andre/Kelly, Gavin, Shareholder Value and the Stakeholder Debate in the UK, Corporate Governance 2001, 110

Griggs, David et al., Sustainable development goals for people and planet, Nature 2013, 496

Hannah, Leslie, The "divorce" of ownership from control from 1900 onwards: re-calibrating imagined global trends, Business History 2007, 404

Hannigan, Brenda, Company Law, 6th ed., Oxford 2021

Hansmann, Henry and Kraakman, Reinier, The end of history for corporate law, Georgetown Law Journal 2001, 439

Hansmann, Henry, Ownership of the firm, Journal of Law, Economics and Organisation 1988, 267

Iqbal, Taskin, The efficacy of the disclosure requirement under s.54 of the Modern Slavery Act, Company Lawyer 2018, 3

Ireland, Paddy, Company Law and the myth of shareholder ownership, MLR 1999, 32

Johnston, Andrew, After the OFR: Can UK Shareholder Value Still be Enlightened?, EBOLR 2006, 817

Johnston, Andrew, Takeover regulation: Historical and theoretical perspectives on the City Code, Cambridge Law Journal 2007, 422

Johnston, Andrew/Segrestin, Blanch and Hatchuel/Armand, From balanced enterprise to hostile takeover: how the law forgot about management, Legal Studies 2019, 75

Johnston, Andrew, Market-Led Sustainability through Information Disclosure: The UK Approach in Sjåfjell, Beate/Bruner, Christopher (eds) The Cambridge Handbook of Corporate Law, Corporate Governance and Sustainability, Cheltenham 2020

Keay, Andrew, Section 172(1) of the Companies Act 2006: an interpretation and assessment, Company Lawyer 2007, 106

Keay, Andrew, Stakeholder Theory in Corporate Law: Has it Got What it Takes?, Richmond Journal of Global Law 2010, 249

Keay, Andrew, Shareholder Primacy in Corporate Law: Can it Survive? Should it Survive?, ECFR 2010, 369

Keay, Andrew, Good faith and directors' duty to promote the success of the company of their company 2011, 138

Keay, Andrew, The Enlightened Shareholder Value Principle and Corporate Governance, Abingdon 2013

Keay, Andrew, The duty to promote the success of the company: is it fit for purpose in a post-financial crisis world?, in Loughrey, Joan (ed), Directors' Duties and Shareholder Litigation in the Wake of the Financial Crisis, Cheltenham 2013

Kelly, Gavin/Parkinson, John, The conceptual foundations of the company: A pluralist approach, CfiLR 1998, 174.

LeBaron, Genevieve/Rühmkorf, Andreas, Steering CSR through home state regulation: A comparison of the impact of the UK bribery act and modern slavery act on global supply chain governance, Global Policy 2017, 15

Millon, David, Communitarians, contractarians, and the crisis in corporate law, Washington & Lee Law Review 1993, 1372

Millon, David, Enlightened shareholder value, social responsibility and the redefinition of corporate purpose without law', in Vasudev, PM/Watson, Susan (eds), Corporate Governance after the Financial Crisis, Cheltenham 2012

Morgan, Bronwen/Yeung, Karen, An Introduction to law and regulation, Cambridge 2007, 96

Okoye, Adaeze, Corporate enterprise principles and UK regulation of modern slavery in supply chains, International Company and Commercial Law Review 2017, 196

Roach, Lee, The legal model of the company and the company law review, Company Lawyer 2005, 98

Rühmkorf, Andreas, Corporate Social Responsibility, Private Law and Global Supply Chains, Cheltenham 2015

Rühmkorf, Andreas (ed) Nachhaltige Entwicklung im deutschen Recht: Möglichkeiten und Grenzen der Förderung, Baden-Baden 2018

Sheikh, Saleem/Rees, William (eds), Corporate Governance & Corporate Control, London 1995

Sjåfjell, Beate/Johnston, Andrew/Anker-Sorensen, Linn/Millon, David, Shareholder primacy: the main barrier to sustainable companies, in Sjåfjell, Beate/Richardson, Benjamin (eds) Company Law and Sustainability: Legal Barriers and Opportunities, Cambridge 2015

Villiers, Charlotte, Corporate Reporting and Company Law, Cambridge 2006

11. The Interest of the Company in Austria: Small but subtle differences from German law

Christoph Schmetterer

A. Introduction

Austrian stock corporation law is so similar to German law that in most respects, it is practically identical. The differences that do exist are, for the most part, not very big. Section 76 (1) of the German Stock Corporation Act of 1965 (deutsches Aktiengesetz – dAktG)[1] stipulates that the management board must "manage the company under its own responsibility", and according to Section 93 (1), the management board must "act for the benefit of the company".

In contrast, Section 70 (1) of the Austrian Stock Corporations Act of 1965 (österreichisches Aktiengesetz – öAktG)[2] reads: "[t]he Management Board shall manage the company under its own responsibility in such a way as is in the best interests of the company, taking into account the interests of the shareholders and employees as well as the public interest". While the German Stock Corporation Act only mentions the good of the company without further explanation, the Austrian Stock Corporation Act mentions other aspects that must be taken into account within the interest of the company.

Interestingly, both regulations go back to the same root: the German Stock Corporation Act of 1937. In general, the development of Austrian stock corporation law since mid-19th century cannot be separated from the German development.

B. The development of Austrian stock corporation law

Until the mid-19th century, while individual stock corporations existed in Austria, there was hardly any stock corporation law in the modern sense. At

1 German Federal Law Gazette (deutsches Bundesgesetzblatt – dBGBl.) 1965 I S. 1089.
2 Austrian Federal Law Gazette (österreichisches Bundesgesetzblatt – öBGBl.) 98/1965.

that time, privileges were the basis for the formation of stock corporations.[3] A new privilege had to be issued for each new corporation, and outside of these privileges, there were only rudimentary general regulations on stock corporations.[4]

In 1787, Austrian law stipulated that stock corporations had to file their articles of association with the competent mercantile court, and in 1821, the law further decreed that the government had to approve stock corporations.[5] In 1840 and 1843, somewhat more comprehensive decrees (Hofkanzleidekrete – HfKD) were issued on the relationship between "private associations" and the state administration.[6] An association patent (Vereinspatent) replaced these decrees in 1852.[7] These regulations did not deal exclusively with stock corporations, but with associations in general. However, stock corporations were handled as associations at the time.[8]

While the focus of the 1840, 1843, and 1852 regulations was on the formation of associations, the internal organization of associations was only dealt with very briefly.[9] These regulations reflected the fact that Austria was governed by an absolute monarch until 1848, and then again from 1852 to 1860. During these time periods, the establishment of associations, and thus of stock corporations, were controlled by the state, meaning the formation of these corporations had to be approved by the government. The state was free to decide whether to approve the formation (concession system);[10] even if the founders fulfilled certain requirements, the state was

3 Thus, the official names of all the examples mentioned contained a reference to the privilege: "privilegirte Oesterreichische National-Bank"; "k.k. privilegierte Erste Eisenbahngesellschaft"; "k.k. ausschließlich privilegierte Kaiser Ferdinands Nordbahn".

4 Kalss/Eckart, p. 50 et sequu; Leixnering/Meyer/Doralt, 103 et sequ., Schennach, p. 91 et sequu.

5 Paurnfeindt, p. 206 et sequ.

6 Collection of Statutes for the Judiciary (Justizgesetzsammlung – JGS) 462/1840 and 763/1843; Kalss/Burger/Eckert, p. 64 et sequu.

7 Austrian Imperial Law Gazette (österreichisches Reichsgesetzblatt – öRGBl.) 253/1852; this patent was remarkably long-lived and was only repealed in 1999 (BGBl. I 191/1999), although its scope of application was already significantly restricted in the 1860s: in relation to stock corporations by the General German Commercial Code (Allgemeines Deutsches Handelsgesetzbuch – ADHGB, see below) and in relation to non-profit associations by the Association Act 1867 (öRGBl. 134/1867); Kalss/Burger/Eckert, p. 68 et sequu.

8 Schennach, p. 93.

9 Kalss/Burger/Eckert, p. 79.

10 Leixnering/Meyer/Doralt, p. 104 et sequ.

not required to approve the formation of a joint-stock company (as would have been the case with a normative system).

These rudimentary provisions (1840, 1843, and 1852) on stock corporations were purely Austrian acts – enacted by the Austrian emperor for Austria only. That was different with the first comprehensive regulation of Austrian stock corporation law, which took place in the context of the German Confederation ("Deutscher Bund") Until 1866, the Austrian Empire was a member of the Confederation (although not all of Austria's territories belonged to it). The German Confederation only had limited legislative powers, but despite this, efforts were made in its last decade to standardise several areas of law in the Confederation states. To this end, the federation's council ("Bundesversammlung") set up commissions to draw up drafts of laws that were then to be enacted as state laws by the individual German states.[11]

Adoption of the draft laws in the individual states only succeeded in one case, the General German Commercial Code (Allgemeines Deutsches Handelsgesetzbuch – ADHGB), before the German Confederation ended: From 1857 to 1861 a commission in Nuremberg drew up the ADHGB.[12] In the years following, the ADHGB was enacted as state law by almost all states of the German Confederation,[13] including Austria.[14] Sections 207–249 of the ADHGB regulated stock corporation law in detail.[15] The ADHGB not only served as the first comprehensive regulation of stock corporations for Austria, but also as a common stock corporation law for the entire German Confederation. The ADHGB remained after the end of the German Confederation and even expanded to Hungary[16] and Bosnia-Herzegovina, who adopted essentially identical laws.[17]

In contrast to the previous Austrian regulations, the ADHGB primarily contained regulations on the internal organization of stock corporations; it only dealt with state approval in two articles. Section 208 (1) ADHGB stated: "[s]tock corporations may only be established with state approval". While this provision alone would call for a licensing system, Section 249 No. 1 ADHGB expressly permitted the individual states to decide whether

11 Löhnig/Wagner/Vogenauer/Schmetterer, 2024 p. 88 et sequu.
12 Löhnig/Wagner/Wagner, 2024 p. 27.
13 Löhnig/Wagner/Wagner, 2024 p. 27 (60).
14 öRGBl. 1/1863.
15 Kalss/Burger/Eckert, p. 99 et sequu.
16 Löhnig/Wagner/Gönczi, 2018 p. 113.
17 Löhnig/Wagner/Löhnig, 2018, p. 139.

to require state authorisation.[18] The decision for a licensing or a normative system was thus left to the individual states.

However, this question shaped the development of stock corporation law over the next few decades in different ways in Germany on the one hand and Austria on the other hand. In 1867, the North German Confederation ("Norddeutscher Bund") was formed and in 1870/71 it was succeeded by the German Reich – both without Austria, which was no longer a part of Germany after the end of the German Confederation in 1866. In the North German Confederation, the concession system was uniformly abolished in 1870 and replaced by a normative system.[19] In 1884, the stock corporation law of the German Reich was comprehensively amended once again.[20] This second amendment to the stock corporation law brought about significantly more changes to the internal structure of stock corporations than the first.[21]

The ADHGB created a common commercial law, but not a common civil law, as it had to be compatible with various civil law systems – the General Civil Code (Allgemeines Bürgerliches Gesetzbuch – ABGB) in Austria, the General State Law (Allgemeines Landrecht – ALR) in parts of Prussia, the Code civil (Cc) in areas on the left bank of the Rhine, the Baden State Law (Badisches Landrecht – BadLR) in Baden, the Codes Maximilianeus Bavaricus Civilis (CMBC) in parts of Bavaria, and the common law in the parts of Germany that had no civil law codification.[22] Accordingly, the ADHGB contained a comparatively large number of civil law provisions that were necessary to lay a foundation for a common commercial law.

This changed for the German Reich with the BGB in 1896/1900. It introduced a standardised civil law that made many of the general civil law provisions in the ADHGB superfluous.[23] Commercial law in the German Reich was recodified in the German Commercial Code (Handelsgesetzbuch – HGB) in 1897, after the BGB was enacted but before it came into force. The HGB built heavily on the ADHGB but dispensed with its general civil law provisions. The HGB did adopt the changes to commercial law that

18 Section 249 No. 1 ADHGB: "The state laws reserve the right to determine that state authorisation is not required for the establishment of stock corporations in general or of individual types thereof."; Söhnchen, p. 173 et sequ.
19 Söhnchen, p. 178 et sequu.
20 Söhnchen, p. 196 et sequu.
21 Bahrenfuss, p. 37 et sequ.
22 In 1863/65, the Saxon Civil Code was added.
23 For example, the provisions on the contracts in general, Sections 317–323 ADHGB.

had been made in the meantime, in addition to making some of its own changes.[24] For stock corporations, the HGB adopted the basic structure of the ADHGB and kept the modifications of 1870 and 1884 but also made some completely new regulations.[25]

The year 1900 simultaneously established and ended legal unity. The BGB gave the German Reich a standardised civil law, however, since the HGB was only introduced in the German Reich, not to Austria and Hungary, the unity of commercial law between Germany on the one hand and Austria and Hungary on the other hand was ended. The end of this unity was not a major turning point, as developments had already differed in Germany and Austria before 1900 due to the German amendments to stock corporation law.

In the last third of the 19th century and the beginning of the 20th century, there were also discussions in Austria about reform of stock corporation law. However, Austria did not amend the ADHGB. Instead, Austria introduced the "Aktienregulativ" in 1899.[26] Formally, the Aktienregulativ was an administrative regulation that implemented the Association Patent 1852 (Ausführungsverordnung). However, in terms of content, it not only concretised the rules of 1852 on the approval of stock corporations but also amended them. As a result, the Aktienregulativ replaced the licensing system with a normative system that standardised the content required in the articles of association of a stock corporation in order for it to be approved.

The debate on the reform of stock corporation law continued in Austria and Germany in the interwar period. Austria considered, but ultimately did not adopt, the German HGB.[27] In Germany, the results were more concrete: in 1930, the Ministry of Justice prepared a draft of a stock corporation law, which ultimately formed the basis for the Stock Corporation Act of 1937.[28] Even though the Stock Corporation Act of 1937 was enacted under National Socialist rule, its contents were specifically National Socialist only

24 For example, in the introduction of a purely subjective system for the delimitation of commercial law, in
contrast to the mixed system of the ADHGB; Löhnig/Wagner/Wagner, 2024, p. 27 (45 et sequu).

25 Bahrenfuss, p. 36 et sequu.

26 öRGBl. 175/1899; Kalss/Burger/Eckert, p. 188 et sequu and 145 et sequu; Leixnering/Meyer/Doralt, p. 107.

27 Wedrac, BRGÖ, p. 350.

28 dRGBl. I 1937 S. 107.

in a few respects,[29] although the language of the act reflects National Socialist ideas in some places.[30]

The German Stock Corporation Act of 1937 initially was not relevant for Austria, but this changed in March 1938 when Austria was annexed to the German Reich. However, the annexation of Austria only resulted in some selective application of German law; German law was not introduced as general law in Austria.[31]

Some of the German laws introduced in Austria after the annexation were particularly characterised by Nazi ideology included the Nuremberg Race Laws.[32] Others, which had been introduced in Germany pre-1933, of course had no Nazi content; these laws included the German Income Tax Act and the Commercial Code, both of which were introduced in Austria following annexation.[33] Still other German laws introduced in Austria after the annexation were enacted during the Nazi era but were only influenced by Nazi ideology in part. Such laws included the Wills Act[34] and the German Stock Corporation Act of 1937.[35]

In contrast to the HGB and the German Stock Corporation Act of 1937, the German BGB was not introduced in Austria during the Nazi era – partly because there were plans for a separate National Socialist codification of private law, the Volksgesetzbuch, which were never finalised. Thus, in 1939, the situation for unification of private law was similar to the pre-1900 situation, albeit under completely different political circumstances. In (former) Austria and the rest of Germany, there was a uniform commercial law (the HGB) but no common civil law (ABGB in Austria and BGB in Germany).

This situation did not change when Austria declared its independence from Germany at the end of World War II. The Second Republic of Austria kept the laws enacted in, or introduced to, Austria following annexation,[36] as long as they were not "incompatible with the existence of a free and

29 Bahrenfuss, p. 45 et sequ.

30 The interests to be taken into account by the Executive Board in accordance with Section 70 AktG were clearly described in National Socialist terms.

31 Davy/Hofmeister, p. 124.

32 On the Nuremberg Race Laws: Essner.

33 dRGBl. I 1938 S. 1428, 1999.

34 dRGBl. I 1938 S. 978; Law Gazette for (former) Austria (Gesetzblatt für das Land Österreich – GBlÖ) 346/1938; Hanel, BRGÖ 230.

35 dRGBl. I 1938 S. 385, 988.

36 Section 2 Legal Transition Act, Austrian Law Gazette (Staatsgesetzblatt – StGBl.) 6/1945.

independent Austrian state or with the principles of a genuine democracy, [...] contradict the Austrian people's sense of justice or contain typical ideas of National Socialism".[37] As the HGB and the German Stock Corporation Act of 1937 met these criteria, they were left in force. (West) Germany also kept the HGB and the German Stock Corporation Act of 1937.[38]

This changed in 1965, when new stock corporation acts were passed in both Germany and Austria that were heavily based on the German Stock Corporation Act of 1937. The new stock corporation acts differed to some extent, ending the uniformity of Austrian and German stock corporation law. However, given their common roots, the laws were not entirely dissimilar. The same degree of similarity can be found in commercial law. The HGB initially developed slowly in both countries due to differing amendments, until it was comprehensively amended in Austria in 2005 and renamed "Unternehmensgesetzbuch" (UGB). The UGB came into force on 1 January 2007.[39]

C. The public interest in the formation of stock corporations

Public interest was at the centre of the Austrian regulations on the formation of stock corporations from the 1840s. The decree of 1840 already stated in the preamble: "[t]his concerns only the legislative provisions with regard to the relationship of private associations to the state and the state administration".[40] The title of the decree of 1843 was even clearer; its subject was the relationship between "private associations that exert a closer influence on public interests and the state administration".[41]

The subject of these regulations was not the internal organisation of associations (including stock corporations) *per se*, but rather their relationship with the state. A distinction was made between associations that had to be licenced and those that did not. Stock corporations always had to be licensed. This remained the case in the association patent of 1852, which

37 Section 1 (1) Legal Transition Act.
38 Bahrenfuss, p. 46 et sequu.
39 öBGBl. I 120/2005.
40 Preamble para. 3 HfKD 1840.
41 Preamble HfKD 1843.

provided a few more details on the internal organization of stock corporations.[42]

Under the Association Patent of 1852, when deciding whether to grant the licence, the state administration first had to consider the object of the business and of the persons involved.[43] In addition, a license would only be granted "if the company's plan and its supporting documents meet the legal requirements [...] and the public considerations involved".[44]

However, the state's influence did not end with the licensing procedure. Even after approval, the state administration retained the right "to inspect the business management of each association, to monitor compliance with the provisions laid down in the approval of the association or by general regulations and, if it is recognised as necessary, to appoint a princely commissioner to the association, to be appointed by the authority appointed for this purpose. The latter must ensure that the association does not exceed the limits of the authorisation granted to it and the provisions of the approved company regulations".[45]

The state could also dissolve stock corporations: "[d]issolution takes place against the will of the company if [...] such circumstances arise under which, according to the law or for public considerations, the withdrawal of an authorisation to exercise an occupation or enterprise also takes place in the case of individual private individuals".[46]

The state was thus able to influence the company's consideration of public interests in all "life phases" of a stock corporation – at the formation, which was only permitted if the project did not violate public interests, during ongoing operations through a monitoring state commissioner, and finally, by dissolving the company for public considerations.

---

42 Kalss/Burger/Eckert, p. 79 et sequ.

43 Para 11 (a) and (b) HfKD 1840; section 11 (a) and (b) HfKD 1843; sections 9 (a) and 14 (b) Association Patent 1852.

44 Section14 (c) Association Patent 1852; para. 11 (c) HfKD 1840: "[i]t must be examined whether the planned statutes contain any provisions that are contrary to the existing laws or violate public considerations, in which respect they must be duly amended"; very similar section 11 (d) HfKD 1843, according to which an association could only be authorised if it was ensured that "the plan of the company and the draft of the statutes comply with the existing laws and the public considerations that arise".

45 Section 22 Association Patent 1852; the possible, but not mandatory, appointment of a commissioner was also provided for in para. 11 (d) HfKD 1840 and Section 15 HfDK 1843.

46 Section 19 HfKD 1843; in the parallel provision in para 13 HfKD 1840 the public considerations were not expressly mentioned; this probably did not mean a difference in content.

The ADHGB did not contain any provisions on stock corporations that referred to the public interest. However, the introduction of the ADHGB did not mean that public interest was no longer relevant for Austrian stock corporations. The ADHGB primarily regulated the internal organisation of stock corporations. Although it required that stock corporations be authorised by the state, the ADHGB did not contain any specific provisions on the requirements or procedures for authorisation. In addition, the ADHGB still allowed dissolving stock corporations by "withdrawing state authorisation", despite not outlining the requirements or procedures for withdrawal.[47] The provisions of the Association Patent of 1852 therefore remained relevant in Austria both for the authorisation of stock corporations and for their dissolution.[48]

The appointment of state commissioners to monitor the ongoing business management of stock corporations was neither explicitly included nor excluded by the ADHGB. The Austrian Introductory Act of the ADHGB did not repeal the section of the Association Patent of 1852 that provided for ongoing supervision; thus, Austria kept the possibility of ongoing supervision even after the introduction of the ADHGB. Accordingly, the ADHGB did not change that stock corporations had to take the public interest into account and that the public interest could thus be monitored by the state at every stage – at the time of formation, during ongoing operations, and on dissolution.

The Aktienregulativ of 1899 transformed the licence system into a normative system, but the ability of the state to monitor each stage did not change. Regarding authorisation for formation, Section 12 (2) of the Aktienregulativ stated: "[a]uthorisation will always be granted if the company's plan complies with the requirements of the existing laws and ordinances, in particular the current regulations, and none of the reasons listed in §14 of the Imperial Patent of 26 November 1852 stand in the way".

Although the Aktienregulativ stipulated that the licence be granted if the requirements listed in the law were met, it also expressly stated that the grounds for refusal from the Association Patent of 1852 were still applicable: general compliance with the law, the applicant's personal and financial circumstances, and "public considerations".

47 Section 242 (2) ADHGB.

48 Argumentum e contrario section 32 of the Austrian Introductory Act to the ADHGB (öRGBl. 1/1863).

Until the German Stock Corporation Act of 1937 was introduced in Austria in 1938/39, Austrian stock corporation law remained two-tiered: the ADHGB regulated the organisation of stock corporations – without reference to the public interest – and the Association Patent of 1852 regulated the approval, monitoring, and withdrawal of approval – with multiple references to the public interest.

D. The public interest and the Management Board

The Austrian regulations from the 1840s and 1850s were very similar to the Stock Corporation Law of the Prussian ALR of 1794, which contained regulations on state control and the public interest;[49] in fact, the Prussian law might have been the model for the Austrian legislation. However, after the general introduction of the normative system in 1870 there was no longer any reference to the public interest in German stock corporation law.[50] Public interest was then reintroduced, in a completely different way, in the German Stock Corporation Act of 1937.

Section 70 (1) of the German Stock Corporation Act of 1937 stated: "[t]he Executive Board shall be responsible for managing the company in a manner that is in the best interests of the company and its following and in the common interest of the people and the Reich".

The German Stock Corporation Act of 1937's major change from the ADHGB and the HGB was the new role of the management board. There was a connection between this new role and the public interest. In the ADHGB and the HGB, the general meeting did not only elect the management board but could also instruct the board in a binding way and dismiss it at any time.[51] Under the German Stock Corporation Act of 1937, the management board was still appointed by the general meeting (now called "Hauptversammlung" instead of "Generalversammlung"), but was now tasked with managing the company on its own.

Previously, resolutions by the general meeting could serve as guidelines for the actions of the management board. This was no longer the case with the board's new autonomy. Instead, three interests the management board should pursue with their actions were included in the law itself: the

49 Mittwoch, Friedmann, p. 1439 (1443 et sequu); Söhnchen, p. 134 et sequ.

50 Kalss/Burger/Eckert, p. 243.

51 A board of directors that was independent of the general meeting was not allowed; Staub, Section 227 mn. 3 a); Art. 231 mn 1.

good of the company, the good of its following ("Gefolgschaft"), and the common good of people and the Reich ("gemeiner Nutzen von Volk und Reich"). The second and third points were written in specifically National Socialist language: "following" was used instead of employees, and the "common good of people and Reich" was used instead of the public interest. Structurally, these three aspects were equally important.

The German Stock Corporation Act of 1937 dealt with public interest in a completely different context than the ALR and the Austrian regulations from the mid-19th century had done. In these earlier laws, it was the responsibility of the state to ensure that the public interest was observed – when corporations were founded, but also through control of existing corporations. In contrast, Section 70 (1) of the German Stock Corporation Act of 1937 handed the task of considering public interest to the management board.

The introduction of the German Stock Corporation Act of 1937 to Austrian law in 1938 finally brought the normative system to Austria, meaning that the provisions of the Association Patent of 1852 were no longer applicable to stock corporations.[52] The old concept of the state-controlled public interest was seamlessly replaced by the new management board responsibility for public interest. From 1870 to 1937 public interest was not mentioned at all in German stock corporation law. In contrast, the public interest has always been mentioned in Austrian stock corporation law: before 1938 as state-controlled public interest and since then as public interest, to be taken into account by the management board.[53]

Germany and Austria both reorganised their stock corporation law in 1965, with only Austria retaining the explicit reference to the public interest. Section 70 (1) of the Austrian Stock Corporation Act, which has remained unchanged since 1965, reads: "[t]he Management Board shall manage the company under its own responsibility in such a way as is required for the good of the company, taking into account the interests of the shareholders and employees as well as the public interest".[54]

The explanations to the government bill on the Austrian Stock Corporation Act were very brief, explaining that : "[i]n eliminating National Social-

52 Section 22 Zweite Verordnung zur Einführung handelsrechtlicher Vorschriften im Lande Österreich (dRGBl. I 1938 S. 988).

53 Kalss/Burger/Eckert, p. 243 et sequ.

54 This wording had been used in a draft version for a new German Stock Corporation Act; Leixnering/Meyer/Doralt, p. 111.

ist ideas and language, the interests of the shareholders would now also have to be given due consideration".[55] Indeed, Section 70 of the Austrian Stock Corporation Act of 1965 brought a change in terminology and an expansion compared to the previous provision in the German Stock Corporation Act of 1937 by mentioning the shareholders' interests.

Additionally, the new version of Section 70 in the Austrian Stock Corporation Act of 1965 introduced a different structure for the individual elements. Under the German Stock Corporation Act of 1937, the interests of the company, its followers, people, and the Reich were of equal but unrelated importance. In contrast, the Austrian Stock Corporation Act of 1965 made the good of the company the decisive guideline for the actions of the management board. The other three aspects, while they do not have the same significance as the good of the company, do not stand in opposition to the good of the company, and thus must be taken into account, albeit within the consideration of the good of the company; to put it bluntly, they can never "beat out" the interest of the company.[56]

The new Austrian Stock Corporation Act of 1965 defined the relationship between the four guidelines (interests of the company, the shareholders, the employees, and the public) but did not directly define the guidelines themselves. Nevertheless, these guidelines are mandatory; corporations' articles of association may specify how they understand the guidelines but may not cancel or restrict them.[57]

The Austrian legal doctrine defines the interests of the company as securing the continued existence of the company and achieving the best possible operating result; accordingly, the long-term development of the company must be taken into account within the scope of the purpose of the company as defined in the articles of association.[58] Having to account for the long-term development of the company means that pursuing exclusively short-term profit maximisation is excluded if it is likely to have a negative impact on long-term profitability of the company.[59] In addition,

55 Government bill, 301 of the supplements to the stenographic records of the National Council. 10th legislative period, p. 69.

56 Artmann/Karollus/Reich-Rohrwig, AktG Section 70 AktG mn. 91.

57 Artmann/Karollus/Reich-Rohrwig, AktG Section 70 AktG mn. 85.

58 Artmann/Karollus/Reich-Rohrwig, Section 70 AktG mn. 83, 91; Eckert/Schopper/Eckert/Schopper, Section 70 mn. 9; this definition does not differ from the German definition; Eckert/Schopper refer to Goette/Habersack/Kalss, Section 76 AktG mn. 162.

59 Artmann/Karollus/Reich-Rohrwig, Section 70 AktG mn. 92, 96.

the management board can forego profitability in the short- or mid- term in favour of achieving profitability in the long term – for example, the management board can choose to engage in a price war, for image or marketing reasons or as part of an investment programme.[60] In any case, it is only possible to determine general limits for the actions of the management board in abstract legal terms, not which measures are required in specific individual cases. This leaves the management board with broad discretion in entrepreneurial decisions.[61]

The very structure of Section 70 the Austrian Stock Corporation Act of 1965 shows that the shareholders' interest is not identical to the company's interest but rather is an aspect that must be considered in the context of the company's interest. Therefore, Austrian stock corporation law does not allow a pure shareholder value approach.[62]

Employees' interests and the company's interests generally coincide in that both are interested in the long-term existence of the company.[63] However, the interests of employees diverge from the company's interest when it comes to the distribution of the profit generated, such as the decision between whether to make investments that build up reserves or to pay higher wages and social security contributions.[64]

The public interest means the general interest as opposed to the individual interest of the corporation i.e. the common good.[65] Occasionally, it is argued in Austrian literature that the management board of a stock corporation considers the public interest sufficiently by complying with existing laws or even just setting up a system to ensure compliance with the law.[66] However, these arguments are not very convincing.[67] If the public interest was not mentioned in Section 70 of the Austrian Stock Corporation Act of 1965, the management board would still have to comply with the law, thus leaving the public interest alone without significance. It must therefore mean more.

60 Artmann/Karollus/Reich-Rohrwig, Section 70 AktG mn. 92.
61 Artmann/Karollus/Reich-Rohrwig, Section 70 AktG mn. 92 et sequ.
62 Artmann/Karollus/Reich-Rohrwig, Section 70 AktG mn. 97.
63 Eckert/Schopper/Eckert/Schopper, Section 70 mn. 11.
64 Artmann/Karollus/Reich-Rohrwig, Section 70 AktG mn. 100.
65 Artmann/Karollus/Reich-Rohrwig, Section 70 AktG mn. 102.
66 Doralt/Nowotny/Kalss/Nowotny, Section 70 AktG mn. 14.
67 Artmann/Karollus/Reich-Rohrwig, Section 70 AktG mn. 103 also comes to this conclusion, albeit with slightly different reasons.

So far, there is no comprehensive academic discussion as to what public interest means for stock corporations in Austria. However, Reich-Rohrwig provides a plausible structure. In terms of content, he distinguishes between measures of corporate social responsibility, donations to charitable organisations, and the promotion of sport, culture, and science.[68] According to the importance of measures within the company, Reich-Rohrwig names three groups of cases: first, the core business activity including the organisation of the company and the management of production processes; second, public relations work; and third, charity in the narrow sense.[69]

According to this categorisation, the weaker the link to the actual business activity, the more strictly the measures must be assessed. Measures associated with corporate social responsibility are therefore even permissible, if they do not lead to higher productivity, higher profitability, or a better image, as long as they are closely linked to the actual business activity. (E.g. the decisions to focus on local production or environmental protection that go beyond the legal requirements or the mandatory monitoring of suppliers.) However, these measures must not jeopardise the company's long-term development.[70]

Public relations measures are also permitted if there is an appropriate cost-benefit ratio. A key aspect here is the level of publicity achieved. The same measure can therefore be permissible if presented to a wide audience, but impermissible if it does not result in greater awareness of the company.[71]

Purely charitable donations not linked to any form of consideration for the company are also permitted, however, the standard for these is much stricter. A guideline for the amount a purely charitable donation is one to two per cent of the balance sheet profit. This means that donations are problematic if the company is unprofitable in the long term.[72]

At the end of his comparatively detailed comments on the public interest, Reich-Rohrwig refers to a major commentary on the German Stock Corporation Act of 1965.[73] This is quite remarkable, as the German Stock Corporation Act of 1965, unlike the Austrian Stock Corporation Act of 1965,

68 Artmann/Karollus/Reich-Rohrwig, Section 70 AktG mn. 104.
69 Artmann/Karollus/Reich-Rohrwig, Section 70 AktG mn. 105 et sequu.
70 Artmann/Karollus/Reich-Rohrwig, Section 70 AktG mn. 105.
71 Artmann/Karollus/Reich-Rohrwig, Section 70 AktG mn. 106.
72 Artmann/Karollus/Reich-Rohrwig, Section 70 AktG mn. 107 et sequ.
73 Artmann/Karollus/Reich-Rohrwig, Section 70 AktG mn. 110 with reference to Hirte/Mülbert/Roth/Kort, Section 76 AktG mn. 106 et sequu.

no longer expressly recognises the public interest. Reference to the German Stock Corporation Act of 1965 helping clarify public interest under the Austrian Stock Corporation Act of 1965 shows that the practical effects of the different regulations are comparatively minor.

However, this does not mean that the different wordings of the Austrian and German Stock Corporation Acts have no effect at all. In my opinion, there is at least one fundamental difference: under German law, it is at least possible to advocate a pure shareholder value approach, even if such an approach would not be for good reasons.[74] In contrast, the explicit stipulation of other interests in section 70 German Stock Corporation Act of 1965 prohibits this in Austria.[75] Therefore, in Germany it is permissible for the management board of a stock corporation to include the public interest in its decisions, while in Austria, it is mandatory to do so, as the objectives of Section 70 of the Austrian Stock Corporation Act of 1965 are binding.[76]

Nevertheless, the practical effects of the difference are small due to both the wording and the systematic categorisation of these provisions. The guidelines of Section 70 of the Austrian Stock Corporation Act of 1965 are very broad terms and cannot be the basis for a claim. Accordingly, there are – as far as can be seen – no Supreme Court decisions based on Section 70 of the Austrian Stock Corporation Act of 1965.

The basis for the liability of the management board is Section 84 (1) of the Austrian Stock Corporation Act of 1965, which states that the management board must exercise the "diligence of a prudent and conscientious manager". This diligence largely coincides with acting in the interests of the company.

Public interest plays practically no role in liability under Section 84 of the Austrian Stock Corporation Act of 1965 due to the construction of this liability; the management board is liable to the company, but not to third parties or even the state. It is likely that a corporation will accuse its management board of not having acted in the interests of the company, but it is much less likely that the company itself will hold the management board liable for not acting in the public interest.

74 Mittwoch, p. 330 et sequu.

75 Kalss, GesRZ 49; Kalss, DRdA 134 et sequ.

76 Leixnering/Doralt about the specific situation of energy supply companies in the public sector.

Thus, the importance of Section 70 of the Austrian Stock Corporation Act of 1965 in the sustainability contexts is ambivalent at best. On the one hand, it is clear that sustainability is part of the public interest. Section 70 of the Austrian Stock Corporation Act of 1965 is particularly relevant in this case for sustainable action, which is not mandatory as such.[77] On the other hand, Section 70 of the Austrian Stock Corporation Act of 1965 is not a suitable way of enforcing sustainable behaviour;[78] actual enforcement of sustainable behaviour would require other instruments.

References

Bahrenfuss, Dirk, Die Entstehung des Aktiengesetzes von 1965 – unter besonderer Berücksichtigung der Bestimmungen über die Kapitalgrundlagen und die Unternehmensverfassung, Berlin 2001

Eckert, Georg/Schopper, Alexander, in: Eckert/Schopper (eds.), AktG-ON

Essner, Cornelia, Die „Nürnberger Gesetze“ oder Die Verwaltung des Rassenwahns 1933–1945, Paderborn 2002

Gönczi, Katalin, Österreich-Ungarn (1867–1918): Transleithanien (mit einem Ausblick auf die Zeit nach 1918), in: Löhnig/Wagner (eds.), Das ADHGB von 1861 als gemeinsames Obligationenrecht in Mitteleuropa, Tübingen 2018, p. 113

Hanel, Stephanie, Das „gesunde Volksempfinden“ und das Testamentsrecht. § 48 Abs. 2 TestG in der Rechtsprechung des LG Wien von 1938–1945, BRGÖ 2017, 239

Hofmeister, Herbert, Privatrechtsgesetzgebung für Österreich unter der Herrschaft des Nationalsozialismus, in: Davy (ed.), Nationalsozialismus und Recht: Rechtssetzung und Rechtswissenschaft in Österreich unter der Herrschaft des Nationalsozialismus, Wien 1990, p. 124

Kalss, Susanne/Burger, Christina/Eckart, Georg, Die Entwicklung des österreichischen Aktienrechts: Geschichte und Materialien, Wien 2003

Kalss, Susanne, in: Goette/Habersack/Kalss (eds.), Münchener Kommentar zum Aktiengesetz V, 4th edition, München 2014

Kalss, Nachhaltigkeit: Die präziser werdenden Pflichten von Vorstand und Aufsichtsrat, GesRZ 2022, 49

Kalss, Nachhaltigkeit im Unternehmensrecht, DRdA 2024, 131

Kort, Michael: in: Hirte/Mülbert/Roth (eds.), Aktiengesetz Großkommentar IV/1, 5th edition, Berlin 2015

Leixnering, Stephan/Meyer, Renate E./Doralt Peter, The Past as Prologue: Purpose Dynamics in the History of the Aktiengesellschaft, Research in the Sociology of Organizations 2022, 97.

77 If a certain form of sustainable action would be mandatory anyway, there would be no need to take the "diversions" via Section 70 öAkt. Kalss, GesRZ 49.

78 Kalss, GesRZ 51 seems to be more optimistic.

Leixnering, Stephan/Doralt, Peter, Die Berücksichtigung des öffentlichen Interesses ist geboten, nicht verboten! Bemerkungen zu § 70 Abs 1 AktG aus Anlass der Energiepreiskrise, Der Gesellschafter 2024, 88.

Löhnig, Martin, Bosnien-Herzegowina (1878–1918): Kondominium, in: Löhnig/Wagner (eds.), Das ADHGB von 1861 als gemeinsames Obligationenrecht in Mitteleuropa, Tübingen 2018, p. 139

Meissel, Franz-Stefan/Bukor, Benjamin, Das ABGB in der Zeit des Nationalsozialismus, in: C. Fischer-Czermak et.al. (eds.), Festschrift 200 Jahre ABGB, Wien 2011, p. 17

Mittwoch, Anne-Christin, Nachhaltigkeit und Unternehmensrecht, Tübingen 2022

Mittwoch, Anne-Christin/Friedmann, Tonio, Nachhaltiges Geschäftsleiterhandeln nach der CSDDD – im Unternehmensinteresse, NZG 2023, 1439

Nowotny, Christian, in Doralt/Nowotny/Kalss, Aktiengesetz, 3rd edition, Wien 2021

Paurnfeindt, Christian Johann, Handbuch der Handelsgesetze und des bei Anwendung derselben bei den Mercantil-Gerichten eintretenden Verfahrens mit besonderer Rücksicht auf das Erzherzogthum Oesterreich unter der Enns, Wien 1836

Reich-Rohrwig, Johannes, in: Artmann, Eveline/Karollus. Martin (eds.), AktG II, 6th edition, Wien 2018

Söhnchen, Markus, Die historische Entwicklung der rechtlichen Gründungsvoraussetzungen von Handels- und Aktiengesellschaften, Berlin 2005

Schennach, Martin P., Rechtsgeschichte der österreichischen Wirtschaft, Wien 2022

Staub, Hermann, Kommentar zum Allgemeinen Deutschen Handelsgesetzbuch, 5th edition, Berlin 1897

Vogenauer, Stefan/Schmetterer, Christoph, Entwurf eines allgemeinen deutschen Gesetzes über Schuldverhältnisse von 1866 – Dresdner Entwurf, in: Löhnig/Wagner (eds.), Deutscher Bund und nationale Rechtseinheit – Symposium für Hans-Jürgen Becker, Tübingen 2024, p. 81.

Wagner, Stephan, Das ADHGB von 1861 – Nürnberger Entwurf, in: Löhnig/Wagner (eds.), Deutscher Bund und nationale Rechtseinheit – Symposium für Hans-Jürgen Becker, Tübingen 2024, p. 27.

Wagner, Stephan, Deutscher Bund, Norddeutscher Bund und Deutsches Reich, in: Löhnig/Wagner (eds.), Das ADHGB von 1861 als gemeinsames Obligationenrecht in Mitteleuropa, Tübingen 2018, p. 79

Wedrac, Stefan, Rechtsangleichung und Handelsrecht in Österreich 1918–1938, BRGÖ 2022, 350.

12. Sustainability and the Company's Interest in Norway: Tensions Between Company Law and Shareholder Primacy

Beate Sjåfjell[1] *and Morten Gullhagen-Revling*

A. Introduction

The introduction of the company form, characterised by the limited liability of the shareholders and the legal distinction between the shareholders and the company, is recognised as one of the most ingenious legal inventions resulting from the industrial revolution. With 'limited liability' for shareholders and a threshold for piercing the corporate veil, the company form has provided the legal infrastructure for risk-taking business. Companies are crucial in most societies' economic development with creation of economic value through production of goods and services, by providing jobs, and by creating revenue, which contributes to the realisation of well-functioning welfare states. At the same time, awareness has been increasing over the last decades concerning the significance of business for sustainability. In globalised business, companies are building blocks in multinational corporate groups and contractual based value chains. In spite of much talk about sustainability, business in aggregate is still based on exploitation of people, degradation of the environment, and undermining of the economic and governance bases for well-functioning societies.

Finding a balance between maintaining the positive aspects of the limited liability company form, and mitigating negative impacts, is the challenge legislators now face. Indeed, business is increasingly called on to contribute actively to meeting global sustainability goals. Therefore, legislative reforms have been introduced both in Norway at the national level[2] and

---

1 The authors gratefully acknowledge the excellent assistance in editing footnotes and bibliography of this chapter by research assistants Armita Sahafiha and Kristina Burkow Vollan, Faculty of Law, University of Oslo.

2 See e.g. Act of 18 June 2022 No. 99, Lov om virksomheters åpenhet og arbeid med grunnleggende menneskerettigheter og anstendige arbeidsforhold (Åpenhetsloven) [Act relating to enterprises' transparency and work on fundamental human rights and decent working conditions (Transparency Act)].

in the European Union (EU)[3] with the aim of facilitating more sustainable companies. While shareholders have interests in a company's adaptation for future existence, and to meet customers' and society's expectations, tension between shareholder interests and sustainability may arise. As we will show, this is very much the case in Norway.

The company is governed by a board, which is obligated to promote the interests of the company in its decision-making. The interests of the company, or the 'company's interest', as it often is referred to in Continental Europe and the Nordics, and which we will use throughout in this chapter, is a core company law concept. The concept is crucial to understanding the scope of action for the board and other corporate decision-makers. The company's interest as an abstract concept of company law should serve to promote the legislative purpose of company law, while the specific concept of company's interest in an individual company should serve to promote that specific company's purpose. In the context of sustainability, the debate on corporate purpose has been revitalised. In this chapter, we concentrate on the company's interest and do not engage in this discussion of corporate purpose.[4]

In this chapter, we analyse the company's interest based on Norwegian legal sources,[5] and, as Norwegian company law does not operate in a vacuum, we also draw on international and EU law and policy developments.

As we show, the company's interest in Norwegian company law is pluralistic and includes sustainability aspects. This gives the board plenty of room for integrating sustainability into corporate governance and decision making. Yet, this room is still undercommunicated and often misunderstood. This underlines the importance of this analysis, with renewed emphasis on the 'company's interest' having the potential to be a key company law element in the fundamental transformation of business towards sustainability. We understand sustainability as securing social foundations for humanity now and for the future while mitigating pressures on planetary boundaries, and 'sustainable business', or corporate sustainability, as being about the

3 Sjåfjell/Cornell European Law Open Vol. 3, 2024, 529–60, provide in section 4.B an overview of key developments from the EU.

4 For a discussion of corporate purpose and sustainability, see Bowman/Mai/Sjåfjell/Mähönen, with further references.

5 Norwegian legal sources and literature that are cited in this chapter have been translated to English by the authors.

contribution of business to achieving these overarching societal sustainability goals.[6]

In this chapter, the concept of the company's interest under Norwegian company law is analysed in abstract, as a key concept in company law. Accordingly, this chapter does not aim to provide answers for specific decisions to be made by the board of a company. Rather, it elaborates on the content of the company's interest as the binding guideline that applies to boards in their decision-making.[7] In Norwegian company law, which has a very hierarchical corporate governance structure, shareholders through the general meeting 'exercise the supreme authority in the company'.[8] The general meeting can change the articles of association of the company, which can shape the board's scope of action in its decision-making, as can any direct instructions that the general meeting chooses to give to the board. The caveat is always that the articles of association and any direct instructions must comply with the law. The board (and the senior executive management) are not allowed to 'comply with any resolution by the general meeting or another company body if the resolution is contrary to law or the company's articles of association'.[9]

The authority of the general meeting also includes the right to replace the board or individual board members (with the caveat that any employee-elected board members cannot be replaced by the general meeting). Knowing that the board can be replaced at the next general meeting may influence the board's decision-making processes. However, as a matter of law, boards have a duty to follow the law and promote the company's interest according to the law, independently of the knowledge that they may be replaced if their decisions do not resonate with the opinions of the most active or controlling shareholders. For listed companies, the Norwegian Corporate Governance Code also emphasises the necessity of the board being independent of all groups, including shareholders, and notably the

6 Elaborated on, with further sources, in Sjåfjell/Cornell European Law Open Vol. 3, 529.

7 See Section B.II in this chapter about this somewhat oxymoronic expression.

8 Act of 13 June 1997 No. 44, Lov om aksjeselskaper (Aksjeloven) Section 5-1(1) [Act on private limited liability companies (Private Companies Act), and Act of 13 June 1997 No. 45, Lov om allmennaksjeselskaper (allmennaksjeloven) [Act on public limited liability companies (Public Companies Act]). In this chapter we refer to both as the Companies Acts.

9 Companies Acts, Section 6–28(2).

majority shareholders.[10] We make this distinction upfront, as we are aware of the argument that often is made, namely that boards *in practice often will* follow what they perceive to be the shareholders' wishes because of the fear of being replaced. This argument does not negate a legal analysis of what boards have a duty to do – rather it underlines the need for such an analysis.

In practice, shareholders may often seek to exert influence outside of formal channels established through company law, including through so-called 'dialogue meetings' or 'ownership meetings'. These are promoted by the Norwegian corporate governance code,[11] and used by the Norwegian state as shareholder (Section C below). However, such meetings are not recognised by company law, and may in some cases also violate company law. Certainly, a board or an individual member of the board cannot lawfully accept 'instructions' through such channels. That this often may happen in practice does not make it lawful. To the contrary, it opens up the board or the individual member to liability, as it does for the shareholder. This is especially clear in Norwegian company law, where the legislation specifically mentions the shareholders as one group of actors that can be held liable for damage caused to the company or to other parties (see below in Section B.II). Of course, again in practice, what is said in these meetings is generally not public, and it is therefore difficult to identify channels of influence and follow up on this.

Ultimately, individual board members can be held liable for not promoting the company's interest, by the company itself,[12] or by others affected

10 See Norsk utvalg for eierstyring og selskapsledelse (NUES), Norwegian Code of Practice for Corporate Governance, 14 October 2021, https://nues.no/eierstyring-og-selskapsledelse-engelsk/, and its comments to clause 8 concerning the Board of directors: composition and independence; '(...) Members of the board, whether elected by the general meeting or the corporate assembly or employees, must not operate as individual representatives for specific shareholders, shareholder groups or other stakeholders. In order to support the stock market's confidence in the independence of the board, at least two of its members should be independent of the company's main shareholder. This principle is particularly important for companies where one or more controlling shareholders could, in practice, decide the outcome of elections to the board'.

11 See Norwegian Code of Practice for Corporate Governance, 14 October 2021, and the comments to clause 13 regarding Information and communication.

12 For example in the Polish case, where the general meeting supported the current board's proposal to sue the previous board, Clark, Polish Energy Company Sues Former Directors for Backing Coal, 2024, https://subscriber.politicopro.com/article/

by the company's business.[13] However, the theme of our chapter is not liability for board members and the conditions for liability claims to be successful.[14] We will therefore not discuss the many obstacles to such claims or the emerging trends that indicate that such claims are increasingly likely to be made and to be successful. Rather, our aim is to discuss the content of the company's interest as core to the duties of the board, to show the possibilities and the direction that company law gives board members in their governance of the company, and the potential that this opens up for in changes in the governance of the company.

In Section B below, we introduce the legal doctrine of the company's interest as the core guideline for corporate decision-making. We present our analysis supporting the view that the company's interest is pluralistic and broad, with room – and arguably even a duty – for the board to integrate sustainability. We also show that the economic prosperity of the company, based on its own interest in its future existence as a legal entity, as a starting point, lies at the core of the board's decision-making. We show how the board's room for integrating sustainability has always been there, while the basis for stating its extent and for stipulating a duty in some cases is stronger now than it was just 10–15 years ago.

In Section C, we discuss the situation in practice, and the tensions between the broad, pluralistic company's interest and the hard-core reality of shareholder power. We illustrate this with the significant corporate governance role of the Norwegian state, which we find promotes the social norm of shareholder primacy in spite of its sustainability talk. This social

---

eenews/2024/02/02/polish-energy-company-sues-former-directors-for-backing-coal -00139156.

13 Such as the external environment, e.g. represented by interest organizations. At the time of writing we do not find examples of such lawsuits in Norway, but they are expected to come. Elsewhere in Europe, there are already such examples, with one being ClientEarth's unsuccessful case against the board of the carbon major Shell, see e.g. Iglesias-Rodríguez, Journal of Environmental Law Vol. 35 no. 3 2023, 445–54. As more and more companies are being held liable for the unsustainabilities across their global value chains, the likelihood increases of companies turning against their previous board, see e.g. R. Carnwath, ClientEarth v Shell: What future for derivative claims? London: Grantham Research Institute on Climate Change and the Environment, London School of Economics and Political Science (February 2024), https://www.lse.ac.uk/granthaminstitute/wp-content/uploads/2024/02/ClientEarth-v-Shell-what-future-for-derivative-claims.pdf.

14 We briefly touch upon the legal basis for liability claims based on Norwegian company law towards the end of Section B.II in this chapter.

norm, informed by postulates from economic theories and financial markets' logic of maximising returns to shareholders, is a major barrier to more sustainable business.[15] We also briefly discuss the possible driver for change in the increasing recognition of risks of unsustainability.

In Section D, we present our concluding reflections.

B. The pluralistic company law concept of the company's interest

I. The legal sources for identifying the company's interest

Identifying the company's interest as a matter of law, entails canvassing a wide range of legal sources.

The starting point is the Private Limited Liability Companies Act and the Public Limited Liability Companies Act.[16] Both of these company forms, the private and the public company, are characterised by the limitation of liability of the shareholders. The main difference between these company forms is that public companies have less restrictions on sale or purchase of shares and only public companies can have their shares (or a class of their shares) listed on a stock exchange. In this chapter, when we refer to companies, and the Companies Acts, this comprises both the private and public companies and the Acts regulating them.

As the wording in the Norwegian company legislation often is kept rather short and general, preparatory works have great importance in the interpretation, in addition to case law, where the Supreme Court decisions have the greatest significance. Concerning case law, court decisions must, of course, always be read in light of the specific facts and legal questions raised in the case. At present, there is no Norwegian case law in modern times concerning the question of whether a board decision violates the company's interest because it favours sustainable value creation over shareholder interests, or challenging the board's prioritisation of environmental or societal interests more generally.[17]

---

15 Sjåfjell/Bruner/Bruner/Sjåfjell, 713; Sjåfjell/Richardson/Sjåfjell/Johnston/Anker-Sørensen/Millon p. 79; Millon, University of St. Thomas Law Journal Vol. 10:4 2013, 1013.

16 See full reference to these Acts in footnote 9.

17 We discuss some seminal cases from the 1920s in B.III.5 in this chapter.

Company law does not operate in a vacuum, and neither can our company law analysis. Accounting law is historically considered a part of company law in the Nordics, which it still is in the EU, and it is therefore directly relevant to company law analyses. Financial market law, especially for listed companies, is also directly relevant. This then gives rise to the question of whether the company's interest can encompass interests regulated in other legislation. One view is that other interests than the shareholders' interests are taken care of by other areas of law, so that employee protection is fully covered by the Norwegian Working Environment Act and environmental protection is covered by the various legislative requirements of environmental law.[18] However, law is not – and should not – be divided up into separate silos, with hard divisions.

Legal compliance is, of course, a duty of the board. And the broader regulatory framework also influences the interpretations of the company law concept of the company's interest. The interests of the employees and societal interests in environmental protection are therefore not excluded from being a part of the company's interest. As we will show below, this is also reflected in company law – in the broad sense of the field – through what has been, for decades, and continues to be included in the reporting rules in Norwegian and gradually also EU accounting law. Another modern example is the Norwegian Transparency Act,[19] which integrates international human rights law and the internationally endorsed OECD Guidelines for Multinational Enterprises on Responsible Business Conduct into legislative requirements for due diligence across the global value chains of Norwegian companies.[20]

The legal sources for the analysis of the concept of the company's interest under Norwegian law also include EU law that is relevant for Norway under the European Economic Area Agreement (the EEA Agreement).[21] The EEA Agreement connects the EFTA states Norway, Liechtenstein and Ice-

18 Aarbakke/Aarbakke/Knudsen/Ofstad/Skåre, comments to section 6–12, item 1.10.

19 For full reference, see fn 2.

20 On the relevance of corporate sustainability due diligence rules for the duties of the board, see e.g. Anton (et al.)/Sjåfjell, Chapter 2; Sjåfjell/Mähönen, Expert Essentials 2025, online edition.

21 Avtale om det europeiske økonomiske samarbeidsområde (EØS-avtalen), the European Economic Area Agreement (EEA Agreement) signed in Portugal in 1992 between the EU member states and the EFTA member states Iceland, Norway and Liechtenstein. Full text of the EEA Agreement can be found here: https://www.efta.int/about-efta/legal-documents/eea-legal-texts.

land, and the EU and its member states. The EEA Agreement encompasses, amongst other things, the freedom of movement of persons, services, goods and capital, and the freedom of establishment, in the EEA market (the EU and the three EFTA states).[22] EU company law, including accounting law, financial market law, and more broadly, EU sustainability law, is therefore directly relevant and implemented or on its way to being implemented in Norwegian law.[23] The EU has, since the beginning of the 2000s, adopted a range of secondary legislation aimed at facilitating sustainable development, and more recently, since 2019 onwards, it has adopted legislation with direct legal duties for both companies and board members, such as the EU Taxonomy[24] and the EU Corporate Sustainability Due Diligence Directive (CSDDD).[25]

International law has traditionally been seen as regulating states, which then, in turn, have the responsibility for regulating companies (as 'non-state actors') within their jurisdictions. Even within such an understanding, the Norwegian state's international obligations may serve as interpretational sources in the analysis of Norwegian law. And further, the understanding that international law does not regulate companies, is now being challenged on several levels. This includes developments such as Advisory Opinions on climate change issued by the Inter-American Court of Human Rights,

---

22 Taxation is one of the few relevant areas excluded from the EEA Agreement, Sejersted (et. al), chapter 15.1.

23 According to the EEA Agreement Article 7, Regulations and Directives which fall within the scope of the EEA Agreement shall be made a part of internal law also in the EFTA members of the EEA. Because of formal requirements, this process takes longer time for the EU legislation with EEA relevance to be implemented and to come in force in the EFTA countries in the EEA compared to the situation in the EU member states.

24 European Parliament and Council, 'Regulation (EU) 2020/852 of the European Parliament and of the Council of 18 June 2020 on the Establishment of a Framework to Facilitate Sustainable Investment, and Amending Regulation (EU) 2019/2088 (Text with EEA Relevance)' (2020) OJ L 198, 22.6.2020, pp. 13–43 <http://data.europa.eu/eli/reg/2020/852/oj/eng> accessed 4 January 2024 (Taxonomy Regulation).

25 European Parliament and the Council, 'Directive (EU) 2024/1760 of the European Parliament and of the Council of 13 June 2024 on Corporate Sustainability Due Diligence and Amending Directive (EU) 2019/1937 and Regulation (EU) 2023/2859Text with EEA Relevance' (2024) OJ L, 2024/1760, 5.7.2024 <http://data.europa.eu/eli/dir/2024/1760/oj/eng>. The Directive is marked as EEA relevant and the inclusion in the EEA Agreement is at present formally being considered by the three EFTA states in the EEA.

and the International Court of Justice,[26] and the discussion concerning the responsibilities of businesses and their investors for involvement in the genocide in Gaza.[27] This also concerns the direct inclusion of international human rights law in the Norwegian Transparency Act, and in the EU Taxonomy Regulation, the Sustainable Finance Disclosure Regulation, the Corporate Sustainability Reporting Directive and the European Sustainability Reporting Standards, as well as the inclusion of international and EU human rights and environmental law in the CSDDD.

These legislative instruments are not only contributing to breaking down the horizontal silo between international law and companies as creatures of national law. They are also breaking down the vertical silo between law and social norms (often denoted 'hard law' and 'soft law'), with the OECD Guidelines and the UN Guiding Principles for Business and Human Rights (UNGPs) being directly integrated into legislation. This means that the internationally endorsed sets of social norms, and, for example, the decisions from the National Contact Points under the OECD Guidelines, are relevant legal sources in our analysis. The OECD Guidelines and the UNGPs may be seen as representing generally accepted ethical norms of society, and thereby giving content to these norms, which historically have been regarded as accepted and relevant sources of Norwegian company law. Locally endorsed sets of social norms may also be relevant. A key example is the Norwegian corporate governance code (NUES),[28] which is directly

26 Carrasco/Pamplona, The Inter-American Court's Advisory Opinion on Climate Emergency and Human Rights: A Breakthrough for the Environment and Business & Human Rights, 2025, www.afronomicslaw.org/category/analysis/inter-american-courts-advisory-opinion-climate-emergency-and-human-rights; Tigre/Bönnemann/De Spiegeleir, The ICJ's Advisory Opinion on Climate Change: An Introduction, 2025, https://blogs.law.columbia.edu/climatechange/2025/07/24/the-icjs-advisory-opinion-on-climate-change-an-introduction/; Wadiwala, Historic Climate Change Ruling from the International Court of Justice: What It Means for Africa, 2025, http://theconversation.com/historic-climate-change-ruling-from-the-international-court-of-justice-what-it-means-for-africa-262047; Tommaso, Profiting from Injustice in the Occupied Palestinian Territory: Reflections on the Report 'From Economy of Occupation to Economy of Genocide', 2025, https://internationallaw.blog/2025/07/14/profiting-from-injustice-in-the-occupied-palestinian-territory-reflections-on-the-report-from-economy-of-occupation-to-economy-of-genocide/.

27 United Nations Human Rights Council, From Economy of Occupation to Economy of Genocide. Report of the Special Rapporteur on the Situation of Human Rights in the Palestinian Territories Occupied since 1967, Francesca Albanese, 30 June 2025, A/HRC/59/23.

28 Reference included in footnote 11.

applicable (on a 'comply or explain' level) to companies listed on the Oslo Stock Exchange.

II. Legal starting points – when the company's interest is relevant

Companies are by law required to have a board, which is responsible for the governance and supervision of the company, which means that it, by definition, has wide powers. Decisions and matters of extraordinary or high importance will fall within the powers of the board except where the decision falls under the general meeting (or another company organ) according to legislation, articles of association or instructions by the general meeting.[29] As examples, the board has the power to represents the company externally, approve decisions by senior executive management; the board can sell or purchase assets such as real estate and shares in subsidiaries, and decide restructuring of the company's business to the extent permitted by the articles of association of the company's determination of its business.

The board must act in the company's interest in its decisions. The duty for board members to act in the company's interest is deduced from the general provision in the Companies Acts section 6–12, providing the legal basis for the board's responsibility for managing the company.[30] The term '*company's interest*' can be found in the Companies Acts section 3–8, which specifies that the board shall declare that an agreement between the company and a shareholder, a holding company, a member of the board or the senior executive manager is entered into in the company's interest. Also, according to the Companies Acts section 8–10 relating to the company's financial assistance for the purchase of shares in the company, the board shall provide a statement which shall include an assessment of the company's interest in such financial assistance from the company.

The board's scope of action in promoting the company's interest is relevant within the following constraints:

1. Law, encompassing company law, and obligations under or in accordance with other areas of law,
2. The articles of association of the company,
3. Instructions and other decisions by the general meeting of the company,

---

29 Aarbakke (et al.), comments to section 6–12, item 1.6.
30 Eg. Aarbakke (et al.),), comments to section 6–12, item 1.9.

4. Contracts the company has entered into,
5. Generally accepted ethical norms in society.

The company's interest is the core guideline for company decision-making within these constraints (which we discuss further below in this section). We therefore refer to the company's interest as a 'binding guideline' for the board, as oxymoronic as that may sound, as it is *binding* in the sense that the board is obligated to follow it, and it is a *guideline* in the sense that it does not dictate the result of the board's specific decisions, but rather sets out the aspects that the board *must* encompass in its decision-making. We distinguish, therefore, between interests that are encompassed in the company's interest and other legitimate interests, which the board *may* include in its decision-making. The distinction between interests included in the company's interest and those that are legitimate interests has a greater practical significance for those who define the company's interest narrowly.

As regards law as a constraint, there is a dual relationship between the concept of the company's interest and relevant law. First, in the sense set out above, the company's interest is relevant only where the law does not dictate the outcome of the board's decision. For example, if the duties for the board to act in cases of loss of equity as set out in the Companies Acts are triggered,[31] the board cannot ignore these rules and decide to continue with business as usual because the members think that would be most beneficial for the shareholders, or because they wish to invest in an upgrade to more environmentally friendly production methods. Second, the regulatory framework provides sources for identifying what is included in the concept of the company's interest.

As regards the articles of association, instructions and other decisions by the general meeting, as well as contracts the company has entered into, these bind the board and constrain their scope of action to the extent that they are in compliance with the law and with generally accepted ethical norms of society.

Articles of association are a company-specific source. Companies comprise a vast variety of business endeavours, with individual purposes, composition of shareholders, geographical presence and financial situation. As the case law of the Norwegian Supreme Court has shown, the articles of association are important in the specific assessment of the company's

31 The Limited Liability Companies Acts Section 3–5.

interest in the situation at hand.[32] This means that the general meeting through amending the articles of association, can contribute to shaping the scope of action for the board's decision-making, and also the understanding of the company's interest for that specific company. This gives rise to questions about the extent to which the abstract company law concept of the company's interest can be deviated from in the articles of association of a particular company. Certainly, the articles of association cannot violate law, so an attempt at codifying the social norm of shareholder primacy (setting out, for example, that the board is to have as its guideline the maximisation of returns to shareholders in all decisions) may collide with legal requirements, especially in light of the evolving regulatory framework. The board would need to interpret such a provision in the articles in light of the evolving regulatory framework and its duty to promote the company's interest, which stands in contrast to the short-term consideration of avenues to maximise returns for shareholders at any point.

As regards generally accepted ethical norms in society, these are of significance for the interpretation of the content of the legal norms and can directly influence how the boundaries of the board's scope of action are drawn up. This is, for example, evident in general clauses such as section 6–28 of the Companies Acts, which stipulates that the board may not give one interest an 'unfair advantage' at the expense of (other) shareholders or the company. Generally accepted ethical norms of society constrain the scope for the board's decision making.[33] The dynamic nature, especially of ethical norms, means that yesterday's answers are not necessarily decisive for tomorrow's questions. As we saw above, we can now draw on internationally endorsed sets of social norms to give content to the reference to generally accepted ethical norms of society, through the OECD Guidelines and the UNGPs.

If the general meeting has violated the law, or the company's articles of association, or, arguably, generally accepted ethical norms in society, in their instructions or other decisions, the board is obligated *not* to comply

32 Eg. Judgment by the Norwegian Supreme Court, 11.11. 1999 – Rt. 1999 page 1682 'Østlendingen' concerning the question of the legality of a board decision denying consent to transfer of shares. The board's decision to deny consent was accepted by the Supreme Court because the board acted in line with the specific company's interest, identified in this concrete assessment. Conversely, in Judgment by the Norwegian Supreme Court, 05.03.2013 – Rt. 2013 page 241 'Stangeskovene', the board was found not to have acted in that company's interest after a concrete assessment.

33 See also Truyen, p. 111.

with these. Similarly, if the board realises that the contracts the company has entered into violate the law or generally accepted ethical norms in society, the contracts must be amended or cancelled. In the quickly evolving regulatory framework, this requires a higher level of vigilance from the board, especially in cross-jurisdictional business.

If a board decision is found to be contrary to the company's interest, this may potentially form the basis for liability claims against board members.[34] Board members could, at least theoretically, be sued for adopting a decision which allegedly violates the company's interest, for example, by promoting environmental protection while reducing the profits of the company and thereby the potential for shareholder returns. Conversely, civil society organisations could file lawsuits where the board has prioritised profits in ways that have led to negative environmental impacts, human rights violations or unsafe working conditions. Norwegian company law recognises claims against board members from the company itself, from shareholders and from the broad category of 'others',[35] with the requirement that damage has been caused to the claimant directly or indirectly by the board's actions or omissions. This means that under Norwegian law, not only damages caused to the company can be recognised, but also damages caused to any other party – including but not limited to shareholders and creditors; also damages caused to employees, workers or communities can be recognised. The prerequisite is that it can be calculated as economic damage. Further, not only members of the board but also other actors with a company law role can be sued, including shareholders and auditors. A successful claim requires that there has been a violation of a duty set out in company law, in the articles of association or in other areas of law. Violating the board's duty to promote the company's interest is a possible legal basis, although it would in most cases be a difficult one to argue before the courts, exactly because of the balancing of various interests that the board is required to do.

At the time of writing, there is no established series of Norwegian court cases concerning claims against board members for violating their duty to promote the company's interest, or for prioritising profit over corporate sustainability. This can partly be explained by Norwegian courts' reluctance

34 See the Companies Acts sections 17–1.
35 Section 17–1 and 17–2 of the Companies Acts.

to overrule business decisions, which is not unique for Norway,[36] and is in comparative research generally recognised as the 'business judgment rule'. Further, most Norwegian cases against board members concern small private companies in financial distress, and it may be presumed that cases regarding large companies are dealt with outside of the court system.[37] Considering the international trend of lawsuits against businesses for environmental and social harm, it seems to be just a question of time before such lawsuits also make their way to the Norwegian courts.[38]

III. Pluralistic approach to the company's interest in Norway

In spite of its practical significance, there has been little research on the company law concept of the company's interest in Norway, especially as concerns the extent to which it encompasses various aspects of sustainability.[39] With the increasing emphasis on corporate sustainability in legislation, the topic has gained more interest also amongst Norwegian scholars.[40] The lack of interest historically may be explained by the dearth of case law on the topic. Also, the business case for corporate sustainability, entailing that at least in the long term, sustainability-oriented decisions are good for shareholders, too, has contributed to a perception that there is no conflict to be analysed. However, with the increasing recognition that contributing to a transformation to a safer and more just future requires major changes, the question of what the board can, should and must do is more topical than ever.

Company law scholarship presents two predominant views in Norway on what the company's interest is. The one view has been that shareholders'

---

36 See e.g. Judgment by the Norwegian Supreme Court, 11.11.1999 -Rt. 1999 s. 1682 (1692) and Judgment by the Norwegian Supreme Court, 22.12.2022 -HR 2022–2484-A (54) stating that the threshold for board liability for 'business misjudgments' is high.

37 Dahlum.

38 Norwegian corporate actors, including board members, may also find themselves recipients of lawsuits in other countries, see e.g. European Coalition for Corporate Justice (ECCJ), Suing Goliath: An Analysis of Civil Cases against EU Companies for Overseas Human Rights and Environmental Abuses, 2021, https://corporatejustice.org/publications/suing-goliath/.

39 Early contributions include Sjåfjell, International and Comparative Corporate Law Journal Vol. 11 issue 1 2013, 1.

40 Recent publications include Christoffersen (et al.)/Reiersen, 157, Bråten/Minde, Oslo Law Review Vol. 10 no. 2 2024, 1.

return on investment is the central element of the company's interest, perhaps constituting the whole of the company's interest.[41] The question of whether other interests can be seen as included is left rather open, as is the question of prioritisation in case of conflict between shareholder interests and other interests, while a long-term shareholder interest is assumed as the guideline in the case of conflicting interests between the shareholders.[42]

The other view, which presents a more pluralistic approach, is that:

> *Profit for shareholders, although it cannot legally be disregarded, may – depending on the concrete situation – be subordinated not only to legal requirements protecting creditors and other contractual parties, employees, the environment and broader society in general, but also to the promotion of such interests beyond the legal requirements.*[43]

In many practical situations, there is not necessarily a conflict between these two views of what the company's interest encompasses, as it is generally acknowledged by the authors representing the more narrow approach, that other interests than the shareholders interest are considered legitimate interests which can be taken into account.[44] However, as we show below in this Section, the pluralistic understanding is more in line with the legal sources than a simplistic approach to the company's interest as being equal to shareholders' interest. A pluralistic understanding also represents a more accurate picture of the complexity of board decision-making in practice.

For example, the Supreme Court of Norway stated in 2018 that:

> *The company's interest is a less clear-cut concept. Naturally, a company must safeguard the interests of its shareholders, but it also has a responsibility to its employees, to its counterparties and creditors, and to fulfil any other obligations it may have to its surroundings and society at large.*

41 Aarbakke (et al.), comments to section 6–12, item 1.9.

42 Aarbakke (et al.), comments to section 6–12, item 1.9.

43 Sjåfjell, International and Comparative Corporate Law Journal Vol. 11 issue 1 2013, 1 (15). See also Sjåfjell, Jussens Venner 2011 Vol. 46, 309. Bråten/Minde, Oslo Law Review Vol. 10 no. 2 2024, 1, state that: 'The company's interest therefore includes the interests of shareholders, employees, counterparties, creditors and society as a whole'. Andenæs (et. al.), p. 345: 'Although the board primarily shall promote the company interest, there is room for safeguarding of other interests, including those of shareholders, employees, or the general public'.

44 Highlighted by e.g. Christoffersen, Tidsskrift for Forretningsjus Vol. 30 no. 1 2024, 75 (84) with reference to Normann, p. 366.

> *Ensuring the company's continued operation can therefore be part of the company's interests.*[45]

The case concerned the validity of a decision by the tax authorities regarding the tax assessment of a listed company after the shares had been sold to a new shareholder. The question was whether the company could claim a deduction for a facilitation fee paid to the company's financial advisor and a termination fee paid to a bidder. The decisive factor regarding the right to deduct the costs was whether there was a sufficient link between the costs and the company's income. The financial advisor's fee was considered by the Supreme Court to fulfil only the shareholders' interests and therefore there was no sufficient link between the cost the fee represented and the company's economic situation. The result was that such cost could not be deducted from the tax assessment. This is in our view a clear example of the company's interest and the shareholders interest being distinguished by the Supreme Court.

Preparatory works for the Companies Acts state that:

> *board members are representatives who act on behalf of their client, i.e. the company*[46]

Newer preparatory works relating to proposed amendments of the Companies Acts also highlight that:

> *The company's interest is often, but not always, corresponding to the shareholders' interests. That the shareholders' interests are a part of the company's interest is, inter alia, set out in the Supreme Court decision HR-2019–515.*[47]

The 2019 Supreme Court decision concerns a shareholder's right to appeal a decision on opening a bankruptcy estate. The Supreme Court stated that '*the shareholders' share in the company's interest and the significance the company's economic situation has for the shareholder, does not in itself pro-*

---

45 Judgment by the Norwegian Supreme Court of 22. 03. 2018 -HR-2018–570-A, (41. Available at www.lovdata.no (subscription necessary; in Norwegian only).

46 Ot.prp. Nr. 23 (1996–1997) Om lov om aksjeselskaper (aksjeloven) og lov om allmennaksjeselskaper (allmennaksjeloven) (*[Proposition to the Storting (the Norwegian Parliament) for the new Companies Acts]* p. 71.

47 Prop. 135 L (2018–2019) Endringer i aksjelovgivningen m.v. (langsiktig eierskap i noterte selskaper) ([Proposition to the Storting (the Norwegian Parliament)] Changes to the companies acts (long term ownership in listed companies) p. 94.

vide a right to appeal'.[48] The decision shows that the shareholders' interests are a part of the company's interest, but does not represent the whole of the company's interest.

The newer preparatory works referred to above also highlight that:

> *The company's interest covers more than the interests of the shareholders, creditors, employees, the market and the society. It is about what is best for the company as an independent legal entity in the short and long term. Even in cases where the company is a part of a group or through acquisition becomes part of a group, it is the company's interest, not the group's interest, which is decisive for whether the company should provide financial assistance for a third party's acquisition of shares. The board must conduct a specific assessment of the company's interest in becoming part of the group.*[49]

The preparatory works go on to state, concerning the situation where a company provides financial assistance for a third party's acquisition of shares:

> *It is important that the board is aware of its role as the company's representative and its duty to act in line with the company's interest.*[50]

Authoritative legal sources clearly show that the company's interest is not equivalent to the shareholders' interests and encompasses a wide range of interests. As we show below, the company's interest in Norwegian company law includes shareholder and creditor interests, the interests of the employees and the local communities, and increasingly, broader environmental and societal interests, including those of workers across global value chains. We start out with presenting the core, the company's own economic interest, before we canvass the inclusion of these other interests.

48 Judgment by the Norwegian Supreme Court of 1403.2019 – HR-2019–515-A, paragraph 58. Available at www.lovdata.no (subscription necessary; in Norwegian only).

49 Prop. 135 L (2018–2019) Endringer i aksjelovgivningen m.v. (langsiktig eierskap i noterte selskaper) [Proposition to the Storting (the Norwegian Parliament)] Changes to the companies acts (long term ownership in listed companies)] on page 95.

50 Ibid. on page 98.

1. The core of the pluralistic concept; the company's own economic interest

In a pluralistic understanding of the company's interest, the business rationale sets the boundaries and gives direction to the board's assessment. The board's decisions must, as a starting point, always have a commercial justification. It is in the nature of the company that the company's financial result is central, as a minimum financial result is a prerequisite for the company's continued existence.

All interests involved, including the interests of employees in good working conditions, living wages, possible salary increases, bonuses and other welfare benefits, of creditors wanting punctual payment, of shareholders in returns, and the company's interest, for example, to invest in environmentally friendly solutions within the company's business, are dependent on the company's own financial situation. The starting point is therefore that the company needs to have a sound economic basis for the various interests to be safeguarded.[51] The company's own interest in securing its continued existence may therefore be perceived as an objective criterion in the board's decision making.

Support for the company's interest having a financial core can be found in section 3–4 of the Companies Acts. The provision requires the company to have sound equity and liquidity, which must be taken into account in all the board's decisions. If the equity is not adequate, the board has a duty to act under section 3–5 of the Companies Acts. These are key limits for the board's scope for action. Together with the Companies Act's restrictions on the ability to distribute funds from the company, this shows that the board must ensure that the company has a healthy and viable economy, which informs our understanding of this as a core aspect of the company's interest.

This is supported by the Supreme Court's decision in 2000, in a case concerning the question of whether the rules on company dividends were applicable for a claim for fees for financial advice which ended with the company's shares being sold to a new share owner:

Although the persons behind the company also had an interest in what they could achieve for their shares, it is fully legitimate to try to take care of

51 This is also indicated in the preparatory works, see e.g. Ot.prp.nr.7 (1971–1972) Om lov om endringer i lov av 6. juli 1957 om aksjeselskaper bedriftsdemokrati [Proposition to the Storting (the Norwegian Parliament) Changes to the Companies Act regarding employee participation in companies] on page 43.

> *the interests of the company as such to survive and keep existing as a legal entity – under the best conditions possible.*[52]

The Supreme Court concluded that the rules on dividends were not applicable to the financial advice in question since the central purpose of the advice was to continue the long-term company's interests.

Other company law scholarship supports the view that the essential element of the company's interest is to actively promote the company's interest in an accountable and prudent manner.[53] The company's interest is regarded as entailing a general and mandatory duty for the board to govern and lead the company on the basis of the company's interest in creating value, and to emphasise the company's value creation when taking action and making decisions on behalf of the company.[54]

This requires the board to ensure the healthy and viable economy of the company, which we see addressed in the Report to the Parliament concerning the Norwegian state's shareholdings and investments in companies:

> *Value creation over time requires that the company is sustainable. A sustainable company balances economic, social and environmental considerations in a way that contributes to long term value creation and that the needs of today are taken care of without destroying future generations' needs.*[55]

Taking the company's economic prosperity and its continued existence as the core of the company's interest and the starting point for the board's decision-making gives a better basis than trying to assume the interests of a hypothetical long-term shareholder.[56] And yet, complex questions still remain where the board needs to decide, based on the purpose and strategy

---

52 Judgment by the Norwegian Supreme Court of 20.12.2000 – HR-2000-141/ Rt. 2000 p. 2033 (2039). Available at www.lovdata.no (subscription necessary; in Norwegian only).

53 Andenæs (et. al.), p. 345. See also newer preparatory works to proposed amendments, Prop. 135 L (2018–2019) Endringer i aksjelovgivningen mv. (langsiktig eierskap i noterte selskaper mv.) [Changes to the company legislation etc. (long-term ownership i listed companies etc.), 21 June 2019, p. 95.

54 Christoffersen (et al.)/Reiersen, 157 (161) in the context of ensuring shareholders' and creditors' interests.

55 St. Meld nr. 8 (2019–2020) Statens direkte eierskap i selskaper, 22 November 2019, p. 76 (*Report from the Norwegian Government to the Norwegian Parliament on the state direct ownership in companies*) on page 76.

56 See further below section B.II.2 in this chapter.

of the company and in light of the evolving regulatory context, what kind of time perspective it will use. Growing recognition of the financial and corporate risks of continued unsustainability also entails that ensuring the basis for the company's continued existence entails considerations of the environmental, social and societal consequences of the business of the company.[57]

Taking the company's own economic interest as the starting point does not mean that it is an overriding priority in all contexts. The obvious legal point, which nevertheless requires reiteration, is that the economic interests of the company cannot be pursued through a lack of legal compliance. In globalised business, this entails careful consideration of what may be perceived as grey areas in cross-jurisdictional issues, with complicated choice of law issues. Further, even in cases that may at first assessment be considered within the law, other factors may be so strong that alternatives to continuing the company in its current form need to be considered. This can be, for example, if the business model of the company is based on the exploitation of workers in other countries, which is contrary to generally accepted ethical norms such as those set out in the OECD Guidelines (with their increasing legal significance).[58] Another example is where a company has based its business on permits to pollute, but where the state's giving of the permit turns out to be illegal.[59]

2. Shareholder interests are included in the company's interest

The interests of the shareholders are clearly a part of the company's interest, as we have already indicated above. According to the Companies Acts

57 Alexander (et al.)/Sjåfjell, 22 (chapter 2); Anton (et al.)/Sjåfjell, chapter 2.

58 See Section B.I in this chapter, and see also for example Malaguti, Oslo Law Review Vol. 10 2024, 1.

59 After the EFTA Court had given its opinion, the Norwegian Appeals Court found the Norwegian permits to pollute illegal, see Christensen, Full Celebration After Victory for Norwegian Fjord, 2025, https://fjordsoksmalet.no/2025/08/13/full-celebration-after-victory-for-norwegian-fjord/. The Norwegian state has not withdrawn these permits, and the company, Nordic Mining, has declared that it will continue basing its business on these permits. At the time of writing, the latest news is that the environmental organisation now has requested that the courts issue an injunction to stop Nordic Mining's dumping of waste in the fjords, NRK, Ber tingretten om å forby Nordic Mining dumping i Førdefjorden [Asking the court to forbid Nordic Mining's dumping in the Fjørde fjord], 2025, https://www.nrk.no/vestland/ber-tingretten-om-a-forby-nordic-mining-dumping-i-fordefjorden-1.17542932.

section 2–2(2), the articles of association must contain clauses on use of profits and assets upon dissolution of the company if the company shall not have a purpose of achieving returns for the shareholders.

According to our analysis of the legal sources, this does not entail that shareholders' interests represent the core of the company's interest, or that it entails a duty to generally prioritise shareholder interests. The legal form of the company can also be used for a business that does not provide returns to shareholders, for example, channelling all profits into specifically designated societal activities (such as protecting rainforests or supporting the local hospital). In such cases, shareholders and potential shareholders must be made aware of this, as they do not, as a matter of company law, have a generally protected right to returns on their shares.

What shareholders do have, where the articles of association do not set out any different, is a legally protected expectation of returns if the company is profitable. It is, however, only in extreme situations that shareholders have any kind of legal claim to returns. This is typically where there is an abuse of power situation between shareholders. A 2016 Supreme Court decision gives us an example of this, in a case concerning a claim for dissolution of the company by a minority shareholder.[60] The Supreme Court found that persistent payment of low or no dividends and financing of dividends for one financial year by issuing shares at a discount with preferential rights to the shareholders represented an abuse of authority that could give the right to demand dissolution under sections 16–19 of the Companies Act. However, the minority shareholder did not succeed with its claim for dissolution because such dissolution requires significant grounds. The minority shareholders' interests could be taken into account in other ways than dissolution of the company, by employing the safety valve in section 8–4 of the Companies Act, which allows the court to set higher dividends in exceptional cases of abuse of power, typically by the majority shareholder.

Shareholders' legally protected expectation of returns is a part of the company's interest. However, as the above-mentioned case shows, breaches of this standard must be persistently low or no dividend at all in spite of the company's profitability. The statement by the Supreme Court quoted above shows that the breach of any lack of dividends must be determined over

60 Judgment by the Norwegian Supreme Court of 29.06.2016 – HR-2016–1439-A. Available at www.lovdata.no (subscription necessary; in Norwegian only).

time, and not related to a specific decision. The company's own economic interest is what the board must concentrate on. Indeed, a principle of Norwegian company law is that the assets of the company are protected against the shareholders, in the sense that shareholders lawfully only can receive any kind of distribution from the company when they are done 'in accordance with the rules regarding dividends, capital reduction, merger or demerger of companies, and repayment following liquidation'.[61] Any kind of transfer of value, which directly or indirectly benefits the shareholder, is covered by this prohibition,[62] and the Supreme Court has determined that it is a criminal offence for shareholders to treat the assets of the company as their own property, even where no other shareholders or creditors were harmed.[63]

In practice, the board's assessment of what is in the individual company's interest will be based on the specific conditions of the company and of the topic at hand. Each company is different in terms of its financial situation, its size, its purpose, possibly defined in the articles of association, the impact the business has on society, the composition and number of shareholders of the company, and whether the general meeting has provided instructions to the board. That shareholder interests are just one element of what needs to be considered is acknowledged as concerns the governance of larger companies, in the preparatory works for the Companies Acts:

> *When a company reaches a certain size, the management of the company is not only a question that concerns its ownership interests, but also such other interests as legislation requires to be taken into account. This applies to considerations of creditors and other counterparties, employees and the broader interests of society.*[64]

The question remains, then, whether the shareholders' interest could be regarded as the core of the company's interest; in other words, encompassing other interests, while using the shareholders' interest as the starting point. As we have shown above, our analysis of the legal sources demonstrates

61 Companies Acts, Section 3–6(1).

62 Companies Acts, Section 3–6(2).

63 Judgment by the Norwegian Supreme Court of 3. 09 2003 -HR-2003–511-A/ Rt. 2003 p. 1112. Available at www.lovdata.no (subscription necessary; in Norwegian only).

64 Ot.prp. nr. 23 (1996–1997) Om lov om aksjeselskaper (aksjeloven) og lov om allmennaksjeselskaper (allmennaksjeloven), 20 December 1996, p. 64 [Proposition to the Storting (the Norwegian Parliament) for the new Companies Acts] on page 64.

that it is the economic interest of the company itself that is at the core.[65] Shareholders' legally protected expectation of returns is derived from the economic interest of the company, and cannot replace it. The company's economic interest is directly connected to its business, and the company has, if nothing else is set out in the articles of association or by law, an eternal timeline.

Shareholders are heterogeneous; they include short term, medium term and long term investors; they encompass the returns-focused investors (e.g. private equity funds, or parent companies), family shareholders interested in maintaining long-term stability for the cornerstone company in the local community, the company's employees, and even civil society organisations or funds investing in shares with the sole purpose of influencing the company through rights provided in the Companies Acts, for example by proposing changes at the general meeting and by voting for investments in more environmentally friendly production or higher pay to workers across global value chains. Although a shareholder typically invests in shares with the intention to receive returns through dividends or by sale of the shares at higher prices, shareholders may also be invested in several companies that may even be in competition with each other. Shareholders' interests may therefore be in contradiction to the company's interests.[66] Universal investors may be more oriented to the general profitability of the sector rather than the individual company. And so on. Governing a company from some kind of hypothetical long-term shareholders' interest is an unnecessarily complicated way of concentrating on the economic prosperity of the company.

3. Creditor protection is central to company law

Creditor protection is central to company law, partly because the legal entity of the company is separate from the shareholders, with the shareholders' limited liability for the company's obligations. The Companies Acts contains a number of rules aimed at safeguarding creditors' interests. The Supreme Court has also, in its 1993 decision, distinguished the share-

65 Aksjelovutvalget, NOU 1996:3 Ny aksjelovgivning, 1 March 1996, p. 133 [Norwegian Official report to the Ministry with proposals for new companies legislation] also clearly differentiate between the company's interest and the shareholders' interest, e.g. on page 133.

66 Anker-Sørensen.

holders' interests from the company's interest in relation to the creditors' interests.[67] The Supreme Court ruled that a bankruptcy estate could sue a board member and claim compensation even if this would not benefit the shareholders.[68]

Companies are not exclusively financed through shareholder contributions (their investments in shares). In most cases, external financing will make the shareholders' contributions a minority in terms of amount. The constant development of new forms of financial instruments, such as hybrids between equity and debt capital, also shows that the share capital itself can play a subordinate role. Since shareholders are not liable for the company's obligations, it has also been argued that trust in the limited liability company form necessitates that creditors' interests are taken into account.[69] Creditors' interests are therefore an independent part of the company's interest.

4. Employees and local communities are also included

Our analysis of the legal sources supports the inclusion of the employee's interest in the company's interest. In Norway, employees in companies with more than 30 employees are entitled to elect one or several members of the board among the employees.[70] A board member elected by the employees does not, as a matter of law, represent employee interests,[71] any more than board members elected by the general meeting as a matter of law represent shareholder interests.[72] All board members have a company law duty to promote the interests of the company. And yet, it is clear that the legislative purpose of the employees' right to elect members of the board is to ensure

67 Judgment by the Norwegian Supreme Court of 30. 11.1993 – HR-1993-130-B Rt. 1993 p. 1399 (known as the Ytternes case). Available at www.lovdata.no (subscription necessary; in Norwegian only).

68 Ibid. on page 1404.

69 Solem, Tidsskrift for Forretningsjus Vol. 7 no. 4 2001, 451 (470).

70 The Companies Acts sections 6–4.

71 Ot. prp. nr. 7 (1971–1972) Om lov om endringer i lov av 6. juli 1957 om aksjeselskaper bedriftsdemokrati, 22 October 1971, p. 43–44 [Proposition to the Storting (the Norwegian Parliament) Changes to the former companies act regarding employee participation in companies].

72 See concerning board members elected by the general meeting, NOU 1992:29 Lov om aksjeselskaper, September 1992, p. 161–162 (Norwegian Official report to the Ministry with revision and proposed changes to the Companies Act).

a broader basis for the board's decision-making to the benefit of both the employees and the company.[73]

In the context of amendments made in the Companies Acts in 2006,[74] it was discussed whether a statutory definition of board members' liability to shareholders and others should be included. The question was raised whether this could entail liability for decisions aimed at preserving jobs, even if the closure and possible dissolution of the company would have given the shareholders greater financial gain. The question was raised specifically related to a case where it was considered to close down the wood processing company Union, which was a cornerstone company in the small town of Skien, in 2005. To this, the Ministry stated, in the preparatory works:

> *In the Ministry's opinion, it will not normally trigger liability for damages if a board member in a private or public limited liability company makes (...) decisions aimed at maintaining operations and jobs, even if a possible closure and dissolution would have given the shareholders a greater financial gain. The situation may be different where the decision in reality means that a loss-making business is maintained at the creditors' expense.*[75]

The statement shows that the interests of the employees and the local community constitute considerations that can be emphasised to a considerable extent, also at the expense of the shareholders' interests, and accordingly constitute an independent part of the company's interest. Employee interests are not only relevant within the scope of the Norwegian Working Environment Act.

The inclusion of local communities, which we return to below,[76] gives an indication of how broad and pluralistic the Norwegian company's interest

73 NOU 1985:1 Videreutvikling av bedriftsdemokrati, 23 January 1985, section 4.8.2 (Norwegian Official report to the Ministry with proposals for further development of the employee participation within companies).

74 Broadening the scope of those who could make liability claims against boards to include 'shareholders' and 'others' in addition to the company itself, see Companies Acts Section 17–1(1), briefly discussed in Section B.II.

75 Ot.prp. Nr. 55 (2005–2006) Om lov om endringer i aksjelovgivningen mv., 7 April 2006, p. 114 ([Proposition to the Storting (the Norwegian Parliament)] Changes to the Companies Act etc.).

76 And which we can find reflected also in EU law, for example in the otherwise very shareholder-oriented Takeover Directive, see e.g. Sjåfjell, Yearbook of European Law Vol. 27, 2008, 387.

also traditionally has been. In the next section, we discuss the aspects of sustainability more broadly and their inclusion in the company's interest in Norwegian company law.

5. The inclusion of broader societal interests historically and now

As highlighted above, the legal sources in Norway support a broad understanding of the company's interest, which also comprises societal interests.

Consideration of broader societal interests was a topic all the way back in the 1920s. In a Supreme Court case, known as the 'Freia' judgement,[77] the question was whether the general meeting of a limited company, with a majority vote, could decide to use NOK 250,000 (which at the time had considerable value) of the profits for the establishment of a fund for medical research (as a gift donation). A minority of the shareholders had challenged this decision. The Supreme Court found that the decision was valid. The Supreme Court emphasised that the donation in the long run also would be in the company's pecuniary interest, and that:

> *The company's purpose is economic activity, but this cannot be understood by the participants of a company to mean that the company shall isolate itself from the society within which it is established and limit itself to only comply with legislation which is applicable when the company's economy is best off in that way.*[78]

Although the judgement relates to a decision of the general meeting, the judgement can in a modern context be used to legitimate decisions from other company organs, notably the board, which are grounded in societal interests.

Two other Supreme Court cases from the 1920s also point in the same direction.

In the first case, the Supreme Court accepted that the board of an insurance company has the authority to provide a considerable guarantee for a local bank as security for loans that the bank provided.[79] Although the

---

77 Judgment by the Norwegian Supreme Court of 11. 03.1922, – Rt. 1922 p. 272 (known as the Freia Chocolate Factory case). Available at www.lovdata.no (subscription necessary; in Norwegian only).

78 Judgment by the Norwegian Supreme Court of 11.03.1922 – Rt. 1922 p. 272, 274.

79 Judgment by the Norwegian Supreme Court of 03.09.1927 – Rt. 1927 p. 588. Available at www.lovdata.no (subscription necessary; in Norwegian only).

guarantee was considered on the face of it to fall outside of the scope of the company's articles of association, the Court stated that:

> *A board of a company is not entitled to go beyond the purpose of the company and what belongs to the operation of its business, but the purpose of the company and the operation of the business require that a board must, by virtue of the nature of the circumstances, have the authority to make dispositions that are not only directly, but also indirectly, necessary or appropriate to promote the purpose of the company.*[80]

The context was that a general request had been made to the local business community in order to provide assistance to two of the city's commercial banks for the common good and to avoid the very difficult consequences that a collapse of these banks would entail for the city. The Supreme Court stated that the insurance company had an immediate and strong interest in ensuring that business in the city where the company operated could avoid the disruption that a bank collapse would cause and that the lack of financial assistance could have direct, detrimental consequences for the company in its future operations and for the company's reputation.

The other case also related to a guarantee, which the board of company A had provided to company B (a local bank) relating to the refinancing of company B. The bankruptcy of company B would have significant consequences in the local community.[81] The question was whether the board had the authority to provide such a guarantee, which the Supreme Court found that the board had, based on the potentially damaging effect a bankruptcy of company B would have on the local community.[82]

Accounting law's reporting requirements concerning broader societal interests also show that the board is meant to take an active approach concerning the company's impact on society. Norway was among the first countries in Europe to have specific reporting requirements concerning the working environment, gender equality, anti-discrimination, and the company's impact on the external environment.[83] The latter was especially

80 Judgment by the Norwegian Supreme Court of 03.09.1927 – Rt. 1927 p. 588, 589.

81 Judgment by the Norwegian Supreme Court of 15.10.1929 – Rt. 1929 p. 857. Available at www.lovdata.no (subscription necessary; in Norwegian only).

82 See also Solem, Tidsskrift for Forretningsjus Vol. 7 no. 42001, 451 (Section 4.4).

83 Act of 17 July 1998 No. 56, Lov om Årsregnskap mv. (regnskapsloven) [the Norwegian Accounting Act]. Today chapter 2 of the Accounting Act has detailed reporting requirements concerning sustainability which shall be included in a company's annual report, as an implementation of EU rules.

progressive in that it originally required that all companies report on their negative impacts on the environment and how these were removed or mitigated.[84] The preparatory works underline that the aim was to enhance the efficiency of compliance with environmental protection rules, and – in line with reflexive theory thinking – to ensure that the board gave attention to the environmental impacts of the company, with the aim of these being reduced year by year, beyond compliance with environmental law.[85]

A reporting mechanism in the annual report relating to the company's corporate social responsibilities[86] was introduced in 2013, and the preparatory works highlight that:

> *Businesses who operate in a socially and environmentally responsible manner will be able to strengthen their competitive advantages nationally and internationally.*[87]

In addition, the preparatory works highlight that the reporting mechanism is intended to contribute to raising the companies' awareness and provide incentives to integrate social responsibility in their daily business and to present the value of such work for investors, shareholders, and society at large.[88]

Today, the reporting mechanisms cover a number of topics such as the external environment, social matters, compliance with human rights and combating corruption and bribery. These mechanisms clearly legitimise the companies' societal responsibilities and serve to justify board decisions which prioritise such responsibilities, also where this could be contrary to the shareholders' (short-term) interests. While the scope of companies has

---

84 Sjåfjell, International and Comparative Corporate Law Journal Vol. 11 issue 1 2013, 1. See also Ikdahl (et. al)/Sjåfjell, Ch. 7. Preprint at SSRN: https://ssrn.com/abstract=4028365.

85 Innst. O. nr. 61 (1997–1998) Innstilling fra finanskomiteen om lov om årsregnskap m.v. en formell innstilling lovforslag *[Recommendation from the Finance Committee in the Storting (Norwegian Parliament) on the Annual Accounts Act, etc.]* Section 10.

86 The Norwegian Accounting Act section 3–3 c.

87 Prop. 48 L (2012–2013) *Endringer i regnskapsloven og enkelte andre lover (rapportering om samfunnsansvar mv.) [Proposition to the Storting (the Norwegian Parliament) Changes to the Accounting Act and certain other acts (reporting on corporate social responsibility, etc.)]* on page 11.

88 Prop. 48 L (2012–2013) Endringer i regnskapsloven og enkelte andre lover (rapportering om samfunnsansvar mv.), 7 December 2012 *[Proposition to the Storting (the Norwegian Parliament)] Changes to the Accounting Act and certain other Acts (reporting on corporate social responsibility, etc.]* on page 11.

been reduced, the Norwegian reporting rules have been strengthened in substance through the implementation of the EU Corporate Sustainability Reporting Directive (CSRD), responding to 'the importance of reliable, comparable and relevant information on sustainability risks, opportunities and impacts',[89] and setting out reporting rules considering both the significance for the performance of the company and 'on information necessary for an understanding of the impact of the undertaking's activities on environmental, social and employee matters, respect for human rights, anti-corruption and bribery matters' ('double materiality').[90] The inclusion of the OECD Guidelines and the UNGPs in the CSRD and the European Sustainability Reporting Standards (ESRS) under the CSRD, as already mentioned earlier, strengthens their legal relevance as generally accepted ethical norms of society.

The Norwegian Transparency Act, which came into force in July 2022, introduces due diligence, reporting and information requirements for larger companies[91] to promote their respect for fundamental human rights and to ensure decent working conditions across the global value chains of Norwegian companies. This Act has, since its adoption, enhanced the awareness of companies' responsibilities for social matters and brought international human rights law directly into the scope of board decision-making. This Act also arguably broadens the inclusion of employee interests, as a part of the company's interest,[92] to encompass workers across global value chains. The Transparency Act is a part of an international trend towards corporate sustainability due diligence as an evolving horizontal norm, supported also by the adoption of the Corporate Sustainability Due Diligence Directive in 2024. As Sjåfjell discusses elsewhere, possible changes through the Omnibus proposals will not be able to reverse the changes made in the perception of what is relevant and necessary for boards to encompass in their decision-making, including the way in which international law and

89 European Parliament and Council, 'Directive (EU) 2022/2464 of the European Parliament and of the Council of 14 December 2022 Amending Regulation (EU) No 537/2014, Directive 2004/109/EC, Directive 2006/43/EC and Directive 2013/34/EU, as Regards Corporate Sustainability Reporting (Text with EEA Relevance)' (2022) OJ L 322, 16.12.2022, pp. 15–80 <http://data.europa.eu/eli/dir/2022/2464/oj/eng> accessed 20 March 2023, Recital 4, see also Recital 5.

90 ibid, Recital 29, referencing Articles 19a and 29a.

91 See the definition of 'larger enterprises' included in the Transparency Act section 3 letter a).

92 See Section B.III.4 in this chapter.

internationally endorsed social norms are integrated into hardcore EU law and national law.[93]

Finally, the Norwegian Corporate Governance Code's inclusion of sustainable value creation in its recommendations also supports a broader and modern approach to what the board of the company should include in its decision-making.[94]

C. A pluralistic company interest clashes with shareholder primacy

The Norwegian company law concept of the company's interest is pluralistic and broad, without any predetermined prioritisation of the interests. Yet, there is strong tension between this pluralistic concept of the company's interest as a matter of company law, and the social norm of shareholder primacy, with its drive for maximisation of returns to shareholders. We see this tension reflected in the context of one of the most powerful shareholders in Norway, the Norwegian state. The state expects corporate sustainability in the governance of Norwegian companies, and, yet, in its own governance of state shareholdings, it does not use – or even appear to recognise – the room there is for more sustainable corporate governance. The state as shareholder promotes shareholder primacy through its emphasis on maximisation of returns. This contributes to explaining the chasm between a company law analysis of the company's interest and corporate governance in practice in Norway.

The state is a particularly significant shareholder in Norway, because of its size and its influence. The state has shareholdings in 69 companies, encompassing listed companies and non-listed ones,[95] and it is one of the largest shareholders on the Oslo Stock Exchange, second in size after the heterogeneous group of 'foreign investors'.[96] It is also a particularly

93 Sjåfjell, Transnational Legal Theory Vol. 16, 2025, 281.

94 The board 'should define clear objectives, strategies and risk profiles for the company's business activities such that the company creates value for shareholders in a sustainable manner'. The board should 'therefore take into account financial, social and environmental considerations', NUES, 2. Business (Section 2).

95 Updated numbers from 'Statens eierrapport 2024 – Statens direkte eierskap i selskaper ['The state's ownership report 2024 – the State's direct ownership of companies'], 15 June 2023, available at www.regjeringen.no/no/dokumenter/statens-eierberetning-2022/id2984565/ (only in Norwegian).

96 The State's 'direct ownership is substantial when concerning both the number of companies and their value, and, when viewed in relative terms, it is more exten-

influential one, and a crucial actor in setting the tone for good corporate governance in Norway – with knock-on effects also outside of Norway, as it is regarded as a role model for state investments.[97]

Through the Norwegian Government Pension Fund Global, the world's largest Sovereign Wealth Fund, Norway is also invested in approximately 8500 companies around the world. The 'Oil Fund', as it is colloquially known in Norway (because of the source of its funding being revenues from petroleum activity), has been regarded as a leading star for responsible investments. In spite of a number of good initiatives by the Oil Fund, it is also under criticism for its unsustainable investments. At the time of writing, many voices, internationally and nationally, have criticised the Fund's investments in companies contributing to Israel's violations of international law in Gaza.[98] In this chapter, we concentrate on the Norwegian state's role as a shareholder in Norwegian companies and its influence on corporate governance in Norway in practice.[99]

The Norwegian state regards itself as a frontrunner in the transformation to sustainability, including mitigating climate change and protecting human rights. Yet, the state's governance of the companies in which it has direct shareholdings may be characterised as a missed opportunity for demonstrating and promoting sustainable corporate governance. Indeed, the state appears 'to act as an idealised version of a private owner that does not really exist in reality',[100] promoting maximisation of returns to investors in the belief that this protects the state as shareholder from accusations of being 'political'.[101]

---

sive than many other Western countries', Meld. St. 6 (2022–2023, A greener and more active state ownership – The State's direct ownership of companies, available in English at ww.regjeringen.no/no/dokumenter/meld.-st.-6–20222023/id2937164/ (hereafter '2022–2023 white paper'); Section 6, figure 6.1.

97 The Norwegian state prides itself on being 'far ahead internationally in terms of the exercise of state ownership', with reference to a 2018 OECD survey, 2022–2023 white paper, Section 8.

98 United Nations Human Rights Council, From Economy of Occupation to Economy of Genocide. Report of the Special Rapporteur on the Situation of Human Rights in the Palestinian Territories Occupied since 1967, Francesca Albanese, 30 June 2025, A/HRC/59/23.

99 The Oil Fund's international influence on corporate governance is discussed inter alia in Sjåfjell/Nilsen/ Richardson, Wake Forest Law Review (2017) 52, 949–79; Sjåfjell/Mähönen/Sjåfjell, 241, (Section 4).

100 Innset, Business History 2025, 496 (511).

101 Innset, Business History 2025, 496 (497) on the 'new paradox of depoliticisation in which the state tries to reach political goals by not having any'.

Sjåfjell has previously undertaken an analysis of the state's corporate governance of Equinor ASA, one of the world's largest energy companies and a carbon major,[102] in which the state owns 67 per cent of the shares.[103] Her analysis shows that there are multiple references to sustainability and to mitigating the climate crisis in the state's documents, yet the state's governance is characterised by a multilayered problematic approach. Generally, the state is satisfied by expressing 'expectations' to companies, rather than using legislation to facilitate sustainable corporate governance generally, or using its corporate governance powers as a majority shareholder specifically. This is especially clear in Equinor, where the state has considerable control through company law. The state prefers 'ownership dialogue', an opaque avenue of influence of the company, which is not recognised by Norwegian company law, rather than using the general meeting. And finally, the state pursues maximum returns on its shareholding. This means that the state is not using its corporate governance to ensure true leadership in the transformation to sustainability, and it is not basing its governance on sustainability research. Ultimately, the corporate governance signal that the Norwegian state, as controlling shareholder in important companies, is sending to shareholders and companies generally in Norway (and beyond) is highly detrimental: no major changes are necessary; maximising returns for shareholders remains the priority.[104]

An emerging recognition of the risks of unsustainability, which started out with the financial risks of climate change, has the potential to mitigate the pressure of shareholder primacy. A specific business-driven understanding of 'sustainability risks' is now an established legal concept in EU legislation, which is being implemented in Norwegian law.[105] The EU's concept of sustainability risks has its weaknesses, but it does represent a powerful push for a more modern and research-based approach to corporate governance.

A full understanding of the financial and corporate risks of continued unsustainability includes risks caused by business contributing to climate change and environmental degradation, to human rights violations and

---

102 Equinor, Emissions ($MtCO_2e$), https://carbonmajors.org/Entity/Equinor-54.

103 Sjåfjell/Mähönen/Sjåfjell, p. 241.

104 Sjåfjell/Mähönen/Sjåfjell, p. 241 (Section 3).

105 These include the Sustainable Finance Disclosure Regulation, the Taxonomy Regulation, the CSRD, the ESRS, and the CSDDD; see Section B.I in this chapter. For a discussion of the sustainability risks approach in EU legislation, see Sjåfjell/Cornell European Law Open Vol. 3, 529–60.

other exploitation of people, to tax evasion and other undermining of the economic and governance bases for well-functioning societies.[106] Such a recognition would bring these aspects fully into the heart of corporate governance and of the duties of the board to promote the company's interest, whether one's view of what the company's interest entails is narrow, limited to shareholder returns, or broad and pluralistic, with the economic prosperity of the company at the core. Although the business case for sustainability has its limitations, much would be achieved if such a research-based understanding of risks was employed.[107]

However, the Norwegian state's follow-up as a powerful and influential shareholder aligns more with a greenwashing approach than with recognising that what historically seemed good is neither sufficient in light of the current situation nor for the future.[108] The state may find itself confronted with this through lawsuits. Litigation is a realisation of the liability risks of unsustainability. The Norwegian state, in its capacity as state, has been sued for facilitating unsustainable business activities, including violation of the rights of the Indigenous Sámi population in Norway,[109] and several rounds concerning its handing out of licences for further petroleum exploitation, thereby contributing to global climate change,[110] and its handing out of pollution permits for dumping of mining waste in Norwegian fjords.[111] There has not yet been a lawsuit against the Norwegian state as shareholder, or against NBIM as the fund manager of the Oil Fund.[112] When that happens

106 Alexander (et. al)/Sjåfjell, 22; Patrick W Keys and others, Nature Sustainability 2019, 2, 667.

107 Alexander (et. al)/Sjåfjell, 22.

108 Sjåfjell/Mähönen/Sjåfjell, p. 241 (Section 3).

109 See e.g. Eide, About the Wind Farms on Fosen and the Supreme Court Judgment, 2023, https://www.nhri.no/en/2023/about-the-wind-farms-on-fosen-and-the-supreme-court-judgment/. The Norwegian Supreme Court decision of 2021 has still not been complied with by the Norwegian state.

110 With the at time of writing latest round involving also an Advisory Opinion from the EFTA Court, see Eide, New EFTA Court Judgment: Combustion Emissions Must Be Assessed and Unlawful Production Licences Must Be Remedied, 2025, https://www.nhri.no/en/2025/new-efta-court-judgment-combustion-emissions-must-be-assessed-and-unlawful-production-licences-must-be-remedied/.

111 See Christensen, Full Celebration After Victory for Norwegian Fjord, 2025, https://fjordsoksmalet.no/2025/08/13/full-celebration-after-victory-for-norwegian-fjord further in fn 59 above.

112 Although NBIM has had several complaints against it before the OECD National Contact Point in Norway, including in the seminal Posco case, see the Norwegian National Contact Point, Norwegian Bank Investment Management Violates OECD

– and it seems to be only a question of time – that may be the game changer. The critical attention to the unsustainable activities that Norway's Oil Fund,[113] and the Norwegian state as a direct shareholder,[114] are involved in, is increasing.

D. Concluding reflections: Towards sustainable corporate governance?

The EU's Sustainable Corporate Governance initiative of 2020 aimed to reform company law and corporate governance to promote long-term sustainable value creation.[115] Because of extensive pushback from shareholder primacy proponents and vested interests, this aim is not expressly included in the CSDDD, which was adopted in 2024. Rather, the CSDDD regulates the key tool of corporate sustainability due diligence. Corporate sustainability due diligence, which the CSRD and the ESRS give reporting rules on, and which the Norwegian Transparency Act regulates aspects of, is evolving as a horizontal norm.[116] Both the EU legislation and the Transparency Act contribute to breaking down silos between international law, on the one hand, and EU and national law on the other, as well as between law and social norms (notably, the OECD Guidelines). With this, and the international trend of lawsuits, the regulatory framework for corporate governance and the duties of the board are rapidly evolving, in spite of pushback and the Omnibus process.

Guidelines, 2013, https://www.responsiblebusiness.no/news/norwegian-bank-investment-management-violates-oecd-guidelines/. See also Malaguti, Maria Chiara, Oslo Law Review, 1 (10).

113 Concerning Gaza, see United Nations Human Rights Council,, From Economy of Occupation to Economy of Genocide. Report of the Special Rapporteur on the Situation of Human Rights in the Palestinian Territories Occupied since 1967, Francesca Albanese, 30 June 2025, A/HRC/59/23'.

114 Concerning Brazil, see Palazzo/Bisschop/Hendlin International Journal of Crime Justice and Social Democracy, 2025, 1.

115 European Commission, Sustainable Corporate Governance. Inception Impact Assessment, 30 July 2020, Ref. Ares(2020)4034032 <https://ec.europa.eu/info/law/better-regulation/have-your-say/initiatives/12548-Sustainable-corporate-governance_en>. See further European Commission, Commission Staff Working Document. Impact Assessment Report. Accompanying the Document Proposal for a Directive of the European Parliament and of the Council on Corporate Sustainability Due Diligence and Amending Directive (EU) 2019/1937, 24 February 2022, SWD(2022) 42 final <https://data.consilium.europa.eu/doc/document/ST-6533-2022-ADD-5/en/pdf>, Section 4.1.

116 Sjåfjell, Transnational Legal Theory, 2025, Section 3.2.3.

The Norwegian state, in its corporate governance, sets out that it wishes to work towards sustainable value creation, which is also supported by the Norwegian corporate governance code for listed companies. And yet, the Norwegian state as shareholder seems to base its corporate governance on a misleading dichotomy between political goals and business goals, and between returns on investment and sustainability. We see a mirror image of this reflected in the Omnibus discussions at the time of writing, where major legislative corporate sustainability reform is suggested 'simplified' for the sake of competitiveness of European business.[117] What is missing is the recognition that competitiveness, economic development, and indeed, the prosperity of all business, all people and our societies, requires working towards a safer and more just world.[118] In an increasingly unstable, unequal and unsafe world, steady returns are not likely in the long run for any actor.

As we have shown in this chapter, there are two opposing viewpoints in Norwegian academic literature of what the company's interest encompasses. One is that the company's interest is equivalent to the shareholders' interests, and the other is that the company's interest is pluralistic, with the economic interest of the company at the core. Those promoting the former understanding typically also claim that shareholder interests need to be understood in the long term (which gives us a hypothetical shareholder interest, rather than an actual one at any time), and that there also are other legitimate interests to be considered (close to the UK enlightened shareholder value). This conceptually reduces the distance between the two understandings. Together with the business case for more sustainable corporate governance, we could envisage that boards following either starting point could end up with the same decision. Boards that wish to do so can, as a matter of company law, integrate sustainable value creation into the aims, strategies and business operations of the company. Increasingly, they will find that law is moving towards requiring that they do so, whether in the form of legislation or in the form of court decisions. However, this

117 Amongst the many reactions and support for existing legislation, IDVO – Initiative for Sustainable & Responsible Business Conduct, Broad Support for the CSDDD, www.we-support-the-csddd.eu/.

118 See e.g. Wester van Gaal, EU-Funded Researchers Urge Rethink of 'Competitiveness' Agenda, 2025, https://euobserver.com/eu-political/ar93b1f197; European Coalition for Corporate Justice, Joint Press Release: Prominent Economists across the EU Warn of the Deep Costs of Weakening Sustainability Regulations, 2025, https://corporatejustice.org/news/joint-press-release-prominent-economists-across-the-eu-warn-of-the-deep-costs-of-weakening-sustainability-regulations/.

space for sustainable value creation is often not used, because there is a vast chasm between the pluralistic understanding of the company's interest and the social norm of shareholder primacy, which dictates, contrary to company law, that returns for shareholders are to be maximised at all costs. Clarifying what Norwegian company law actually allows, expects and requires is, we hope, a step in pushing back against this social norm.

References

Aarbakke, Magnus/Aarbakke, Asle/Knudsen, Gudmund/Ofstad, Tone/Skåre, Jan, Lovkommentarer aksjeloven og allmennaksjeloven (Commentary Public and Private Limited Liability Companies Acts), 5th ed., Oslo 2024

Albanese, Francesca, 'From Economy of Occupation to Economy of Genocide. Report of the Special Rapporteur on the Situation of Human Rights in the Palestinian Territories Occupied since 1967 (Advance Edited Version)' (United Nations Human Rights Office of the High Commissioner 2025) Country Report A/HRC/59/23 <https://www.ohchr.org/en/documents/country-reports/ahrc5923-economy-occupation-economy-genocide-report-special-rapporteur> accessed 15 August 2025

Andenæs, Mads Henry/Andenæs, Ole/Berge, Stig/Christoffersen, Margrethe B., Aksjeselskaper og allmennaksjeselskaper (Private and public limited liability companies), 3rd ed., Oslo 2017

Anker-Sørensen, Linn, Corporate Groups and Shadow Business Practices, Cambridge University Press, 2022

Bråten Tore/Minde, Stine Winger, To What Extent Must, and Can, the Boards of Norwegian Limited Liability Companies and Public Limited Liability Companies Consider Sustainability?, Oslo Law Review Vol. 10 no. 2 2024, 1

Bruner, Christopher M./Sjåfjell, Beate, Corporate Law, Corporate Governance and the Pursuit of Sustainability, in Sjåfjell, Beate/Christopher M. Bruner (eds.), The Cambridge Handbook of Corporate Law, Corporate Governance and Sustainability, Cambridge University Press, 2019, 7139

Carnwath R, 'ClientEarth v Shell: What Future for Derivative Claims?', Grantham Research Institute on Climate Change and the Environment, London School of Economics and Political Science 2024 <https://www.lse.ac.uk/granthaminstitute/wp-content/uploads/2024/02/ClientEarth-v-Shell-what-future-for-derivative-claims.pdf>

Christensen, Tor Bjarne, 'Full Celebration After Victory for Norwegian Fjord', 13 August 2025 <https://fjordsoksmalet.no/2025/08/13/full-celebration-after-victory-for-norwegian-fjord/> accessed 26 August 2025

Christoffersen, Margrethe B., Erstatningsansvar for styremedlemmer i aksjeselskaper – blir det stadig strengere? (Liability for board members in companies – it is getting ever stricter?), Tidsskrift for Forretningsjus Vol. 30 no. 1 2024, 75

Clark, Lesley, Polish Energy Company Sues Former Directors for Backing Coal, 2024, https://subscriber.politicopro.com/article/eenews/2024/02/02/polish-energy-company-sues-former-directors-for-backing-coal-00139156 (last accessed: 5 February 2024)

Dahlum, Andrea, Styreansvar i praksis ('Liability for board members in practice'), Oslo, 2021

De Tommaso, Alessandra, Profiting from Injustice in the Occupied Palestinian Territory: Reflections on the Report 'From Economy of Occupation to Economy of Genocide', 2025, https://internationallaw.blog/2025/07/14/profiting-from-injustice-in-the-occupied-palestinian-territory-reflections-on-the-report-from-economy-of-occupation-to-economy-of-genocidehttps://internationallaw.blog/2025/07/14/profiting-from-injustice-in-the-occupied-palestinian-territory-reflections-on-the-report-from-economy-of-occupation-to-economy-of-genocide/ (last accessed: 4 August 2025)

Eide, Magnus, About the Wind Farms on Fosen and the Supreme Court, 2023, https://www.nhri.no/en/2023/about-the-wind-farms-on-fosen-and-the-supreme-court-judgment/ (last accessed: 28 August 2025)

Eide, Magnus, New EFTA Court Judgment: Combustion Emissions Must Be Assessed and Unlawful Production Licences Must Be Remedied, 2025, <https://www.nhri.no/en/2025/new-efta-court-judgment-combustion-emissions-must-be-assessed-and-unlawful-production-licences-must-be-remedied/ (last accessed: 28 August 2025)

Equinor, https://carbonmajors.org/Entity/Equinor-54 (last accessed: 21 August 2025)

European Coalition for Corporate Justice (ECCJ), Suing Goliath: An Analysis of Civil Cases against EU Companies for Overseas Human Rights and Environmental Abuses, 2021, https://corporatejustice.org/publications/suing-goliath/ (last accessed: 18 April 2022)

Herencia-Carrasco, Salvador/ Pamplona, Danielle Anne, The Inter-American Court's Advisory Opinion on Climate Emergency and Human Rights: A Breakthrough for the Environment and Business & Human Rights, 2025, www.afronomicslaw.org/category/analysis/inter-american-courts-advisory-opinion-climate-emergency-and-human-rights (last accessed: 31 July 2025)

Iglesias-Rodríguez, Pablo P, 'ClientEarth v Shell Plc and the (Un)Suitability of UK Company Law and Litigation to Pursue Climate-Related Goals' (2023) 35 Journal of Environmental Law Vol. 35 no. 3, 445

Innset, Ola, State-owned enterprises after the market turn: Hybridisation and the historical development of nested paradoxes in the case of Norway, Business History 2025, 496

Joint Press Release: Prominent Economists across the EU Warn of the Deep Costs of Weakening Sustainability Regulations, 2025, https://corporatejustice.org/news/joint-press-release-prominent-economists-across-the-eu-warn-of-the-deep-costs-of-weakening-sustainability-regulations/ (last accessed: 21 May 2025)

Keys, Patrick/Galaz, Victor/Dyer, Michelle/Matthews, Nathaniel/Folke, Carl/Nyström, Magnus/Cornell, Sarah E., Anthropocene Risk, Nature Sustainability 2019, 667

Malaguti, Maria Chiara, From Soft to Hard Law and Interpretation: The Case of the OECD Guidelines for Multinational Enterprises and the Role of the National Contact Points, Oslo Law Review Vol. 10 2024, 1

Millon, David, Radical Shareholder Primacy, 10 University of St. Thomas Law Journal Vol. 10:4 2013, 1013

Normann, Kristin Aarum, Styremedlemmers erstatningsansvar i aksjeselskaper (Liability for members of the board in limited liability companies), Oslo 1994

Norwegian Bank Investment Management Violates OECD Guidelines, 2013, https://www.responsiblebusiness.no/news/norwegian-bank-investment-management-violates-oecd-guidelineshttps://www.responsiblebusiness.no/news/norwegian-bank-investment-management-violates-oecd-guidelines/ (last accessed: 28 August 2025)

NRK, Ber tingretten om å forby Nordic Mining dumping i Førdefjorden, 2025, https://www.nrk.no/vestland/ber-tingretten-om-a-forby-nordic-mining-dumping-i-fordefjorden-1.17542932 (last accessed: 26 August 2025)

Palazzo, Fernando Procópio/ Bisschop, Lieselot/Hendlin, Yogi Hale, Polluter by Proxy: Norwegian Environmentally Harmful Mining Activities in Brazil as State-Corporate Crime, International Journal for Crime, Justice and Social Democracy 2025, 1

Reiersen, Hedvig B., «Selskapsinteressen» i norsk aksjeselskapsrett ('The company interest' in Norwegian company law) in Christoffersen, Margrethe B./Høgberg, Alf/Irgens-Jensen, Harald/Knudsen, Gudmund (eds.), Juss og Mangfold – Festskrift til Geir Woxholth 70 år, Oslo 2023, 157

Sejersted, Fredrik/Arnesen, Finn/Rognstad, Ole-Andreas/Foyn, Sten/Kolstad, Olav, EØS-rett (EEA law), 3rd ed., Oslo 2011

Sjåfjell Beate/ Mähönen, Jukka T., Reimagining Corporate Purpose for a Safe and Just World in Bowman, Megan/Mai, Laura (eds.), A Research Agenda for Finance and the Environment: Reimagining Law and Regulation, Edward Elgar, in print 2025. Preprint available at http://dx.doi.org/10.2139/ssrn.5255480

Sjåfjell, Beate/Johnston, Andrew/Anker-Sørensen, Linn/Millon, David, Shareholder Primacy: The Main Barrier to Sustainable Companies in Sjåfjell, Beate/Richardson, Benjamin (eds.), Company Law and Sustainability: Legal Barriers and Opportunities, Cambridge University Press, 2015, 79

Sjåfjell, Beate, Kan Aksjeselskaper Sette Miljø Foran Profitt? [Can Companies Prioritise Environment Over Profit?] Jussens Venner 2011 Vol. 46, 309

Sjåfjell, Beate, Sustainable Value Creation in the Land of Oil and Honey, in Sjåfjell, Beate/Mähönen, Jukka T. (eds), Nordic Company Law: Broadening the Horizon, Oslo 2023, 241

Sjåfjell, Beate, Conceptualising Corporate Sustainability Law, Transnational Legal Theory Vol. 16, 2025, 281, https://www.tandfonline.com/doi/full/10.1080/20414005.2025.2559542https://www.tandfonline.com/doi/full/10.1080/20414005.2025.2559542

Sjåfjell, Beate, Exploring Corporate Sustainability Law in Global Value Chains, in Anton, Ricardia/Bose, Debadatte/Lafarre, Anne/Rombouts, Bas/Verbruggen, Paul (eds.), The Cambridge Handbook of Law and Responsible Business: Legal Strategies for Sustainability in Global Value Chains, Cambridge University Press, forthcoming 2026, Chapter 2

Sjåfjell, Beate, Political Path Dependency in Practice: The Takeover Directive, Yearbook of European Law Vol. 27 2008, 387

Sjåfjell, Beate, Selskapsrett og et Feministisk Bærekraftsperspektiv (Company Law and a Feminist Sustainability Perspective), in Ikdahl, Ingunn/Hellum, Anne/Asland, John/Bruserud, Herman/Hjort, Maria A./Gudmundsdottir Jonassen, Bjørk/Skilbrei, May-Len (eds.), Kjønn og rett. Kvinne-, kjønns- og likestillingsperspektiver i jusstudiet, Oslo 2022

Sjåfjell, Beate, Sustainable Companies: Possibilities and Barriers in Norwegian Company Law, International and Comparative Corporate Law Journal Vol. 11 no. 1 2013, 1–58, available at http://dx.doi.org/10.2139/ssrn.2311433

Sjåfjell, Beate, Taking Finance Seriously: Understanding the Financial Risks of Unsustainability, in Alexander, Kern/Gargantini, Matteo/Michele, Siri (eds), The Cambridge Handbook of EU Sustainable Finance: Regulation, Supervision and Governance, Cambridge University Press 2025, Ch. 2

Sjåfjell, Beate/Mähönen, Jukka T., 'Sustainable Corporate Governance for Boards and Their Lawyers,' in Sam De Silva and others (eds), Expert Essentials, online edition, Oxford Law Pro 2025, https://doi.org/10.1093/9780198972877.003.0048

Sjåfjell, Beate/Cornell, Sarah E., 'What the Actual ....? Tensions in the Science-Business-Policy Interface for Global Sustainability, ' (2024) 3 European Law Open Vol. 3 2024, 529, https://doi.org/10.1017/elo.2024.34

Sjåfjell, Beate/Nilsen, Heidi Rapp/Richardson, Benjamin J., Investing in Sustainability or Feeding on Stranded Assets? The Norwegian Government Pension Fund Global, Wake Forest Law Review Vol. 52 no. 4 2017, 949

Solem, Eirik, Salg av kronjuveler (Sale of Crown Jewels), Tidsskrift for Forretningsjus Vol. 7 no. 4 2001, 451.

Tigre, Maria Antonia/Bönnemann, Maxim/De Spiegeleir, Antoine, The ICJ's Advisory Opinion on Climate Change: An Introduction, 2025, https://blogs.law.columbia.edu/climatechange/2025/07/24/the-icjs-advisory-opinion-on-climate-change-an-introductionhttps://blogs.law.columbia.edu/climatechange/2025/07/24/the-icjs-advisory-opinion-on-climate-change-an-introduction/ (last accessed: 31 July 2025)

Truyen, Filip, Aksjonærenes myndighetsmisbruk (Shareholder abuse of authority), Oslo 2005

Van Gaal, Wester, EU-Funded Researchers Urge Rethink of 'Competitiveness' Agenda, 2025, https://euobserver.com/eu-political/ar93b1f197 (last accessed: 9 April 2025)

Wadiwala, Zunaida Moosa, Historic Climate Change Ruling from the International Court of Justice: What It Means for Africa, 2025, http://theconversation.com/historic-climate-change-ruling-from-the-international-court-of-justice-what-it-means-for-africa-262047http://theconversation.com/historic-climate-change-ruling-from-the-international-court-of-justice-what-it-means-for-africa-262047 (last accessed: 31 July 2025)

Authors

Tonio Friedmann

Tonio Friedmann studied law at the University of Mainz and passed the first state examination. He holds a Master's degree in International Commercial Law (LL.M.) from the University of Glasgow. After completing his legal clerkship at the Wiesbaden District Court in 2022, he passed the second state examination.

He is a PhD candidate at the Chair of Civil Law, European and International Business Law at Martin Luther University Halle-Wittenberg and a research assistant at the Chair of Civil Law and Civil Procedure at Johannes Gutenberg University Mainz.

Géraldine Goffaux Callebaut

Géraldine Goffaux Callebaut is Professor of Private Law at the University of Orléans and a member of the Centre de recherche juridique Pothier (CRJP), where she heads the Organisations and Governance section. She is co-director of the Master's Degree in Cultural Heritage Law (Université Paris Saclay) and the Master Degree in Art Market (École du Louvre). She is also an associate researcher at the Institut Droit Éthique Patrimoine (Université Paris Saclay) and at the Public Law Research (CRDP) at the University of Montréal.

Her research and teaching focus on business law and cultural and artistic heritage law. In business law, she has conducted numerous research projects on company's interest, ethics and corporate social responsibility. She is also interested in the legal issues raised by new technologies (electronic voting, blockchain, AI). She is currently leading a regional project *Law & Ethics of Digital Transformations.*

Morten Gullhagen-Revling

Morten Gullhagen-Revling is a Norwegian lawyer at DLA Piper Norway where he is a part of the company's regulatory department working within a broad range of EEA law related matters. Morten was in 2012 research assistant in the project Sustainable Companies led by Professor Sjåfjell.

Diletta Lenzi

Diletta Lenzi is an Assistant Professor of Business Law at the University of Genoa since 2024. Before joining the University of Genoa, she worked at the University of Trento and the University of Florence. She has conducted research at Georgetown University and at the University of Oxford. She worked as a consultant for the World Bank Group, and at the UNIDROIT Secretariat as the *Sir Roy Goode Scholar 2023*. She earned a PhD in Business Law from Ca' Foscari University of Venice, with a dissertation on corporate law and the risk of environmental damage. She has held the Italian National Academic Qualification as Associate Professor of Business Law since 2023. She is an Academic Member of the ECGI, the Jean Monnet Centre on EU Sustainable Finance and Law, and the Genoa Centre for Law and Finance. Her main areas of research include company law and insolvency law, and the intersection of business and sustainability.

Lela Mélon

Dr. Lela Mélon is an expert in EU corporate law and sustainability, recognized for her academic and consultancy work at the intersection of law, policy, and sustainable business. With a background in law and economics, she has held prestigious roles including Marie Curie Research Fellow at Pompeu Fabra University and recipient of the 2021 Emerging Sustainability Leader Award. Her scholarly work focuses on policy coherence for sustainability, reflected in her books *Shareholder Primacy and Global Business* (Routledge, 2018) and *Sustainability in Public Procurement, Corporate Law and Higher Education* (Routledge, 2024). Dr. Mélon has been instrumental in embedding sustainability into higher education curricula and has lectured at universities and institutions worldwide. As a senior sustainability consultant, she works closely with industry stakeholders and policymakers to foster systemic change toward sustainable corporate governance.

Lina Mikalonienė

Dr. Lina Mikalonienė is a professor at Mykolas Romeris University, Law School. Her main research interests are in company law, with a focus on closely held companies. She is the author and co-author of number of academic publications in the field of company law (https://cris.mruni.eu/cris/entities/person/linamikaloniene/publications).

Anne-Christin Mittwoch

Anne-Christin Mittwoch holds the chair of Private Law, European and International Business Law and is the Executive Director of the Institute of Economic Law at the faculty of Law, Economics and Business at Martin Luther University Halle-Wittenberg. She is founder and Director of the Research Institute of Sustainable Economic Law (RISE) and author of the monograph 'Nachhaltigkeit und Unternehmensrecht' ('Sustainability and Company Law'), that was published in 2022. She is also an Of Counsel at GvW Graf von Westphalen, one of Germany'a largest independent law firms. From February to July 2025, she was a Visiting Professor at the University Brest in France. Mittwoch's main areas of research include company law and financial markets law, and the intersection of business and sustainability in the EU internal market.

Andreas Rühmkorf

Andreas Rühmkorf is Professor of German and International Commercial Law at Westfälische Hochschule Gelsenkirchen, Bochholt, Recklinghausen. He is also an Honorary Professor at the University of Sheffield. His research focusses on the legal regulation of human rights in global supply chains from a private law perspective. He has published extensively in this area. He is also publishing on corporate governance and company law as well as the interface of sustainable development and private law. He is currently Co-PI of the research project 'Human rights in global supply chains: Measuring the effectiveness of home state regulatory models on corporate behaviour' which he runs jointly with the British Institute of International & Comparative Law (BIICL). The project is funded by the Deutsche Forschungsgemeinschaft (DFG, German Research Foundation) – Projektnummer: 527798519.

Christoph Schmetterer

Christoph Schmetterer studied law and history/political science at the Unviersity of Vienna, earning his doctorate in both subjects. He has worked as an attorney and is currently completing his habilitation on legal history and civil law at the Martin Luther University Halle (Saale).

Beate Sjåfjell

Beate Sjåfjell is Professor of Law at the University of Oslo, Centre for Global Sustainability & Faculty of Law, Academic Chair in the European University Alliance Circle U, and Visiting Professor at College of Europe.

Professor Sjåfjell is head of the University of Oslo's Research Group Sustainability Law, and coordinator of Daughters of Themis: International Network of Women Business Scholars. Her research has become increasingly interdisciplinary, and she publishes extensively on topics related to the integration of sustainability into business, including in the field of corporate law, corporate governance, and sustainability.

Aleksandra Szczęsna

Aleksandra Szczęsna is a doctoral candidate at the Doctoral School of Social Sciences of the University of Warsaw. She holds a Master's degree in Law from the Faculty of Law and Administration of the University of Warsaw and a Master's degree (*Droit des affaires*), completed as part of a Polish–French program in cooperation with the University of Poitiers in France. She is a recipient of a research grant from the Polish National Science Centre (NCN) to fund her doctoral project.

Anne-Marie Weber

Dr. Anne-Marie Weber, LL.M., is an Assistant Professor at the Chair of Commercial Law at the Faculty of Law and Administration, University of Warsaw, where she obtained her Master of Laws degree and defended her doctoral dissertation. She also holds a Master's degree from Berkeley School of Law, University of California. She has been a Visiting Scholar at Berkeley School of Law and a recurring Research Fellow at the Max Planck Institute for Comparative and International Private Law in Hamburg. She is a recipient of scholarships from the Max Planck Gesellschaft, the French Government, the Polish National Agency for Academic Exchange, and the Polish National Science Centre. Dr. Weber is a Fellow of the European Banking Institute and the European Law Institute, and an Academic Member of the European Corporate Governance Institute.